Intellectual Property Law Handbook

Related titles available from Law Society Publishing:

Company Law Handbook
Stephen Griffin

Data Protection Handbook
General Editor: Peter Carey

Design Law: Protecting and Exploiting Rights
Margaret Briffa and Lee Gage

Drafting Confidentiality Agreements (Second Edition)
Mark Anderson and Simon Keevey-Kothari

Entertainment Law Handbook
Richard Verow, Nick Kanaar, Estelle Overs and Vincent Scheurer

Execution of Documents
Mark Anderson and Victor Warner

Freedom of Information Handbook
General Editors: Peter Carey and Marcus Turle

Insolvency Law Handbook (Second Edition)
Vernon Dennis

Technology Outsourcing: A Practitioner's Guide
General Editor: John Angel

Titles from Law Society Publishing can be ordered from all good legal bookshops or direct from our distributors, Prolog (tel. 0870 850 1422 or email **lawsociety@prolog.uk.com**). For further information or a catalogue, email our editorial and marketing office at **publishing@lawsociety.org.uk**.

INTELLECTUAL PROPERTY LAW HANDBOOK

BIRD & BIRD

Edited by **Lorna Brazell**

The Law Society

ISBN: 978-1-85328-996-5

Published in 2008 by the Law Society
113 Chancery Lane, London WC2A 1PL

Typeset by J&L Composition, Filey, North Yorkshire
Printed by Antony Rowe Ltd, Chippenham, Wiltshire

Contents

About the editor and contributors

EDITOR

Lorna Brazell

Partner

Lorna specialises in the protection of intellectual property in all its forms. Her experience spans both drafting and negotiating commercial contracts for the creation, transfer or licensing of intellectual property and the enforcement of rights through mediation, arbitration and litigation in the High Court and Patents County Court across a range of industries.

Lorna has a BSc (first class honours) in geophysics from Edinburgh University and an LLM in corporate and commercial law from King's College London. She qualified as a solicitor in 1994, as a solicitor-advocate for the higher courts in 2005 and is an Associate of the Chartered Institute of Patent Agents.

Lorna's reported cases include:

- *Union Carbide Corp* v. *BP Chemicals Ltd* (1997) on a process for the production of polyethylene, including a significant project on the assessment of damages.
- *The Horne Engineering Company* v. *Reliance Water Controls* (1999) on thermostatic valves.
- *Oxford Gene Technology Ltd* v. *Affymetrix* (2000) on the synthesis of DNA and manufacture of DNA microarrays. This case made new law on privilege in relation to disclosure of documents in connection with the amendment of granted patents.
- *Intel* v. *VIA Technologies* (2002) on computer chipsets.
- *Oakley Inc* v. *H Young (Operations) Ltd & Ors* (2004) on registered design.
- *The Procter & Gamble Co* v. *Reckitt Benckiser (UK) Ltd* (2007), the first UK case on the new Community Registered Design.

Lorna has also worked on a variety of issues relating to e-commerce, including the establishment of certification authorities, the legal status of encryption technology and the use of digital signatures.

She is the author of *Electronic Signatures: Law and Regulation* (Sweet & Maxwell, 2004) and co-author with Trevor Cook of *The Copyright Directive: UK Implementation* (Jordans, 2004). She has contributed articles to a variety of publications, and wrote chapters in *Database Law* (Rees and Chalton (eds), 1998) and *The Pharmaceutical Pricing Compendium* (Urch, 2003).

CONTRIBUTORS

Peter Brownlow

Partner

Peter is a partner specialising in intellectual property law. Although involved in a wide range of contentious and non-contentious intellectual property work, Peter has particular experience in passing off, trade mark, copyright, design and patent litigation and regularly speaks and writes on a number of these subjects.

His experience includes acting for the claimants in *Micro Matic A/S* v. *DSI & others*; *Mercury Communications* v. *Mercury Interactive (UK) Ltd*; *Chocosuisse & others* v. *Cadbury Ltd* both in the High Court and in the Court of Appeal; *Associated Newspapers Ltd* v. *Metro News Ltd*; and the defendants in *Manchester Evening News Ltd and Guardian Newspapers* v. *Associated Newspapers Ltd* both in the High Court and Court of Appeal; *David West (trading as Eastenders)* v. *Fuller Smith and Turner plc* (trade mark revocation) and *Saint Gobain* v. *Electrosteel Casting Ltd and Fusion Provida Ltd* also in the High Court and Court of Appeal.

Peter is an associate member of the Institute of Trade Mark Agents and has sat on their Designs and Copyright Committee since 1996. Since 1998 Peter has been co-editor of the INTA publication *The Community Trade Mark – Regulations Practice and Procedure*.

Mathew Oliver

Partner

Mathew Oliver is a partner in the International Corporate Group at Bird & Bird who specialises in corporate and business taxation. He heads up the UK Tax Group. He joined Bird & Bird in November 2005. Before joining, Mathew worked in another large City firm and one of the big 4 accountants.

Mathew has extensive experience in mergers & acquisitions, reorganisations and reconstructions, joint ventures, private equity, finance and property transactions. He has acted for a wide variety of clients across a broad spectrum of business sectors.

Mathew is a member of the Chartered Institute of Taxation.

Jeremy Robinson

Associate

Jeremy Robinson is a solicitor (England and Wales) with substantial experience across all areas of EU and UK competition law and economic regulation. He has both contentious and non-contentious experience of the application of competition law to intellectual property and technology transfer matters, across different sectors including pharmaceuticals and communications. His non-contentious practice also spans cartels, merger control, the analysis of commercial agreements for their effects on competition and abuse of dominance. In the course of his work he represents clients before EU and UK competition authorities and sector regulators (water, energy, communications).

Jeremy has published several articles in legal and industry papers, and speaks regularly on competition law and regulatory matters.

Sally Shorthose

Partner

Sally joined Bird & Bird in September 2006 as a partner in the Intellectual Property/Life Sciences Groups, based in London.

After studying law at Manchester University and the College of Law, she qualified in 1988. After a period as a solicitor at Herbert Smith, Sally worked in-house, first as senior legal advisor at ICI/Zeneca, and latterly as Legal Director of Novartis UK, where she had particular responsibility for intellectual property protection and competition law compliance. She was Head of IP and Life Sciences at another City firm before joining Bird & Bird.

Sally has been involved in providing advice in relation to the protection and exploitation of a full range of intellectual property rights, from design rights to patents, trade marks, copyright and confidentiality across a range of jurisdictions. Her experience has given her significant insight into the high-tech, pharmaceutical and IT sectors. She regularly advises clients on regulatory and freedom to operate matters.

She is a regular speaker on IP issues, particularly licensing and exploitation matters. She is described as an 'expert' in regulatory and life sciences in the most recent *Global Life Sciences Review*.

Ingrid Toth

Associate

Ingrid is an Australian qualified lawyer in the corporate department of Bird & Bird, practising exclusively in taxation law.

Ingrid joined Bird & Bird in September 2006. Prior to that time, Ingrid worked in the tax practices of Arthur Andersen and Thomson Playford for more than eight years.

Ingrid handles a broad range of corporate tax work with a particular emphasis on international taxation. She has recently completed the examination requirements for membership of the Association of Taxation Technicians in the UK.

Preface

From having been an esoteric and exotic subject which most practitioners rarely needed to consider, intellectual property has become the engine underlying an increasing proportion of the commercial and industrial activities making up the economy of the United Kingdom. As a result, it has moved into the foreground in a wider range of transactions and developments than ever before and can no longer safely be ignored or treated as a side issue. Despite this, the majority of commercial lawyers successfully qualify and practice without any formal education in intellectual property, or if any then focussed almost exclusively on the academics' favourite topic of copyright, and have to pick it up in oddments as and when encountered in practice.

The books previously available on intellectual property have tended either to be academic texts written for undergraduate teaching purposes, with little context as to when and how intellectual property may be relevant in commerce, or specialist tomes on the various sub-categories of intellectual property – *Kerly on Trade Marks*, *Terrell on Patents*, *The Modern Law of Copyright and Designs* – which, though comprehensive and authoritative, are hardly accessible to a general practitioner. This book is intended to fill the gap, looking at intellectual property in all its forms (albeit treating some of the less common species rather briefly, in Chapter 1 alone) and in its commercial context. Thus, in addition to the chapters discussing the key rights there are chapters on commercial transactions in intellectual property and the detailed competition and tax issues which may need to be considered in developing, exploiting or selling intellectual property rights. We have tried to make complex provisions as lucid as possible while covering all of the essential information.

Due to the on-going efforts of the European Commission to harmonise intellectual property law across the European Union, there is a steady stream of new Directives and Regulations affecting all areas other than patents, confidential information and taxation. The law is stated here as it stands at 1 October 2007, from which vantage point there are no major legislative changes immediately expected. However, the European Commission is considering introducing criminal penalties for intellectual property infringements and there is still some prospect of establishment of a centralised

European court for the determination of patent disputes, both of which may be introduced in the next few years. Meanwhile, new case law is constantly being handed down, at national level and by the European Court of Justice, as to the interpretation of the recently revised laws of copyright, trade marks and designs.

The book is a joint effort between a number of Bird & Bird authors, as identified on the contents pages. But it would not have reached the light of day without the sterling efforts of our secretaries, particularly Angela Hill and Nicola Brewer, in reducing the text into publishable form, and the invaluable patience, understanding and support of my partner Stephen Lee.

Lorna Brazell
October 2007
www.twobirds.com

Table of cases

Table of statutes

Table of statutory instruments

Table of international treaties, conventions, regulations and directives

List of abbreviations

ADR	alternative dispute resolution
AQE	available qualifying expenditure
BERR	Department for Business, Enterprise and Regulatory Reform
CA 1998	Competition Act 1998
CAA 2001	Capital Allowances Act 2001
CDPA 1988	Copyright, Designs and Patents Act 1988
CFC	controlled foreign company
Community Design Regulation	Council Regulation (EC) No.6/2002 of 12 December 2001 on Community designs
Community Trade Mark Regulation	Council Regulation (EC) No.40/94 of 20 December 1993 on the Community trade mark
Comparative Advertising Directive	Directive 97/55/EC of European Parliament and of the Council of 6 October 1997 amending Directive 84/450/EEC concerning misleading advertising so as to include comparative advertising
Copyright Directive	Directive 2001/29/EC of the European Parliament and of the Council of 22 May 2001 on the harmonisation of certain aspects of copyright and related rights in the information society
CTM	Community Trade Mark
CUP	comparable uncontrolled prices
Database Directive	Directive 96/9/EC of the European Parliament and of the Council of 11 March 1996 on the legal protection of databases
Database Regulations 1997	Copyright and Rights in Databases Regulations 1997, SI 1997/3032
Designs Directive	Directive 98/71/EC of the European Parliament and of the Council of 13 October 1998 on the legal protection of designs
DTT	double tax treaty

EA 2002	Enterprise Act 2002
EC Interest and Royalties Directive	Council Directive 2003/49/EC of 3 June 2003 on a common system of taxation applicable to interest and royalty payments made between associated companies of different Member States
ECHR	European Convention for the Protection of Human Rights and Fundamental Freedoms.
ECMR	Council Regulation (EC) No.139/2004 of 20 January 2004 on the control of concentrations between undertakings
E-Commerce Directive	Directive 2000/31/EC of the European Parliament and of the Council of 8 June 2000 on certain legal aspects of information society services, in particular electronic commerce, in the Internal Market
E-Commerce VAT Directive	Council Directive 2002/38/EC of 7 May 2002 amending and amending temporarily Directive 77/388/EEC as regards the value added tax arrangements applicable to radio and television broadcasting services and certain electronically supplied services
EPC	European Patent Convention 1973
EPO	European Patent Office
EU	European Union
FA 2000	Finance Act 2000
FA 2002	Finance Act 2002
FA 2003	Finance Act 2003
FACT	Federation Against Copyright Theft
FAST	Federation Against Software Theft
Franchising Code	European Code of Ethics for Franchising
FRAND	fair, reasonable and non-discriminatory
FRS 10	Financial Reporting Standard 10
GAAP	generally accepted accounting practice
GPL	General Public Licence
HMRC	Her Majesty's Revenue and Customs
HRA 1998	Human Rights Act 1998
Human Rights Convention	Convention for the Protection of Human Rights and Fundamental Freedoms of the Council of Europe
ICANN	Internet Corporation for Assigned Names and Numbers
ICTA 1988	Income and Corporation Taxes Act 1988
IFRS	International Financial Reporting Standards
ISP	internet service provider

ITA 2007	Income Tax Act 2007
ITTOIA 2005	Income Tax (Trading and Other Income) Act 2005
JV	joint venture
LOA Right	London Olympics Association Right
Madrid Protocol	Protocol Relating to the Madrid Agreement Concerning the International Registration of Marks
MCPS	Mechanical Copyright Protection Society
Modernisation Regulation	Council Regulation (EC) No.1/2003 of 16 December 2002 on the implementation of the rules on competition laid down in Articles 81 and 82 of the Treaty
OA Right	Olympics Association Right
OHIM	Office of Harmonisation for the Internal Market
P2P	peer-to-peer
PA 1977	Patents Act 1977
Paris Convention	Paris Convention for the Protection of Industrial Property of 20 March 1883
pma	*post mortem auctoris*
PPL	Phonographic Performance Limited
PRS	Performing Rights Society
R&D	Research and development
R&DBE	block exemption created by Commission Regulation (EC) No.2659/2000 of 29 November 2000 on the application of Article 81(3) of the Treaty to categories of research and development agreements (R&D block exemption)
RDA 1949	Registered Designs Act 1949
RIPA 2000	Regulation of Investigatory Powers Act 2000
SMEs	small and medium-sized companies
Software Directive	Council Directive 91/250/EEC of 14 May 1991 on the legal protection of computer programs
TCGA 1992	Taxation of Chargeable Gains Act 1992
TDR	total disposal receipts
TDV	total disposal value
TMA 1994	Trade Marks Act 1994
Trade Marks Directive	First Council Directive 89/104/EEC of 21 December 1988 to approximate the laws of the Member States relating to trade marks
TRIPS Agreement	Agreement on Trade-Related Aspects of Intellectual Property
TTBE	Technology Transfer block exemption (Commission Regulation (EC) No.772/2004 of

	27 April 2004 on the application of Article 81(3) of the Treaty to categories of technology transfer agreements (Technology Transfer Block Exemption Regulation))
TTBE Guidelines	Guidelines on the application of the EC Treaty, Art.81 to Technology Transfer Agreements
UDRP	Uniform Dispute Resolution Policy
UKIPO	UK Intellectual Property Office
url	uniform resource locator
VAT	value added tax
VATA 1994	Value Added Tax Act 1944
VRBE	block exemption created by Commission Regulation (EC) No.2790/1999 of 22 December 1999 on the application of Article 81(3) of the Treaty to categories of vertical agreements and concerted practices
WPPT	1996 World Performances and Phonograms Treaty
WTO	World Trade Organisation

CHAPTER 1

What is intellectual property?

Lorna Brazell

1.1 THE SIGNIFICANCE OF INTELLECTUAL PROPERTY IN COMMERCIAL TRANSACTIONS

Intellectual property as a core asset

For any organisation more complex than a corner shop, intellectual property should be the very keystone of its strategic planning. All companies own at least some intellectual property, whether or not they are aware of it and whether or not it has market value. Intellectual property is recognised worldwide as a key incentive to technical and commercial development. There has already been a degree of international harmonisation since the World Trade Organisation (WTO) established its Agreement on Trade-Related Aspects of Intellectual Property (known as the TRIPS Agreement), building on earlier international treaties in relation to copyright, patents and trade marks. The World Intellectual Property Organisation (WIPO) in Geneva campaigns tirelessly to increase standards of protection across all forms of intellectual property, and international protection is the norm rather than the exception.

But closer to home, even a corner shop with ambition needs to be aware of the strategic potential of its branding. Facing up to increasing consumer choices and decreasing customer loyalty, businesses need to sell not merely products but also an identity with which consumers choose to identify, or to which they may aspire. The gulf between the book value and the market value of most consumer or high technology businesses today is the best evidence of the growing importance of intangible assets, amongst which intellectual property rights are central. In the contracts which give effect to issues such as buying and selling businesses, developing new products or managing a workforce, intellectual property issues are coming increasingly to the fore.

Brand identity, then, is one of the most important elements of any business whose ultimate end-product is a consumer item, or which trades at the retail level. Trade marks, in both their registered and unregistered forms, are the building blocks from which a brand is constructed. But intellectual property is critical in other respects as well. Although a brand is a marketing tool of enormous power, it cannot entirely compensate for mediocre or outdated products: businesses have to innovate as regards both the design and performance of their products if they are to retain or increase market share, and the value invested in both these forms of innovation needs to be protected. A range of different protections are available for novel designs, collectively referred to as 'design rights'. Developments in the actual technology of a product are protected through 'patent rights'. Businesses whose activities are situated further upstream may be less dependent upon brand recognition, but more dependent upon cost reduction, improved environmental compliance or performance issues which can only be maintained through innovation. Once again, investment in these forms of innovation are protected by patent rights.

The functions of intellectual property

Intellectual property is the system of legal rights which governs the world of products of the mind: ideas and expressions of human creativity. The essence of any property right is the ability to control access to and use of the property and its resources and facilities. Intellectual property, therefore, is about the control of use of ideas and the products of human creativity in all its manifestations, ranging from technical inventions in every field of science and technology through to the ingenuity of traders in improving their position in any market and the works of artists and performers in all fields of the arts.

The diversity of subject matter potentially or actually protected by intellectual property is bewildering. Consequently, the various forms of intellectual property devised to provide appropriate protection can seem to add up to a bewildering collection of overlapping rights, the relevance of any one of which in any particular transaction is impossible to fathom. As a result, in many contracts every possible kind of right or material which might have some bearing on intellectual property is included in an all-encompassing definition which is then used in a single clause to deal with all subsequent intellectual property issues.

This 'one size fits all' approach is not necessarily either appropriate or adequate. Intellectual property rights, and the related equitable rights in confidential information, come in all shapes and sizes for very good reason. They have been developed to provide suitable protection for the products of mental labour in a variety of different contexts, which are seen as a matter of public policy as deserving different qualities of protection.

Categorising intellectual property rights

Some intellectual property rights, such as patents and registered designs, are absolute monopoly rights. Even someone who comes up with the same product or design wholly independently can be prevented by the rightholder from exploiting his or her own work. This is a deliberate public policy to encourage financial investment in the sort of research activity whose fruits may be protected by such rights.

Other rights, such as copyright and rights in confidential information, are only partial monopolies, where a truly independent devisor of the same work has the right to exploit his or her own work regardless of the prior rightholder. Such rights can only be used to stop those who have in some way derived benefit from the rightholder's prior effort. But since all forms of intellectual property rights are monopolies of one kind or another, there is an inevitable tension between their exploitation and the functioning of a truly competitive market. Transacting in intellectual property on any but the very smallest scale requires a weather eye to be kept on the potential implications for competition.

The formalities associated with the various rights also differ widely. Some rights, most notably copyrights, arise automatically as soon as the new work comes into existence, whereas other rights have to be applied for and come into existence only when registered with a government authority. Some rights, again most notably copyrights, are effectively global rights; others, namely certain trade mark and design rights, may have limited international effect; but most are strictly national rights. Very few businesses today can be satisfied with rights limited to a single jurisdiction, so it may be necessary to apply for and obtain equivalent national rights in many countries.

Exploiting intellectual property effectively

Given the potential range of intellectual property which may be relevant to any given business and its dealings, the temptation to sweep it all up in a single definition is understandable. It is, however, increasingly unlikely to be seen as an adequate approach as businesses' reliance on intellectual property for their competitive advantage increases.

Owners of intellectual property have a range of freedoms to deal with their rights as they see fit, similar to the range of rights which an owner of real property has. The form of the rights available to be granted depends upon the characteristics of the property being dealt with. Permissions to use all or a subset of the rights can be granted for a single defined purpose or for all manner of purposes, for any period of time, and on an exclusive, sole or non-exclusive basis. It is up to the holders to decide how assiduously they wish to maximise the exploitation of their rights. The important thing is to appreciate the multiplicity of options and to decide whether or not to identify and manage each of them, or treat them as a whole to be worked out by a licensee.

To deal with intellectual property issues effectively it is important to appreciate which rights really matter in a given transaction and to ensure that those are properly addressed. This means understanding what kind of context each right was designed for, and asking questions about the business underlying the transaction to identify the rights which are going to be material. It may have the added bonus that some rights can be ignored altogether, simplifying the text and enhancing the likelihood that not only will the contract say more precisely what it means, it will be relatively easy for anyone, including a court, who is subsequently faced with trying to interpret the contract to identify that meaning.

Limitations of intellectual property

Intellectual property has its limitations, of course. For a start, the TRIPS Agreement mandates only a minimum standard of protection and there is only limited international consensus as to what intellectual property ought to protect. The most notorious example of this is that business methods are considered to be patentable in the USA, whereas in every other country they are not, leaving the financial services industries in particular dependent upon trade secrecy and copyright to protect their latest ideas. Since patent protection is conditional upon publication of the invention, this means that US banks and brokers face a dilemma: obtaining strong protection at home means disclosing the invention without protection in the rest of the world.

Secondly, the protections available in the form of the various different legal rights are in most cases the *only* form of protection available for the 'property' concerned. Ownership of a car in the UK is protected not only by a contract of sale and registration with the DVLA but also by a key which bars access to all but those with conscious criminal intent. As a result, the owner is unlikely ever to have to resort to the civil courts to prevent law-abiding third parties from using that car without consent. In contrast, ownership of a trade mark is protected only through the legal rights adhering to the mark which may, but need not, be signalled to the rest of the world through an entry in the Trade Marks Registry. The result is that otherwise law-abiding third parties, seeing the mark in use and knowing nothing of the system of trade mark rights, may well decide that the same or a very similar mark would be useful in promoting their own businesses – and without any awareness of potential wrong-doing, proceed to do so. This multiple use may have been in progress for some time before it comes to the attention of the trade mark owner, by which time the 'borrower' has itself invested significantly in promoting the new mark, and is reluctant to cease using it. Consequently, the owners of intellectual property need to exercise far more active vigilance than the owners of physical property, and are very much more reliant upon the civil courts to enforce their rights.

The protection afforded by intellectual property is also capable of being undermined by an inexperienced judiciary. Thus, although most countries apart from the least developed now have a framework of modern intellectual property laws in place which are compliant with the global norms, very few countries have courts which are really familiar with this branch of commercial law, leaving them more susceptible to persuasion by a skilful advocate than they would be on better understood subjects. The impact of low levels of judicial expertise is far greater upon intellectual property assets than upon a business's other assets. The English courts have developed significant expertise in intellectual property issues over recent decades and represent one of the most sophisticated systems available globally for determining related issues. Nevertheless, the constant evolution of the law under the flow of European harmonisation and other initiatives means that the scope of rights has for the last decade been uncertain in one respect or another, as yet more changes must be tried out through the courts.

1.2 IDENTIFYING THE RELEVANT INTELLECTUAL PROPERTY RIGHTS

The exercise should start from the pragmatic question of whether or not a particular kind of right is realistically likely to be encountered and whether it will matter in practice. There are numerous exotic species of intellectual property (such as semiconductor topography rights, plant variety rights and performers' rights) which apply exclusively to extremely specific industries and will simply never be relevant except in contracts directly relating to those industries. As regards these, all that the non-specialist needs to know is when they might conceivably be relevant, in order to do further research or seek expert advice if necessary. If they are not relevant, there is no need to include them in any definition or provide for the formalities to be completed. The rights falling into this category are each described in outline in the section on exotic intellectual property rights in this chapter, but are not otherwise dealt with in this handbook.

The remaining classes, such as patents, copyright and trade marks, are liable to be encountered frequently in transactions in almost any kind of industry. The relative *importance* of each kind of right will very much depend upon the particular industry and transaction in question. Even a start-up biotechnology company will own a significant amount of copyright, but the total value of that copyright pales into insignificance beside that of even a single key biotech patent. Each of these rights is the subject of a subsequent chapter of this handbook. The following section aims only to highlight which rights are likely to be important in any given context, and to give a flavour of their different characters.

1.3 THE PRINCIPAL FORMS OF INTELLECTUAL PROPERTY

Copyright

Copyright must qualify as the most widely known form of intellectual property. It is also possibly currently the most contentious as the music industry seeks to enforce its rights by suing numerous file-sharing operations worldwide and the individuals who use them.

In addition to being widely known, copyright is the most ubiquitous form of intellectual property: since copyright arises so easily, all businesses own copyright in numerous works. But most of these 'accidental' copyrights have no market value whatsoever. It is principally in industries which rely upon some form of artistic creativity (whether as a product in itself, such as newspapers, fashion or music, or as in advertising) that the copyrights have any significance.

Copyright is also important in protecting computer software, reflecting an historical initial assessment of computer programs as being a species of literary work rather than an industrial technology. It is also, of course, important in businesses which rely upon the written word even if they are not generally classified as 'creative', such as the precedents used in legal and financial services.

In other industries, copyright is generally a right of secondary importance, if any. The exception is where copyright and rights in confidential information overlap. It is commonplace for a business operating complex technologies to own or be licensed under multiple patents, but these will not necessarily incorporate every detail of the technology. 'Know how' as to how to optimise performance may be found partially in the form of operating manuals, stock records and quality monitoring test logs which, although mundane, nevertheless attract copyright protection under the English test for originality. The contents will also be protected as confidential information of the business, which provides a more effective form of protection since it protects the information itself, not merely the form in which it is recorded. Nevertheless, confidentiality is a leaky form of protection: once information has been disclosed it may lose its confidential status, whereas copyright remains in effect no matter to whom the information recorded may have been passed. Accordingly, copyright can be a worthwhile back-up to confidentiality in transactions relating to established technological processes, as well as in the opposite extreme of the creative arts.

The protection given by copyright is the longest-lasting of any intellectual property right other than trade marks. For most works it continues in effect for the entire lifetime of the author of the work, and for a period thereafter which varies from country to country but is generally between 50 and 70 years. As a result, it may be necessary to look further back through the annals of a business in order to be sure that all relevant rights have been identified and assigned, than will be needed in relation to shorter-lived forms of intellectual property.

It is less well known as having the dubious distinction of the greatest legal complexity. Copyright is, however, a relatively weak right. In order to establish infringement it is necessary to show that the alleged infringer has actually copied from the original. In some cases this may be straightforward – it is common to include deliberate errors such as spelling mistakes in order to demonstrate that copying must have taken place. But in many cases it requires the court to draw an inference from a striking similarity and for the owner to show that the alleged infringer has had some opportunity to copy the original. This can be both costly and uncertain.

Trade marks

Any sort of mark which a trader uses to distinguish its goods or services in the eyes of the relevant public can function as a trade mark. Words, logos and sounds are commonly used, and trade mark rights may accrue to these even without registration, provided they achieve a sufficient level of consumer recognition. Brands of all kinds are very valuable in many industries, but particularly in consumer goods and services, where the underlying product may be practically identical to its competitors but command twice the price because of its prestigious label. The extreme example of this is in the highly technical field of pharmaceuticals, where once patent protection has expired a trusted brand can retain market share because of its recognition amongst patients, in the face of very substantially cheaper and chemically identical alternatives.

Apart from the special case of the Community Trade Mark (CTM), a registered right which takes effect in all EU Member States, registered trade mark rights are strictly national in effect. Unregistered rights may have some international effect since WTO Member States are required by the Paris Convention of 1883 to provide protection to 'well-known' marks even if these are not registered in their territory. What is required to achieve 'well-known' status is a matter left to each Member State to decide, however, and as a result the test is highly variable.

Trade marks are the only potentially perpetual form of intellectual property rights. Provided a trade mark remains in use and does not become the generic term for the products it is used to promote (think of 'Hoovering' the floor), it can continue in effect indefinitely.

The strength, and hence normally value, of the rights obtained under a trade mark depends upon whether or not it is registered.

A registered trade mark confers an absolute monopoly on the use of the same mark for the same goods and services. Ignorance of the registration is no defence: anyone can check the register, and so is taken to have notice. The registration also enables the holder to prevent the same mark being used on similar goods or services, or to prevent a similar mark being used on the same or similar goods or services, if as a matter of fact consumers are likely to be confused by such use. A CTM is effective throughout all Member States of the EU through a single registration.

The rights of a proprietor of an unregistered trade mark depend upon the level of recognition of the mark amongst the relevant public, which is infinitely variable. The most widely recognised mark in the world is apparently the Mercedes badge, since although few other trade marks penetrate the Dark Continent, Mercedes cars are used throughout Africa for their durability and longevity. Such a level of recognition could confer a standard of protection similar to that of a registered trade mark. Other unregistered marks may only be able to retain exclusivity in a restricted geographical area, or for a very limited category of goods or services.

A final point: the relevant European legislation is the Trade Marks Directive EC/89/104 and refers to 'trade marks'. The equivalent statute in the USA uses the spelling 'trademark', which is often incorrectly applied in the European media.

Confidential information

Like copyright, most businesses will generate some information which they consider warrants protection through maintaining its confidentiality. Some information may have transient value, for instance plans leading up to a new product launch, while other may represent the core of the holder's business, as in the case of the famously secret formula for Coca-Cola.

Unlike copyright, there is no particular category of business for which confidential information is more or less likely to matter. These rights need to be considered in any transaction, in any context.

Under English law, no confidential information attracts protection in the form of a true property right: rights in information are purely rights to prevent the unauthorised use or disclosure of the information as a matter of equity. Rights in confidential information are therefore less flexible from the point of view of transacting in them than the intellectual property rights properly so called – they cannot be assigned or mortgaged in the usual senses. This is in contrast to the rights under the laws of various of States of the USA, where statutory 'proprietary information rights' may exist and be assigned, mortgaged and so on as property. It is particularly important not to allow intellectual property definitions to include proprietary information as a substitute for a clause specifically addressing confidential information as it is recognised under English law, although in practice this can be difficult when faced with a precedent of US origin and a counterparty who does not appreciate that difference.

Again like copyright, confidential information is only a partial monopoly right: an independent development leading to the same information cannot be prevented, the monopoly is only effective against the use or disclosure of information if it has been obtained from the person to whom it is confidential. It is however potentially even weaker than copyright, in that a business which wishes to assert that information is truly confidential needs to be able to demonstrate that it has made at least minimum efforts to ensure that it is kept confidential and that employees are aware of this. Mere assertion is not enough. Consequently, not only legal policing but practical measures need to be in place if confidential information is to retain its status and thus its value. If this is done effectively, information can remain confidential indefinitely, but a single instance of information reaching the public domain may result in confidentiality being lost forever.

Designs

Lack of harmonisation

Designs are key to the success of many consumer products, from household cleaning to luxury cars, but less important in industries where function or simple cost dictate the choice of a product.

Unfortunately, there is less international harmonisation for design law than for any other category of intellectual property. New designs in the UK can be protected by a series of overlapping rights: registered Community and national rights, unregistered Community and national rights, and in some aspects also by copyright. This adds up to a surprisingly complicated regime even within the EU.

Registered designs

Registered designs, like the other registered rights, provide an absolute monopoly. This can be used to prevent manufacture, import or sale of any product incorporating a design which creates the same overall impression on an informed user. Unlike registered trade marks or patents, there is no examination of an application to register a design, which means that this very strong right can be obtained simply by completing the appropriate forms and paying a filing fee. It will, however, be more vulnerable to validity challenges throughout its life than patent or trade mark rights precisely because it has not passed any formal verification process. Design rights can therefore be harder to value accurately than other registered rights.

The rights last for up to 25 years (subject to payment of renewal fees). In consumer products this will in many cases be longer than the shelf-life of the product. These are therefore potentially very powerful rights – and in the case of the Community registration, effective throughout all Member States of the EU.

Unregistered design rights

In contrast, unregistered design rights (whether Community or national) provide only a partial monopoly in that they protect only against copying, not against independent development of the same design. Other than this common feature, they fall into two categories of differing strength.

The unregistered community design right lasts only for three years. It is intended for very short-lived products such as fashion items, or to enable a company to 'road test' its design before deciding whether to invest in a design registration.

By contrast, unregistered design right under national law in the UK last up to 15 years but is subject to a compulsory licensing regime for the final five years. It is intended to provide protection for relatively utilitarian designs which may not meet the standard of novelty and individual character required for the other categories of design right. It is, however, unique in having virtually no international counterparts and in consequence the criteria for design protection include nationality requirements which, though present in respect of most intellectual property rights, have little significance where other rights are concerned because mutual recognition means that most countries' nationals will qualify. The design must also be original and 'not commonplace in the design field in question', and is subject to a number of exceptions (for instance, surface decorations cannot be protected by this right).

Patents

Patents, which protect technical inventions, are traditionally considered the strongest, and in many cases are the only effective, form of intellectual property. Their principal relevance is to manufacturing industries of all kinds, where they protect inventions either in the form of processes or products, and to the delivery of services which depend on technology, such as telecommunications networks. They provide an absolute monopoly against either copying or independent development, and give a relatively harmonised level of protection wherever in the world applied for. Protection lasts for up to 20 years (save in the case of pharmaceuticals, where an extension of up to a further five years may be available).

Despite the existence of a European Patent Office, unlike the position for trade marks and designs there is no such thing as a *unitary* European patent. The application process is centralised, but the end result is a bundle of identically worded national patents. This has been a target for reform for many years but to date political consensus has not emerged. Thus, references to European patents and UK patents are essentially a matter of nomenclature. A patent will be referred to as a European patent if the application passed through the centralised application process. It is likely to have identical equivalents in two or more other European countries. The rights conferred by the resulting grant are identical to those conferred by an application to the UK Intellectual Property Office.

Partly because they relate to technological developments and partly because of the legal conventions surrounding their drafting and interpretation, patents are seldom easy to understand. The accurate distillation of a technical idea from its description over tens or hundreds of pages is fraught with difficulties. Few non-specialists make any effort to understand specific patents despite their high market value. This can also translate into a failure to take care to ensure that the formalities of registering assignments and making sure renewal fees are paid, actually get executed. Patents lapse regularly through apparent oversight in these matters, and can be restored to the Register only in very limited circumstances.

1.4 THE EXOTICS: INTELLECTUAL PROPERTY RIGHTS UNLIKELY TO BE ENCOUNTERED IN MOST CIRCUMSTANCES

Plant variety rights

The European Patent Convention explicitly excludes from patentability 'any variety of animal or plant or any essentially biological process for the production of animals or plants, not being a micro-biological process or the product of such a process'. This exclusion arises because there is an entirely separate system of rights for the protection of plant and animal varieties which have been developed by use of the traditional techniques of breeding rather than genetic engineering.

It follows that this species of intellectual property is only ever relevant in transactions concerning agricultural businesses or commercial horticulture. Otherwise, it can safely be omitted.

Plant variety rights have never reached great prominence in the United Kingdom, being an import from the Dutch system of intellectual property. As may be imagined, plant varieties are an important issue in the Dutch economy and appropriate protection was developed many years ago.

Under the English implementation by the Plant Varieties Act 1997, a plant grouping within a single botanical taxon of the lowest known rank (i.e. a variety) can be protected. To qualify, the variety must be able to be:

(a) defined by the expression of the characteristics resulting from a given genotype or combination of genotypes;

(b) distinguished from any other plant grouping by the expression of at least one of those characteristics; and
(c) considered as a unit with regard to its suitability for being propagated unchanged.

A variety meeting these criteria qualifies for plant variety right if it is distinct, uniform, stable, and new. The person who breeds it, or discovers and develops it is entitled to apply for the right (unless he or she is an employee, in which case the employer has the right). Once granted the right lasts:

(a) in the case of potatoes, trees and vines, for 30 years from the date of the grant; and
(b) in other cases, for 25 years from that date.

The right entitles the holder to prevent anyone else without authorisation from:

(a) producing or reproducing propagating material of the protected variety or a dependent variety whose existence was not common knowledge immediately before the coming into force of the Act;
(b) conditioning it for the purpose of propagation;
(c) offering for sale, selling or other marketing;
(d) importing or exporting; or
(e) stocking for any of the purposes mentioned.

The right is subject to important exceptions. The rightholder cannot prevent a farmer using for propagating purposes the product of the harvest which he has obtained by planting on his own holding propagating material of either the protected or a dependent variety. The seed must also be planted in a field on his own holding. The rightholder is, however, entitled to equitable remuneration for such use. Nor can the rightholder object to acts done for private and non-commercial purposes (e.g. amateur gardening), acts done for experimental purposes, or acts done for the purpose of breeding another variety.

Further, there is a compulsory licensing regime if the Controller is satisfied on application that the holder of any plant breeders' rights:

(a) has unreasonably refused to grant a licence to the applicant; or
(b) has imposed or put forward unreasonable terms in granting, or offering to grant, a licence to the applicant.

Geographical indications of origin

This form of quasi-intellectual property arises from the French and Italian 'appellation d'origine controlée' system. The object is to protect local designations of agricultural produce and foodstuffs (for example champagne and other wines, cheeses, meat products and so forth) which have a quality or characteristics which are essentially or exclusively due to the geographical environment in which they are produced. The system has been elevated to an international regime such that any WTO contracting country must provide such a system of protection.

The process for the UK is that at the request of an individual or group, the Department of the Environment, Food and Rural Affairs must make an application to the European Commission for a given identifiable product to receive protection, designating the area or areas in which it can be produced and the characteristics which define the protected product. So far, products such as Stilton Cheese, Scotch Beef, Whitstable Oysters, Cornish Clotted Cream and Newcastle Brown Ale have been designated from the UK. An application is being made in respect of Melton Mowbray pork pies.

Once a particular designation of origin has been registered, only products complying with the characteristics specified and produced in the designated geographical area can use the designation. Misleading evocations of the indication, such as 'style', 'imitation' or 'as produced in', are also prohibited.

The right is not, however, exclusive to any enterprise or trade association; the designation of origin is available to any producer whose products meet the criteria. Thus, this is not a private intellectual property right capable of private ownership or assignment. The most that an individual enterprise can claim is that it produces products which are entitled to use a given indication of origin, so that for instance a purchaser of the business will be entitled to use the same indication provided that it maintains the production process and location as previously established.

Utility models

Another form of intellectual property right frequently mentioned but rarely discussed is the utility model (sometimes known as a 'petty patent'). In countries which provide for it, this is a form of protection for technology again, but applicable to inventions or improvements which do not meet the criteria for patentability, for instance by not being sufficiently inventive. The application is generally registered without being examined. Accordingly, the protection lasts for a shorter period than patent protection, usually six or 10 years.

This form of protection is, however, available only in some countries, and these do not include the United Kingdom. The European Commission consulted with industry in the late 1990s as to whether there would be support for harmonising the system of utility model protection by extending it to all Member States, and found that there was not. In the United Kingdom, therefore, it remains the case that either an invention is patentable or, if it is not, the only form of protection available is secrecy.

English companies are of course eligible to apply for utility model protection in those countries, such as Germany and Australia, where this is available. Indeed it is common in Germany to file an application for a utility model while the patent application is being prosecuted through the Patent Office, to provide interim coverage. If such rights are then sought to be enforced, their validity has to be considered as well as whether or not they are infringed, in contrast to patents, which the German infringement courts generally treat as valid unless shown a clear and compelling reason why they are not. As a result, though utility model protection is relatively cheap to obtain there may be additional costs when enforcing. However, English companies rarely register such rights. Unless a transaction has an international dimension including research carried out in such countries, utility models are likely to be irrelevant.

Semiconductor topography rights/'mask rights'

Semiconductor topography rights, known to US lawyers as 'mask rights', are, as their name suggests, specific to the semiconductor industry. They are a special protection introduced by countries worldwide in the 1970s under heavy pressure from the US and Japanese governments. In the UK, they are implemented by the Designs (Semiconductor Topographies) Regulations 1989, SI 1989/1100.

The US and Japan were in the 1970s the only countries with the expertise to design and build commercial silicon chips. Laying out electronic circuits in three dimensions configured such that they could be built in a solid state format, and then chemically doping the silicon to produce the structures required, is highly skilled. In practice the process of doping and layering is performed by applying a series of lithographic masks across the surface of the silicon so that only the area being worked on at any one time is exposed to the chemical doping. The masks therefore embody the exact structures to be embedded into the silicon – hence the name 'mask rights'.

However, it is possible, if anyone is prepared to invest the necessary time and expense, to slice a silicon chip up finely and determine exactly how it has been structured and chemically altered in order for the various gates, capacitors and circuit connections to function. The US and Japanese governments feared that other countries' industries could by such analysis take advantage of the work that went into their products.

Semiconductor topography rights will never be relevant to any company other than a designer or manufacturer of semiconductor chips. In practice, they may not be relevant even to those working in that industry. Despite the fears of the US and Japanese industries, once the principle of how to treat silicon had become well known it was found to be both quicker and cheaper for competitors to design their own masks and structures rather than painstakingly to reverse engineer existing chips. There has never been a litigation over mask rights, and they remain on the statute book essentially through inertia.

Exclusivity rights over regulatory data

This is a form of protection, although (like rights over confidential information) not a property right as such, which has significant value in the pharmaceutical, veterinary medicine and agrichemicals industries. It has no application whatsoever outside these industries, and so is wholly irrelevant to the vast majority of commercial transactions involving intellectual property.

It arises because of the strict regulatory regime which applies before any medicinal or veterinary product or pesticide can be put on the market. In order to obtain a marketing authorisation, the applicant must first demonstrate the product's safety, efficacy and quality to the required standards. Demonstrating safety and efficacy of medicines involves very extensive preclinical and clinical testing, all of which must itself be conducted in accordance with stipulated standards and procedures. To demonstrate that the product is of the necessary quality, data must be supplied showing the manufacturing processes to be used for the product, their stability, characterisation and control. In the case of pesticides and herbicides, field trials are necessary which will measure the effect on surrounding plants and animals, the soil and the residues in food products such as meat and milk. All of this information must be presented in a specified format with an overview and summaries. The process takes years and costs millions of pounds.

Special protection for this data is necessary since the applicant does not have the option of keeping it secret: it has to be supplied to the regulatory authority. Once the regulator is satisfied that the new product is indeed safe and effective, there would in principle be no barrier (other than concerns over the manufacturing process used by a second applicant) to the regulator granting further marketing authorisations without requiring the tests to be repeated. Indeed, it would arguably be unethical to require further clinical tests to be carried out, in the interests of patient health. Understandably, the first applicant would view any such second grant as an unfair exploitation of the initial work in devising and carrying out the required tests.

Under Directive 2004/27/EU all Member States must grant 10 years' exclusivity to the first applicant's regulatory data in respect of a new medicinal product. Similar protection is provided for agrichemicals under Arts.13 and 14 of Directive 91/414/EC concerning the placing of plant protection products on the market.

The system has some additional subtleties.

First, regulatory data provided in support of an application for marketing authorisation for medicinal products for human use will only have eight years of absolute protection. After that, an applicant for an authorisation for a generic version can rely upon the originator's data in support of their application. However, the products themselves have at least a 10-year period of marketing protection. Hence, even once a marketing authorisation has been granted to a second applicant in reliance on the originator's clinical data, the generic applicant cannot start selling until the remaining two years have elapsed. Further, this period of marketing exclusivity can be extended to a maximum of 11 years if, during the first eight years after authorisation, the marketing authorisation holder obtains an authorisation for one or more new therapeutic indications which, during the scientific evaluation prior to their authorisation, are held to bring significant clinical benefit in comparison with existing therapies.

There is also a new provision providing a non-cumulative period of data exclusivity of one year in respect of data submitted in support of an authorisation for marketing a well-established substance for the treatment of a new indication, where such data has been generated by carrying out 'significant' pre-clinical or clinical studies, and special provision for medicines for pædiatric use and orphan drugs.

Performers' rights and other neighbouring rights

The evolution of sound recording, film and video led for the first time to the permanent recording, and subsequent repetition and exploitation, of formerly evanescent performances, which accordingly became capable of protection as 'works'. Since all of these new types of works have individual characteristics unlike those of the 'traditional' copyright works, they have been granted protection under rights specifically crafted to reflect the particular needs of the respective industries: performers' rights, rental and lending rights, for example. These are often referred to as 'neighbouring rights' since, in terms of subject matter at least, they are close neighbours of copyright.

These rights are therefore relevant only in the field of the performing arts and the recording industry. They are substantially harmonised at the international level through the Rome Convention, which provides for performers to have rights in respect of the recording and exploitation of recordings of their performances, as well as rights for phonogram producers. In the UK, these rights are implemented in the Copyright, Designs and Patents Act (CDPA) 1988 (as amended).

Performers have both property and non-property rights as regards recordings of their performances, set out in CDPA 1988, ss.182–4. The property rights are the rights to authorise the reproduction, distribution, rental and lending of copies of a recording. The remaining rights (i.e. to consent to recording or transmission of a performance, to consent to the use or making available of a recording or to consent to importation, possession of and dealing with a recording, and to receive equitable remuneration for the playing of commercially produced sound recordings) are not property rights. The distinction is important since an injunction is available as well as damages in respect of infringement of the property rights, whereas the action for infringement of the non-property rights is an action in breach of statutory duty for which the remedies are limited to damages and the delivery up or seizure of illicit recordings. Further, the property rights can be assigned, mortgaged or passed by inheritance. In contrast, the non-property rights are not assignable (although they can become exercisable by an heir).

The performances that these provisions aim to protect are dramatic or musical performances (including variety acts) and the reading or recitation of a literary work. Although there have been attempts to argue that the scope should include sporting moves, these have not met with general acceptance.

The protection is extended to nationals of, or performances which take place in, qualifying countries. These are defined by inclusion in the Copyright and Performances (Application to Other Countries) Order 2005, SI 2005/852. The list is long, but not as comprehensive as the list of countries recognised in respect of copyright itself. Care should therefore be taken where a performance by a non-EU citizen has taken place outside the EU to check whether the country concerned is one in respect of which performers' rights will arise.

1.5 CONCLUSION

The rights falling into the specialist categories of intellectual property described in **1.4** are relevant only in agreements relating to the specific industries for which they were devised, and can safely be ignored in all other agreements.

The principal intellectual property rights, discussed further in the remaining chapters of this handbook, are likely to be important across a range of industries and should be considered on a case-by-case basis.

In particular, the provisions governing first ownership of the various rights and what formalities are involved in completing ownership on a transfer of title are often overlooked. This frequently leads to problems in proving title as and when any dispute arises such that the right has to be enforced. A right which cannot be enforced has little or none of its potential market value.

CHAPTER 2

Copyright

Lorna Brazell

2.1 INTRODUCTION

Historical background

The first statutory copyright was introduced in the early eighteenth century to improve the protection of printers from the commercial depredations caused by 'pirate' copying of the literary works they produced. Initially, the right was obtained through a registration of a work at the Stationers' Company of the City of London. The requirement of registration in order for a work to be protected by copyright was abolished many years ago, however, and the register therefore fell into disuse.

Copyright is the most international of intellectual property rights. Works by British nationals or residents, or which are first published in the UK, are automatically protected by copyright in almost all industrialised and most developing countries thanks to the Berne Convention on Copyright of 1885. This sets a minimum standard of protection for copyright works and in particular requires all signatories to grant the same protection to works of foreign authorship (as long as the foreign author comes from another Berne member country) as to works of its own nationals. Even countries which have not actually joined Berne are generally required under the World Trade Organisation rules to give foreign works at least as good protection as Berne would require.

As technology has developed, a variety of different forms of work and their propagation have evolved which were not protected by the original copyrights (for example, sound, film and video recording, cable and satellite broadcasting). Copyright has therefore been progressively extended.

Common law and civil law

Although copyright in the UK originated as a protection for commercial interests, there has always been another approach taken in continental legal systems: that the right aims to protect not the printer but the author. Thus, whereas the UK initially gave a copyright with a term of only 28 years in total (sufficient for the printer to recoup his investment in producing the book), the continental systems based the term of protection on the lifetimes of the author and the author's heirs. Today, all EU countries give copyright lasting for a minimum of 70 years after the author's death (*post mortem auctoris* or 'pma') – potentially, for a work written today by a person in their twenties, a total in the region of 150 years. This is wholly disproportionate to the value of the right itself in the majority of cases.

Copyright works and physical possession

Copyright is completely independent of the physical medium in which the work has been recorded. Thus, the owner of a painting or a book does not acquire any rights at all to copy that image or text, unless a separate licence for the purpose is obtained. The failure of the general public to appreciate and respect this distinction has led, now that means of perfect, instantaneous copying and transmission have become widely available, to a crisis of the copyright-based industries as to what business model may in future enable them to supply works in a form for which consumers will pay, while simultaneously allowing them to retain control and the ability to profit from such supply.

2.2 SUBJECT MATTER OF PROTECTION

Copyright subsists only in the types of work listed in CDPA 1988, s.1. There are eight categories: literary, dramatic, musical or artistic works; sound recordings; films; broadcasts; and typographical arrangements.

Traditional copyright works

Artistic works

An artistic work is comprehensively defined by CDPA 1988, s.4 as being either:

(a) a graphic work, photograph (including X-rays or holograms), sculpture or collage;
(b) a work of architecture; or
(c) a work of artistic craftsmanship (such as clothing, ceramics or other craftworks)

A 'graphic work' is further defined as:

(a) any painting, drawing, diagram, map, chart or plan; and
(b) any engraving, etching, lithograph, woodcut or similar work.

This definition has required little clarification by case law.

Dramatic works

Dramatic works include dance and mime, provided that the work is capable of being performed in front of an audience. In *Norowzian* v. *Arks Ltd (No.2)* [2000] FSR 363 a claim of infringement failed in respect of a film of a solo dancer. The film itself had not been copied but reconstructed, so the claim had to be brought in respect of the dramatic work which was its subject. However, the 'dance' in that case was not shown in full; by use of an editing technique called jump cutting the dancer was made to appear to perform a series of moves which no human could in fact have performed as shown. The claim that there was an underlying dramatic work which had been copied therefore failed. Nevertheless, in recognition of the genuine creativity involved in its production, the Court of Appeal held that the film itself was a dramatic work and therefore protected.

Literary works

Literary works include any work which is written, spoken or sung, and therefore covers tables and compilations, and computer programs and preparatory works therefore (for example, flow diagrams), but not single words no matter how original nor at what cost invented. Slogans are also on the edge, the question being whether they qualify as a 'work' in the first place, that is, something intended to give either 'information and instruction or pleasure in the form of literary enjoyment' (*Hollinrake* v. *Tryuswell* [1884] 3 Ch 420). For example, the name 'Exxon' was selected after extensive research to confirm that it had no meaning in any major human language – but even so it was not protectable as a copyright 'work' (*Exxon Corp* v. *Exxon International Consultants Ltd* [1982] Ch 119). Similarly, the slogan 'youthful appearances are social necessities, not luxuries' was considered too trivial to attract copyright (*Sianamid* v. *La Maison Kosmeo* (1928) 139 LT 365). Exactly where the threshold lies is a matter of judgment in each case. There is no doubt that a poem of only four lines would be protected, but two lines of rhyming advertising jingle might be highly debatable.

Databases are capable of protection by copyright provided that they reach a minimum standard of creativity such that they can be considered 'the author's own intellectual creation'. This rather curious carve-out arises from the introduction by the EU of a harmonised database right, a specific form of protection for databases which is discussed in **Chapter 10**. Prior to this right being introduced in 1998, English law protected all original databases as copyright works; the remaining copyright is intended to cover only those databases which do not qualify for protection under the new right.

Musical works

A musical work is any work consisting of music, but it does not exclude the work of editors of pre-existing (but incompletely recorded) works. In *Sawkins* v. *Hyperion Records Ltd* [2005] EWCA 565 the Court of Appeal confirmed that the editor of a 'performing score' of the works of Lalande, a seventeenth century composer many of whose works were available only in the form of parts for some of the voices and/or instruments, was entitled to copyright in his scores even though (as Hyperion argued) the more accurate his work in reconstructing what Lalande had originally written, the less 'original' the resulting complete score. Considerable skill, labour and judgement had been expended in preparing the complete scores for performance and the resulting work attracted copyright.

No aesthetic standard

The *Sawkins* case highlights an important point. Under UK law, copyright is for most categories of work independent of any kind of aesthetic or artistic 'minimum standard'. Thus, a child's scribble and a watercolour by a Royal Academician qualify equally for protection. An electrical circuit diagram is capable of being copyright (*Anacon Corp Ltd* v. *Environmental Research Technology Ltd* [1994] FSR 659). What qualifies a work for protection in the UK is the mental effort which went into its production, not any value judgement as to what that effort produced. This is not the position in some other countries, notably France, where protection is only given to works of some aesthetic quality. It is also subject to a single exception: in the case of works of artistic craftsmanship, an aesthetic threshold must be exceeded for copyright to subsist. This arises from the combination of terms 'craftsmanship' with 'artistic'. In the leading case, concerning mass market furniture, the artistry of the work appears to have impressed the House of Lords so little that they concluded it was not capable of attracting copyright protection (*Hensher* v. *Restawhile Upholstery (Lancs) Ltd* [1976] AC 64). Subsequent case law has confirmed that the issue here is the intention of the maker: the courts will not attempt to judge the artistic merits of a work, but a piece by a recognised ceramic artist such as Bernard Leach is more likely to be accepted as satisfying the test than those produced by Ideal Standard.

Idea/expression dichotomy and non-textual copying

The subject matter of the copyright is not the idea or information itself conveyed by the words, but the form in which they are expressed. This distinction, known as the 'idea/expression dichotomy' is not the end of the debate, however. The plot of a novel, or the sequence of presentation of information, may in themselves be copyright works capable of being infringed even though there has been no copying of the actual text in which the novel or history was expounded (*Harman Pictures NV* v. *Osborne* [1967] 2 All ER 367). This theory, sometimes referred to as 'non-textual copying', appears to offer a means to monopolise information or argument in the abstract and is consequently asserted for that purpose, with repeated lack of success. The most high profile case was *Baigent & Leigh* v. *Random House* [2007] EWCA Civ 247, which asserted that despite little evidence of copying of text, Dan Brown's novel *The Da Vinci Code* had copied the 'Central Theme' of a book published some 20 years earlier entitled *The Holy Blood and the Holy Grail*. The weakness of the case was apparent from the difficulty the claimants had in formulating what it was that was said to have been copied. The Central Theme as eventually formulated consisted of a series of 15 propositions concerning the life of Christ and subsequent history, all of which appeared in the novel. Unfortunately, not all of them appeared in *The Holy Blood and the Holy Grail*, and several of those which did appear in both works had also appeared in a number of publications independently of their proposition in that book. The claim inevitably failed, even though Mr Brown freely admitted that *The Holy Blood and the Holy Grail* had been one of the research sources for his novel.

The theory of infringement by non-textual copying remains intact (though the Court of Appeal disapproved that nomenclature), but allegations of such copying should generally be treated with a substantial degree of scepticism unless there is no other plausible explanation for striking similarities between two works.

Modern technologies

Sound recordings, films and broadcasts

Sound recordings are any recording from which sounds or the whole or part of a literary, dramatic or musical work may be reproduced. The definition is technology neutral and so applies to any medium or recording technique, whether or not known at the date of CDPA 1988. The right subsists in the master tape, although of course copies made of copies from that tape will still infringe. The right is independent both of the physical object in which the recording is embodied, and of the copyright in any music or other work which is the subject of the recording.

Under CDPA 1988, a film is any recording from which a moving image may be produced, irrespective of the medium on which the recording is made or the technology required to produce the moving image. Interestingly, the film's soundtrack is treated as part of the film copyright rather than a separate sound recording copyright. Once again, the copyright is independent of the physical object or the rights in any works the subject of the recording – and will subsist even if there is no underlying work. Thus a film of live events is as much entitled to film copyright as a film made to a script with a screenplay. Under the Copyright Act 1956 the position was considerably more complex but is beyond the scope of this handbook. Care should be taken where pre-1989 film copyright is concerned.

A broadcast is an electronic transmission of information for simultaneous reception by members of the public and capable of being lawfully received, or transmitted at a time determined solely by the transmitter for presentation to the public. Broadcasts over the internet are excepted from this protection *unless* they are effectively broadcasts save for the medium of transmission. So internet transmissions made simultaneously over the airwaves or cable and also over the internet, or transmitted over the internet as part of a scheduled programme service, will be included in the definition. This regime was considerably revised by the implementation of the Copyright Directive (Directive 2001/29/EC of the European Parliament and of the Council of 22 May 2001 on the harmonisation of certain aspects of copyright and related rights in the information society), and is discussed further in **Chapter 10** below.

Typographic arrangements of published editions

The subject matter being protected by this category of copyright work is the arrangement of the words and images on a page, i.e. the layout of a book or newspaper. Thus, a book which is a facsimile reproduction of an earlier edition of the same work will not attract protection; but if the publisher has decided upon a particular font, margin spacings, positioning of pictures and captions and so forth, these elements attract a copyright independent from that in the words and images being reproduced. This means that it provides a limited protection for a new edition of an out-of-copyright work. The font itself has a separate copyright as an artistic work, which is not part of the copyright in the typographic arrangement.

Moral rights

In addition to the commercial copyrights, an author may have certain additional rights, known as 'moral' rights over the work. These rights were first introduced in CDPA 1988 in order to harmonise English law with the continental treatment of copyright. They apply only to the traditional categories of copyright work (literary, dramatic, musical and artistic works) and to films. The beneficiary is the author or, in the case of films, the principal director. The moral rights are not property rights in the sense that they are not assignable, although the principal rights do pass by inheritance either along with the copyright or, if expressly treated separately, independently of it. Further, the moral rights can be waived by a signed, written instrument, either in respect of specified works or generally and for the future.

The principal moral rights, which last as long as the work is in copyright, are:

(a) the right to be identified as the author ('right of paternity': CDPA 1988, s.77);
(b) the right not to have the work subjected to derogatory treatment ('right of integrity': CDPA 1988, s.80).

The right of paternity is more-or-less self-evident (although, notably, it only applies to literary, dramatic and musical works if the author 'asserts' it either in a signed written statement or in any assignment of the copyright; in respect of artistic works, identification of the artist on the work or any frame is sufficient). It applies when the work is published commercially, performed in or communicated to the public (or in the case of artistic works, exhibited in public), or included in a film which is issued to the public. However, if the work was made in the course of the author's employment, then the employer obtains the right to ignore the paternity right (CDPA 1988, s.79(3)).

The right of integrity is a little harder to interpret, since it is unclear what treatment might be derogatory of a work. 'Treatment' is any addition or alteration to, deletion from, or adaptation of the work. 'Derogatory' is defined as including anything which distorts or mutilates the work or is otherwise prejudicial to the honour or reputation of the author – but authors are famously touchy people, and may feel themselves dishonoured more easily than less creative spirits. The test for what has been derogatory treatment is therefore likely to be an objective one, taking third parties' views rather than the participants. There has as yet been no useful case law as to what, objectively speaking, may amount to a distortion or mutilation or prejudicial to honour and reputation. Minor changes the identification of which was likened to 'a child's game of "spot the difference"' were held not to amount to derogatory treatment (*Tidy* v. *Trustees of the Natural History Museum* (1997) 39 IPR 501).

This right accrues to the same categories of persons (i.e. authors and directors) as the paternity right, but it does not need to be asserted.

In addition, there is a moral right, pertaining to anyone who may need to make use of it, not to have works *falsely* attributed to them as author or director (CDPA 1988, s.84). It applies either to straightforward false attribution of a work, or to false attribution that a work is an adaptation of another's work.

Finally, there is a limited 'right of privacy' whereby the commissioner of personal photographs (weddings, funerals and the like) may object to these being published, broadcast or shown in public even though, in the absence of an express assignment, the photographer will own the actual copyright (CDPA 1988, s.85). This is intended to balance the change implemented by CDPA 1988 whereby the commissioner ceased to be the automatic owner of copyright in such photographs. The right lasts as long as the copyright, and although not assignable can pass by inheritance.

Any other persons who happen to appear in the photographs have no right to object; only the commissioner can enforce the right. This is consistent with the absence from English law of any image or personality rights: unlike many other countries, no one in England has any right to object to being photographed, or to having photographs taken of them being used for any purpose, provided that the taking of the photograph was not an invasion of privacy in the first place. Thus most people are 'fair game' at any time when they are in a public place. This is discussed further in **Chapter 6** in the context of the Article 8 right to private life.

Equivalent moral rights accrue to performers, i.e. the right to be identified as the performer and to object to any distortion, mutilation or modification of a performance which would be prejudicial to the performer's reputation (Performances (Moral Rights etc.) Regulations 2006, SI 2006/18). Curiously, these rights apply only in respect of the sound element of a performance not to the visual elements. The right of identification, like the right of paternity, needs to be asserted.

2.3 QUALIFICATION FOR PROTECTION

Originality

To be protected by copyright, a work must be original, which means no more than that it is not a copy of a previous work. It is generally enough that the work is the production of something in a new form as a result of the skill, labour and judgement of the author, even if another had already achieved the same result by a different method. There is a bottom line: a work will not be protected if its creation was a matter of routine such as arranging names in alphabetical order, or filling in colours according to existing instructions. But beyond this, any degree of originality is sufficient.

It does not even matter if the end result is identical to an existing work. For example, a table of trigonometric functions or logarithms, if individually calculated afresh, could be a copyright work notwithstanding that the answers have been known for over a century. Similarly, copyright may subsist in a compilation of data, a translation of a work from another language (including a computer code in one language into a computer code in another), an anthology or a collage if enough work was put into their production. Where the 'new' work is an abridgment, consisting of selections from an existing work, there may or may not be any copyright depending upon the skill and judgement needed to perform the selection.

One area where uncertainty lingers is in the case of photographs, which may in effect be a mere reproduction of a pre-existing work. Parliament was in no doubt when passing the 1862 Fine Arts Act which conferred copyright on photographs that a photograph of a pre-existing work, such as an ancient fresco in a distant country, could properly be the subject of copyright, and this was reflected in early case law (*Graves' case* (1869) 4 LR QB 715). However, this has not been tested for many years, during which the level of skill and labour, if not judgement, needed to take a good photograph have dramatically diminished. In the US, the decision in *Bridgman Art Library Ltd* v. *Corel Corp* 36 F Supp. 2d [9] (SDNY 1998) concluded that a photograph faithfully reproducing a painting was not sufficiently original to attract copyright, but no equivalent case has yet arisen to establish whether the English courts would now take a similar position.

Note that the lower the degree of originality that a work possesses, the more slavish or direct a copy will have to be to infringe the copyright. Thus, all that the logarithm table copyright in the above example is likely to protect against is exact reproduction of virtually the whole table, whereas copyright in a striking modern painting will protect not only against complete reproduction but also potentially against copying of significant details, or borrowing of the underlying structure or of the colour scheme.

Fixation

A further problematic area is the question of ownership of copyright in a work recorded by an amanuensis. Since the category of literary work includes anything 'spoken or sung' it is not incumbent upon an author to write down his or her work, but CDPA 1988, s.3 requires literary, dramatic and musical works to be fixed in some tangible form in order for copyright to arise. Up until that point, the work may be reproduced without any infringement. To whom, then, does the copyright belong once the work has been 'fixed'? The normal interpretation is that it belongs to the author rather than to the secretary or transcript writer who happens to record the work in tangible form. However, this natural interpretation has been subject to contrary interpretation in a number of cases. In *Walter* v. *Lane* [1900] AC 539 copyright in detailed notes of a politician's *ex tempore* public speech was awarded to the journalist on the grounds that the transcription of a speech into shorthand and subsequently into a newspaper article is an original work which requires skill and labour, and can therefore be protected against copyright, notwithstanding that any other shorthand writer who might have been present could equally have produced a substantially identical report. This decision was upheld in the 1990s, although despite this there is no suggestion that a secretary who took a letter by dictation would obtain copyright – the margin of skill involved being insufficient.

Notably, there is no requirement of fixation in respect of artistic works. Installations attract protection although there has not yet been any case law as to whether copyright in such a work would be infringed by the re-creation of the same combination of elements in a different space.

Nationality

In order to be protected under English law, a copyright work must qualify by reference either to its (human) author, country of first publication or, for a broadcast, the country of origination of the broadcast.

The author is a qualifying person if at the material time (of making or publication of the work) he or she was a national of an EEA country or another country to which CDPA 1988 has been extended or applied by Order in Council. The current Order is the Copyright (Application to Other Countries) Order 1999, SI 1999/1751, which covers most jurisdictions.

Similarly, first publication in any of the same countries will qualify the work for copyright protection, even if the work is simultaneously (meaning 'within 30 days') published in a non-listed country. Publication is sufficient if it is intended to satisfy the reasonable requirements of the public, which in the case of little-known or esoteric works may require as few as six copies to be put on sale (*Francis, Day and Hunter* v. *Feldman & Co* [1914] 2 Ch 728). However, performance of a literary, dramatic or musical work is not a publication for this purpose, nor is playing or showing a sound recording or film in public a publication. By CDPA 1988, s.175(4)(c) works of architecture, sculptures and works of artistic craftsmanship are not published for this purpose if merely exhibited or if copies of images of them are issued to the public (either graphical or on film).

2.4 SCOPE OF PROTECTION

Introduction

Copyright, although by statute a property right, is essentially a negative right: to prevent others from carrying out a number of acts, known as the restricted acts (CDPA 1988, s.2). In addition, there are a number of acts which may infringe copyright if carried out in knowledge of the copyright: these are known as the secondary acts of infringement. It is an infringement to perform any of the restricted acts, without the copyright owner's permission. The effect of this exclusivity is to enable the owner to license or sell that right. However, it is not an absolute monopoly, since it does not give exclusivity against independent creation of the same or a very similar work. Further, any use of copyright material which is neither a restricted act nor a secondary act of infringement cannot be prevented using copyright law. A good example is the use of a directory to create a mailing list. Whilst it would clearly infringe copyright in the directory to print off a run of envelope labels bearing a substantial proportion of the names and addresses from the directory, it does not infringe copyright in any way to cut up the directory and stick the names and addresses onto envelopes.

Nor, indeed, does copyright give the author the right to stop absolutely all kinds of copying. There are a lengthy series of exceptions which permit limited copying in certain circumstances.

Infringement does not depend upon the alleged infringer having intended any harm to the copyright owner, nor even having obtained any commercial advantage from his or her act.

Restricted acts

Statutory definition

The acts restricted by CDPA 1988, s.16 are:

(a) copying the work;
(b) issuing copies of the work to the public;
(c) renting or lending copies of literary, dramatic, musical or artistic works to the public;
(d) performing, showing or playing the work in public;
(e) communicating the work to the public;
(f) making an adaptation of the work or doing any of the restricted acts in relation to an adaptation of the work; and
(g) authorising any person to do any of the restricted acts.

Copying

Copying includes reproducing the work in any material form, including a computer memory. A transient electronic copy in a computer memory infringes (CDPA 1988, s.17) as does a single handwritten copy. A recording of someone reading a book aloud is a copy of the book, as would be a silent film of it without benefit of any words at all. Similarly, copying includes making a copy in three dimensions of a two-dimensional work and the making of a copy in two dimensions of a three-dimensional work. Thus, manufacturers used to be able to claim that companies who copied their product were actually infringing copyright in the engineering drawings of that product by reproducing it in three dimensions. However, for designs created on or after 1 August 1989 it is no longer an infringement in the copyright in any record of a design for an article to make an article to that design or copy an article made to that design or issue copies to the public (CDPA 1988, s.51). Instead, a special limited protection for the design of three-dimensional articles was introduced (see **Chapter 5**).

To infringe, the copy has to be a copy of the *whole or a substantial part* of the work, and must be a sufficiently close copy that it can clearly be described as a reproduction or adaptation of the original.

(A) WHAT IS A SUBSTANTIAL PART?

The test of substantiality is one of quality as much as quantity: even if only a few lines are taken from a text, or only a detail from a drawing, if those are the memorable and acclaimed aspects of the particular work in question, then copyright may be infringed. On the other hand, a lengthier extract which comprises only trite and mundane material may not infringe. There is necessarily a degree of subjectivity involved in deciding exactly how much of a work amounts to a substantial part. For example, small amounts taken regularly from a serial publication are likely to infringe if the result is to reduce the market for the original in a particular field or area.

A substantial part of a work may consist equally in the underlying form of the work as in the actual words or lines used to express it. Where the skill and judgement which went into the original lay in the selection or arrangement of information, then copyright may be infringed by taking the selection or arrangement, even if the result is recast in different form.

Parodies, which deliberately attempt to recall the original but with intent to ridicule, are generally granted a degree of latitude but may still infringe copyright if they come close enough to the original to be said to have taken a substantial part.

(B) CONNECTION WITH THE ORIGINAL

It is also necessary to show that the alleged infringement has *in fact* been copied – that the infringer had had access to the original at some point and in some form before the alleged copy was produced, even if the infringer has now forgotten that he or she had ever seen it. There must be a causative link between the two works. This can be fulfilled if, for example, a manufacturer sees the original and later gives instructions to their designers to create a design, describing to them the object which they should produce. Even though the designers never see the original, nevertheless there is a clear link between original and copy, in the form of the instructions given by the manufacturer. Thus, to avoid any possibility of copyright infringement, the best way to proceed is to give only a general instruction and leave the designers free to develop as much as possible of the eventual product on their own: the 'clean room' approach. Issues relating to copying works in digital form are discussed in **Chapter 10**.

Issuing copies to the public

This refers to any copy not yet in public circulation, so that once an infringing copy (or a copy produced under a licence which has expired since its production) has been released, this does not render subsequent infringing copies any less infringing. On the other hand, it is not a primary infringement to resell an infringing copy which is already in circulation, although in some circumstances (discussed below) it may be a secondary infringement. Note also that where the work is a film, sound recording or computer program, any subsequent rental or lending of the work even after it has been put into circulation is still an infringement of the copyright owner's rental or lending right.

The effect of the EU provisions on free movement of goods under the EC Treaty, Arts.28–30, needs to be considered. In brief, UK copyright cannot be used to prevent the import into the UK of copies which had already been placed on the market in the EEA by the copyright holder or with the copyright holder's consent. The copyright is said to be exhausted by the first permitted sale in any EEA country. However, copyright is not exhausted by sales made without consent in the EEA, or by any sale (permitted or not) outside the EEA.

Rental and lending

Rental and lending are the same acts, distinguished only by whether the institution providing the copy to the borrower is doing the act for commercial advantage. The authors of works to which these rights apply have an inalienable right to equitable remuneration from the rental of the works, although they can assign the right to a collecting society to administer collection of the income on their behalf.

Performance, showing or playing a work in public

Performance of a work in public is restricted in respect of literary, dramatic or musical works, while showing or playing a work in public is restricted in respect of sound recordings, films and broadcasts. Performance includes showing a film or broadcast, playing a recording, reading a work or an unreasonable extract from it aloud. A performance/show is in public if the people attending are there in their public as opposed to domestic capacity. The numbers involved need not be great: playing music in a factory has been decided to be 'in public', as has showing an instructional video to a group of only 11 employees. Nor is the requirement to pay an entrance fee decisive (*Jennings* v. *Stephens* [1936] 1 All ER 409).

Communication to the public

Communication of a work to the public by electronic transmission is a restricted act either where the work is broadcast (i.e. a scheduled transmission, over the internet or otherwise) or made available for on-demand or other interactive access by members of the public. The audience for a broadcast need not be assembled together: individual guests in their hotel rooms can, collectively, amount to the public for this purpose so that a broadcast over an hotel entertainment system infringes (ECJ Case C-306/05 *Sociedad General de Autores y Editores de España (SGAE)* v. *Rafael Hoteles SL*).

This restricted act is discussed further in **Chapter 10**.

Adaptation

Adaptation is a restricted act in respect of literary, dramatic or musical works. What acts infringe depends upon the category of copyright work concerned. Adaptation of musical works is the creation of a new arrangement or transcription, whereas adaptation of a literary work includes translation, the making of a dramatic version of a non-dramatic work or vice versa, or the production of a cartoon or similar version. Translation of a computer program covers translation of source code from one computer language to another or from a computer language into a non-code form. As any or all of these acts may require considerable skill and judgement, the resulting adaptation may have sufficient originality to itself attract copyright protection – but it will nonetheless be an infringement of the adapted original.

Under US law, the owner of copyright in the underlying work has a claim to partial ownership of the adapted ('derivative') work. There is no such provision under English law.

Authorisation of an infringing act

It is as much an infringement to purport to authorise someone else to carry out an infringing act (for instance, directing a colleague to make a copy of a journal article) as it is to perform the act oneself. There may not need to be an express direction to do something which involves copying: in a noted Australian case, the University of New South Wales was held to be authorising its students to infringe copyright by providing photocopiers for their use in the library without restriction as to what the photocopiers could be used for, or supervision of their use (*Moorhouse* v. *University of New South Wales* [1976] RPC 151). However, it is not clear that this would have reached the same result under English law, which seems to require something more than merely enabling infringement. When Amstrad manufactured a tape cassette recorder capable of recording from one tape to another at high speed, they advertised it saying that it would 'enable you to make duplicate recordings from one cassette to another, record direct from any source and then make a copy and you can even make a copy of your favourite cassette'. The advertisement was held not to amount to an authorisation as such. It highlighted the ability to copy, but did not grant any right to do so in respect of copyright works. The court pointed out that the cassette recorders were equally capable of being used for entirely legitimate, non-infringing purposes (*CBS Songs Ltd* v. *Amstrad Consumer Electronics plc* [1988] AC 1013). This case is the basis for the English refusal to establish a system of charging levies on the manufacturers of equipment which is capable of being used for infringing purposes. Such levies are the norm in continental Europe.

Secondary acts of infringement

The secondary acts of infringement are set out in CDPA 1988, ss.22–4. They consist of dealings in infringing copies or articles designed or adapted for making infringing copies. Such acts will infringe only if the person concerned knows or has reason to believe that the copy in question is an infringing copy. If not, then the act does not infringe. Thus secondary infringement is considerably harder for the copyright owner to prove. In practice, when coming across an importer or dealer for the first time, it is essential to notify them of the existence of copyright so that they can thereafter no longer rely upon this let-out. This can be done in forceful terms since, unlike most other intellectual property rights, someone threatened with legal proceedings for copyright infringement cannot turn around and bring an action for an injunction against continued unjustified threats.

Infringing copies are not restricted to copies the making of which actually did infringe copyright. A copy will also be an infringing copy if its making would have been an infringement or a breach of an exclusive licence, had it taken place in the UK. Importation of such copies is therefore an infringing act – except where the copy is imported from elsewhere in the EU.

Similarly, dealing in infringing copies even by possession of them in the course of a business, as well as selling, offering for sale, hiring or offering for hire will all infringe. Distributing infringing copies non-commercially will also infringe if this is done to the extent that the copyright owner's interests are prejudiced.

There are further possible acts of secondary infringement relating to infringing public performances of copyright works. Finally, it is a secondary infringement to transmit infringing copies by a telecommunication system – for instance, by fax or e-mail or as an attachment to an e-mail – knowing or having reason to believe that an infringing copy will be made by the recipient in the UK or elsewhere. The very reception of a signal by a computer or fax machine causes an image or text to be produced on that apparatus, so this act is not dependent upon the recipient deciding to make further copies which also infringe; the simple automated reception of the copies completes the infringement.

Exceptions

Transient or incidental copies

The Copyright Directive attempted with limited success to harmonise the national copyright laws of the EU with regard to which acts were excepted from copyright protection. Its success was limited since the plethora of national exceptions recognised by different Member States had evolved from the different ways business has developed in those jurisdictions. Accordingly, the negotiations of the Directive resulted in many of the national exemptions being retained as options.

Only one, narrow, exception to copyright is mandated by the Directive, and that is an exception to the exclusive right of reproduction for certain *temporary* acts of copying which:

(a) are transient or incidental;
(b) are an integral and essential part of a technological process;
(c) have as their sole purpose to enable:

    (i) a transmission in a network between third parties by an intermediary; or
    (ii) a lawful use,

    of a work or other subject matter to be made; and

(d) which have no independent economic significance.

This exception is discussed further in **Chapter 10**.

Educational and public administration

Of the optional exceptions, CDPA 1988 permits a limited amount of copying for educational purposes, or by libraries and archives, since this is considered to be in the public interest. It does not extend to teachers being permitted to copy whole books and distribute them to pupils; a maximum of one per cent per quarter is allowed from any given work. Similarly, educational establishments may perform or show works in the course of their activities, record broadcasts and produce anthologies for educational use (CDPA 1988, ss.33–9). The exceptions only apply to educational establishments, so commercial course providers and conference organisers cannot rely upon it.

Copying within public administration (for parliamentary or legal proceedings, or of material on a public register) is also permitted.

Fair dealing

Limited copying may be permitted as 'fair dealing' for the purposes of private research or private study. Again, this relates to the use of abstracts and small excerpts from a complete work, not wholesale copying of texts. No commercial research is capable of being exempt on this basis.

It may equally be fair to copy for the purpose of criticism or review, provided that the work has already been lawfully made available to the public. Copying of a complete work, with the addition only of occasional marginal notes, is unlikely to qualify as fair dealing for the purpose of criticism; but a long passage with detailed commentary may.

Thirdly, it may be fair dealing to use copies in the course of reporting current events (as long as a sufficient acknowledgement is made as to the source of the material copied, unless this is impractical). Notably, the current events exception does not apply to photographs; this is to prevent newspapers from 'borrowing' each other's best shots for their own reports of the same event.

The test for what is 'fair' is a matter of degree and the impression the court forms of the defendant's conduct. The amount taken is clearly highly pertinent, as well as the use made of it. The more substantial the amount taken, the harder it will be to convince a court that it really is fair to do so. For instance, in *Time Warner Entertainment* v. *C4 TV* [1994] EMLR 1, Channel 4 had used 12 minutes (8 per cent) of the film *A Clockwork Orange* in a late-night programme discussing it. The excerpts amounted to 40 per cent of the programme. The Court of Appeal accepted Channel 4's 'fair dealing' defence holding that fair means fair: it is 'a common sense judgment based on amount, proportion, audience, genuineness of intention and motive'. In this case the use was fair because the programme quite clearly was a work of art criticism, the film was not commercially available at the time; nor was the use misrepresentative of the film as a whole since 'Criticism can be of the Work or the thought or philosophy behind the Work or just one aspect of the work'. The Court of Appeal also acknowledged Channel 4's regard of the film as a work of 'long-term social significance'. In these circumstances the total length of the extracts was within fair dealing.

Any use of a copyright work under such an exception must still satisfy the 'three-step test' set out in Art.9(2) of the Berne Convention for the Protection of Literary and Artistic Works, which provides the international framework for copyright protection. It requires that the exceptions:

(a) shall only be implied in certain special cases;
(b) which do not conflict with a normal exploitation of the work or other subject matter; and
(c) do not unreasonably prejudice the legitimate interests of the rightholder.

Thus any dealing which may have an impact on the copyright owner's ability to exploit the work is very unlikely to be considered 'fair'. Similarly, if the material has been published in breach of confidence, then it is unlikely to be considered fair (*Hyde Park Residence Ltd* v. *Yelland* [2000] 3 WLR 215), although leaking information which it is in the public interest to reveal may survive this hurdle.

Special exceptions to computer program copyright

Computer programs have always been protected as literary works, but several special provisions have had to be made. For a start, it would clearly be a major hindrance to the development of the software industry if a software house could effectively tie any customer to using their software only, by preventing other programmers from having any access to the source code, as is necessary in order to write compatible programs. Thus, an exception has been made to allow lawful users to decompile any program (from object code (readable only by computers) to source code (readable by humans)) where and to the extent necessary in order to make different programs interoperable. It is therefore allowed, for example, to decompile a software package in order to identify the correct parameters and addresses within the existing program, to which an interoperable program would need to refer, if this information is not readily available from the supplier of the software.

Further, it is permissible to run any program for the purpose of working out how it operates, despite the fact that this will infringe any copyright in the program (by creating transient copies in the computer's memory). It is also expressly permitted to lawful users of the program to make backup copies of a program legitimately obtained, to alter the source code to remove small errors or 'bugs', and to make minor changes to keep the software up-to-date. For example, if a design program incorporated safety standards and these were changed, it would be necessary to alter the values incorporated in the program. However, the copyright owner can by contract exclude this right, thus requiring all users to come back to them for any maintenance or development work.

This exception is discussed further in **Chapter 10**.

Time-shifting

In contrast to most other European countries, which provide a generalised exception for private copying, coupled with a levy on recording media and equipment the proceeds of which are distributed to copyright holders, there is no generalised exception for private copying in the UK. Nevertheless, CDPA 1988, ss.70 and 71 permit private recording of broadcasts for the purpose of time-shifting, i.e. watching at a time other than that at which it is broadcast, or photographing images from broadcasts. However, such a recording or photograph is exempt only if it is made for private and domestic purposes in domestic premises. If the recording is subsequently sold or let for hire, offered for the same or communicated to the public it becomes an infringing copy. The right covers rights in performances in so far as a performance is incorporated in a broadcast. Although Art.5.2(b) of the Copyright Directive requires that for private copying the rights holders 'receive fair compensation', s.70 is considered compatible since the prejudice to the rightholder is minimal.

Other exceptions

There are numerous exceptions of limited application, some more important in the commercial sphere than others. For instance, there is a special exception for commercial art galleries, to use copyright works for advertising the public exhibition or sale of artistic works, as necessary to promote the event but excluding other commercial use. The effect is that a sale catalogue which is not an infringement until the day of the sale becomes an infringing work the day after.

Including a copyright work incidentally in a photograph, film or broadcast does not amount to infringement. This exception is clearly necessary, since it would be impossible to record interviews or make documentaries without including some copyright work or other (many buildings are still covered by architectural copyright, for example). However, although the inclusion does not have to be accidental to be incidental, it is less likely to be considered incidental if it was done for a commercial reason (*FA Premier League & Ors* v. *Panini* [2003] EWCA Cw 995). The exception is applied less liberally in respect of musical works, since 'incidental' addition of music can add substantial value to a film or report. If music is included, it needs to be genuinely incidental, such as a report of a public ceremony including footage of a military band playing.

A similar exception applies to copies of buildings or models for buildings, sculptures, and works of artistic craftsmanship where on permanent public display. These can be included in a graphic work, photograph, film or broadcast without infringing the copyright.

The playing of sound recordings in charitable, religious, educational or social welfare clubs or societies is permitted without infringing copyright but only under very limited circumstances. The proceeds of any charge for admission to the place where the recording was to be heard and the proceeds of any goods or services sold by or on behalf of the organisation at the time must be applied solely for the purposes of the organisation. Further, the sound recording must be played by a person who is acting primarily and directly for the benefit of the organisation and not with a view to profit (i.e. not by commercial DJs at club social events). Provided that these conditions are met, there will be no infringement of copyright.

Likewise, where a broadcast is played in public but to a non-paying audience copyright will not be infringed if certain restrictions are complied with. This exception was formerly drafted inclusively, so as to permit the showing of a broadcast in public generally save in specified circumstances. It was revised following the Copyright Directive so that it now permits only not-for-profit organisations and TV or hi-fi sales and repair shops to play broadcasts without paying a royalty. All other organisations can now expect to be visited by the relevant collecting societies.

There is a right for the visually impaired to make a single copy for personal use; for instance in order to enlarge the font size. However, this exception does not create a loophole for the production of accessible copies: such a copy in the possession of anyone who is not visually impaired for any purpose for transfer to anyone other than a visually impaired person will be an infringement. The provisions are complex in order to make this exception workable.

2.5 DURATION

Works created under CDPA 1988

The basic period of protection under UK law for literary, dramatic, musical or artistic works and films created on or after 1 August 1989 (the date of commencement of CDPA 1988), the author of which is within the Berne Convention, is 70 years from the end of the calendar year in which the author dies. Where a work has joint authors (discussed under ownership, below) the term runs from the end of the calendar year in which the last survivor dies. This rule applies whether or not the work is published during the author's lifetime.

The moral rights, other than right to object to false attribution, also last until this point. The right to object to false attribution lasts only 20 years after the death of the falsely attributed 'author'.

If the author of a work is not known, the copyright period is reduced to 70 years from the end either of the year the work was written (if known) or the year in which it was made available to the public. Once the authorship is discovered, the normal rule applies.

For sound recordings, computer-generated works and broadcasts, the period of protection is only 50 years from the end of the calendar year in which the recording/broadcast was made (or, if a recording was not released immediately, 50 years from the end of the year when it was released).

The shortest period of protection relates to typographical arrangements, which are protected only for 25 years from the end of the calendar year in which the edition was first published.

Works created prior to the commencement of CDPA 1988

The superficially straightforward regime applicable to works created since 1 August 1989 is complicated by the variety of different terms which applied to different categories of works prior to CDPA 1988, the transitional provisions relating to the change in the term, and the existence of 'revived copyrights' in the works of authors who died between 1925 and 1945. Some works which were created when the Copyright Act 1911 was in force are still under copyright protection. A new Copyright Act was passed in 1956, including transitional provisions in respect of works already in existence and still in copyright. Works created while the 1956 Act was in effect have subtly different protection in some cases from works created since CDPA 1988. The ensuing complexities are beyond the scope of this chapter.

The term of copyright was extended to 70 years pma only in 1995, prior to which it had been 50 years pma. A provision therefore had to be made as to what would be done about works in which copyright had already expired but in respect of which it then came into existence once more. The owner of such revived rights was given the right to a reasonable royalty on uses of the works, but provided that notice is given of an intention to use such a work, the copyright owner no longer has a right to injunct any uses (Duration of Copyright and Rights in Performances Regulations 1995, SI 1995/3297).

There are also special transitional provisions to protect the rights of authors of works which were not published in their author's lifetime, where the author died before CDPA 1988 came into force. Such works and engravings (but not other artistic works) enjoy a period of 50 years' protection from the entry into force of CDPA 1988 (i.e. copyright will expire in 2039) unless the period would have been longer under the pre-1989 arrangements, in which case the longer period will apply. The same expiry applies to pre-1989 photographs which had been published before 1 August 1989, but pre-1989 photographs which were unpublished at that date have either their original copyright term *or* 70 years pma, whichever is longer.

Likewise, pre-1989 films and sound recordings and works of unknown authorship have special provisions which depend on whether they had been released or published at commencement of CDPA 1988. Works of unknown authorship produced between 1 August 1989 and 1 January 1996 have potentially perpetual copyright until they are made available to the public, after which the copyright lasts 70 years.

Publication right

A special pseudo-copyright applies where copyright has expired in a work without its having been published. This new right was introduced in 1996. The rights it confers are equivalent to copyright (i.e. to copy, issue to the public, adapt etc.), and last for 25 years from the end of the year of first publication. It accrues to the first lawful publisher (defined to include rental, lending or exhibiting in public) of any previously unpublished work in which copyright would have subsisted. This right is therefore significant to any library, university, gallery or museum holding a collection of materials, perhaps by bequest, which have never been displayed or published. The first publication does require the consent of the owner of the physical medium embodying the work.

The right is relevant in respect of any artist who died on or before 31 December 1956, since until commencement of CDPA 1988 the term of copyright in artistic works was life plus 50 years. Copyright has thus already expired in respect of any unpublished works of such an artist. In respect of writers and musicians, however, copyright in unpublished works will not expire until the end of 2039, so this right has no real value until that date.

Crown and Parliamentary copyright

The term of literary, dramatic, artistic or musical copyrights made by the sovereign or an officer or servant of the Crown is 125 years from the end of the year of making, unless published commercially, in which case it is 50 years from the end of the year of first publication. Any form of making available for electronic retrieval counts as commercial publication.

Acts of Parliament are copyright for 50 years from the end of the year of giving of Royal Assent, while other literary, dramatic, artistic or musical works of Parliament are copyright for 50 years from the year of making. Other categories of work get the normal period of protection.

2.6 OWNERSHIP

General principles

As previously mentioned, ownership of copyright (the legal right to prevent copying and other infringing acts) is not necessarily, and rarely will be, in any way associated with ownership of the physical object in which the copyright subsists. Purchase of a Howard Hodgkin painting does not, despite the expense, confer upon the owner any rights whatsoever under the copyright.

Ownership of copyright can only derive from the author. The 'author' of any work is the person who creates it, or, in the case of computer-generated works, the person who makes the arrangements for the work to be produced. The first owner of copyright is the author, unless the author is an employee who creates a literary, dramatic, musical or artistic work or film in the course of his employment, in which case the employer is the first owner of copyright in the work, subject to any agreement to the contrary. It is not necessary to stipulate this in any contract of employment, save to avoid any possible argument that any other provision in the contract is intended to exclude it.

Ascertaining what acts fall within the course of an author's employment is not always straightforward. Difficult issues arise wherever a person is employed to do a skilled and creative job, in trying to decide how far their employment should be considered to continue outside their normal working hours. For instance, a computer programmer who writes programs in his or her spare time may be developing on from the work he or she was instructed to do at work, but if the work is not done under instructions, not on work-supplied equipment, and not during the hours the employer is entitled to call upon the employee, then it is not evident that the work is in the course of employment. The line is blurred where the form of employment ordinarily entails irregular working hours. For instance, a teacher who prepares and marks lessons in the evenings and at weekends is arguably still working in the course of his or her employment in writing teaching materials wherever and whenever it is done. If, however, the normal teaching preparation is actually done during free periods at school but the teacher is also 'moonlighting' as a private tutor and preparing separate materials for this purpose, then those separate materials which are neither intended nor used for the employer's business are less likely to be considered within the course of the teacher's employment, even though they could be so used.

It is also necessary to distinguish between employment and arrangements more akin to contracting or consultancy roles. Where an author is hired to provide particular services, such as plan a particular advertising campaign, the relationship is not necessarily that of employer–employee and the copyright in any works created will not necessarily vest in the hirer. This needs to be tested by reference to the principles of employment law: does the hirer have the right under the contract to direct not only what is to be done but how; does the author provide his or her own equipment and bear any share of the risk; are paid holidays included in the arrangement; who pays National Insurance, and so on.

Finally, issues can arise in connection with directors and other officers of a company, who in many cases may have no contract of employment as such. However, a director owes a fiduciary duty to the company to act in its best interests, and the usual principle is that a director will hold any design or copyrights on trust for the company he or she works for, unless there is some reason to infer that he had any intention to do otherwise than that which his obligations as a director demand of him (*Ultraframe (UK) Limited* v. *Clayton (No.2)* [2003] RPC 23).

Joint ownership

If a work has been produced by collaboration such that separate contributions cannot be identified, and each of the collaborators has had significant creative input, then it is a work of joint authorship and the copyright is owned jointly between all the contributors. This does not apply to the position where different authors' contributions *can* be identified (for example, contributors of separate chapters to a book, or of the lyrics and music to a song). In that case, each contributor has a separate copyright in his or her own text.

Issues frequently arise as to the extent of contribution which is required to found a claim to be recognised as a joint author and therefore co-owner. Many works are the product of more than one mind, in the sense that an author may be inspired by an idea suggested by someone else, or a band may create a new song through a process of improvisation from a rough melodic line. There is a continuum between the slightest possible input ('let's do a song about breaking up a relationship') and a contribution which is just short of 50 per cent of the total work. Accordingly, what contribution will warrant a claim to joint authorship is a question of fact and degree in each case. A mere suggestion certainly will not entitle the contributor to any share in the copyright; a contribution of significant skill and labour which is reflected in the finished work certainly will. Performance suggestions, either in the form of tinkering with a script by a theatre director or a band member's contributions during rehearsal, will not normally qualify (*Hadley* v. *Kemp* [1999] EMLR 589).

Where, however, a building company executive gave very detailed instructions to a firm of technical draughtsmen as to the design of some new houses, including the materials which were to be used in their eventual construction, the court held that the skill and effort involved in 'creating, selecting or gathering together the detailed concepts, data or emotions which th[e] words or lines have fixed in some tangible form' deserved protection as much as the physical skill and labour in reducing them into written form (*Cala Homes (South) Ltd* v. *Alfred McAlpine Homes East Ltd* [1995] FSR 818).

This decision is consistent with the principle that a secretary who takes a dictated note does not obtain copyright in the work merely through being the instrument who gave it physical form. However, in *Cala Homes* the executive who directed what the drawings should contain was clearly very close to the final work in the same way as is a person giving dictation of a letter. Where only general direction is given leaving much of the detail and creative decision making to the person actually carrying out the work, the latter will qualify as the author.

Commissioned works

There is no automatic vesting of copyright in a commissioned work in the commissioner: contracts commissioning works in which copyright may subsist need to provide expressly for the right to be owned by the commissioner.

This provision gives rise to widespread confusion, partly because it is exactly the opposite of the law before CDPA 1988, under which the commissioner owned the copyright in a commissioned work. A licence will inevitably be implied for the commissioner to use the work for the purpose for which it was commissioned. For example, if an architect is commissioned to produce plans for a building, the contract may only require the architect to pass over the drawings themselves, but a licence will be implied to permit the commissioner to build a building to those plans (as this would otherwise infringe the copyright in the drawings). Similarly, an author who sends a manuscript to a journal will be implied to have licensed the publisher to include it in the journal. However, under the rule in *Liverpool City Council* v. *Irwin* [1977] AC 239, that licence will extend no further than is strictly necessary for the business purpose then contemplated. Thus, for example, art commissioned for an advertising campaign which is successful cannot subsequently be used for other campaigns without obtaining a further licence from the artist.

In rare instances, an author commissioned to produce a work may be found to hold the copyright on a constructive trust for the commissioning party (*Robin Ray* v. *Classic FM* [1998] FSR 622). Where the commissioned work is specific to the commissioner's business and the terms agreed include payment to the full value of the copyright, then the parties are taken to have intended that the copyright be transferred to the commissioner in due course. Consequently, even though there is no assignment the author retains no beneficial interest in the copyright and can be called upon to assign the legal title at a later stage. This analysis works by analogy with the position between a seller and buyer of land, where the seller holds the property on trust for the buyer from the point at which a contract is entered into until completion by conveyance of the legal estate. The trust is a legal mechanism invoked to prevent the seller (or, in the copyright situation, the author) from dealing with the property in a manner inconsistent with the buyer's (commissioner's) interests and to ensure that the seller takes reasonable care of the property.

This argument is the more likely to succeed where the copyright work concerned has a purely commercial function, for instance to be used as a company's logo. In such circumstances implying the grant of a licence to the commissioner would be inadequate, as the client would need some right to prevent others from reproducing the logo (*R Griggs Group Ltd and Others* v. *Ross Evans and Others* [2004] FSR 31).

The Court in *Griggs Group* listed some other examples of where an assignment of copyright could be required:

(a) where the artist works from sketches of the client, so could not use his or her own drawing without infringing the rights in those underlying works; or
(b) where the purpose of the commission is to produce a work which the client will sell copies of so that competition from the artist would undermine the whole purpose of the contract; or
(c) the artist works with the client to produce a composite work.

Formalities

Copyright can be assigned; by CDPA 1988, s.90 any assignment must be in writing, signed by or on behalf of the owner. If there are joint owners then all owners must be parties for the assignment to be effective. An assignment should specify which of the several rights in any work (for example, the right to copy, to perform, to make recordings and so on) are being assigned and in what territories of the world, as there is a separate copyright in every country. It is advisable, when taking an assignment of copyright, to include in the rights assigned the right to sue for past infringements, in case the value of the copyright turns out to be under siege from existing pirate copiers. If not expressly assigned, this right will remain with the former holder of the copyright.

It is a curiosity of the copyright regime in the UK that copyright in a work can be assigned before the work has come into existence (CDPA 1988, s.91(1)). Thus a contract commissioning the production of an original work can include an assignment of the copyright as and when it arises.

Copyright can also be licensed. Note that, in contrast to usage in US legal documents, under English law the terms 'sole' and 'exclusive' are mutually contradictory and should never be used in the form 'sole and exclusive'. A sole licence is one which excludes the copyright owner from granting any further licences to third parties, but does not exclude them from exploiting the work themselves. An exclusive licence excludes not only further third party licensing but also the copyright owner's own use of the work.

Similar considerations apply to the scope of licences as to assignments, so that for example a licence may give permission only to copy, or to translate but without the right to issue copies of the resulting translation to the public. In addition, terms need to be included as to how long the licence is to last.

Although ordinary (non-exclusive) licences can be granted orally, it makes for greater certainty, and thus enforceability, if the terms are written down. Any exclusive licence *must* be in writing (CDPA 1988, s.92).

Like other property rights, copyright passes by operation of law to a trustee in bankruptcy of the owner, or to his or her personal representatives on death. However, in order for it to become the legal property of any beneficiary a vesting assent must be executed.

Moral rights, on the other hand, cannot be assigned but can be inherited. They can also be waived under CDPA 1988, s.87, either generally or in respect of specified acts or occasions. This has substantially weakened their effectiveness, since in most cases an author has minimal bargaining power *vis-à-vis* the publisher, record or film producer, and it is standard in copyright assignments for many purposes to include a waiver of all moral rights so that assignees are free to deal with the copyright in any way they wish.

2.7 COLLECTIVE ADMINISTRATION OF ARTISTIC COPYRIGHTS

Once gramophones had been invented and the widespread reproduction of recorded music became possible, it soon became apparent that music performers and broadcasters would not be able to function if it were necessary in each instance to trace the copyright owner for each work and obtain a licence. Rather, it would be more efficient if a single organisation could hold all copyrights on behalf of the composers and grant block licences to radio stations, concert halls, record producers and so on. Thus, between 1910 and 1915 the Mechanical Copyright Licences Company (now the Mechanical Copyright Protection Society (MCPS), and covering TV, film and video as well as records) and the Performing Rights Society (PRS) were established, and have since been joined by Phonographic Performance Limited (PPL) (broadcasting of sound recordings). These organisations are known as 'collecting societies'. The author of a work assigns the relevant aspects of copyright to the relevant collecting society, which thereafter:

(a) negotiates licences with anyone interested in using the work;
(b) monitors broadcasters and anyone else using the work (for example, anywhere where music is played over a public address system such as cafes, shopping centres or airports needs a licence) to ensure that they obtain and abide by their licence – and sues them if they do not;
(c) collects licence fees and royalties and distributes them to the appropriate composers; and

(d) lobbies for any changes in the law which appear necessary to preserve or enhance their members' rights.

Similar problems began to arise in respect of written or printed works once 'reprographic copying' methods such as photocopying became commonplace. As a result the Design and Artists Copyright Society (in respect of artistic works) and more recently the Copyright Licensing Agency (in respect of literary works, in particular newspapers and magazines of all kinds) have been established.

Once the collecting societies had come into existence, however, they began to wield very substantial market power in their related industries. An inability to obtain a licence from the necessary collective administrator puts a business at risk of having to close down if it cannot operate without using the copyright works. There is therefore a dedicated Copyright Tribunal, a court whose principal function is to regulate the licensing schemes administered by the collecting societies to ensure that they do not abuse their power by charging extortionate fees or applying discriminatory terms in licences without due cause. Any party dissatisfied with the performance of a collecting society can bring proceedings at the Copyright Tribunal to have its activities and licence terms reviewed.

2.8 INFRINGEMENT

Introduction

Copyright infringement may be tackled by using either civil or criminal law, or both. The civil approach is at the option of the copyright owner, which has advantages in terms of control and speed, but also leaves the entire costs to be borne by the owner.

Criminal enforcement is carried out by local Trading Standards Officers and HM Revenue and Customs (HMRC), usually at the request and with the cooperation of the copyright owner (since there is no other means by which they might know what goods are pirate copies and which are not). There are several advantages to the copyright owner if criminal measures are used: costs savings because any investigation and prosecution is funded publicly; the increase in manpower which is made available by bringing in these authorities; and the potential application of criminal remedies including prison sentences. However, this approach is most suited to stopping relatively large-scale pirate copying of consumer items such as music CDs, clothing and so on: it is not suitable for preventing other unauthorised uses of copyright works, such as advertising. Further, there will often be a need for action to be taken swiftly, in which case a private (civil) action may be the only option.

Civil infringement

Who can sue and be sued?

The legal owner of any aspect of copyright in a work can sue for infringement of that aspect of the right. An exclusive licensee can bring proceedings as of right. Where an exclusive licence has been granted, if the copyright owner wishes to bring proceedings over an infringement which includes infringement of all or part of the rights covered by the exclusive licence, then the licensee must also be included as a party to the proceedings.

Sole or non-exclusive licensees do not obtain any right to enforce in their own name as of right. If such powers are required, the licence must expressly give the licensee the right to bring proceedings in the copyright owner's name.

If the copyright is jointly owned, any one or more of the co-owners can bring proceedings in their own right but must also join the co-owners. If one co-owner alone purports to grant a licence to a third party, then the licence will be invalid and the co-owner themselves may be sued for authorising an infringement.

In respect of moral rights, only the original creator of the work is entitled to sue for infringement – an assignee of the copyright has no rights and can obtain none.

Anyone who infringes copyright may be sued, whether the infringement is primary or secondary.

Preliminary relief – DIY seizures, search orders and freezing injunctions

(A) SEIZURE BY COPYRIGHT HOLDER

The copyright holder or anyone authorised by the copyright holder is allowed to pre-empt the need for court proceedings by seizing infringing articles under CDPA 1988, s.100 without any court order having been made (if the infringing copy was exposed for sale or hire), on condition that proceedings for copyright infringement are then started. The copyright holder:

(a) must inform the local police station in advance of what action is planned, in case there is a risk of a breach of the peace;
(b) can enter private land to which the public have access but cannot seize from a 'permanent place of business' (e.g. a shop);
(c) cannot use force; and
(d) must leave a prescribed notice at the place of seizure.

This section allows copyright holders to seize infringing goods from street traders and is classically used in relation to pop concerts, sporting events and tournaments. It is effective, but the drawback of not being able to seize from permanent place of business is limiting.

Since the power can only be exercised in public or on premises to which the public have access, it is most useful for dealing with, for example, traders selling counterfeit memorabilia outside stadia or concert halls. However, it is prudent only to exercise this right when it is absolutely obvious that the goods are counterfeit; if goods are seized which prove not to be infringing copies, then the copyright owner may be ordered to return them and, if unable, may have to pay damages instead.

The copyright owner is entitled to have an order for all infringing copies to be disposed of, so that these copies cannot find their way back onto the market.

(B) SEARCH ORDER

The search order (formerly known as an Anton Piller order) can be a relatively cheap and very effective means of recovering counterfeit or otherwise infringing goods and other evidence. The order acts in effect as a civil search warrant, requiring the suspected infringer to allow representatives of the claimant to enter and search their premises for specified goods or information. It is obtained by the rights owner without notice to the suspected infringer, although it will be necessary to issue proceedings simultaneously if not beforehand and to return to court within seven days for the order to be continued, and the respondent is entitled to apply in the meantime (generally on notice) for the order to be varied or discharged.

The search order is now governed by a Practice Direction under Part 25 of the CPR, which sets out an approved form of draft order on which the application should be based, and the judge's attention should be drawn to any deviation from it. Due to past abuses by search parties, the order will now be executable only during working hours and by a limited number of people. In addition a requirement for supervision of the searchers by an independent solicitor experienced in search work has been introduced, which adds to the cost and has correspondingly reduced the popularity of the order.

No force can be used – it is not a search warrant as such, just an order for the occupier to give their permission for a search, and even then subject to the occupier's right to seek legal advice before permitting entry. The search party must also keep a complete and detailed list of what is seized. The claimants themselves or their employees may not be permitted to participate if there is a risk that they will gain access to a trade competitor's documents; and steps must be taken to make sure the confidential information disclosed is not abused.

To obtain such an order it is necessary to have a very strong case and to be able to show a likelihood that the defendants will destroy evidence if proceedings on the usual (slower) timetable are followed. It is especially useful against fly-by-night operators. The 'Doorstep Piller' (formerly so named because no one actually enters the infringer's premises, but instead the infringer is ordered to produce and hand over the required items) can be used where there is less evidence available, and can be similarly effective.

The privilege against self-incrimination for criminal purposes does not apply to search orders in intellectual property cases. Instead, the information obtained is excluded from admissibility in criminal proceedings, so the infringer's civil liberties are protected, even though somewhat artificially.

(C) FREEZING INJUNCTION

A freezing injunction is an interlocutory order of the court restraining the party enjoined from disposing of or dealing with its own assets. The assets to be covered may be specified, but more usually are all assets falling within one or more specified categories. The order is intended to prevent the defendant taking action designed to ensure that an existing or future judgment is made less effective than it would otherwise be – although there is no need to prove nefarious intent on the part of the defendant.

The injunction may be expressed to affect the assets only to the value of a certain sum, leaving the defendant free to deal with the assets insofar as their value exceeds that sum.

Applications are made without notice but, as with applications for search orders, should be made in the form of the relevant approved draft in the Practice Direction.

To obtain an injunction the applicant must establish that:

(a) an action on the merits is proceeding in which the applicant has a good arguable case against the party to be restrained;
(b) there is a real risk that judgement will go unsatisfied by reason of that party's disposal of their assets, unless restrained (for example evidence of dishonesty or past incidents of debt default); and
(c) it would be 'just and convenient' in the circumstances of the case to grant the relief sought.

In applications for both search orders and freezing injunctions, the applicant has a duty to make a full disclosure of all relevant facts, including those unfavourable to the applicant's case.

Civil remedies

(A) DAMAGES

Damages are available to compensate the copyright owners by putting them in the position they would have been in had the infringement not taken place. This may be, for example, the profits the copyright owner would have made from selling the same number of original articles as the pirate has sold copies; although if the copyright owner cannot show that absent the piracy they would have sold those copies, they may only get a reasonable royalty on them instead (*Blayney* v. *Clogau St David's Gold Mines Ltd* [2003] FSR 19). Damages may also compensate for the suppression of the price the copyright owner can command for originals, due to the presence of pirate copies on the market. The damages available are limited to compensating for the six years prior to the proceedings being started, however, so where a long-standing pirate is only identified after some years it is essential to bring proceedings immediately or compensation for earlier infringement may be foregone.

Additional damages may be available in some cases where, for example, the infringer has done more than merely cause the copyright owner to lose a measurable amount of money, but has also damaged the market, or acted in the expectation that the amount to be made from infringement would outweigh any damages to be awarded against them. Flagrancy (deliberate or deceptive conduct, for example) of the infringement will be taken into account under CDPA 1988, s.97(2). The amount awarded under this head will vary widely according to the nature of the deliberate act. Cases where an infringer has a well-founded belief that on-going negotiations will lead to a licence in the usual way are at the opposite end of the spectrum from a cynical decision to infringe regardless of the copyright (*Ludlow* v. *Williams* [2002] FSR 57).

Damages are available for infringement of moral rights in the form of compensation for the creator's loss of goodwill and reputation (as economic rights) and for injury to feelings (in line with the damages awarded in libel cases).

(B) INJUNCTION

The infringer will also be permanently injuncted from either committing, or continuing to commit, the infringing acts. An application for an injunction pending trial can be made simultaneously with the issue of a claim form or at any later stage; a permanent injunction will only be granted after trial. This may not be granted if the copyright owner has acquiesced in the pirates' activities, or has delayed bringing proceedings to the extent that the defendant was seriously prejudiced (for example, where a former authorised dealer is led to believe that it has been permitted to continue dealing in copies).

Likewise, an injunction is available for the infringement of the moral rights.

(C) DELIVERY UP

Delivery up of the infringing articles may be ordered.

Criminal infringement

Criminal offences

By CDPA 1988, s.107 it is a criminal offence to do any of the following in respect of an article which the dealer knows or has reason to believe is an infringing copy:

(a) make it, for sale or hire;
(b) import it other than for private, domestic use;
(c) possess it in the course of business with a view to doing any infringing act;
(d) sell, let, offer, exhibit or distribute it in the course of a business; or
(e) distribute it, even if not in the course of a business, if it is to such a great extent that it prejudices the owner's rights.

It is also an offence to possess anything specifically designed or adapted for making infringing copies, if the holder knows or has reason to believe it is to be used for that purpose.

Mere denial of knowledge is unlikely to be a successful defence in intellectual property rights cases. However, the prosecution have to prove that the defendant was in the possession of sufficient facts from which a reasonable man would arrive at a relevant belief and also that the defendant had these facts for a reasonable time, so as to convert those facts into a belief.

The penalties for criminal copyright infringement are still relatively light. On summary conviction, the defendant may be fined up to £5,000 and/or sentenced to up to six months' imprisonment (the same as the penalties in respect of trade mark counterfeits). On indictment the defendant may be ordered to pay a higher fine and/or sentenced to up to two years' imprisonment (less than the penalties for trade marks).

Other forms of relief

The copyright owner can:

(a) apply for an order for delivery up (criminal) under CDPA 1988, s.108;
(b) prosecute under CDPA 1988, s.108 a 'conniving or consenting director' where a company has committed an offence under s.107;
(c) ask the court to order that goods seized under ss.99, 100 and 108 shall be forfeited to the copyright owner or destroyed (s.114); and
(d) where musical works are being performed the copyright owner can under CDPA 1988, s.198 prevent bootleggers from making illicit recordings.

Private prosecutions

A company can always invoke its own private prosecution under CDPA 1988, s.107 if the Trading Standards Departments or the police (for whatever reason) are not prepared to get involved. Bringing a private prosecution enables the intellectual property rights owner to retain control of how its intellectual property rights are used in the prosecution; and possibly avoid expensive civil litigation (although having instead to meet the higher criminal standard of proof).

However, costs awards in criminal cases tend to be of the order of £500. Alternatively, the Federation Against Copyright Theft (FACT) and Federation Against Software Theft (FAST) can now bring private prosecutions on behalf of their members.

Note that the prosecution will have to prove that the dealer knew or had reason to believe that the article was an infringing copy. Thus, these provisions can only be successfully invoked after the dealer has been notified that the copyright owner considers the articles to be infringing copies – up until then, dealers are free to argue that they had no idea what they were selling. It may also be possible to give notice to the world in general, for example by advertising in the trade press, with enough information to enable traders to distinguish the originals from the counterfeits. Of course, in any given case there may be other circumstances which would lead to a dealer being shown to have had the necessary knowledge even in the absence of specific notice having been given.

2.9 PRACTICAL PROTECTION

Copyright notices

Since registration is neither necessary nor, in the UK, available for copyright works, copyright owners, unlike patent or trade mark holders, face the problem of how to let the public know that their works are not available for use or reproduction without authorisation. The best available solution is to ensure that all copies of the work bear or are linked to a notice pointing out the subsistence of copyright.

Since the copyright notice is not required either by statute or treaty, there is no constraint as to the form such a notice can take. At the minimum, it should include either the statement 'protected by copyright' or the '©' symbol to prevent infringers denying all knowledge of the possibility that copyright might still be in force. No damages will be awarded against an innocent infringer.

Beyond this, it is merely a question of how much additional information can usefully be included in the space available. It is useful wherever possible to include the date from which copyright is being asserted, since this will enable the reader to calculate whether it is still in effect in their jurisdiction. It is customary to include the name of the person or entity which owns the copyright, in case the reader wishes to try to obtain a suitable licence and needs to know where to ask. United States copyright notices tend to go into detail about the consequences of infringement and which acts are prohibited, but since ignorance of the law (as opposed to the subsistence of copyright) is no defence this does not add anything from an English legal point of view – unless of course the notice is simultaneously performing the function of a unilateral licence permitting certain uses without further formality, in which case it is essential to spell out which these are, and equally which uses are restricted.

Invoking the statutory presumptions

In addition, it is useful to incorporate certain information stipulated by CDPA 1988, ss.104–6, the appearance of which on a copy will bring into effect statutory presumptions concerning the ownership and subsistence of copyright. These are extremely helpful (although rarely sufficient) when a dispute arises where, as is inevitable for most works, the copyright has passed through a number of hands. The chain of title is frequently muddied and sometimes completely lost to obscurity.

In the case of literary, dramatic, musical or artistic works, it is presumed that a person named, on copies as published or on the work when made, as the author or publisher, or in the case of sound recordings and films as the copyright owner or director, was indeed the author, publisher or director (as the case may be). In respect of computer programs, under s.105(3) it is presumed that a person named as owner of copyright in the program in electronic copies was the copyright owner at the date of issue of the copies, or that the program was first published in a specified country or that copies of it were first issued to the public in electronic form in a specified year. Section 105(3) also includes a direction that such statements are admissible as evidence of the facts stated. Notably, it is only the software presumption which refers to the work being issued to the public in electronic form. However, any argument that none of the other presumptions apply where the work and the rights management information are electronic would be very unlikely to succeed.

CHAPTER 3

Trade marks

Peter Brownlow

3.1 INTRODUCTION

English law relating to the protection of trade marks can conveniently be divided into two parts:

(a) registered trade marks; and
(b) unregistered trade marks.

Registered trade marks

A registered trade mark gives its proprietor certain rights to prevent unauthorised third parties using identical or confusingly similar trade marks. It is acquired by applying to a particular registry, meeting the requirements for registration and paying the requisite fee. It is possible for an individual or company to make the application themselves, although it is advisable to have a qualified trade mark professional, such as a qualified trade mark attorney to assist.

Registration routes

There are three registration schemes which can result in a trade mark registration having effect in the UK:

1. A national trade mark registration which has effect just in the UK (a UK Mark).

2. A Community Trade Mark (CTM) registration which has effect in all EU Member States.
3. An international trade mark registration, which takes effect as a registered mark in the jurisdictions designated in the application, so long as the jurisdiction is a signatory to the relevant convention (i.e. the Protocol Relating to the Madrid Agreement Concerning the International Registration of Marks, adopted at Madrid on 27 June 1989 ('the Madrid Protocol')).

National registered trade mark law in the EU was harmonised by the Trade Marks Directive (First Directive 89/104/EEC of the Council, of 21 December 1988, to Approximate the Laws of the Member States Relating to Trade Marks). The Trade Marks Directive was implemented in the UK by TMA 1994. The UK Trade Marks register is administered by the Trade Marks Section of the UK Intellectual Property Office (UKIPO), formerly the Trade Marks Registry.

The Community Trade Mark (CTM) Regulation (Council Regulation (EC) No 40/94 of 20 December 1993 on the Community trade mark) is the legislation governing CTMs. The language of the CTM Regulation closely follows that of the Trade Marks Directive and although there are minor differences, the law for UK marks and CTMs is broadly the same as regards registrability and infringement. Community Trade Marks and the CTM register are administered by the Office of Harmonization for the Internal Market (OHIM) which has its seat in Alicante, Spain. Once registered, a CTM has effect in the UK without the applicant having to take any further steps.

The international trade mark registration system is governed by the Madrid Agreement and Madrid Protocol. It is essentially a mechanism for filing trade marks in a large number of countries at a lower cost than if the applicant applied separately to each country's trade mark office. The applicant must hold a trade mark registration or application in the member country where the applicant is domiciled, has an establishment or is a national. The international application is made at the trade mark office in this country. The trade mark office passes the application to the International Bureau at the World Intellectual Property Organization (WIPO) in Geneva which in turn notifies the trade mark offices of the countries designated in the application. The trade mark office of each country has a time limit in which to object to registration of the international application under their national trade mark law. If no objection is received within the relevant time limit the international trade mark registration takes effect as if the mark had been registered as a national trade mark (Madrid Protocol, Art.4(1)(a)). It is possible to designate a CTM in an application for international trade mark. As a consequence the law as to registrability, infringement and invalidity as it affects national marks or CTMs will apply to the international registration. For further information regarding the procedure for filing an application for an international mark, see the WIPO website (**www.wipo.int**).

Unless the contrary is stated the law as regards registered trade marks set out in this chapter applies equally to UK marks and CTMs, as well as to international trade marks.

Goods and services

Trade marks are registered in respect of specific goods and services or classes of goods and services.

Goods and services are classified and the current classification system (International Classification of Goods and Services: Nice Agreement) contains 34 classes of goods and nine classes of services. For instance, DVDs are included in class 9, and telecommunication services in class 38. The complete list can be found at the WIPO website (see **www.wipo.int**).

Unregistered trade marks

Where a trade mark has not been registered but has been used in the course of trade and acquired goodwill, it may be possible to prevent an unauthorised third party using that mark or a similar one by way of the tort of passing off. The requirements for this tort are set out at the end of this chapter.

Where possible it is advisable to file for trade mark registration rather than rely on passing off. As a general rule the hurdles to overcome to succeed in a passing off action are greater than in a trade mark infringement action. In passing off it is necessary to prove that the trade mark has acquired goodwill and that the proprietor has suffered damage. Neither of these is necessary to establish trade mark infringement (at least under TMA 1994, s.10(1) or (2)).

There is also specific protection granted to 'well known marks' under the Paris Convention (Paris Convention for the Protection of Industrial Property of 20 March 1883), Art.6*bis*, but this also requires proof that the mark is indeed well known.

Certain marks related to the Olympic Games and the 2012 London Olympics have special protection under English law.

Trade libel may provide protection in certain specific circumstances but this is beyond the scope of this chapter.

Application process for registered trade marks

For ease of reference the basic procedure for filing a UK national mark is illustrated in Figure 3.1.

Further information on the procedure for filing an application for a UK Mark is available from the Intellectual Property Office website (**www.ipo.gov.uk**).

The equivalent steps for filing a CTM application are shown in Figure 3.2.

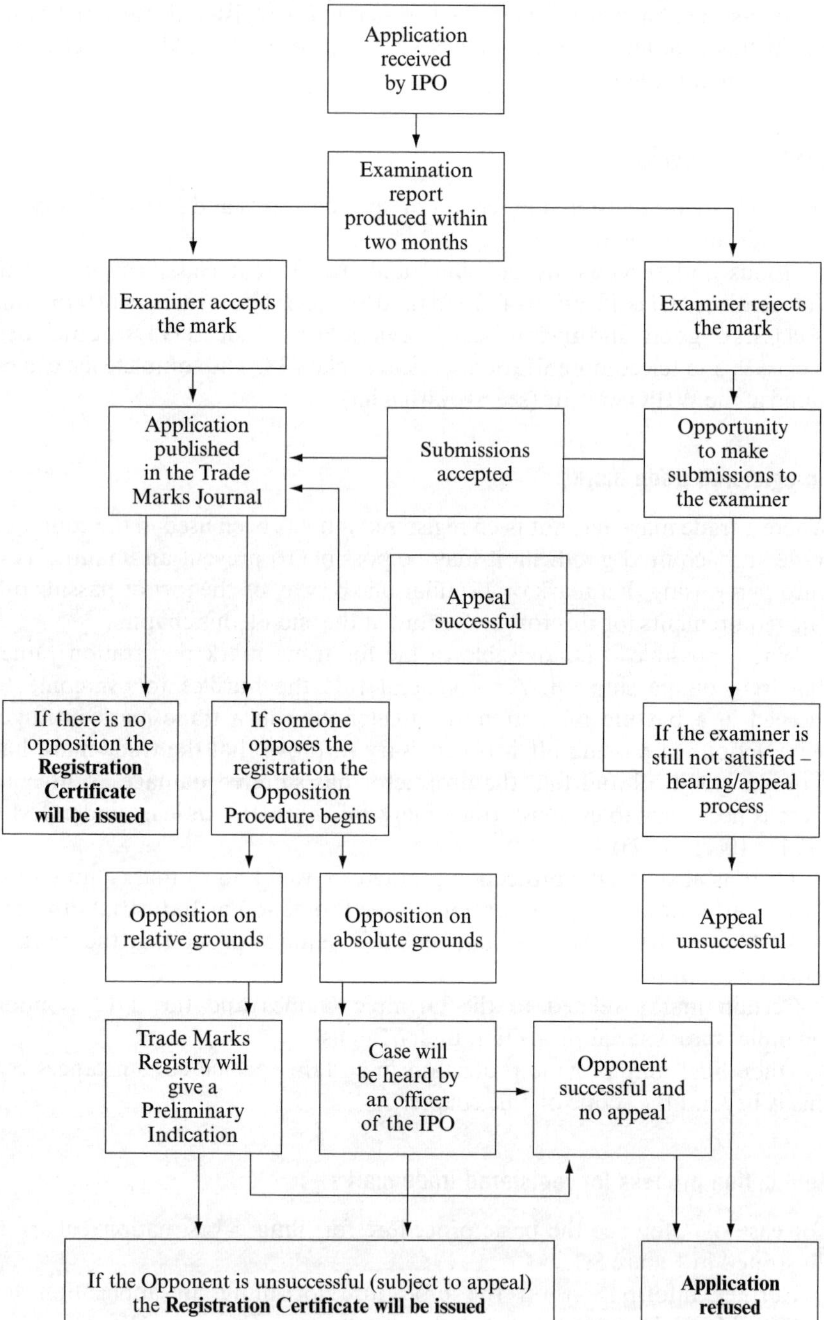

Figure 3.1 Procedure for registration of UK trade mark

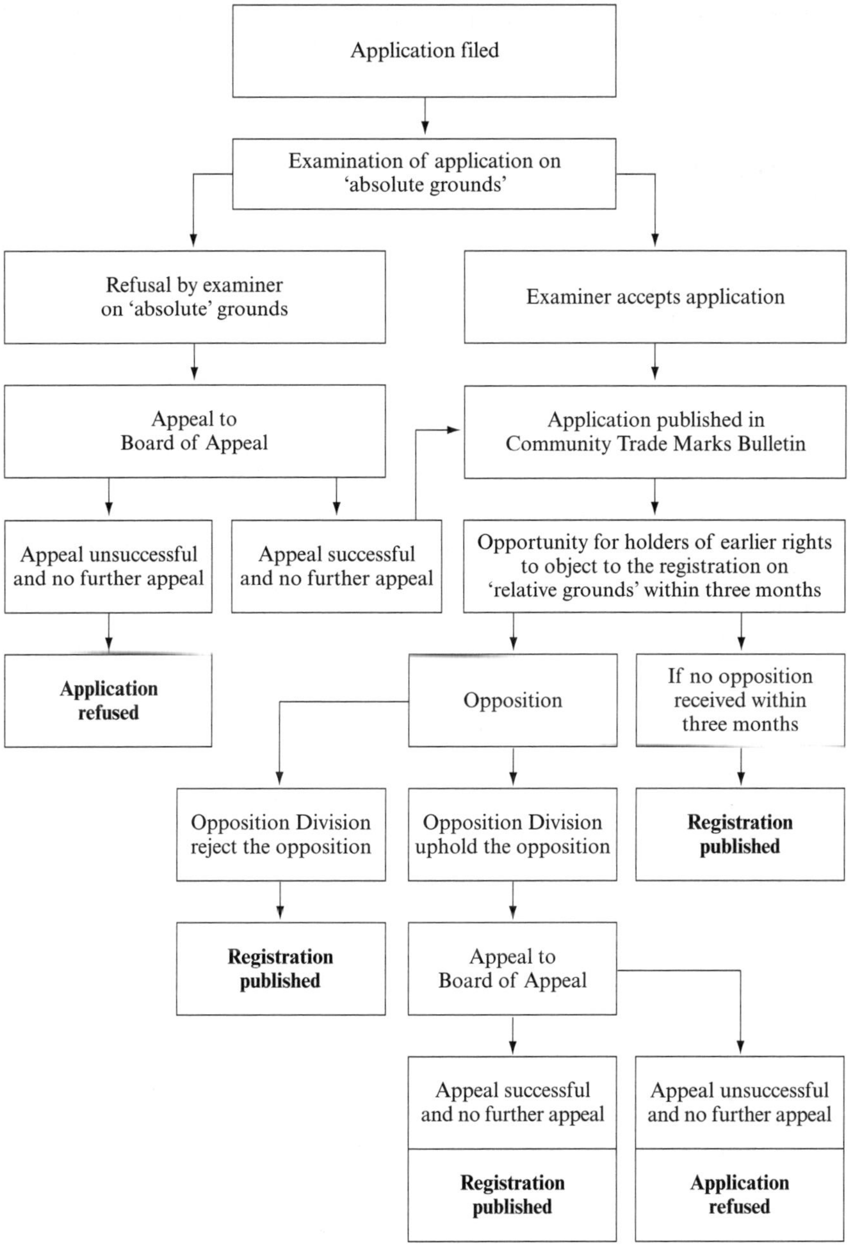

Figure 3.2 Procedure for registration of Community Trade Mark

Further information on the procedure for filing an application for a CTM is available from the OHIM website (see **http://oami.europa.eu/en/mark/default.htm**).

3.2 REGISTERED TRADE MARKS

Requirements for registration

Both the national and Community registration systems list two categories of grounds on which a trade mark will be refused registration. These are:

(a) absolute grounds; and
(b) relative grounds.

Absolute grounds for refusal relate to the nature of the mark being applied for. For instance, one absolute ground is that the proposed mark is a descriptive term that other traders will legitimately want to use in relation to other goods and services. Relative grounds for refusal relate to whether the proposed trade mark conflicts with any existing earlier rights.

Under both the UK and CTM systems the relevant office examines applications as to whether there are any absolute grounds for refusal. At the time of writing the UKIPO also examines applications as to whether there are any relative grounds for refusal, but examination on relative grounds is to be discontinued in October 2007. CTM applications are not examined by OHIM on relative grounds and it is left to third parties to object to the application through the opposition procedure.

Absolute grounds for refusal of a trade mark

Signs which can constitute a trade mark

By TMA 1994, s.1(1) any sign that can be represented graphically and which is capable of distinguishing the goods or services of one undertaking from those of other undertakings, can function as a trade mark. In particular, words, including personal names, designs, letters, numerals, the shape of goods or of their packaging are commonly used. Signs which do not satisfy the requirements of s.1(1) cannot be registered as a trade mark (TMA 1994, s.3(1)).

(A) NON-TRADITIONAL MARKS

Colours and sounds have been held to qualify as signs. While a few registrations were granted for smells it is unlikely that subsequent attempts will be successful given the requirements for graphical representation explained below.

The function of the graphical representation is to enable the sign in question to be represented visually, so that it can be precisely identified. The representation must be: clear, precise, easily accessible, intelligible, self-contained and durable (ECJ Case C-273/00 *Sieckmann* [2002] ECR I-11737).

These criteria have been held to apply to colours in the following way (ECJ Case C-104/01 *Libertel* [2003] ECR I-3793):

1. A mere sample of a colour is unlikely to be sufficiently durable.
2. A written description of a colour *may* suffice, but it depends on the circumstances and the description. Designating a colour using an internationally recognised identification code (e.g. Pantone) will constitute a graphic representation.
3. A combination of a sample of the colour with a written description may suffice provided it meets the general criteria – clear, precise, self-contained, easily accessible, intelligible and objective.

The registration of sounds is possible. Musical notation has been accepted as a clear and precise graphical representation of a sound mark (ECJ Case C-283/01 *Sheild Mark BV* v. *Joost Kist h.o.d.n. Memax* (27 November 2003)).

The requirement for graphical representation has been held not to be satisfied by a chemical formula, by a description in words, by a deposit of an odour sample or by a combination of any of these elements (*Sieckmann* (above)). It is difficult to conceive of another way of graphically representing a smell and therefore unlikely that a smell will be registrable as a trade mark.

The reasoning applied to smells also applies to tastes; again it is unlikely a taste would be registrable as a trade mark.

One reason that tastes and smells are difficult to graphically represent is that individuals' perception of these non-visual sensations differs making it hard to define them in a clear and precise way that is intelligible to others.

(B) CAPABLE OF DISTINGUISHING

The other requirement for a sign to be a 'trade mark' is that the sign must be 'capable of distinguishing' the goods and services of one undertaking from another. The distinctiveness requirement is important. It is the subject of three further overlapping absolute grounds for refusal.

The ECJ has summarised the distinctiveness requirement as the mark serving to identify the product in respect of which registration is applied for as originating from a particular undertaking, and thus to distinguish that product from products of other undertakings (ECJ Joined Cases C-53/01 to C-55/01 *Linde and Others* [2003] ECR I-3161).

It serves to prevent signs achieving registration which the relevant public would not understand as being trade marks.

The other absolute grounds dealing with lack of distinctiveness approach the issue in different ways.

Signs which cannot constitute a trade mark

SIGNS OR INDICATIONS WHICH MAY SERVE IN THE COURSE OF TRADE TO DESIGNATE CHARACTERISTICS OF GOODS AND SERVICES

It is not possible to register:

> trade marks which consist exclusively of signs or indications which may serve, in trade, to designate the kind, quality, quantity, intended purpose, value, geographical origin, the time of production of goods or of rendering of services, or other characteristics of goods or services (TMA 1994, s.3(1)(c)).

This ground prevents signs being registered that are descriptive of the goods or services for which registration is sought or characteristics of such goods or services. The reasoning behind this provision is that it is in the general interest that such descriptive terms should be freely available for use by traders.

By way of example, 'METAL' for nails or 'PAPER' for newspapers would be refused registration under this ground. It is not necessary that the descriptive term is actually in use, it is sufficient that the sign could be used to designate a characteristic of the goods.

A sign will be refused even if it has a number of possible meanings and only one of its meanings could be used to indicate a characteristic of the goods. In ECJ Case C-191/01 *Doublemint* [2004] RPC 18 the sign was applied for in respect of confectionery. It was argued that the public would not view it as descriptive because it had a number of possible meanings, for example, it could mean two types of mint or double the strength of mint flavour. The ECJ held that it fell within this absolute ground even if only one of the possible meanings was descriptive.

It is also irrelevant if there are other descriptive terms or indications in use to identify the particular characteristics. It is not necessary that the objected sign is the only way to describe that characteristic.

SIGNS OR INDICATIONS CUSTOMARY IN THE CURRENT LANGUAGE OR ESTABLISHED PRACTICES OF THE TRADE

It is not possible to register:

> trade marks which consist exclusively of signs or indications which have become customary in the current language or in the *bona fide* and established practices of the trade (TMA 1994, s.3(1)(d)).

Signs which are generic terms, that is, terms that are currently in general use in the relevant trade, cannot be registered. For a term to fall foul of this ground it needs to be perceived as a generic term principally by end users and consumers of the relevant goods and services, although the perceptions of the trade will also be relevant in relation to certain goods and services (ECJ Case C-371/02 *Björnekulla Fruktindustrier AB* v. *Pocordia Food AB*).

In contrast to the descriptiveness ground, the term has to be in the current use. Examples include stars for hotel services and a representation of a spanner for mechanic services (see *Trade Mark Registry Work Manual*).

DEVOID OF DISTINCTIVE CHARACTER

It is not possible to register 'trade marks which are devoid of any distinctive character' (TMA 1994, s.3(1)(b)).

This is essentially a 'sweeping up' provision catching non-distinctive signs that have not been caught by the descriptive or generic grounds of refusal described above. It is possible for a sign to fall foul of more than one ground of refusal and it is likely that any sign caught by the descriptiveness ground referred to above would also be caught under this head.

Examples of marks found to be devoid of distinctive character which might not fall within the generic and descriptive grounds include signs deemed to be laudatory of the goods or services, such as 'EXCELLENT' or 'BEST'.

It is also used to object to signs which comprise of the shape of the goods or their packaging. This is dealt with in the discussion on 'shapes' below.

ACQUIRED DISTINCTIVENESS

The lack of distinctiveness objections above do not apply if the mark has become distinctive in relation to the goods and services for which registration is requested in consequence of the use which has been made of it (TMA 1994, s.3(1) proviso). In other words, although the sign may lack inherent distinctiveness, for instance, because it is a descriptive term, it may have been used sufficiently by the proprietor so that the public have come to understand it to indicate goods or services originating from one business.

Whether the sign has acquired distinctive character is determined by making an overall assessment of the evidence that the mark has come to identify the product concerned as originating from a particular undertaking, and to distinguish that product from goods of other undertakings.

The following can be taken into account in assessing distinctive character:

(a) the market share held by the mark;
(b) how intensive, geographically widespread and long-standing has been the use of the mark;
(c) the amount invested by the undertaking in promoting the mark;
(d) the proportion of the relevant class of persons who, because of the mark, identify goods as originating from a particular undertaking;

(e) statements from chambers of commerce and industry or other trade professional associations (ECJ Case C-108/97 *Windsurfing Chiemsee* [1999] ETMR 585).

It is however necessary to establish that the sign had acquired distinctive character through use before the application for registration was filed (Case T-247/01 *eCopy* v. *OHIM (ECOPY)* [2002] ECR II-5301).

To prove acquired distinctiveness in relation to an application for a CTM, distinctiveness must be shown to have been acquired in the part of the Community where the absolute ground for refusal was established.

CONTRARY TO PUBLIC POLICY OR TO ACCEPTED PRINCIPLES OF MORALITY

A trade mark cannot be registered if it is 'contrary to public policy or to accepted principles of morality' (TMA 1994, s.3(3)(a)).

This ground is aimed at preventing the registration of marks that would cause offence to a section of the public. Marks which encouraged or promoted drugs, counterfeiting, and pornography would be likely to be refused under this ground. Examples of marks rejected include 'JESUS' for a range of goods and 'FOOK' for clothing. In contrast applications for 'RAATZ PIZS' for beer and 'KRAP' in a device mark have been accepted on the basis they merely amounted to 'fairly mild bad language' and would therefore presumably not cause offence to the public.

LIKELY TO DECEIVE THE PUBLIC

A trade mark cannot be registered if it is 'of such a nature as to deceive the public (for instance as to the nature, quality or geographical origin of the goods or service)' (TMA 1994, s.3(3)(b)).

This ground relates to signs which are likely to inherently deceive customers. An example is the 'INTERNATIONAL STAR REGISTRY' which was refused as being likely to mislead consumers into believing that the organisation which uses it is an authoritative body empowered to give names to stars (of the heavenly body variety) (OHIM, Case R-468/1999-1, Decision of the First Board of Appeal (4 April 2001)). 'POUDRE LIBRE NATURELLE' was held deceptive for cosmetics which were not powders (*L'Oreal* v. *Beiersdorf*, Decision of the First Cancellation Division (2000)).

In some cases applicants will be caught between this ground of objection and the descriptiveness objection. Under the English law predating the Trade Marks Directive and CTM Regulation 'ORLWOOLA' was refused registration for suits as it was found to be descriptive if the suits were all wool, or deceptive if they were not (*Re HN Brock* [1910] Ch 130).

USE IS PROHIBITED BY ANY ENACTMENT OR RULE OF LAW OR BY ANY PROVISION OF COMMUNITY LAW (OTHER THAN TRADE MARK LAW)

> A trade mark shall not be registered if or to the extent that its use is prohibited in the United Kingdom by any enactment or rule of law or by any provision of Community law (TMA 1994, s.3(4)).

This ground of refusal relates to the trade mark itself rather than the existence of any third party rights. As a consequence an objection based on passing off would not arise under this ground, such objections fall within the relative grounds for refusal.

The ground requires the identification of a specific law or statutory provision.

This provision does not appear in the CTM Regulation but only in TMA 1994 and the Trade Marks Directive. Instead, the CTM Regulation contains a much more limited prohibition on registrations of trade marks which contain or consist of geographical indications identifying wines or spirits (CTM Regulation, Art.7(1)(j)).

SPECIALLY PROTECTED EMBLEMS

> A trade mark shall not be registered in the cases specified, or referred to, in section 4 (specially protected emblems) (TMA 1994, s.3(5)).

Certain specific categories of emblems will be refused registration on the grounds they are specially protected. These are listed in TMA 1994, including: Royal Arms; Royal crown; representations of the Royal family; words likely to lead persons to think the applicant has had Royal patronage or authorisation; national flags of the UK if the use would be misleading or grossly offensive; national emblems of countries which are part of the Paris Convention and emblems of certain international organisations; and Olympic symbols.

The CTM Regulation does not list the categories of emblems but Art.7(1)(h) restricts registration of marks which have not been authorised by the competent authorities and are to be refused under Article 6*ter* of the Paris Convention. Article 6*ter* applies to national emblems of Convention countries and international organisations. Article 7(1)(i) of the CTM Regulation restricts registrations of badges, emblems or escutcheons (other than those covered by Article 6*ter*) which are of particular public interest, unless the consent of the appropriate authorities has been given.

APPLIED FOR IN BAD FAITH

> A trade mark shall not be registered if or to the extent that the application is made in bad faith (TMA 1994, s.3(6)).

This is not a ground for refusal under the CTM Regulation. Instead there is a relative ground for refusal that prevents a registration in the name of an agent of the proprietor without consent (CTM Regulation, Art.8.3). Bad faith of an applicant when filing an application is also a ground of invalidity under CTM Regulation, Art.51.1(b).

The test for 'bad faith' in this context is whether, having regards to the facts, the application falls short of acceptable commercial behaviour found by reasonable and experienced individuals in the particular field in question (*Harrison* v. *Teton Valley Trading Co* [2004] EWCA Civ 1028 ('Chinawhite')).

Applications have been found to be in bad faith where someone other than the owner of the goodwill in the mark applies for registration, where there is no bona fide intention to use the mark and where unduly broad specifications of goods and services have been applied for.

Shapes

Section 1(1) of TMA 1994 confirms that a trade mark may consist of a shape.

For a shape to be a registered trade mark, it has to avoid not only the absolute grounds above and relative grounds for refusal discussed below, but also the specific prohibitions relating to shapes (TMA 1994, s.3(2)).

The additional absolute grounds for refusal of shape marks are as follows.

(a) Signs which consist exclusively of the shape which results from the nature of the goods themselves (TMA 1994, s.3(2)(a)). The issue here is whether the shape results from the 'nature of the goods'. This provision does not exclude signs merely because they consist of the shape of the goods themselves. There may well be manufactured goods which have a very distinctive shape which would fall outside this prohibition. Shapes which would fall foul of this objection would be the shape of bananas for bananas or the shape of a lemon for lemons.

(b) Signs which consist exclusively of the shape of goods which is necessary to obtain a technical result (TMA 1994, s.3(2)(b)). This ground excludes shapes which perform a technical function even if there are other shapes that would achieve the same function. In ECJ Case C-299/99 *Philips* v. *Remington* [2003] RPC 2 the shape in question was a drawing of the top of a three-headed rotary shaver. The heads were arranged in the shape of equilateral triangle. It was proved that other arrangements of the heads would achieve the same technical function. It was argued that the shape was therefore not necessary to obtain the technical function. The ECJ dismissed this argument on the basis that the shape performed a technical function and nothing else. It was therefore irrelevant whether other shapes could achieve the same result. Other examples of shapes which have fallen foul of this prohibition include the 'lego' brick registered for playthings and a yoghurt pot with two triangular compartments (one for the yogurt and the other for the flavouring).

(c) Signs which consist exclusively of the shape which gives substantial value to the goods (TMA 1994, s.3(2)(c)). It is unclear how this prohibition should be applied, and there is little guidance from the courts to assist. The Court of Appeal in *Philips* (above) stated that the purpose of this provision was to exclude 'aesthetic-type shapes' and that a comparison should be made between the shape sought to be registered and shapes of equivalent articles. It is only if the shape has, in relative terms, substantial value that it will be excluded from registration. An example of a shape that has been rejected on the basis of this provision is the Dualit toaster. It was held by the hearing officer that the eye appeal of the toaster designs gave substantial value to the goods (*Dualit Ltd's (Toaster Shapes) Trade Mark Applications* [1999] RPC 304).

Relative grounds for refusal

The relative grounds for refusal of a trade mark in TMA 1994 apply where the trade mark applied for conflicts with an earlier right.

Three relative grounds for refusal relate to earlier registered rights. These three grounds closely mirror the infringement provisions. To avoid duplication these will be dealt with in the infringement section. They are however set out here in full for completeness.

1. Section 5(1):

> A trade mark shall not be registered if it is identical with an earlier trade mark and the goods or services for which the trade mark is applied for are identical with the goods or services for which the earlier trade mark is protected.

2. Section 5(2):

> A trade mark shall not be registered if because –
>
> (a) it is identical with an earlier trade mark and is to be registered for goods or services similar to those for which the earlier trade mark is protected, or
> (b) it is similar to an earlier trade mark and is to be registered for goods or services identical with or similar to those for which the earlier trade mark is protected,
>
> there exists a likelihood of confusion on the part of the public, which includes the likelihood of association with the earlier trade mark.

3. Section 5(3):

> A trade mark which –
>
> (a) is identical with or similar to an earlier trade mark, and
> (b) is to be registered for goods or services which are not similar to those for which the earlier trade mark is protected,
>
> shall not be registered if, or to the extent that, the earlier trade mark has a reputation in the United Kingdom (or, in the case of a Community trade mark, in the European Community) and the use of the later mark without due cause would take unfair advantage of, or be detrimental to, the distinctive character or the repute of the earlier trade mark.

For the purposes of these three relative grounds, an 'earlier trade mark' includes:

(a) a UK mark, CTM, or international mark which has an application date earlier than the trade mark in question;
(b) an application for such a mark; or
(c) a trade mark protected under the Paris Convention as a well-known mark.

In addition, TMA 1994 and the CTM Regulation both contain relative grounds for refusal where the conflict is with earlier rights other than registered trade marks. Section 5(4) of TMA 1994 provides:

> A trade mark shall not be registered if, or to the extent that, its use in the United Kingdom is liable to be prevented –
>
> (a) by virtue of any rule of law (in particular, the law of passing off) protecting an unregistered trade mark or other sign used in the course of trade, or
> (b) by virtue of an earlier right other than those referred to in subsections (1) to (3) [earlier registered trade marks] or paragraph (a) above, in particular by virtue of the law of copyright, design right or registered designs.
>
> A person thus entitled to prevent the use of a trade mark is referred to in this Act as the proprietor of an 'earlier right' in relation to the trade mark.

Rights under the law of passing off are those most often brought into play under subsection (a), although other rights such as those of well-known marks under TMA 1994, s.56 could also form the basis of an objection (see **3.8**). As regards a UK mark it is not necessary to be the owner of the earlier right in order to make the objection.

The position as regards relative grounds for refusal in respect of a CTM under the Regulation is slightly different for the following reasons.

1. The opposition can only be brought by the proprietor of the earlier right or by a person authorised under the relevant law to enforce it.
2. The rights are only those based on or acquired by use of a sign, it does not include rights such as copyright, or designs.
3. It is necessary that the earlier right is of more than mere local significance. A sign could merely have local significance if its geographical spread is substantially less than the whole EU (*Compass Publishing* v. *Compass Logistics* [2004] RPC 41). If correct, this could exclude rights existing in just one EU Member State.

Consent

Under TMA 1994, s.5(5) and CTM Regulation, Art.4(5), an objection based on relative grounds can be overcome if the proprietor of the earlier trade mark or right consents to the registration of the later trade mark.

3.3 INFRINGEMENT OF REGISTERED TRADE MARKS

A proprietor of a UK mark has exclusive rights in the trade mark which are infringed by use of the trade mark in the United Kingdom without his consent.

The acts which amount to infringement of a registered trade mark to a large extent mirror the relative rights of refusal (as regards earlier registered trade marks) set out above. In all cases, the use must be in the course of trade in order to infringe.

Identical sign/identical goods and services

> A person infringes a registered trade mark if he uses in the course of trade a sign which is identical with the trade mark in relation to goods or services which are identical with those for which it is registered (TMA 1994, s.10(1)).

The proprietor of a registered trade mark is given the exclusive right to use the mark in relation to goods and services which are identical with those for which it is registered. Thus, the proprietor can prevent third parties without his consent from using in the course of trade a sign which is identical with the trade mark in relation to such goods and services.

Similar marks/similar goods or services

By TMA 1994, s.10(2) a person infringes a registered trade mark if he or she uses in the course of trade a sign where because:

(a) the sign is identical with the trade mark and is used in relation to goods or services similar to those for which the trade mark is registered; or
(b) the sign is similar to the trade mark and is used in relation to goods and services identical with or similar to those for which the trade mark is registered,

there exists a likelihood of confusion on the part of the public, which includes the likelihood of association with the trade mark.

Unfair advantage/detriment

By CTM Regulation, Art.9(1)(c) the proprietor is entitled to prevent third parties not having the proprietor's consent from using in the course of trade any sign which is identical with or similar to a CTM in relation to goods or services which are *not* similar to those for which the CTM is registered, where:

(a) the latter has a reputation in the Community; and
(b) use of that sign without due cause takes unfair advantage of, or is detrimental to, the distinctive character or repute of the CTM.

Following the ECJ's decision in Case C-408/01 *Adidas Salomon AG* v. *Fitnessworld Trading Limited*, where it was held that this ground of infringement also applied to goods and services that were identical and similar as well as to those that were different from those for which the earlier trade mark was registered, the equivalent section in TMA 1994, s.10(3) was amended to cover all goods and services:

> A person infringes a registered trade mark if he uses in the course of trade in relation to goods or services a sign which is identical with or similar to the trade mark . . . where the trade mark has a reputation in the UK and the use of the sign, being without due cause, takes unfair advantage of or is detrimental to, the distinctive character or the repute of the trade mark.

There has been judicial comment that this change was entirely unnecessary (*Intel Corporation Inc* v. *CPM UK Limited* [2007] EWCA Civ 431 *per* Jacob LJ). Should the Act be amended for each court decision interpreting the Directive or Regulation? What if the ECJ changes its mind? There has been no corresponding change to the CTM Regulation, which remains as set out above.

What acts amount to 'use in the course of trade'?

Acts which amount to 'using a sign' for the purposes of infringement under TMA 1994, s.10 include:

(a) affixing the sign to goods or its packaging;
(b) offering or exposing goods for sale, putting them on the market or stocking them for those purposes under the sign, or offering or supplying services under the sign;
(c) importing or exporting goods under the sign;
(d) using the sign on business paper or in advertising (TMA 1994, s.10(4)).

The list is not exhaustive. Further, TMA 1994, s.103(2) states that use of a trade mark includes use otherwise than by means of a graphic representation. This includes oral use of a sign.

Under TMA 1994, s.10(5), a person who applies a registered trade mark to material intended to be used:

(a) for labelling or packaging goods;
(b) as a business paper; or
(c) for advertising goods or services,

will be treated as a party to any use of the material which infringes the registered trade mark. This is so long as that person knew or had reason to believe when he or she applied the mark that the application of the mark was not duly authorised.

The 'reason to believe' requirement is an objective test. The person must have sufficient facts from which a reasonable man would have believed that the application of the mark was not authorised.

Is 'use as a trade mark' necessary?

There has been considerable discussion in the case law as to whether it is necessary for a sign to be used as a trade mark for there to be infringement. In other words for the purposes of infringement, is it necessary for the defendant to use the mark to indicate origin, i.e. use the sign in a trade mark sense rather than, for instance, descriptively.

In Case C-206/01 *Arsenal Football Club* v. *Reed* (12 November 2002) the ECJ held that for there to be infringement there must be use of a sign by a third party which affects or is liable to affect the functions of the trade mark, in particular its essential function of guaranteeing to consumers the origin of the goods.

This would occur whenever the use of the sign by the third party creates an impression that there is a material link in trade between the third party's goods and the trade mark proprietor.

There may still be use as a trade mark where, although purchasers themselves do not interpret the sign as indicating origin, consumers who come into contact with the goods sometime after the point of sale will interpret the sign in this way. The example given in the *Arsenal* case was of scarves bearing the mark 'ARSENAL'. The purchaser of the scarf may understand 'ARSENAL' to be used merely as a badge of allegiance and not indicating origin, particularly if the scarf was sold from a clearly unofficial stall. However if the scarf was then given to the purchaser's nephew as a gift, without the knowledge of the circumstances surrounding the purchase, the nephew may believe the use of 'ARSENAL' indicated it to be an official product.

The requirement for 'trade mark use' has recently been confirmed by the ECJ in its decision in Case C-48/05 *Adam Opel* (25 January 2007). That case indicated, however, that while this was a requirement for infringement under s.10(1) and (2), it may not be a requirement for s.10(3) infringement.

Meaning of 'identical' under s.10(1)

To assess whether a sign is identical to a trade mark it is first necessary to identify the sign being used by the defendant. This has to be considered from the perception of the average consumer. *Reed Executive plc* v. *Reed Business Information Limited* [2004] RPC 40 involved an allegation of infringement of the registered trade mark REED by the term 'Reed Business Information'. It was held by the Court of Appeal that the sign being used by the defendant was 'Reed Business Information' not 'REED' (Jacob LJ at para.36):

> . . . the name as a whole is 'Reed Business Information'. The use of capital letters is of some visual significance – it conveys to the average user that 'Business Information' is part of the name. If the added words had been wholly and specifically descriptive – really adding nothing at all (e.g. 'Palmolive Soap' compared with 'Palmolive') the position might have been different. But 'Business Information' is not so descriptive – it is too general for that.

Once the sign being used by the defendant has been identified it is then necessary to assess whether it is identical to the mark. A sign will be identical with the registered mark where it reproduces, without any modification or addition, all the elements constituting the mark or where, viewed as a whole, it contains differences so insignificant they go unnoticed by the average consumer (Case C-291/00 *LTJ Diffusion SA* v. *Sadas Vertbaudet SA ('Arthur et Felice')* (20 March 2003)).

A sign is only identical to a mark if using the above criteria there is both aural and visual identity (*Reed*, above).

The assessment of 'likelihood of confusion' – s.10(2)

The assessment of whether there is confusion is a global assessment taking all factors relevant to the circumstances of the case into account including:

(a) the similarity of the sign to the mark;
(b) the similarity of the goods or services; and

(c) any reputation attaching to the earlier trade mark (ECJ Case C-251/95 *Sabel BV* v. *Puma AG* [1998] ETMR 1).

To assess similarity of the sign and mark the court must assess the degree of visual, aural and conceptual similarity between the mark and sign. The court must also assess whether greater importance should be placed on one of these factors given the relevant goods or services (*Lloyd Schuhfabrik Meyer* [2000] FSR 77).

The assessment is to be conducted through the eyes of the average consumer of the relevant goods or services. This person is deemed to be reasonably well informed and reasonably observant and circumspect.

The global appreciation of the visual, aural and conceptual similarity of the marks in question must be based on the overall impression given by the marks, bearing in mind, in particular, their distinctive and dominant components. The average consumer normally perceives a mark as a whole and does not proceed to analyse its various details (*Sabel* v. *Puma*, above).

The more distinctive the earlier mark, the greater will be the likelihood of confusion. This distinctive character can be either as a result of its inherent distinctiveness or the reputation it has with members of the public.

The court will also take account of the fact that the consumer will rarely see the mark and sign side by side and when seeing the sign will be comparing it with the imperfect recollection he has of the mark (*Lloyd Schuhfabrik*, above).

As it is a global assessment, there is an interdependence of the various factors. For instance, a lesser degree of similarity between the goods and services may be offset by a greater similarity between the sign and the mark (*Canon* v. *MGM* [1998] ECR I-5507).

What type of confusion?

The Act refers to 'a likelihood of confusion on the part of the public, which includes the likelihood of association with the trade mark'.

Confusion in this context is confusion as to the origin of the goods and services. In *Sabel* v. *Puma* (above) the ECJ held that mere association which the public might make between a mark and a sign as a consequence of their similarity is not in itself sufficient grounds for finding a likelihood of confusion.

Confusion as to origin includes situations where the consumer incorrectly believes the goods or services originate from the same undertaking or otherwise consider there is an economic link between the proprietors of the sign and those of the mark. An example would be where consumers believe the sign is licensed by the proprietor of the mark.

What is a mark with a reputation?

For infringement under TMA 1994, s.10(3), the registered mark must have a reputation. For the purpose of infringement under TMA 1994 this reputation must be in the UK; for the purpose of the Regulation, it must be in the EU. Further, the reputation must exist in a substantial part of the UK (*General Motors* v. *Yplon* [1999] All ER (EC) 865). A significant proportion of the public must be concerned by the goods or services covered by the registration.

Requirement for a 'link' in the mind of the public

There must also be a degree of similarity between the mark and the sign such that the relevant members of the public make a connection or establish a link between them even though it does not confuse them. The existence of such a link must, just like a likelihood of confusion, be assessed globally taking into account all factors relevant to the circumstances of the case (ECJ Case C-408/01 *Adidas-Salomon* v. *Fitness World* [2004] FSR 21).

The presence in the marketplace of marks and signs which call each other to mind is not, of itself, sufficient for that purpose (*Electrocoin Automatics* v. *Hitachi Credit* [2005] FSR 7).

The scope of infringement under TMA 1994, s.10(3) is still not clear. At the time of writing the question of whether a link alone was sufficient for infringement under s.10(3) has been referred to the ECJ in *Intel Corporation Inc.* v. *CPM UK Ltd* [2007] EWCA Civ 431.

What amounts to detriment/unfair advantage?

The requirement that use of a sign without due cause take unfair advantage of, or be detrimental to, the distinctive character or repute of the trade mark is at the heart of s.10(3). It prevents proprietors of marks with a reputation from objecting to the use of any sign by a third party merely because it reminds people of the mark (*Premier Brands* v. *Typhoon* [2000] FSR 767).

Detriment to and unfair advantage of distinctive character or repute must be proved by evidence. Mere speculation about harm will not be enough. To assess both detriment and unfair advantage it is necessary for there to be a global assessment of the relevant factors.

The precise ambit of what amounts to taking unfair advantage and detriment is unclear. The English cases suggest that, at least for 'unfair advantage' and perhaps also for 'detrimental to distinctive character or repute' the later mark should have an effect or be likely to have an effect on the economic behaviour of the consumer (*Electrocoin Automatics Ltd* v. *Coinworld Ltd* [2004] EWHC 1498 (Ch); *Mastercard International* v. *Hitachi Credit (UK) Plc* [2004] EWHC 1623 (Ch)).

Unfair advantage requires a benefit accruing to the defendant through use of the registered mark. It is intended to encompass instances where there is clear exploitation and free-riding on the coat-tails of a famous mark or an attempt to trade upon its reputation (Advocate General's Opinion in *Adidas* v. *Fitnessworld*, above).

Detriment may be caused in at least two ways. The use of the later mark may erode the distinctiveness of the earlier mark. This is sometimes described as 'dilution', which is the blurring of the distinctiveness of a mark. The other type of detriment is tarnishment. An example of tarnishment may be where the use of the later mark on certain goods may give rise to unpleasant mental associations with the goods for which the earlier mark is reputed (*Premier Brands* v. *Typhoon* (above); see also *Ferrero* v. *Kindercare Learning* [2005] OHIM Board of Appeal).

The Court of Appeal in *Intel Corporation Inc.* v. *CPM UK Ltd* (above) suggested the following non-exhaustive list of factors should be considered when making the global assessment of whether there has been detriment to distinctive character:

(a) whether the 'pulling power' of the earlier mark for its specific goods or services is really likely to be affected by the use of the later mark for its specific goods or service;
(b) whether the user of the later mark is likely to get a real commercial advantage from its use for its specific goods or services by reason of the repute of the earlier mark for its specific goods or services;
(c) whether, if the earlier mark is unique, it really matters that it is used for the dissimilar goods or services of the later mark;
(d) where the later mark is not the same as the earlier mark what difference that it will make on the average consumer and in particular whether there is merely a calling to mind of the earlier mark;
(e) whether the economic behaviour of the average consumer in relation to the earlier mark when used for its goods and services is likely to be affected;
(f) how inherently distinctive the earlier mark is; and
(g) how strong the reputation of the earlier mark for its goods and services is.

The question of what factors should be taken into account in assessing unfair advantage and detriment have also been referred to the ECJ in *Intel*. It is hoped that this will clarify the position, but at the time of writing the ECJ's decision was still pending.

Limitations on the effects of a trade mark – defences to infringement

Use of a registered trade mark

Under TMA 1994, s.11(1) a trade mark is not infringed by the use of another UK registered trade mark in relation to goods or services for which the latter is registered. This defence only applies to an infringement of a national mark, and it is not a defence to infringement of a CTM.

Use of person's own name or address

A registered trade mark is not infringed by the use of a person of his own name or address, provided the use is in accordance with honest practices in industrial or commercial matters (TMA 1994, s.11(2)(a)).

The defence applies to an individual's name and address but also to the use of a trading name (ECJ Case C-245/02 *Anheuser-Busch* v. *Budejovicky Budvar*); it also includes company or firm names (*Scandecor Development AB* v. *Scandecor Marketing AB* [2002] FSR 7).

The defence does not arise where the defendant has registered a company name for the purposes of taking advantage of the reputation of a registered trade mark. This would not fall within the requirement of honest practices (*Asprey & Garrard* v. *WRA (Guns)* [2002] FSR 31).

A person's name is the name which they are known by or called. It will include the name by which they are usually known even if it is not the name they are christened. The name of a company will also include the name by which it is usually known to its customers, for example, omitting 'limited' or 'plc' (*Mercury Communications* v. *Mercury Interactive* [1995] FSR 850).

Use of the name as a trade mark does not prevent the defence applying.

Is the use within honest practices?

The test for whether something is within honest practices in industrial and commercial matters is an objective test. It is an expression of the duty to act fairly in relation to the legitimate interest of the trade mark owner (Case C-100/02 *Gerolsteiner Brunnen* (7 January 2004)). The test is whether reasonable members of the relevant trade would think, upon knowing all the relevant facts, that the defendant knew that the use complained of was honest (*Volvo* v. *Heritage* [2000] FSR 253).

Use of a trade mark will not comply with honest practices where it is done in such a manner that it may give the impression that there is a commercial connection between the user and the trade mark proprietor. It is also not within honest practices where the use affects the value of the trade mark by taking unfair advantage of its reputation; or discredits or denigrates the mark; or where the user presents its product as an imitation or replica of the product bearing the trade mark of which it is not the owner (Case C-228/03 *Gillette* v. *LA-Laboratoires* [2005] ETMR 67).

In assessing honest practices the court also needs to take into account the following factors.

1. The overall presentation of the product marketed by the third party, particularly the circumstances in which the mark of which the third party is not owner is displayed in that presentation.
2. The circumstances in which a distinction is made between that mark and the mark or sign of the third party.
3. The effort made by that third party to ensure that consumers distinguish its products from those of which it is not the trade mark owner (*Gillette* v. *LA-Laboratoires* (above)).

Indications concerning the kind, quality, quantity, intended purpose or other characteristics

A registered trade mark is not infringed by the use of indications concerning the kind, quality, quantity, intended purpose, value, geographical origin, the time of production of goods or of rendering of services, or other characteristics of goods or services – provided that the use is in accordance with honest practices in industrial and commercial matters (TMA 1994, s.11(2)(b)).

Use of terms as trade marks rather than exclusively as descriptors can still fall within the defence so long as the sign had some descriptive significance. In *Gerolsetiner* there was a conflict between the registered trade mark GERRI (for, among other things, mineral water) and an alleged infringement 'Kerry Spring' for Irish mineral water from the Kerry Spring sold by a company called Kerry Spring Water. It was held that it was enough for the operation of the defence (under Art.6 of the Directive) that 'Kerry' was of geographical significance even though it also had some trade mark significance.

Use necessary to indicate the intended purpose of a product or service

A registered trade mark is not infringed by the use of the trade mark where it is necessary to indicate the intended purpose of a product or service (in particular, accessories or spare parts) (TMA 1994, s.11(2)(c)). This is again provided the use is in accordance with honest practices in industrial and commercial matters.

In *Gillette* v. *LA-Laboratoires* (above) the defendant's use of Gillette's trade marks was held to be necessary in order to indicate the intended purpose of the defendant's product. The defendant sold replaceable blades under the mark PARASON FLEXOR. The packaging of that product had a sticker affixed to it with the words: 'All PARASON FLEXOR and GILLETTE SENSOR handles are compatible with this blade'.

The ECJ held that use of Gillette's trade mark by a defendant in practice constituted the only means of providing the public with comprehensible and complete information on that intended purpose for that product.

Use of an earlier right in a locality

A registered trade mark is not infringed by the use in the course of trade in a particular locality of an earlier right which applies only in that locality (TMA 1994, s.11(3)).

The earlier right has to be an unregistered trade mark or sign which has been used continuously in relation to goods or services. The use has to have commenced from prior to either:

(a) the use of the registered trade mark by the proprietor or a predecessor in title; or
(b) the registration of the registered trade mark.

The earlier right is regarded as applying in a locality if, or to the extent that, its use in that locality is protected by virtue of any rule of law (in particular, the law of passing off). Thus, if the earlier user could have succeeded in an action in passing off against the use of the trade mark, then they are entitled to continue to use the mark in that locality.

Unjustified threats

As with designs and patents, there is a remedy under TMA 1994 for any third party against anyone who makes unjustified threats of trade mark infringement proceedings.

Section 21 states that where a person threatens another with proceedings for trade mark infringement any person aggrieved may bring proceedings to obtain an injunction to prevent further threats, damages and a declaration that the threats are unjustified.

The provision does not apply where the threats relate to:

(a) the application of the mark to goods or their packaging;
(b) the importation of goods to which, or to the packaging of which, the mark has been applied; or
(c) the supply of services under the mark.

It is a defence to a 'threats' action if the defendant can show that the acts in respect of which proceedings were threatened constituted an infringement of the relevant trade mark. However, if the trade mark is shown to be invalid or liable to be revoked the recipient of the letter is still entitled to relief.

The mere notification that a trade mark is registered or that an application has been made does not constitute a threat.

Invalidity/revocation

It is a defence to trade mark infringement proceedings that the registered trade mark is invalid or should be revoked. If a mark is found to be invalid, the mark should never have been registered and the registration is deemed never to have existed. However, this does not affect any transactions which are 'past and closed' (TMA 1994, s.47(6)). Revocation, on the other hand, deals with matters that have arisen since registration. An order for revocation has effect from the date of the order unless the court decides the ground existed from an earlier date.

For national marks, a declaration of invalidity or order for revocation can also be sought independently of an infringement action either at the IPO or through the courts.

Invalidity

The grounds on which a trade mark can be declared invalid are set out in TMA 1994, s.47.

A registered trade mark may be declared invalid on the ground that the trade mark was registered in breach of the absolute grounds of refusal of registration. There is, however, a caveat: if the trade mark was registered in breach of one of the distinctiveness grounds for refusal (devoid of distinctive character/descriptive/common term) then the mark will *not* be invalid if, in consequence of the use made of it following registration, it has acquired distinctive character in relation to the goods and services for which it is registered.

A registered trade mark may also be declared invalid on the ground that:

- there is an earlier registered trade mark which fulfils the conditions set out in the Relative Grounds of refusal section above; or
- there is an earlier right in relation to which the condition set out in the Relative Grounds of Refusal section above applies.

A proprietor of an earlier trade mark or earlier right cannot seek invalidity where the proprietor has acquiesced for a continuous period of five years in the use of a registered trade mark in the UK, knowing of that use. In such a case, the proprietor of the earlier right loses his right to seek to invalidate the registered trade mark unless the registration was applied for in bad faith (TMA 1994, s.48(1)).

Partial invalidity

If grounds of invalidity are established in respect of only some of the goods and services for which the trade mark is registered, the trade mark will only be declared invalid as regards those goods or services only.

Revocation

There are four grounds of revocation under TMA 1994, s.46. The first two relate to non-use of the trade mark for five years. We will deal with each of these in turn.

Non use after registration

> [T]hat within the period of five years following the date of completion of the registration procedure it has not been put to genuine use in the United Kingdom, by the proprietor or with his consent, in relation to the goods or services for which it is registered, and there are no proper reasons for non-use (TMA 1994, s.46(1)(a)).

Section 46(1)(a) gives rise to a number of issues:

1. *What amounts to genuine use?* Genuine use of the mark is use which is not 'token' use – that is merely to preserve the rights conferred by the registration and avoid a revocation attack. The use also has to be use of the mark on the market for goods and services protected by the registration and not just internal use by the business concerned. In assessing whether the use is genuine, consideration should be given to:

   (a) the nature of the goods or services;
   (b) the characteristics of the market; and
   (c) the scale and frequency of the use of the mark (*Ansul BV* v. *Ajax Braandbeveiliging BV* [2003] RPC 40).

   Even minimal use can be sufficient to qualify as genuine on condition that it is deemed to be justified, in the economic sector concerned, for the purpose of preserving or creating market share for the goods or services protected by the mark (*Laboratories Goemar SA* v. *La Mer Technology Inc* [2004] EWHC 2960).
2. *Date of completion of the registration procedure?* The five-year period runs from the date on which the trade mark appears on the relevant register. It is not the date on which the trade mark application was filed or the date on which the application was published.
3. *Proper reasons for non-use.* 'Proper reasons' is intended to cover abnormal situations in the industry or market, or even temporary but serious disruption affecting the proprietor's business. Normal delays caused by some unavoidable regulatory requirements, such as the

approval of a medicine, might be acceptable but not the normal delays found, for example, within the marketing function (*Invermont* [1997] RPC 125).

4. *Use of variants of the mark.* The use of a trade mark for these purposes includes use in a form differing in elements which do not alter the distinctive character of the mark (TMA 1994, s.46(2)).

Non use for five years

> [T]hat such use has been suspended for an uninterrupted period of five years, and there are no proper reasons for non-use (TMA 1994, s.46(1)(b)).

This subsection deals with the situation where the mark has been used after registration but that use has subsequently ceased.

Resumption/commencement of use

Under both s.46(1)(a) and (b), if use is resumed/commenced after the five-year period of non-use the mark will not be revoked. Any use after the expiry of the five-year period but within three months of an application to revoke shall be disregarded. Such use will, however, be taken into account where the preparations for the use began before the proprietor became aware that the application might be made (TMA 1994, s.46(3)).

Common name in the trade

> [T]hat, in consequence of acts or inactivity of the proprietor, it has become the common name in the trade for a product or service for which it is registered (TMA 1994, s.46(1)(c)).

Whether a mark has become the common name in the trade for a product or service is a question of fact to be decided in the circumstances. It is a qualitative test rather than quantitative (*Hormel Foods Corporation* v. *Antilles Landscape Investments NV* [2005] ETMR 54). Famous examples include 'HOOVER' which became the common name for vacuum cleaners and 'BIRO' for ballpoint pens.

The focus of the enquiry as to what is a 'common name in the trade' is whether the trade mark can still function as an indication of origin. The class of persons whose views are to be taken into account in determining whether the trade mark has become the common name in the trade for the product comprises all consumers and end users and, depending on the features of the relevant market, all those in the trade who deal with the product commercially. Depending on the circumstances, this can include intermediaries in the supply chain to the consumer (Case C-371/02 *Bjornekulla Fruktindustrier AB* v. *Procordia Food AB*).

The mark becoming 'generic' needs to be as a result of the acts or inactivity of the proprietor. This may arise in circumstances where the proprietor's own advertising campaigns have resulted in the mark becoming a descriptive term, especially where the mark was composed of descriptive elements. Alternatively the proprietor may have failed to properly police the use of the trade mark as a generic term by competitors.

Likely to be misleading

> [T]hat in consequence of the use made of it by the proprietor or with his consent in relation to the goods or services for which it is registered, it is liable to mislead the public, particularly as to the nature, quality or geographical origin of those goods or services (TMA 1994, s.46(1)(d)).

For a mark to be misleading there must be a real risk of the economic behaviour of consumers being affected. The reason for this provision (or its equivalent in the Directive) is consumer protection, but mere confusion on the part of the average consumer is not sufficient to trigger it (Case C-259/04 *Elizabeth Emanuel* v. *Continental Shelf 128 Ltd* (AG Ruiz-Jarabo Colomer; OJ 2006 C-134 18)).

The case involved a well-known designer of bridal wear who had ceased to have any involvement with the company which carried her name. The company owned a trade mark registration for 'ELIZABETH EMANUEL'. The designer argued that the average consumer believed she was still involved in the business and this was misleading. The ECJ held that even if the average consumer were to be influenced into buying garments sold under the mark 'ELIZABETH EMANUEL' by imagining that Elizabeth Emanuel designed them, the characteristics and the qualities of those garments would remain guaranteed by the trade mark owner. Consequently, the name 'ELIZABETH EMANUEL' was not in itself deceptive as to the origin of the goods.

The provision presupposes the existence of actual deceit or a sufficiently serious risk that the consumer would be deceived (see also Case C-87/97 *Consorzio per la tutela del formaggio Gorgonzola* (4 March 1999)).

3.4 COMPARATIVE ADVERTISING

Comparative advertising gives rise to some particular problems when considering whether the use of a registered trade mark (or one confusingly similar thereto) within a comparative advertisement to refer to a competitor amounts to trade mark infringement.

Various potential defences to an allegation of infringement are available in such circumstances.

1. The use is not trade mark use as it does not jeopardise the essential function of the trade mark to guarantee origin.
2. The use falls within TMA 1994, s.10(6), i.e. it does not fall within any of the infringement provisions since the use is for the purpose of identifying goods or services as those of the proprietor or a licensee. The defence is only effective if the use is in accordance with honest practices in industrial or commercial matters and does not without due cause take unfair advantage of or cause detriment to, the distinctive character or repute of the trade mark. This defence only applies to an infringement claim based on a national mark.
3. The use is permitted by the Directive on Misleading and Comparative Advertising (Directive 97/55/EC, the 'Comparative Advertising Directive') which permits comparative advertising where:

   (a) it is not misleading;
   (b) it compares goods and services meeting the same needs or intended for the same purpose;
   (c) it objectively compares one or more material features of the goods and services which may include price;
   (d) it does not discredit or denigrate the trade marks;
   (e) it does not create confusion between the advertiser and the competitor;
   (f) it does not take unfair advantage of the reputation of a trade mark;
   (g) it does not present goods as imitations or replicas bearing the trade mark.

4. The use falls within the s.11(2)(b) defence referred to above, i.e. that the use is of indications of characteristics of the goods or services (*O2 Holdings Ltd and O2 (UK) Ltd* v. *Hutchison 3G Ltd* [2006] EWCA Civ 1656).

The *O2* case is currently pending before the ECJ for preliminary rulings on the following three questions.

1. Whether comparative advertising amounted to trade mark use for the purpose of infringement.
2. Whether to fall within the Comparative Advertising Directive a defendant had to show it was necessary or indispensable to use its competitor's mark. (O2 argued that on the facts, 3G did not need to use the bubble images.)
3. Whether the Comparative Advertising Directive required the identical mark to be used or permitted the use of a confusingly similar mark.

3.5 EXHAUSTION OF RIGHTS

Under TMA 1994, s.12(1) a registered trade mark is not infringed by the use of the trade mark in relation to goods which have been put on the market in the European Economic Area under that trade mark by the proprietor or with its consent.

Nevertheless, where there exist legitimate reasons for the proprietor to oppose further dealings in the goods, for instance, where the condition of the goods have been changed or impaired, the defence does not apply (s.12(2)).

This section prevents the trade mark proprietor from stopping further circulation of goods bearing its trade mark, once the proprietor (or someone with his consent) has placed them on the market.

Three issues arise out of this section (and the equivalent articles in the Directive and Regulation).

First, it only applies where goods are placed on the market in the EEA with the proprietor's consent. If the proprietor places the goods bearing the trade mark on the market outside the EEA, and someone purchases them and then without consent tries to import them into the UK, the proprietor can still use his UK registered trade mark rights to prevent the import or sale of the goods in the UK (*Silhouette International Schmied Gmbh & Co KG* v. *Hartlauer Handelsgesellshaft Gmbh* [1998] 2 CMLR 953)

Secondly, the proprietor's consent to have the goods placed on the market in the EEA will normally have to be express because it equates to the proprietor giving up his exclusive rights in the registered trade mark in respect of the goods in question. Consent cannot be inferred from mere silence on the part of the trade mark proprietor. Consent will also rarely be implied, and will certainly *not* be implied from the mere fact that the goods carry no warning that they are not to be resold in the EEA or that the proprietor has not contractually limited the right of resale in the EEA under its contract of sale with a third party (Joined Cases C-414/99 to C-416/99 *Zino Davidoff* v. *A&G Imports Ltd, Levi Strauss* v. *Tesco, Levi Strauss* v. *Costco*).

There will, however, be cases where the facts give rise to an implication of consent. For instance in *Mastercigars Direct Limited* v. *Hunters & Frankau* and *Corporacion Habanos SA* v. *Mastercigars Direct Limited* [2007] EWCA Civ 176 it was held that the trade mark owner knew and encouraged the sale of cigars in Cuba to Europeans for resale abroad; consent was implied.

Thirdly, even where the goods have been placed on the market in the EEA with consent of the proprietor, the proprietor may still be able to prevent the importation of the goods bearing the trade mark into the UK if there are legitimate reasons to do so. 'Legitimate reasons' are often raised where the goods that were placed on the market by the proprietor are altered or where their packaging has been changed.

It is a legitimate reason to oppose further dealings where the goods are changed by adding another component that is not approved by the proprietor.

Repackaging gives rise to more difficult issues. In the pharmaceutical industry it may be necessary to repackage or re-label goods to be able to market them in other EU countries. For instance, drugs originally packaged for sale in Greece would need to have instructions and any descriptions on the packaging translated into English for sale in the UK.

The courts have sought to strike a balance between the interests of the trade mark proprietor in not permitting the reputation of his trade mark to be damaged by the repackaging or re-labelling with the principle of free movement of goods within the EU (EC Treaty, Art.28).

In the case of *Bristol-Myers Squibb* v. *Paranova* [1996] ECR I-3457 the ECJ laid down the so-called '*BMS* conditions' as to when a trade mark owner may legitimately enforce his rights under Art.7(2) of the Trade Marks Directive 89/104/EEC notwithstanding the principle of exhaustion of rights under Art.7(1) of the Directive and Art.28 of the EC Treaty. In short (as summarised by Lord Justice Jacob in this case) 'the importer who repackages and re-applies the mark will infringe unless he satisfies all five of the *BMS* conditions . . .' by showing that:

(a) it is necessary to repackage to market the product;
(b) there is no effect on the original condition of the product or on the instructions;
(c) the repackaging includes clear identification of manufacturer and importer;
(d) the presentation is non-damaging; and
(e) notice has been given to the trade mark owner in advance of importing the repackaged goods.

These conditions have been elaborated in subsequent cases. A parallel importer must fulfil all the *BMS* conditions even if the repackaging causes no harm to the specific subject matter of a trade mark; and must also show that repackaging is necessary because effective access to the market is hindered as a result of strong resistance from a significant proportion of consumers to re-labelled products.

The ECJ in its second judgment in this case in April 2007 (ECJ Case C-348/04 *Boehringer Ingelheim KG & Anr* v. *Swingward Ltd; Boehringer Ingelheim KG & Anr* v. *Dowelhurst Ltd and Others*) has explained the position still further and confirmed that:

1. All the *BMS* conditions apply to overstickering (i.e. placing a sticker over the old packaging bearing the new information and the original trade mark, rather than producing a complete new package).
2. The requirement of necessity only applies to the fact of repackaging, not the manner of repackaging.
3. The requirement that the repackaging should not be damaging is not limited to cases where the repackaging is defective, of poor quality or untidy.

4. Whether de-branding, co-branding or failure to identify the owner of the trade mark are damaging is a question of fact for the national courts.
5. The onus of proving that the repackaging complies with the *BMS* conditions lies with the parallel importer (who must supply a sample if requested) although the burden of proof can be reversed by providing evidence that 'leads to the reasonable presumption that the condition has been fulfilled'.
6. If the parallel trader fails to give notice to the trade mark owner of the repackaged product then the trade mark is infringed on any subsequent importation of the product.

3.6 DEALING WITH REGISTERED TRADE MARKS

Assignment of trade marks

A national UK registration is transmissible by assignment, testamentary disposition or operation of law in the same way as other personal or moveable property. It is transmissible either together with or separately from the goodwill of the business (TMA 1994, s.24(1)). An assignment of a registered trade mark is not effective, however, unless it is in writing signed by or on behalf of the assignor (TMA 1994, s.24(3)).

An application for a national trade mark is transferable in the same way as a registered trade mark (TMA 1994, s.27).

With certain exceptions, a registered CTM is dealt with in its entirety as an object of property as if it were a national trade mark registered in the EU Member State in which the proprietor has its seat or domicile. Where the proprietor does not have its seat or domicile in a Member State, the laws of the Member State where the proprietor has an establishment apply. If the proprietor does not even have an establishment in a Member State then it will be treated as a national trade mark in Spain (Regulation, Art.16(i)).

An assignment of a CTM must be made in writing and requires the signature of the parties to the contract (except when it is a result of a judgment) otherwise it is void (Regulation, Art.17(3)). The only exception to this is where there is a transfer of the whole of a business when special rules apply.

A CTM application is treated in the same way as a CTM registration.

Licensing trade marks

Licences may be exclusive or non-exclusive and may relate to some or all of the goods or services for which the mark concerned is registered.

Under TMA 1994 a licence is not effective unless it is in writing signed by or on behalf of the grantor (TMA 1994, s.28(2)).

Registration of assignments and licences

Assignments and licences of UK national trade marks are registrable transactions. Details of them may be entered in the UK Trade Marks Register on application of the proprietor.

Registration is not necessary for the assignment or licence to be valid. However registration protects the individual who acquires an interest in a trade mark from any third party who acquires a conflicting interest. Until registration is made the transaction is ineffective against a person acquiring a conflicting interest in or under the registered trade mark in ignorance of the prior transaction (TMA 1994, s.25(3)).

Registration also permits a licensee or assignee to bring infringement proceedings.

3.7 PASSING OFF

English law has no law of unfair competition or any proprietary right in company names as such. Nevertheless, where a trader has used a trade mark in the course of trade, the trader may be able to rely on the tort of passing off to prevent unauthorised use of the trade mark by a third party.

Unlike registered trade mark law, passing off is not created by statute: it is purely a creature of common law.

Definition of passing off

The elements of the tort of passing off were restated in *Reckitt & Colman Products Ltd* v. *Borden* [1990] 1 All ER 873. They are:

Goodwill

The claimant must prove the existence of a reputation attached to his goods or services in the mind of the purchasing public by association with the identifying 'get-up' (whether it consists simply of a brand name or a trade description, or the individual features of labelling or packaging) under which particular goods or services are offered to the public, such that the get-up is recognised by the public as distinctive of the claimant's goods or services.

Misrepresentation

The claimant must demonstrate a misrepresentation by the defendant to the public (whether or not intentional) leading or likely to lead the public to the belief that the goods or services offered by the defendant are the goods or services of the claimant.

Damage

The claimant must demonstrate that he suffers, or, in a *quia timet* action, that he is likely to suffer, damage by reason of the erroneous belief engendered by the defendant's misrepresentation that the source of the goods or services is the same as the source offered by the claimant.

This formulation is referred to as the 'Classical Trinity'.

Extended form

There have been a number of cases where the goodwill in the mark is not owned by one claimant but belongs to a class of persons whose goods share common characteristics. Examples of this include SWISS for chocolate; and ADVOCAAT and CHAMPAGNE for alcoholic drinks. This is known as the 'Extended Form' of passing off. Claimants in this type of case are able to prevent a defendant using the term in respect of products that do not share the relevant characteristics.

Goodwill

The purpose of a passing off claim is to protect the goodwill of a proprietor. Goodwill is the 'attractive force which brings in the custom' (*IRC* v. *Muller's Margarine* [1901] AC 217).

To establish passing off, it is not necessary that the trade name is known throughout the UK. The relevant date for establishing the existence of goodwill is the date of the start of the alleged infringement (*Schweppes Property Ltd* v. *The Pub Squash Company Ltd* [1981] RPC 429). There is no set period over which goodwill has to be established – each case depends on its facts – the only requirement is that sufficient reputation has been established that it will be damaged by the acts of the defendant.

It is not necessary to show that the public knew the identity of the owner of the goodwill when purchasing goods under the trade mark. It is only necessary that they understood the trade mark to indicate the origin of the goods i.e. that the goods were from a particular source.

Goodwill is personal property. It can be assigned and the transfer of a business as a whole will necessarily also transfer the goodwill to the assignee.

Goodwill can survive the cessation of the underlying business and may persist for a number of years after the business has ceased.

Misrepresentation

It is not necessary that the misrepresentation was intentional. Fraud is not a necessary element to the tort (*Reddaway* v. *Bentham* (1892) 12 RPC 83).

However, if it is proved that the defendant set out intentionally to deceive the public then the court will strain to infer that the defendant succeeded.

There have been a variety of different types of misrepresentation established in the cases:

- misrepresentation by the defendant that the goods he sells are those of the claimant;
- misrepresentation that the defendant's business is the claimant's business;
- misrepresentation where the defendant has pretended to be agent for the sale of the claimant's goods.

Unlike registered trade mark infringement, for a claim in passing off the misrepresentation needs to occur at the point of sale.

Passing off is however a flexible tort and is not limited to specific types of misrepresentation.

Other examples of misrepresentation include a misrepresentation that an individual (who has a reputation) has endorsed another business or its products. In *Irvine* v. *Talksport* [2002] 2 All ER 414, Eddie Irvine, a highly successful racing driver, was pictured in promotional material for the Talksport radio station shortly before the British Grand Prix. The photograph had been doctored so he was shown holding a Talksport radio. Irvine succeeded in his claim for passing off against Talksport. The court held that the actions of Talksport gave rise to a false message which would be understood by a not insignificant section of the relevant public that Talksport had been endorsed by Irvine.

It is not possible to classify all the possible ways in which a false representation might amount to passing off, and the courts avoid doing this.

Damage

It is essential that the misrepresentation should be such as to be likely to cause substantial damage to the claimant's goodwill.

There are two main types of damage likely to be suffered:

(a) diverting trade from the claimant to the defendant; or
(b) injuring the trade reputation of the claimant.

While confusion can be helpful in establishing misrepresentation and damage, confusion on its own is not sufficient to establish passing off. When Midland Bank changed its name to HSBC, this resulted in many customers confusing the bank with HFC. The court held, however, that the confusion was not sufficient to amount to passing off, due to the limited recognition of the HFC brand (*HFC Bank* v. *Midland Bank* [2000] FSR 176):

> People make assumptions, jump to unjustified conclusions, and put two and two together to make five.

This is not enough to establish passing off unless the use by the defendant will be taken by consumers as a representation that his business is or has some connection to the business of the claimant so giving rise to harm or a risk of harm to the claimant's goodwill or reputation (Chadwick LJ in *Premier Luggage and Bags* v. *Premier Co* [2003] FSR 5).

3.8 MISCELLANEOUS

Well-known marks

A well-known mark is a mark that is well known in the UK and is the mark of a person who:

(a) is a national of a convention country; or
(b) is domiciled in, or has a real and effective industrial or commercial establishment in, a convention country (TMA 1994, s.56, implementing Art.6*bis* Paris Convention).

It is not necessary that the person carries on business or has any goodwill in the UK.

The proprietor of a mark which qualifies for such protection is entitled to restrain by injunction the use in the UK of a trade mark which, or the essential part of which, is identical or similar to his mark, in relation to identical or similar goods or services, where the use is likely to cause confusion. However, there is no clear guidance as to what level of recognition must be established in order to meet the requirement of being 'well known'.

The section is rarely used in the UK.

Olympic Marks

Olympic Symbol etc. (Protection) Act 1995

The 1995 Act created an Olympics Association Right ('OA Right') to control the unauthorised use in the course of trade of the following signs and symbols:

(a) the Olympic five-ring symbol ('Symbol');
(b) the Olympic motto: '*Citius, altius, fortius*' ('Motto');
(c) particular variations of 'Olympic' such as 'Olympiad' and 'Olympian' ('the Protected Words'); and
(d) any representation that is so similar to the Symbol or Motto as to be likely to create an association with it in the public mind.

The owner of the OA Right was the British Olympic Society.

London Olympic Games and Paralympic Games Act 2006

The 2006 Act widens the ambit of rights granted. It prohibits the use of words that are so similar to any of the Protected Words as to be likely to create, in the mind of the public, an association with the Olympic Games or Olympic movement.

Additionally, the 2006 Act creates a London Olympics Association Right ('the LOA Right'). The LOA Right is aimed at dealing with those who attempt to claim an association with the 2012 Olympics *without* using the specific words or symbols already protected by the OA Right.

The main features of LOA Right are as follows.

1. The owner of the LOA Right has the exclusive right to use (and so can prevent others from using) any representation in a manner likely to create an association in the public mind between the London Olympics and goods/services.
2. In considering whether someone has infringed the LOA Right, a court may, in particular, take account of his use of a combination of expressions, as set out below:

   (a) Any combination of two or more of: games, two thousand and twelve, 2012, twenty twelve.
   (b) Any combination of any of the expressions set out above with any of the following: gold, silver, bronze, London, medals, sponsor, and summer.

An 'association' can be any kind of contractual, commercial, corporate or financial connection between goods/services and the London Olympics. However, an association is not suggested by a statement which:

(a) accords with honest practices in industrial or commercial matters; and
(b) does not make promotional or other commercial use of any of the Words by incorporating it in a text to which the Olympic Games and the Olympic movement are substantively irrelevant.

Defences

The OA and LOA Rights are not infringed by certain uses of a representation:

(a) in the course of publishing/broadcasting a report of a sporting event or other event forming part of the London Olympics;
(b) in the course of publishing/broadcasting information about the London Olympics;
(c) as an incidental inclusion in a literary or artistic work, sound recording, film or broadcast; or
(d) in the course of advertising any of these.

The LOA Right is also not infringed by:

(a) use of a trade mark in relation to goods/services for which it is registered;
(b) a trader's use of the trader's own name or address;
(c) use of indications of characteristics of goods/services; or
(d) use to indicate intended purpose of goods/services.

These defences are similar to those relevant to trade mark infringement, discussed above.

CHAPTER 4

Patents

Lorna Brazell

4.1 ESSENTIALS

Theory

A patent is the grant by a State to an inventor of an absolute monopoly over the exploitation of an innovative technical device or process, for a limited period, in return for a complete written disclosure of how to carry out the invention. The consideration theory justifies this monopoly, which would otherwise be plainly undesirable in a free market economy, by reference to the benefits hoped to be received by the State in return:

(a) encouraging innovation; and
(b) the commercial exploitation of the innovation in that State, leading to increased employment and trade.

Effect of a patent

The monopoly given by a patent is not a positive right to do something. Ownership of a patent does not imply freedom to operate the invention. In any developed field of technology, it is likely that there will be underlying technology upon which the new invention builds. If it is necessary to use that underlying technology in order to work the invention, but the underlying technology is still protected by patent or other rights, then the grant of a patent does *not* give freedom to operate. The patent holder will need to obtain a licence of any valid rights over the underlying technology in order to avoid the risk of proceedings for infringement. Of course, ownership of a patented improvement on the existing technology may well be a valuable bargaining chip in such negotiations. But on its own, it is insufficient.

Conversely, everyone has the right to make and (subject to infringement of third party rights) use their own inventions; there is no need to meet any legal standards and obtain a grant of a monopoly merely to do that.

The key issue is what impact imitators will have on the business, over what timescale, if the invention is left unprotected. Some inventions, such as the optimal fermentation conditions for a particular biotechnology-derived compound, may not be capable of being deduced from the end product. In such a case, secrecy may be an equally effective means of maintaining a monopoly. Secrecy, whilst far harder to maintain in practice than a patent, is also potentially perpetual compared to the time-limited patent monopoly. It is then a commercial decision whether to protect the invention by applying for a patent over it, or to attempt to keep it secret.

Alternatively, in some fast-moving fields, simple reliance upon first mover advantage may be more cost-effective than the expense and delays of prosecuting a patent application.

Limitations of patents

A patent, then, is a purely negative right to stop other people doing that which is within the scope of the patent, whether or not they come by that invention independently. But the commercial effectiveness of any given patent depends both on the scope of the claims (is it a complete road block, or merely an obstacle which with a little effort may be designed around?) and on the validity of the grant. No Patent Office is perfect; for reasons which will be examined in more detail below, a granted patent is not necessarily a valid patent. In any discussion over the value of a particular patent, it is important to come prepared not only with an interpretation as to the true scope of the claims but also as to the strengths and weaknesses of the whole.

Sources of patent law

Patents in the United Kingdom are governed by the Patents Act (PA) 1977, which was introduced to implement the 1973 European Patent Convention (EPC). That Convention established a European Patent Office in Munich, but it is not a treaty of the European Union. All Member States of the European Union are also signatories to the EPC and their national laws accordingly reflect its provisions. However, a number of other countries are also signatories, such as the EEA countries, Switzerland, Turkey and so on.

In consequence, as a court solely of the European Union, the European Court of Justice has no jurisdiction in patent matters. This lack of a single centralised decision-making body has led to unresolved divergences in national interpretations of the EPC, and hence the interpretation of patents, in national law. This is a problem continually under scrutiny at European level – so far without a solution, although a European Patent Litigation Agreement has been close to finalisation several times.

4.2 OWNERSHIP

Unlike copyright and certain design and trade mark rights, a patent does not just come into existence at the moment the invention is made: a patent has to be applied for. The application must be made before the invention has been disclosed to the public, with certain limited exceptions.

The application process

An application including a detailed specification describing the invention must be submitted to the appropriate Patent Office. The geographical scope of protection required will determine which Patent Office should be chosen. This handbook is concerned only with the UK, in which case an application at the UK Intellectual Property Office (UKIPO) leading to grant in the UK alone will suffice, but typically protection is sought in more than one country. Even if the inventor only has capacity to exploit the invention in the UK, it is important to consider the possibility of obtaining protection abroad since it may be possible to license rights under the patent to other businesses in return for a royalty stream, or to sell the foreign rights. If so, an application will be 'first filed' in the UKIPO or the European Patent Office, an international 'second filing' being lodged within the subsequent year at the World Intellectual Property Organisation (WIPO) in Geneva.

This period of a year for international filing derives from the Paris Convention for the protection of industrial property of 1883, which began the process of harmonising patent law at international level. The process has ultimately led to the inclusion in the World Trade Organisation (WTO) statutes of a minimum standard of protection for inventions to be provided by all WTO members. However, patent law is not entirely harmonised worldwide; work continues on a Substantive Patent Law Treaty at the WIPO but this is unlikely to reach a conclusion in the near future.

The application process is described in more detail at **4.3**.

Valuing a patent application

Not every application leads to the grant of a patent. Even where it does, most patent applications are amended to some degree in the course of prosecution. As a result of concessions and amendments made in the face of the examiner's objections, the patent ultimately granted may have a materially different focus and scope from the application as originally filed, although it can only be narrower than the initial application not broader.

An application in the early stages of prosecution is therefore of very little value in trying to establish the likely scope and strength – and hence value – of any patent which may be granted. At best, it gives some indication of the very broadest monopoly that may conceivably result.

The right to apply for a patent

As mentioned above, no patent rights at all arise in an invention unless and until a patent application is filed. References to the right to apply for a patent, which often appear in contractual documents, are meaningless: there are no legal limitations as to who can *apply* for a patent although under PA 1977, s.7 (as amended) a legal right to ownership, implying some connection with the inventor, is necessary for a grant.

The inventor is defined in PA 1977, s.7(3) as the actual deviser of the invention. Where two or more persons were involved in devising the invention, they are considered to be joint inventors. A patent can be granted to the inventor or joint inventors unless another person has a better entitlement to it. For example, in some circumstances (discussed below) an invention made by an employee belongs by law to his or her employer.

Disputes in this area are common. For instance, a person who, or organisation which, commissioned the research which led to the invention may have an equitable claim to the benefit accruing from the patent as a matter of contract. The principle is that the deviser of the 'heart of the invention' is entitled to the patent rights (*Markem* v. *Zipher* [2005] EWCA Civ 267). However, even in the context of collaborative research, the parties may hold different views as to who contributed what to the actual inventive step. In *Stanleco Fibre Optics* v. *Bioprogress* [2004] EWHC 2187 (Pat), Bioprogress claimed entitlement to various patents granted in Stanleco's name. The patents had arisen from a project Bioprogress had instituted to find a way of preparing ingestible capsules from water-soluble polymeric film materials using radio frequency welding. Bioprogress did not have the technology to make the capsules itself. Stanleco demonstrated sufficient likelihood that the idea would work for the parties to enter into a collaboration, during which Stanleco filed the patent applications in dispute, naming one of its own employees as sole inventor. Stanleco's position was that since Bioprogress had not been able to implement the 'core inventive concept' they had not made any invention but had rather compiled merely a 'wish list'. This position is somewhat persuasive, since many more people are capable of dreaming up good ideas than are capable of making them work. Nonetheless, the court held that as Bioprogress's employee had come up with the basic idea, he could justifiably claim to be the actual deviser of that invention, despite the fact that he had not reduced the invention to practice because he could not. Stanleco's employee had contributed the practical knowledge necessary to demonstrate that the idea worked, but this did not amount to an inventive contribution sufficient to make him a co-inventor of the principal invention, although he had made creative contributions to other claimed inventions.

There is a presumption (which can, however, be challenged) that the person making the application is entitled to the grant of the patent. The patent can also be granted to a successor in title to the person who would otherwise have been entitled.

The person to whom the patent is granted and who thus has the exclusive right to work the invention is known as the proprietor. The inventor has, however, an absolute right to be mentioned as being the inventor in any published application and in any patent granted.

Employee inventions and compensation

A very large proportion of patent applications will concern employee inventors. By PA 1977, s.39(1) an employee's invention belongs to the employer if either:

(a) the invention was made in the course of the employee's normal duties as an employee (or in the course of duties specifically assigned to the employee), provided that in either case an invention might reasonably be expected to result from the carrying out of those duties; or
(b) the employee had a special obligation to further the interests of the employer's undertaking and the invention was made in the course of the employee's duties (whether or not an invention might be expected to result from the carrying out of those duties).

In all other circumstances, the invention belongs to the employee. By s.42, the contract of employment cannot exclude this.

What precisely falls within the scope of an employee's employment can be a vexed question. The second category, of employees having a special obligation to further the employer's interests, is easier in this respect. Employees falling in this group include directors or other very senior figures, whose duties are likely to be expressed in relatively broad terms which may well encompass anything they do which relates to the employer's undertaking.

In all cases, the courts will look at the reality of the employment rather than treat the wording of an employment contract as definitive. In *Greater Glasgow Health Board's Application* [1996] RPC 207 the employer health authority argued that it was entitled to a patent over an invention relating to an ophthalmological instrument, made by a junior registrar at Glasgow Eye Infirmary. The registrar's job description included an expectation that he would avail himself of the research facilities available to the department and assist with post-graduate teaching of ophthalmology. However, his Head of Department testified that this was intended to function as an informal invitation to become involved with the University side of matters, thus making his career appear more interesting and hopefully opening up opportunities for the future. Making inventions fell outside the actual scope of his duties. Conversely, in *LIFFE* v. *Pinkava* [2007] EWCA Civ 217, an employee of LIFFE, whose normal duties as defined in his contract of employment involved the marketing of financial instruments already in use on the exchange, invented a mechanism which enabled a new class of financial instruments to be devised. The employee claimed the rights to the patent since the invention fell outside his normal contractual duties. The Court of Appeal found that the invention related to the employer's potential expansion of its business, and the employee had been permitted to work on his invention during business hours on LIFFE's computer systems. Accordingly, the employee's normal duties had evolved since the contract was entered into so that the project was within the course of his employment. Consequently, LIFFE, the employer, was entitled to any resulting patents.

Employee compensation

If an employee devises an invention which is patented and of outstanding benefit to his or her employer, PA 1977, s.40 provides that the employee may apply for compensation. The employer cannot enforce any term in the employee's contract to the extent that the term reduces the employee's right to compensation. However, the UK courts have interpreted 'outstanding benefit' extremely strictly. For instance, an employee whose patented invention had generated revenues of £5 million was not awarded any compensation since this was not outstanding in a £5 billion industry (*GEC Avionics Ltd's Patent* (1992) 6 RPC 107). As a result, there have in the past been only one or two applications for employee compensation each year. This contrasts strikingly with the position in France and Germany, where employee inventors are often entitled to a significant payment in respect of their inventions. It remains to be seen whether the slight change to the wording of this section which was introduced by the Patents Act 2004, s.10(1) (removing the requirement for the employee to show that the benefit arose from the *patent* rather than from the invention) will have any effect.

Commissioned work

In the light of the rule that only the inventor or their employer can be the first owner of rights in any potential patent, care is needed in drafting any other kind of contract which may result in an invention being made. A commissioner of product development work may be entitled to an implied licence to use the invention, but will not be entitled to own any patent unless the contract expressly so provides. Joint development contracts and contracts commissioning research work therefore must expressly deal with the ownership of any rights arising.

This in turn requires close attention to the conduct of the research, to ensure that the chain of title will be good. For instance, contract research may be carried out not only by employees of the contracting party but also by outside consultants brought in on a temporary basis because of their particular expertise. Ownership of rights in their work will be their own, unless the consultancy contracts provide otherwise. If the contractor is a university or research institution, members of the academic staff may be employed to teach rather than to invent, such that any invention is not made in the course of employment. Students (unless perhaps research students) may not be employed at all. It is essential to undertake due diligence investigations to assess the nature of any prior potentially conflicting interests (for instance, of charitable or industrial sponsors which fund the operation of the laboratory) in the fruits of such research. Finally, research work carried out in a facility located abroad may be subject to the rules as to ownership of inventions quite different from the 'employer takes all' principle.

Clearly it is not practical to review the contractual arrangements of each and every individual researcher or subcontractor of the contractor, but the agreement should entitle the commissioning company to inspect all such contracts if it so requires. In practice, the arrangements for any specific key personnel should be reviewed prior to entering into the agreement.

A warranty that all personnel working on the project through the contractor must have entered into a written contract with their respective employer will provide some protection. However a warranty provides only a right to claim damages for a breach. This may not be sufficient if the commissioner needs the right not only to use the invention but later to assign or mortgage such rights.

Co-ownership

Where two or more people are jointly responsible for devising the invention, by PA 1977, s.36 they will be considered joint inventors and jointly entitled to the grant of a patent. This seemingly natural and logical arrangement is, however, fraught with disadvantages. The co-owners can each exercise the right to exploit the invention, but they cannot independently assign or license their interest in it: all co-owners' consent is required for this (s.36(3)). Even sub-contracting manufacture requires the grant of a licence. Accordingly, co-ownership is extremely restrictive on all parties, and it is more effective in most cases to agree sole ownership by one party, which also assumes responsibility for maintenance of the registration and prosecution of any foreign application, while the other parties are granted licences permitting them to exploit the invention and even to sub-license in their respective fields of interest.

The Court of Appeal has recently sought to relax the restrictiveness of s.36 by ruling that the power granted to the Comptroller of Patents to determine ownership of a patent under s.9 implied that the Comptroller's powers under s.37 also included the right to order the grant of a licence at the behest of one co-owner (*Paxman* v. *Hughes* [2006] EWCA Civ 818 and [2006] EWCA Civ 887). Although this was contrary to the face of the statute, the Court noted that, under the 1907 and 1949 patent statutes the Comptroller had had power to order the grant of such a licence. The Court saw no reason why there should have been any change in the law in this respect. This decision potentially breaks the deadlock which otherwise arises between co-owners who are unable to agree as to how a patent should be exploited. However, it appears potentially inconsistent with the traditional approach to statutory construction, which would impute to Parliament an intention not to change the law in passing any consolidating act but no such intention where the new primary legislation brings in a revised regime. The latter was certainly the case with the passage of PA 1977, which was the UK's implementation of the EPC and the then-anticipated Community Patent Convention. The Act changed the law relating to patents in a number of significant ways from the previous UK practice. In the circumstances, although the Court of Appeal's approach is clearly pragmatic and likely to be welcome to patent holders, it may be vulnerable on any future review by the House of Lords.

4.3 PROSECUTION OF A PATENT APPLICATION

Principles

A patent can be granted for any technological invention. Inventions are generally classed as either products or processes.

Drafting and prosecuting applications for patents is one of the principal functions of patent attorneys. The process is governed by the Patents (Amendment) Rules 2005, SI 2005/2496.

The application is not merely taken at face value and rubber-stamped, as are applications for design registrations for example. Rather, the patent examiner, who is technically qualified in the relevant scientific field, will carry out a detailed assessment as to whether the invention meets the necessary legal criteria for patentability by reference to databases of existing technical publications. The process of prosecution of the application is a negotiation with the patent examiner as to the correct interpretation of any previous publications that the examiner finds to have a bearing upon the supposed invention, and the true extent of the inventor's contribution to the field.

The patent document, known as a 'specification', must disclose the invention clearly enough and completely enough to enable the invention to be performed by a person skilled in the art. Failure to do so may result in the patent being found invalid on the ground of 'insufficiency'. There is however no requirement under UK law for the specification to disclose the 'best mode' of working the invention; that requirement is a feature only of US law.

The claims themselves must:

(a) define the matter for which the applicant seeks patent protection;
(b) be clear and concise;
(c) be limited to material disclosed in the description; and
(d) relate only to one invention or to a series of inventions so linked as to form a single inventive concept (for instance a product and the process by which it is made).

As a consequence of this last requirement, a separate application must be made for each separate invention. It is possible to divide new applications out of an existing filing, if the patent examiner objects that the application covers more than one invention. As a result, any given product may fall within the claims of numerous patents, each relating to a different aspect of its construction, operation or the processes by which it is manufactured.

Stages of prosecution

After filing, the Patent Office checks the application for completeness and other formalities. The fact (though not the substance) of the application is published in the Official Journal. There is then an 18-month period before publication of the application as filed. This is intended to allow the applicant time to continue the development of the product and decide whether the application is worth pursuing further. If the invention turns out not to be commercially viable, the application can be dropped before ever becoming public.

If at the end of this period the applicant decides to proceed, the application as filed is published as the 'A' specification of the patent. A patent examiner will then carry out a *search* for pre-existing material which anticipates the claimed invention, and *examine* the application against the results. It may be necessary to amend the application at this stage to exclude any elements of the invention which the search results reveal to have been already known. The application will also be examined to see if it complies with the four conditions for grant of a patent (discussed at **4.6**). The examiner notifies any objections to the applicant's patent attorney, who will either attempt to persuade the examiner to take a different view, or propose further amendments to take account of the objection.

During the examination stage, any third party is entitled to inform the Patent Office of any reason of which they are aware (but which the examiner may have missed) why the patent ought not to be granted. This is a relatively cheap process for influencing the scope of any patent ultimately granted. The applicant is notified of all such objections and may once more amend, or attempt to persuade the examiner, in writing or at an oral hearing, as to the merits of the application despite the objections raised. Since the Patent Office's *raison d'être* is to grant rather than to refuse patents, such arguments generally succeed. Strategically, therefore, unless costs dictate otherwise it may be advisable not to object before grant but wait to raise the new material in a revocation application to the court after grant.

The complete procedure takes typically two to four years in the UKIPO. By statute, after four and a half years the UKIPO has to decide either to grant or to reject the application.

The procedure at the EPO is broadly similar, but has no cut-off date and, in addition, permits third parties not merely to tell the examiner that he or she has missed something but actually to bring proceedings opposing the patent at any time up to nine months after it has been granted. These opposition proceedings may involve contested hearings with both parties, and appeals to the Board of Appeal of the EPO. If opposed, a European patent can take considerably longer to reach final approval (although it remains in force during the opposition proceedings). In one or two extreme cases, patents have expired before the final decision had been given on their valid scope. However, the validity of a patent which has survived a determined opposition in the EPO is considerably more certain than that of one which has simply been granted unopposed.

Renewal and duration

Initially, a patent is granted for four years. Thereafter, it is renewable annually, on payment of a renewal fee, up to a maximum of 20 years in total (with limited exceptions). Renewal fees vary on a sliding scale which increases over time, so that patentees who continue to renew their patents, presumably having made a commercial success of their inventions, subsidise the cost of processing applications.

There is six months' grace for payment of each renewal fee for a patent, during which the patent may be restored to the register by late payment of the fee. However if any infringement takes place during this period the right to financial remedies such as damages is discretionary. It is therefore always prudent to renew before the current period of subsistence expires, rather than rely on the grace period.

The international patent system

There are several geographical options open to a person applying for a patent, depending on the territorial scope of protection required.

(a) United Kingdom patent only

To obtain a UK patent, an application should be made to the UK Intellectual Property Office (UKIPO) in Newport.

(b) European patent

As yet, there is no such thing as a unified European Patent. Although discussions on a Community Patent (equivalent to the Registered Community Design or CTM) have been underway for many years, political issues derailed these in 2005 and they have yet to be re-started. An application to the European Patent Office (EPO) results in law in a direction to the patent offices of the EPC Contracting States nominated by the applicant for the grant of a bundle of national patents, all identical.

The application is made to the EPO in either Munich or The Hague, or through the UKIPO (which acts as a post-box for the EPO). The EPO will carry out the search and examination, and adjudicate any oppositions third parties bring against the grant of the patent. Once it has approved the patent for grant, the designated national patent offices grant the individual but identical national patents.

(c) 'World-wide' or 'international' patent

Over 80 countries are members of the Patent Co-operation Treaty, administered by WIPO in Geneva. A patent can be applied for in any number of them through the UKIPO. However, the patents obtained will *not* necessarily all be identical. After the initial search for prior art is carried out by WIPO, the application proceeds as a national application in each designated country so that the vagaries of the different examiners will produce small, but occasionally critical, variations in wording in the final grants. A European patent can designated as one application under an international application.

Supplementary Protection Certificates

The 20-year maximum term of a patent is extended to a limited extent in the special case of the pharmaceutical and veterinary medicines and agrichemicals industries, where the marketing of the product may be subject to considerable delay as a result of the need to demonstrate the product's compliance with regulatory requirements of quality, safety and efficacy. This involves the carrying out of extensive trials which can take years and many millions of pounds, before approval to market is granted. The effective life of the patent protection is therefore curtailed. To compensate for this, a limited extension of protection, in the form of a Supplementary Protection Certificate, may be granted in respect of the product for which marketing approval has been obtained (Council Regulation 1768/92, Art.3 implemented by the Patents (Supplementary Protection Certificates) Rules 1997, SI 1997/64). Supplementary protection lasts up to 15 years from the grant of the first marketing authorisation anywhere in the European Union, but no more than five years from the expiry of the original patent.

Post-grant amendment

Substantive amendment of a patent after grant is only possible in limited circumstances (although mere clerical errors can always be corrected). It may happen quite innocently that neither the applicant nor the patent examiner picks up certain prior art during the prosecution of the application, but that it later comes to light. The proprietor of the patent can apply at any point during the lifetime of the patent to amend to avoid such materials.

Post-grant amendment must not extend the technological monopoly granted, however, and cannot add new material into the specification (PA 1977, s.72). If the patent is infringed before an amendment to the specification is allowed, damages are not available for the period before amendment unless it can be shown that the specification was initially framed in good faith and with reasonable skill and knowledge (PA 1977, s.62(3)(b)).

4.4 FORMALITIES

Registration of transactions

A patent is a form of personal property, but not a thing in action (PA 1977, s.30). Since it is a creature of statute, it may be granted or transferred only in accordance with s.30.

Patents and patent applications may be assigned or licensed, either before or after grant and either exclusively or otherwise. They may also be mortgaged or vest by operation of law in a personal representative or trustee in bankruptcy, for example, like other personal property. An assignment or mortgage of a patent or patent application is void unless it is in writing and signed by or on behalf of the parties to the transaction (s.30(6)).

All transactions affecting property rights in patents must be entered on the Register of Patents. Failure to register means a potential loss of priority over any later assignee or mortgagee who does not have notice of the earlier transaction and who registers first (PA 1977, s.33). Further, an assignee or exclusive licensee may be unable to obtain damages or an account of profits for any infringement of the patent if the transaction is not registered within six months (unless the court or the Comptroller is satisfied that it was not then practicable to register and registration took place as soon as it became practicable) (PA 1977, s.68). This is an area where errors frequently arise, as the parties lose interest once the transaction has been completed. It is essential to include in any transaction disposing of patents a covenant of further assurance to ensure that if, on a later assignment, it transpires that the previous assignment has not been registered, the former owner can be required to assist in setting the record straight. However, obtaining the practical cooperation necessary for this years after the event tends to be difficult.

Licences of right

The issues and formalities of commercial patent licensing are dealt with in depth in **Chapter 7**. It is worth mentioning here a special form of licence specific only to patents and UK design right.

A 'licence of right' over a patent may arise in one of two ways.

First, at any time after the patent has been granted, the proprietor may apply to the Comptroller of Patents under PA 1977, s.46 to indicate on the register that 'licences as of right' are available; that is, licences are available to all comers without discrimination. If this is done, subsequent renewal fees are reduced to half for as long as the concession remains in effect. The proprietor may later cancel this concession (s.47). If the proprietor is unable to agree terms for a licence of right with any prospective licensee, the Comptroller has the power to settle a licence on such terms as a hypothetical willing licensor and willing licensee would have agreed.

Second, if the Monopolies and Mergers Commission gives an adverse report on the patentee, then the Comptroller of Patents may unilaterally make an entry on the register to the effect that licences are available as of right even without the patentee's consent (s.51).

Where a licence of right is available, then if allegations of infringement are raised the defendant has the option of giving to the court an undertaking to take a licence if necessary. If this is done, no injunction will be granted and a cap is placed on any damages that may later be awarded against them. The cap is twice the royalties that would have been payable under a licence of right – which may be considerably more favourable than damages calculated on the usual scale.

Impact of competition law

Since patents provide an absolute monopoly to their holders, there is frequently a risk that any transaction with either suppliers, customers or potential licensees could infringe one of the prohibitions on restricting or distorting competition laid down by EU and UK law. **Chapter 8** addresses the impact of competition law on the freedom of patent owners in both exercising and licensing their rights under any patent.

4.5 SCOPE OF PROTECTION

Exclusive rights

A UK patent, whether granted by the UKIPO or through the EPO, gives a commercial monopoly for a limited period. During this time, the registered proprietor has the exclusive rights to work the patented invention in the United Kingdom, by manufacturing, importing, keeping, offering for disposal, disposing of or using the patented product, using the patented process, or importing, keeping, offering for disposal, disposing of or using goods directly produced by using the patented process (PA 1977, s.60(1)). Any person who undertakes any of these activities without the patentee's authorisation is said to 'infringe' the patent. Infringement may be prevented by the issue of an injunction, as well as creating a liability to pay damages or give an account of any profits obtained by the infringement (discussed in **4.7**).

The patentee is also able, by PA 1977, s.60(2), to prevent an unauthorised person from supplying or offering to supply in the UK means relating to essential elements of the invention when they know, or a reasonable person would have known, that the elements were suitable for *and intended to be used to* put the invention into effect in the UK. This is known as contributory infringement. Staple commercial products are excepted from this – a patentee cannot stop someone selling standard nails or washers, just because they could be used in assembling an infringing machine, even if the supplier knows that they are intended for that purpose.

The principles set out above are simple enough; the difficulty lies in assessing exactly what product or process is legitimately monopolised by the patent. Assessing the extent of protection conferred by a patent is an exercise in finding the correct legal construction of a legally and technically complex document. It could reasonably be compared with the construction of a contract written in a foreign language: the reader needs to take care in ascertaining the meaning of the words used, as well as in then forming a conclusion as to the legal effect of those words.

Structure of a patent

A patent consists of a document called a *specification*, which comprises two sections: first, a *description* of the area of technology with which the invention is concerned and the problems with existing technology in that area. The description will explain the principles of the invention and may include specific examples of different embodiments of the invention, and drawings. It is followed by one or more *claims*. The totality of the information in the description and claims is often referred to as the *teaching* of the patent.

The description is written discursively, explaining the relevant field of technology ('art') to which the invention relates, the problem that the invention overcomes and how the invention overcomes it. In complex technologies such as biotechnology the description may take hundreds of pages; in electronics and mechanics, the descriptions are generally quite short. The purpose of the description is to ensure that the invention is disclosed clearly and completely enough to enable the invention to be performed by a person skilled in the appropriate art. The drawings and examples are intended to ensure that the skilled person has a thorough grasp of what it is the patent is trying to describe.

It is the claims alone, however, which define the precise scope of the legal monopoly. The description is principally used to help with interpretation of the claims, illustrating what the patentee meant by the particular words used. Hence, the precise wording of the patent, and in particular the claims, is extremely important.

Traditionally, claims are written in 'cascades', or series, each beginning with an *independent claim* to 'a device for . . . in which . . .' or 'a method of . . .'. From each independent claim depend a series of narrower claims, the *dependent claims*, each giving more and more detail as to the parameters of the monopoly. The dependent claims are therefore by definition narrower than the independent claim from which they depend. For instance, in a chemical process claim one might start with an independent claim to 'a method of synthesising molecule X by causing compounds Y and Z to react under electromagnetic radiation at high temperature'. A dependent claim to such a claim might then be to 'a method according to claim 1/2/3/. . . in which the heating step is carried out at a temperature of 55°C'. This is narrower than the independent claim, which would cover the process carried out at any temperature which could be described as 'high'. Similarly, a further dependent claim might specify that the electromagnetic radiation should be ultraviolet light, thereby excluding infrared and X-rays. The independent claim, in contrast, would include the whole spectrum.

Everything included in a dependent claim is taken to be included in the independent claim from which it depends even though not there specified. This does not, however, exclude a dependent claim from having validity independent of the claim from which it depends. It may be that the broader claim is invalid as a result of some publication which describes only a part of what the broad claim covers – such as a synthesis process carried out under infrared light. A dependent claim to carrying out the same process under ultraviolet light could still be an invention despite that publication, although in many cases the minor details spelled out in the dependent claims will not amount to inventions in themselves.

The addressee of the patent

A patent is considered to be written so as to be read by a hypothetical 'person skilled in the art', that is, someone working in the relevant field who has an interest in the problem allegedly solved by the invention. Although a legal document in itself, it is not addressed to lawyers and should not be read as though it were. In many technical fields a particular meaning may be attributed to terms of art, which are different from their meaning in everyday parlance, but nevertheless well understood by practitioners. If so, those terms must be given that meaning in the patent. In practice, much of the language of the patent will consist of scientific terminology which may well be used in its ordinary sense but which may still need to be explained to the legal reader.

The identity of the person 'skilled in the art' therefore needs to be established before the document can be construed. The hypothetical 'person skilled in the art' is taken to have the necessary technical knowledge and skills to understand and be able to apply the invention. They do not need to have extensive academic credentials – they may be, for example, a skilled mechanic or plumber. Equally, in today's world of highly complex research carried out by large teams of researchers, where each member brings the skills of different disciplines to bear on a single problem, the 'skilled person' may in fact be a 'skilled team' (*Lilly-ICOS* v. *Pfizer* [2001] IP&T 190).

Either way, however well informed he or she may be, the 'skilled person' is assumed to be 'normally skilled but unimaginative', with no spark of inventiveness, the ability to jump intuitively over apparent hurdles, which characterises the inventor. Thus, the 'skilled person' reads documents in a dogmatic, technically competent fashion, but unable to surmount any significant gaps or flaws without further teaching.

The monopoly – literal and purposive infringement

A patent claim, however broadly it has been expressed, cannot realistically describe every possible way of implementing a technological mechanism or process. It is therefore accepted that, generally, the patentee may intend the patent claim wording to have to some extent a figurative meaning, and that the literal wording simply describes the best known or most striking example of the class he or she is defining.

Of course, any product or process which falls within the class literally described by the claim will infringe the monopoly right. However, products or processes which do not fit the exact wording may equally infringe under the so-called 'purposive' approach to construction of the claims. This approach is stipulated by EPC, Art.69. The problem is how to strike a balance between giving patentees full credit for their inventions by construing the claims sufficiently broadly to include any product or process which in reality does use the invention, while also giving third parties reasonable certainty as to what they can and cannot do without infringing. The German and English courts, in particular, formerly took very divergent approaches to this task. Accordingly, a Protocol to Art.69 has been introduced which cites both English and German approaches as incorrect:

> Article 69 should not be interpreted in the sense that the extent of the protection conferred by a European patent is to be understood as that defined by the strict, literal meaning of the wording used in the claims, the description and drawings being employed only for the purpose of resolving an ambiguity found in the claims. Neither should it be interpreted in the sense that the claims serve only as a guideline and that the actual protection may extend to what, from a consideration of the description and drawings by a person skilled in the art, the patentee has contemplated. On the contrary, it is to be interpreted as defining a position between these extremes which combines a fair protection for the patentee with a reasonable degree of certainty for third parties.

The Protocol appears at PA 1977, s.125(3).

The current interpretation of this approach in English law was laid down by the House of Lords in their 2005 judgment in *Kirin-Amgen* v. *Transkaryotic Therapies Inc & Anr* [2004] UKHL 46. Lord Hoffmann concluded that to establish whether a product infringes, the reader needs to decide what a skilled person, reading the patent at the time when it was published, would have understood the patentee meant by the words he or she chose to use for the claim. This test throws the onus onto the reader to consider the claims in the light of the teaching of the patent in the context of its own time: both its own text, and the publications which were available to the addressee at that time. Avoiding hindsight in this way is never easy. It is particularly difficult where the invention represents a breakthrough in its field, in that the terminology which later developed to describe the field may not yet have been adopted so that the patent uses its own set of terms which were unfamiliar to the reader at the time and are not the standard terms used today. It is nevertheless essential to avoid applying hindsight, since this risks either unfairly extending the patent monopoly or unfairly limiting it.

The test also highlights the fact that apart from the application of a few legal rules and principles of construction, the interpretation of a claim can ultimately only be done with the aid of a person skilled in the appropriate technical field. Notably, the patentee's own intention as to what the words should mean is irrelevant; thus, any correspondence with the granting Patent Office explaining the meaning is not available as an aid to construction. This is diametrically opposite to the approach applied in the United States, where prosecution history estoppel is a major doctrine of patent construction.

Until the decision of the House of Lords in *Kirin-Amgen*, the test established in *Catnic* v. *Hill & Smith* [1982] RPC 183 was generally used. In *Kirin-Amgen* the House of Lords indicated that over-reliance on the *Catnic* test was to be avoided, but it remains a useful approach particularly in simpler cases. This approach involves asking the following series of questions:

(a) Does the variant – the difference between the literal meaning and the alleged infringement – have a material effect upon the way the invention works?
If yes, the variant is outside the scope of the claim.
If not, continue to the next question:

(b) Would the fact that the variant has no material effect have been obvious at the date of publication of the patent to a reader skilled in the art?
If not, the variant is outside the scope of the claim.
If yes, ask:

(c) Would the reader skilled in the art nevertheless have understood from the language of the claim that the patentee intended that strict compliance with the primary meaning was an essential requirement of the invention?
If yes, the variant is outside the claim.
If no, the patent is infringed.

Exceptions and defences

Exhaustion of rights

Once a patented object has been sold by the patentee or with their authority, a licence is implied for the purchaser to use it, repair it or dispose of it to a third party (*United Wire* v. *Screen Repair Services (Scotland)* [2001] FSR 365). This 'franking' applies equally where a product has been put on the market outside the United Kingdom or even the European Union (*Roussel-Uclaf* v. *Hockley* [1996] RPC 441).

Experimental use

Section 60(5) of PA 1977 sets out a number of uses which can be made of patented inventions without infringing the legal monopoly. One of the most important is that experimental work relating to the subject matter of a patent does not infringe the monopoly (s.60(5)(b)). The work must be truly experimental, in the sense of having as its objective to find out something that is not already known (*Auchinloss* v. *Agricultural and Veterinary Supplies Ltd* [1997] RPC 649, reversed in part [1999] RPC 397). It must also relate to the specific, claimed subject of the patent, not merely the same general areas of technology. For instance, in the case of a patent relating to a new process for making a known chemical product, experiments which use the process but are in fact directed towards better understanding the reactive or other chemical properties of the product will not fall within the exception, whereas experiments aiming to find improvements to the synthesis process would.

Vehicles in transit

Acts done on or with ships and aircraft in transit through the UK's territorial waters or airspace do not infringe, even if the delay in the territorial space is measured in hours rather than minutes: what counts is the intention of being in transit, whether or not marine conditions prevent departure (*Stena Line* v. *Irish Ferries* [2003] EWCA Civ 66).

Making up prescriptions

The extemporaneous making up of prescriptions does not infringe.

Private non-commercial use

Private, non-commercial use of a patented invention (such as for instance carrying out experiments for use in court proceedings) is not an infringement.

Prior use

A defence is also available to anyone who, prior to the filing of the patent application, had either done in good faith something which would be an infringement if the patent were in force, or made serious and effective preparations to do such an act. This defence is known as 'prior use', and PA 1977, s.64 gives such a person the right to continue the act after the patent has been granted. It is however a personal, non-assignable and non-licensable right. There is little case law addressing this defence, and what case law exists is inconsistent (compare *Helitune* v. *Stewart Hughes* [1991] RPC 78 with *Lubrizol Corp* v. *Esso Petroleum (No.5)* [1998] RPC 727, CA). The more recent authority is inconclusive (since on the facts there were found to have been not 'serious and effective preparations' but only preliminary planning) so that there is uncertainty as to what if any leeway is allowed.

The authority available as to what constitutes 'serious and effective preparations' is restrictive: something considerably closer to initiating production is required than merely showing that the infringer had had the same idea as the patentee and was investigating its commercial viability or carrying out research directed at implementing it.

If the prior user has since developed its product into a new variation which also falls within the claims, the new variant is likely to be found to infringe. However, where there may be inherent minor variations in starting materials or other factors outside the user's control, the defence must at least extend to the resulting minor variations in product or process or its protection would be illusory. There is no reason, however, to believe that any deliberate modification could be introduced without losing the protection.

The 'Bolar' exemption for clinical trials

Finally, for the benefit of the generic pharmaceutical industry there is a special exemption for the acts necessary for carrying out clinical trials with a view to submitting the resulting data to the regulator in order to obtain a marketing authorisation for a medicinal product. Clinical trials carried out by generic pharmaceutical manufacturers in preparation for launch of generic versions of drugs upon expiry of the relevant patents are unlikely to fall within the experimental use exemption since they do not involve discovering any new information, unless related to the production of a 'super generic' such as a combination product or new formulation. The drug's originator would therefore be able to forestall launch of a generic version within a considerable period after the patent's expiry by preventing the necessary clinical trials from being performed. This new exception was introduced in 2005 as part of the UK's implementation of the revisions to the EU's pharmaceutical regime (Directive 2004/27/EC, amending Directive 2001/83/EC on the Community Code relating to Medicinal Products for Human Use) and has not yet been tested in court. There is therefore still significant uncertainty as to exactly what acts are covered.

Crown use and compulsory licences

The Crown has a right to use any patented product or process subject only to the payment to the patentee of compensation in the form of a reasonable royalty (PA 1977, ss.55–9). The Act also provides for the grant of compulsory licences under patents which are not being worked in the UK, or whose existence is stifling the development of other products, in certain limited circumstances (ss.48–54) but these have very rarely been invoked. Working within the EU is sufficient to avoid these provisions.

4.6 PATENTABILITY

Introduction

A patent is purely a creature of registration; and initial and continued registration are in turn conditional upon the invention meeting the criteria for patentability. At any stage, even after expiry, a patent can be *revoked* if it is proved that it did not meet one or more of these criteria. If revoked, the patent ceases ever to have had legal effect. A patent which is *surrendered*, however, ceases to exist only from the moment of its surrender, so that the possibility remains that the former proprietor could sue for damages for up to six years after that date.

The conditions imposed by PA 1977, s.1 for the grant of a patent over an invention are that:

(a) the device or process is novel;
(b) it involves an inventive step (that is, the invention is not obvious);
(c) it is capable of industrial application; and
(d) the subject matter is not excluded from patentability.

Of these, the criteria most often used as the basis for validity challenges are novelty and obviousness. However, the question of whether the subject matter is patentable at all is a logical precursor to considering whether those criteria are met.

Exclusions

The principal exclusions from patentability are set out in PA 1977, s.1(2) and (3). They are an assortment of unrelated categories mainly relating to things which are protected by other intellectual property rights (for example, copyright works or plant varieties) or are not considered to be technical, such as:

(a) pure scientific theories or discoveries, or mathematical methods;
(b) methods for performing any mental act, playing games or doing business; or
(c) computer programs.

Further categories are excluded on moral or social grounds, such as inventions which would be generally expected to encourage offensive, immoral or anti-social behaviour. Varieties of animal or any essentially biological process for the production of any animal or plant (other than micro-biological processes) are also excluded. A separate system exists to protect plant varieties produced by breeding and selection.

Software and business methods

Each of the exclusions applies only to the extent that a patent application relates to that thing 'as such'. The precise scope of this exclusion has been highly controversial in the cases of computer programs and methods of doing business. Both of these are patentable under US law, with the result that patent applications are constantly being filed in Europe which fall very close to the line dividing the patentable invention from the non-patentable.

An application of a computer program (for instance, the control of an industrial process) is patentable, and many thousands of such patents have been granted. The EPO's approach has been to find software patentable provided that it displays some 'technical effect' beyond the normal interactions of software and machine. Identifying such a technical effect has therefore become critical. It is often possible to do so where the claims cover the software running on a computer; but for the purposes of the software industry (other than the open source lobby) the crucial aspect was to have patent rights over the software before it was ever loaded, so that distributors rather than end users could be targeted for enforcement. In 1997, the EPO succumbed to prolonged pressure from industry and granted to IBM two patents in respect of software for operating a computer (including for instance overlay of one window on another), which not only covered a computer in operation under the control of the program but also the program itself recorded on a physical medium, such as a floppy disk (*IBM/Computer Programs* T935/97 and T1173/97 [1999] EPOR 301 and 219). However, other cases decided by differently constituted Boards have assessed the issue differently and the Technical Board of Appeal declined to give any further clarification (*PBS Partnership/Controlling Pension Benefits System* T0931/95).

This decision sparked a move for the EPC to be reformed, but so highly politicised has the issue become, with extensive lobbying against any form of patent protection for software by interest groups such as the Free Software Foundation, that it has been impossible to reach any consensus as to what the reforms should be. Neither the Diplomatic Conference responsible for the Convention nor the European Commission has yet been able to carry through any changes to the wording.

In the meantime, however, both the Boards of Appeal of the EPO and the national courts which are responsible for the interpretation of patents after grant, have retreated from the liberal interpretation of the EPC endorsed in *Pension Benefits* (above) towards a more restrictive stance. The English courts therefore regularly have to grapple with the issue of what technical effect is sufficient to render a software invention patentable. A series of first instance decisions in the High Court culminated in the Court of Appeal reconsidering this issue in the joined cases *Aerotel* v. *Telco; Macrossan's Application* [2006] EWCA Civ 1371. The appeals gave the Court of Appeal its first opportunity since *Fujitsu* [1997] RPC 608 to consider the effect of EPC, Art.52(2) and (3) (required by s.130(7) to have the same effect as s.1(2) under UK law).

Before considering the individual nature of the patent and application in issue, the opportunity was taken to review the current state of the law. This analysis placed the Court of Appeal in a quandary. On the one hand, this Court is constitutionally bound to follow its earlier decisions. On the other hand, judges are exhorted to pay great attention to decisions of the EPO Boards of Appeal. However, here these were seen to be mutually contradictory. The Court therefore urged the EPO President to refer to the EPO's Enlarged Board of Appeal this conflict of decisions, but the EPO President subsequently declined to do so.

The UK and EPO case law had given rise to two basic approaches to the effect of Art.52(2).

1. The contribution approach, asking whether the invention's contribution to the state of the art fell within excluded subject matter (adopted by

Falconer J in *Merrill Lynch* [1988] RPC 1, but expressly rejected on appeal in that case [1989] RPC 561).
2. The technical effect approach, asking whether the invention produced a technical effect in the physical world. This was the approach adopted by the Court of Appeal in the *Merrill Lynch* appeal, following the EPO in *Vicom* (T208/84).

The court plainly preferred the 'contribution approach' but was precluded by the *Merrill Lynch* appeal decision from following it. Therefore the 'technical effect' approach set out in *Merrill Lynch* on appeal has to be accepted. However, the Comptroller suggested that this 'technical effect' approach involved four steps:

(1) properly construe the claim;
(2) identify the actual contribution;
(3) ask whether it falls solely within the excluded subject matter; and
(4) check whether the actual or alleged contribution is actually technical in nature.

This was accepted, with the effect that if the contribution to the art falls solely within the excluded subject matter the invention is not patentable since there is no reason to progress to the fourth question. This four-stage approach must now therefore be followed in all subsequent UK decisions unless and until it is overturned by the House of Lords.

Of the two cases actually being considered at that appeal, the *Aerotel* patent (which had been granted in 1988 and had expired in January 2006) involved a telephone system for calls made from a public call box involving a special exchange from which the cost of a call can be downloaded according to actual usage, rather than by pre-payment of an estimated amount. This system as a whole was a new physical combination of hardware and was therefore, clearly, 'more than just a method of doing business as such'. Since the invention passed the third step of the test the court considered whether the invention was technical in nature and decided that it was. The appeal was therefore allowed.

The *Macrossan* invention was an automated method of producing the documents necessary to incorporate a company. The Court of Appeal was 'firmly of the opinion that the patent is both for a method of doing business as such and for a computer program as such'. The invention therefore failed the third step of the test. The court noted that in addition there was nothing technical about the contribution made, beyond the mere fact of the running of a computer program. The *Macrossan* appeal was therefore dismissed.

Novelty

The state of the art

An invention is new if, at the *priority date* of the application, it does not form part of the 'state of the art' (PA 1977, s.2(1)). The priority date is normally the date of filing, although earlier priority can be claimed from a foreign patent application in respect of the same invention made within the previous 12 months. The 'state of the art' includes all matter which, at that time, has been made available to the public anywhere in the world by written or oral description, by use or in any other way (PA 1977, s.2(2)). This would include a demonstration to visitors to a laboratory, or a prototype left in a position where it could legitimately be seen by passers-by.

Co-pending patent applications which have been filed before the priority date form part of the state of the art for this purpose (PA 1977, s.2(3)), even if they are not published until after that date. The state of the art therefore includes not only material which the applicant may not happen to be aware of, it also includes material which the applicant (and the patent examiner) cannot possibly be aware of during the prosecution.

The state of the art does not, however, include information which became public in the six months before the date of filing due to:

(a) being obtained or disclosed in breach of confidence; or
(b) being disclosed by display at an international exhibition, i.e. any trade show designated by the Department for Business, Enterprise and Regulatory Reform (BERR) as an international exhibition for this purpose. A list is available on the BERR website (**www.berr.gov.uk**).

Test for anticipation

If the supposed invention as claimed has been completely, clearly and unambiguously described in an earlier publication, then the invention is said to have been *anticipated* and a patent will not be granted, or will be invalid and liable to revocation. To anticipate, the prior description or use must involve an enabling disclosure, that is a disclosure which would enable any skilled person to make or obtain the invention.

A clear and unambiguous explanation of how to do something, coupled with an instruction not to do it for some reason, will not anticipate. Nor is it sufficient for the prior publication to describe most aspects of the claimed new invention leaving the reader only to fill in minor details. As the House of Lords in *General Tire* v. *Firestone Tire* [1975] RPC 197 put it:

> A signpost, however clear, upon the road to the patentee's invention will not suffice. The prior inventor must be clearly shown to have planted his flag at the precise destination before the patentee.

The prior disclosure does not have to be on a wide scale, nor need it have been acted upon. It does not matter if no one, in fact, gains access (*Lux Traffic Controls Ltd* v. *Pike Signals Ltd* [1993] RPC 107). A single disclosure in non-confidential circumstances is sufficient, provided that *at the date of that disclosure* a skilled person could have used it to implement the patentee's invention.

Given this condition, it is essential that the person applying for a patent does not divulge any details publicly before filing the application, since such a disclosure, unless confidential, will then be part of the state of the art and could itself anticipate the patent. (This is in marked contrast to the position in the United States, where there is a grace period of a year after first disclosure in which the invention may be exploited without losing novelty, before the patent application is filed. The effect has been that US inventors frequently 'prior disclosed' their inventions in the US and lost the right to obtain a patent in Europe. As a result, the US has brought heavy pressure to bear to have a grace period introduced into patent laws worldwide. This has been under negotiation at the WTO for some years.)

Obviousness – has it an inventive step?

Principles

If the invention passes the test for novelty, it reaches the second test: whether it is inventive – meaning 'not obvious to a person skilled in the art' (PA 1977, s.77) having regard to the state of the art. Obvious simply means 'very plain'. This is a question of fact, but there is an irreducible subjectivity to this test: what is obvious to one person may well not be obvious to another even if the two share identical background knowledge.

A prior description which encompasses all of the salient features of the invention, but leaves unstated elementary technical details, will not anticipate a patent but may well render it obvious since the skilled person would be able to fill in the basic techniques for themselves.

As with the test for novelty, ultimately what is or is not obvious can only be assessed with the assistance of a person familiar with the relevant technical field. In particular, patent and scientific literature is unlikely to disclose the prejudices held in the art, which may render an approach that looks obvious to the lay person fraught with imagined (or even real) problems.

Co-pending but unpublished patent applications are ignored for the purpose of this test, even though they form part of the state of the art for the novelty test. However, unlike the state of the art for the novelty test, the state of the art for the purpose of establishing inventive step includes the common general knowledge in the art.

Common general knowledge

The identity of the person skilled in the art is key to applying the test for inventive step, since it defines the information which may be said to be common general knowledge.

In addition to the material published in learned journals, technical bulletins and the like, there will in any industry be a certain amount of information which forms the matrix into which the occasional strikingly new idea falls. This may include: the skilled technician's 'know how' as to how to make a process operate under genuine industrial rather than laboratory conditions; the fundamental elements of the art which may come to have new application in light of recent developments; and the background understanding of the hows and whys of the subject that every practitioner or researcher in the field carries around with them. Anything which skilled addressees in general can be taken both to have known and to have accepted as a sound basis for action falls within the definition of common general knowledge.

The skilled addressee necessarily has this knowledge available. Such knowledge can render a claimed invention obvious, if in fact it turns out that many industrial operators do as the patent teaches as a matter of course – or would, in the light of a particular prior art disclosure. Unfortunately, it is in the nature of common general knowledge that it is frequently difficult to identify precisely. Certainly the contents of the leading undergraduate textbooks are likely to qualify as common general knowledge, as may standard laboratory handbooks. But much may be shared through teaching and discussion without ever being reduced to writing. This sort of general knowledge is inaccessible to a patent examiner and therefore ordinarily ignored in examining a patent application. Conversely, an article in a scientific journal may be widely circulated but that does not give rise to an automatic inference that the average person working in the field accepted its contents without question and would have assumed that its techniques could reliably be adopted.

As a result, many patents are granted which are vulnerable to later challenge, since a commercial competitor is invariably in a better position than the Patent Office to know what was common general knowledge at the time and to persuade a court to revoke the patent on the grounds of obviousness. Once again, however, it is important to beware hindsight.

The Windsurfing test

Although the courts have attempted to approach the question of inventive step in a systematic fashion, at the end of any analysis there is a judgment call to be made. An approach to assessing 'inventive step' was set out in *Windsurfing* v. *Tabur Marine* [1985] RPC 59:

- identify the inventive concept in the alleged invention;
- put yourself in the shoes of the unimaginative skilled person with the common general knowledge in the art at the priority date;
- identify what, if any, differences exist between the prior art identified and the alleged invention; and
- ask whether, viewed without any knowledge of the alleged invention, those differences constitute steps which would have been obvious to the skilled person or whether they required any degree of invention.

This is, of course, impossible. Hindsight will always affect the way a technician will look at a problem, making everything more obvious than it might have seemed at the time as a result. But this test, although relegated in more recent cases to the status of a guideline rather than a gold standard, does provide a helpful framework for focussing on the most relevant aspects of the question – the need to read the patent with an eye to identifying what exactly the patentee is claiming to have invented. Patents often include considerable discussion of the field of technology concerned, its limitations and other attempts to solve the problems, as preliminaries or part of their explanation of how the invention works. The invention, described as a whole, may well include elements from the state of the art as well as the entirely new component or combinations which are in fact the nub of the inventive concept.

A patent drafting convention which is helpful in this respect (although not universally followed) is to break the claim into two sections: the first 'setting the scene' as to what was in the prior art and often described as the preamble to the claim; and the other identifying the inventive component, introducing it with the words 'characterised in that' or similar.

Commercial success as evidence of inventive step

Patentees are often attracted by the argument that the commercial success of their product demonstrates that it cannot have been obvious: there demonstrably being money to be made by exploiting it, someone would have done so if it had been obvious how to do it.

This argument can be raised in response to an attack based upon an allegation of obviousness, but should be treated with caution. The first hurdle is to demonstrate that, as assumed by the patentee, there was in fact a long-felt want for this solution had it only been available. If there was no such want, then no matter how obvious the solution there was no need for anyone to produce it. Further, commercial success is a result of many complex interactions and the courts are slow to assume that all that is needed is a good technical innovation in order to succeed. The failure of the Betamax video standard, despite its being generally agreed to be technically superior to VHS but let down by inadequate marketing, is a vivid illustration of this. Good marketing, fashion and many other factors contribute to making any product commercially successful and it is generally an uphill struggle to demonstrate that in this particular case it was the technical improvement that was paramount (*Raychem Corp's Patents* [1998] RPC 31).

Insufficiency

A third ground on which a patent may be refused or held invalid is if it does not describe the invention claimed clearly and completely enough for it to be performed by a person skilled in the art (PA 1977, s.72(1)(c)). Since the skilled addressee brings the common general knowledge available at the date of filing the application to bear upon the interpretation of the specification, it is not necessary to describe every single aspect where these would not cause the skilled person any difficulty. Indeed, the skilled person is considered to be prepared to display a reasonable degree of skill in making trials, and to be able to correct obvious errors in the specification if this can readily be done (*Mentor* v. *Hollister* [1993] RPC 7). But if reasonable addressees can come to different conclusions as to what the patent means, then it is not sufficiently described.

A second form of insufficiency arises where the patentee, believing himself to have made a breakthrough in the field, claims the invention in terms broad enough to cover several different ways of achieving it – some of which may not yet have been devised. If such claims were then enforced, the effect would be to stifle future research. The claim must be enabled by the specification across its whole scope. This is a delicate balancing act to perform, since a truly groundbreaking invention may well open the path to numerous variants not foreseen by the patentee which, however, might not have been arrived at without drawing upon the disclosure he or she has given. The critical issue is 'not whether the invention could deliver the goods [across the full width of the patent] but whether the claims cover other ways in which they might be delivered: methods which owe nothing to the teaching or any principle which was disclosed' (*Biogen* v. *Medeva* [1997] RPC 1).

Industrial application

An invention is capable of industrial application if it can be made or used in any kind of industry, including agriculture. Surgery, therapy and diagnosis in relation to human or animal bodies are excluded from the meaning of industrial application. Thus, new drugs are patentable in themselves, but the way that they are used is not. However, this exclusion is most commonly invoked by patent examiners faced with the never-ending trickle of applications for patents over inventions which defy the laws of physics, such as variations on the perpetual motion machine which generates energy from nothing.

4.7 DISPUTES AND REMEDIES FOR INFRINGEMENT

Dispute resolution: options before legal action is taken

Threats actions

It is permissible to threaten a supposed infringer with legal action for making or importing a patented product or for using a patented process, the so-called primary acts of infringement. However, where any person (normally the patentee or their representatives) makes threats that they will bring proceedings for any other form of infringement, such as offering for sale or selling an infringing product, the alleged infringer or any other person aggrieved by the threats can bring an action for an injunction to stop the threats being repeated (PA 1977, s.70). The exception to the rule that only an importer or manufacturer may be threatened is where the patentee has made efforts to identify the manufacturer or importer but has not been able to do so. In these circumstances, the Patents Act 2004, s.12 relaxed the rule on threats to provide that a patentee can write to the highest point it is able to identify in the supply chain, setting out the efforts that the patentee has made to identify the ultimate source of the infringement, and requesting information as to the ultimate source on pain of proceedings for infringement, without being liable for making unjustified threats.

It does not matter whether the alleged threat was addressed to the alleged infringer themselves or to third parties such as their customers or suppliers: they will still be entitled to relief, as an aggrieved party. The objective of this provision is to prevent patentees from 'spoiling the market' for a product by putting retailers off dealing in it, without tackling the manufacturer or importer who is the real source of the infringing goods.

As further discussed in **5.2**, the courts' interpretation of what amounts to a threat has been liberal. Mere factual information about the existence of a patent does not amount to a threat falling within this provision (PA 1977, s.70(5)(a)), but almost anything more than notification does if it conveys to the recipient the impression that legal action for infringement may follow, no matter how remotely. If the recipient is particularly timid, the suggestion of legal action may be read into the most cautious of letters. Threats are actionable whether or not a patent has been granted and whether or not the product complained of is or could be an infringement – so it is no defence to argue that no-one could reasonably have felt threatened. 'Cease and desist' letters and letters before action in patents cases therefore need to be drafted with extreme care.

The 'without prejudice' principle will protect against the possibility of a threats action, but it is important that the correspondence is genuinely aiming to negotiate a settlement of a genuine dispute – merely labelling a threatening letter 'without prejudice' will have no such effect (*Kooltrade Ltd* v. *XTS Ltd* [2001] IP&T 116).

Damages can also be available, if it can be shown that the threats have in themselves caused actual loss. Loss caused by infringement proceedings brought subsequent to actionable threats are not recoverable on the basis of a threats action (*Carflow Products (UK) Ltd* v. *Linwood Securities (Birmingham) Ltd* [1998] FSR 691).

The patentee's only defence is to prove that the threats were justified by showing that there was indeed infringement.

Intellectual Property Office opinions

A further innovation introduced by the Patents Act 2004 was the option to apply to the UKIPO for an opinion as to whether a patent is valid and/or infringed. The intention was to promote settlement of disputes by giving the parties some assessment of their prospects of success in court. These have been popular, enabling small companies and individuals to obtain an informed opinion at a very modest fee and reasonably promptly. There is so far no data available as to whether the opinions actually issued have had the effect of promoting settlements.

The process has limitations. In particular, the UKIPO does not conduct an investigation into the surrounding facts; it delivers an opinion based upon the information provided to it – which in a number of cases has simply been insufficient to reach a conclusion either way. In such circumstances, the opinion given is often that 'infringement has not been established', which is a very different thing from 'the patent is not infringed'.

There have nevertheless been some opinions to the effect that the patent was not valid in the light of the prior art and arguments put forward, which must materially affect the parties' bargaining positions.

Application for a declaration of non-infringement and/or revocation

Where there is uncertainty as to whether a proposed course of action will involve infringing a patent or not, one pragmatic option is to write to the patentee requesting their confirmation that the proposed product or process does not infringe. Obviously, sufficient information needs to be given as to what is proposed to enable the patentee to assess this proposition, so such a letter risks precipitating proceedings for infringement. However, where the patentee has declined, or simply failed after a decent period to confirm that the patent will not be infringed, it is possible to apply to the Comptroller of Patents or the High Court for a declaration that the proposed course of action will not infringe (PA 1977, s.71). This enables the potential infringer to resolve the question without incurring any damages or risking an injunction being granted against them. It also enables a party to prevent the patentee stalling in a state of uncertainty for an indefinite period.

The patentee will normally be the defendant to such an action and may well counterclaim for infringement. Whether unprovoked or in the face of such a counterclaim, the claimant can also apply for the patent to be revoked.

Legal actions for infringement

Civil and criminal options

At present, the vast majority of patent enforcement proceedings take the form of actions for damages in the civil courts. Limited criminal remedies are available in respect of specific false claims of rights under a patent or patent application (PA 1977, ss.110–11), but these are rarely invoked. The European Commission is, however, in the process of evaluating the use of criminal measures EU-wide to prevent intellectual property infringement and it may be that new offences will be introduced in the future.

Civil actions: who can sue and be sued

The proprietor of a granted patent has the right to bring proceedings for infringement of any claim. This includes the right to sue for infringements which occurred between the publication of the application and the grant of the patent, provided that they fall within the scope of the claims as filed, but the proceedings cannot be started until the patent has been granted.

Importantly, an exclusive licensee of a patent automatically has the same right as the proprietor to bring proceedings in respect of any infringement after the date of the licence agreement (PA 1977, s.67). Non-exclusive licensees cannot, unless their licences give this right.

An infringement action can also be launched by an equitable owner, although the legal title will have to be transferred in the course of the proceedings.

Anyone who does or threatens to do any of the infringing acts in the UK (including a licensee who goes beyond the acts permitted under the licence) may be sued for infringement. Ignorance of the patent's existence is not a complete defence, but will protect an infringer from liability for damages over the period before the infringer became aware of the patent (for example, through receipt of a letter notifying them of it) (PA 1977, s.62). Simply marking the product 'patent' or 'patented' is not enough to defeat this innocence argument: the full patent number needs to be present, to put potential copiers on notice.

Civil remedies

Overview

The remedies available for infringement of a patent are:

(a) an injunction against continued infringement;
(b) damages or alternatively an account of the infringer's profits;
(c) an order for delivery up or destruction of infringing goods, and any tools or dies for making them;
(d) a declaration that the patent is valid and has been infringed by the defendant.

The question of infringement may, if both parties (the proprietor and any alleged infringer) are willing, be referred to the Comptroller of Patents at the UKIPO, in which case the only remedies available are damages and/or a declaration of validity/infringement. In practice such references are infrequent despite the possible costs savings: the Comptroller has limited powers as regards disclosure of documents and cross-examination of witnesses, leading most parties to conclude that the courts offer a better option.

Actions must be brought in the Intellectual Property Court of the Chancery Division of the High Court or the Patents County Court for England and Wales, the Scottish Court of Session or the High Court of Northern Ireland.

Injunctions

The basis for an award of an injunction is that the infringer threatens to continue to infringe unless restrained. The proprietor will normally apply for an injunction as part of the final order at trial, but can also ask for a temporary or 'interim' injunction at the outset of proceedings, if the effect of the infringer continuing to infringe until trial will seriously damage the proprietor's business.

Interim injunctions are not common, the courts often preferring instead to order that a trial be held under the 'speedy trial' procedure which can lead to a final determination in around six months (although the length of the Intellectual Property Court list often makes this more of a theoretical than a practical possibility). The exception is where the patentee is likely to suffer damage as a result of the infringement which will not be remediable after trial – for instance, a permanent price depression as a result of the second source of supply being temporarily available. This argument is most often raised in pharmaceutical cases, where the price drop resulting from the launch of a generic product is unlikely to be reversible.

The court has, however, a discretion to award damages instead of a final injunction, taking into consideration whether the proprietor can be adequately compensated by money and whether it would be oppressive to grant an injunction. For example, if the proprietor routinely licenses the technology, then it is assumed that damages in the sum of the licence fees the infringer ought to have paid will be adequate compensation. In these circumstances an interim injunction is highly unlikely. Further, the UK has implemented Directive 2004/48/EC of the European Parliament and of the Council of 29 April 2004 on the Enforcement of Intellectual Property Rights by amending CPR Part 25 such that the infringer may now apply to be permitted to continue to infringe pending trial on the basis of providing a guarantee against any future damages award. There is as yet no case law as to how this will work in practice.

An injunction may similarly be refused if the proprietor, despite knowing of the infringing activity, has delayed to the point where the alleged infringer was entitled to believe it was free to continue to act.

Finally, no injunction will be granted against a defendant who undertakes to take a licence, where there is an entry on the Register of Patents to the effect that 'licences of right' are available in respect of the patent.

Any final injunction granted after trial will last until the patent expires or is revoked.

Damages/account of profits

Once infringement has been proved, the patentee has to choose what form of monetary compensation they want. One option is damages, to compensate for loss or injury by, so far as possible, putting the injured party in the same position as it would have been in if there had been no infringement. Alternatively, where the patentee might not have been in a position to make the same sales as the infringer has done, and therefore has suffered little or no actual damage, the patentee may instead request an account of the profits the infringer made by virtue of the infringement.

The calculation of damages can be complex, but case law is scant since most actions settle once liability has been established.

If the proprietor has been exploiting the patent by granting licences, then its loss is the capitalised value of the royalties that the infringer would have paid had it taken a licence. This convenient method becomes less easy to use if (as is often the case) the proprietor has granted various licences of the patent at different royalty rates.

The royalty method is not so appropriate if the proprietor does not grant licences but works the patent itself. In this case it is a question of the profits lost as a result of the infringer's activities. Here, many factors may be relevant including the effect on the market place of the infringement, such as:

(a) whether every sale of an infringing article represents a lost sale for the proprietor (this is assumed, unless the defendant can show otherwise);

(b) whether the proprietor would have sold other articles along with those lost sales (for example, the buyer may have also purchased non-patented articles in addition to the patented article, damages for which are often referred to as 'parasitic' damages): these lost sales will also be recoverable provided that the associated damage was foreseeably caused by the infringement;
(c) whether the infringer had generated additional interest in the patented article through its marketing efforts;
(d) what the effect on the market was of changing a monopoly into a duopoly (for example, where the proprietor had to reduce its prices to compete with the infringer);
(e) typical profit margins for the category of article concerned; and
(f) whether the infringer had deliberately undercut the proprietor's sale price.

On sales which the proprietor would not have made even absent the infringement, the proprietor is entitled to a reasonable royalty. A proper notional royalty rate is that which a potential licensee who had not yet entered the market would pay after a negotiation between willing licensor and willing licensee although the 'profits available' approach (disregarding costs of research and development and fixed costs) may also be used where appropriate (*Gerber* v. *Lectra* [1995] RPC 383).

Exemplary damages (i.e. damages above and beyond the loss suffered by the patentee) cannot be awarded. The patentee is, however, entitled to simple interest on the damages awarded, calculated at clearing bank base rate plus two per cent.

As mentioned above, neither damages nor an account of profits is available if the defendant can prove that, at the time of the infringement, it was not aware and had no reasonable grounds for supposing that the patent existed – the 'innocent infringement' defence.

Delivery up/destruction

If the infringer has produced infringing products and still has stocks of them, then the proprietor is entitled to have the remaining stock delivered over to them or destroyed, to ensure that it does not filter back onto the market. Likewise, the tools and any moulds used to make the infringing products must be delivered up or destroyed to ensure that the defendant does not simply pass them on to another entity or return to manufacturing, perhaps in another jurisdiction.

Certificate of contested validity

This is a precautionary remedy. The winner in any legal action will normally be awarded an order for their costs to be assessed by the court and a proportion, generally between 65 and 75 per cent, to be paid by the loser. If the patent's validity is challenged and successfully defended, then the proprietor is entitled to a declaration that it is valid. Should some third party later challenge the patent's validity in court on the same grounds and lose, a certificate of contested validity granted after the first successful defence will entitle the proprietor to a greater proportion of the legal costs of defending the patent than would ordinarily be reimbursed.

Defences to civil actions

Possible defences in addition to the exceptions to the patentee's rights discussed at **4.5** include the following.

1. That there is an implied licence to use the patent (for example, to repair goods made using it).
2. That the alleged infringing variant is in fact described in the prior art. If the allegedly infringing product is both previously described and within the claims of the patent, then the claims must be invalid for lack of novelty over the particular prior art. Alternatively, if the product is not within the claims, there is no infringement (but the patent is valid) (*Gillette Safety Razor Co* v. *Anglo-American Trading Co. Ltd* (1913) 30 RPC 465). This is known as the '*Gillette*' or 'squeeze' defence.

Criminal offences

Unauthorised dealing with patented products or products obtained from patented processes may constitute a criminal offence under trade descriptions or forgery legislation.

There are also a number of specific offences.

1. Making false representations that anything disposed of for value is a patented product (PA 1977, s.110).
2. Making representations that a patent has been applied for in respect of any article disposed of for value when this is not true or if the patent application has been withdrawn or refused (PA 1977, s.111).
3. Making, or causing to be made, a false entry on the Register of Patents. This extends to written material purporting to be copies of such entries (PA 1977, s.109).

It is a defence to the first two of these offences to show that the accused person had used due diligence to prevent the false representation being made.

These offences are rarely called upon, however, since patent issues tend to be somewhat more complex to determine than the enforcement authorities for criminal matters (i.e. the police and trading standards departments) are generally equipped to do. Although private prosecutions are possible, the magistrates' courts are not accustomed to deal with the issues involved. Nor are these issues perceived as being as serious as other criminal activities such as offences against the person or against property.

CHAPTER 5

Design rights

Lorna Brazell

5.1 OVERVIEW

Categories of design protection

As outlined in **Chapter 1**, the regime for legal protection of designs is woefully complicated. There are five possible forms of protection:

(a) registered designs at national level;
(b) registered designs at Community level;
(c) unregistered Community design rights arising automatically in respect of registrable designs;
(d) UK unregistered design rights, a unique domestic system of protection also arising automatically but in respect of an overlapping but differently defined class of designs; and
(e) copyright, which may protect certain designs.

Of these, the first three options apply to essentially the same designs. The choices to be made are between the geographical scope of protection (EU-wide or UK-only) and duration (three years for unregistered Community design rights or up to 25 years for the registered rights).

The remaining forms of protection apply only to limited categories of design. UK unregistered design right has an effective duration of 10 years, while copyright can last for 25 years in some cases or the life of the author plus 70 years in others.

Ownership issues

The complexity does not end there, however. Public policy as regards the UK national design rights (registered and unregistered) has led to a system which encourages retention of both rights in a single entity's ownership. It is not impossible for them to be split, but the law potentially penalises multiple ownership. Similarly, any assignment or licence of national registered design rights is effective as regards any copyright in the design.

As regards the Community design rights, the first owner of both registered and unregistered Community designs will be the same since the rights will arise in the same designs and the first ownership rules are the same.

However, the rules governing first ownership of the Community designs are different from those governing first ownership of a national registered design, or UK unregistered design right or copyright. There is therefore no legal reason why ownership of a Community design and a national registered or unregistered design over the same product could not be in different hands.

Ultimately, the only way to assess the legal rights which may subsist in any given design at a given point in time is to look at all of the possibilities in turn, and review the duration, criteria for first ownership and any assignments for each right found to subsist, to produce a definitive statement of currently subsisting rights and the ownership of each.

Validity of 'old' designs

This system is yet further complicated by the fact that the new law of UK national registered designs was introduced only in December 2001 and the old law continues to apply as to the validity of all designs on the register at that date. All new national registrations after that date will be governed by the new law on validity. Since registrations may (subject to payment of renewal fees) last up to 25 years, the dual law governing the validity of national registered designs will persist until December 2026.

5.2 REGISTERED COMMUNITY DESIGNS

Origins

The Community Design Regulation (Council Regulation (EC) No 6/2002 of 12 December 2001 on Community designs) was adopted by the EU Council of Ministers on 12 December 2001 and came into effect on 6 March 2002.

The Regulation introduced two new rights: an unregistered Community design and a registered Community design. Both of these new Community rights exist in tandem with the protection already afforded to designs under national laws. Both unregistered and registered Community designs have what is called 'unitary character'. In essence, this means the general rule is that everything which is done in relation to a Community design is done in relation to the whole of the EU. For example, a Community design can only be assigned or declared invalid for the whole of the EU (although licences can be granted for part only of the Community, subject to competition law considerations). On the other hand, the Community design owner can bring one action in one country in order to enforce the rights throughout the EU.

Application and duration

The registered Community design is obtained through an application to OHIM in Alicante, Spain whose website (**http://oami.europa.eu/en/design/default.htm**) contains all necessary application forms and details of current fees, and a searchable register of designs registered so far. Once registered, the right can last for up to a period of 25 years (subject to payment of renewal fees).

Designs capable of qualifying for registration

A 'design' is defined as the appearance of the whole or a part of a product resulting from the features of, in particular, the lines, contours, colours, shape, texture and/or materials of the product itself and/or its ornamentation (Community Design Regulation, Art.3(a)). The essence is thus directed to protection of appearance not function – indeed, features which are solely dictated by the product's technical function are excluded from protection under a design registration (Art.8(1), discussed further below). OHIM's Examination Practice Note states that colours, smells, sounds, plants and building plans are not considered to be designs.

The design must relate to a 'product', which is defined as any industrial or handicraft item (including parts intended to be assembled into a complex product), packaging, get-up, graphic symbols and typographic typefaces (Art.3(b)). Computer programs are expressly excluded; although screen images, icons and so on may be included. The inclusion of parts of complex products is a significant change from the previous UK law. Component parts are protected only if they are visible during normal use of the whole into which the part has been incorporated, and it is those features remaining visible which must meet the criteria for registrability (Art.4(2)–(3)). It is not yet clear what 'visible during normal use' may mean: are the parts of a car engine which are seen when the bonnet is lifted to check the oil, visible in normal use?

Notably, the protection conferred by the registration is not limited to the product in respect of which it was developed. Thus, the indication on the register of the kind of product to which the design relates may be relevant for indicating the classes of products amongst which prior art designs might be sought, but it does not constrain the rightholder from asserting the registration against use of the design on any other category of product. Community design registrations are therefore very much broader than registrations under the previous UK design law.

Substantive requirements

The criteria for the protection of a design, set out in Art.4(1) of the Community Design Regulation, are that the design:

(a) is new, i.e. no identical design has been made available to the relevant public before the date of application for registration; and
(b) has individual character, i.e. the overall impression it produces on an informed user differs from the overall impression produced on such a user by any design which has previously been made available to the public.

Since the Community Design Regulation came into effect only five years ago there has as yet been no guidance on the interpretation of these criteria by the European Court of Justice (ECJ), although the Invalidity Division of OHIM, which has jurisdiction over actions solely for a declaration of invalidity of registered Community designs, has given a number of decisions.

Novelty

The question of what it takes to make a design available to the public is more subtle in this context than in that of patents. Whilst publication outside the EU is no bar to a design having been made available such as to destroy novelty, it will not do so if it 'could not reasonably have become known in the normal course of business' to the businesses concerned operating inside the EU (Art.7(1)). OHIM's Invalidity Division has opined that designs on a publicly available register in Japan can reasonably have become known, and so will destroy novelty (*Sunstar* v. *Dentaid* ICD 0420), since this is the official journal of one of the world's most important intellectual property offices. In other words, businesses for which design is a significant feature are expected to carry out searches of major jurisdictions' design publications. But it could well be argued that publication only in a specialist Japanese journal would not destroy novelty.

Confidential disclosures, naturally, do not make the design available to the public.

Individual character

The second test raises the question of who is the informed user and what forms his or her overall impression.

The question of what amounts to 'individual character' is further expanded in the Regulation to take into account the degree of freedom available to the designer: if there is little freedom, then otherwise minor details may assume significance. Constraints on design freedom may be issues such as health and safety considerations, but will not include purely commercial constraints (*Procter & Gamble Co.* v. *Reckitt Benckiser (UK) Ltd* [2006] EWHC 3154 (Ch)).

The informed user takes such constraints into account when considering a design. He or she is taken to be more than a mere consumer of the products to which the design is applied, but not a design specialist who may consider every feature from a professional angle. He or she is someone aware of the existing design corpus in the relevant product category. Thus, in a case relating to a national registered design for street furniture (streetlights in particular), where the same question as to the characteristics of the informed user arose, the judge suggested *obiter* that the informed user was to be someone whose role involved buying such products for a local council, rather than either an ordinary pedestrian or a manufacturer of the goods (*Woodhouse* v. *Architectural Lighting Systems* [2005] EWPCC (Des 25)). This approach was approved as regards the informed user of a Community registered design by the Court of Appeal, in *Procter & Gamble* v. *Reckitt Benckiser (UK) Ltd* (A3/2007/0072). The court there held that the informed user was a user of the product class indicated in the registration (which in this case meant users of sprayers), rather than, for example, informed users of the infringing product. He or she was more familiar with what was relevant than might be expected of the average consumer, having some awareness of product trends and what was available in the recent past, and will be reasonably discriminatory – more so than the 'average consumer' of trade mark law. He or she also had some basic knowledge of technical considerations. Bearing all of this in mind, his or her 'overall impression' of a design is 'what stikes the mind when a design is carefully viewed' (discussed further under Infringement, below).

Grace period

These criteria are subject to a one-year grace period (Art.7(2)). This means that disclosures (e.g. marketing and selling products made to the design) which have been made either by the applicant for registration, or as a result of information provided by the applicant (e.g. photographs appearing in a trade magazine of samples provided by the applicant), during the one-year period prior to registration are not taken into account when determining whether the design is new and has individual character.

Further, the application can claim priority from an application for design protection filed up to six months previously in another Paris Convention contracting State. If so, the date for assessing novelty is the date of that earlier application.

Exclusions

Technical function

The first case to consider exclusion from protection of features dictated solely by their technical function related to the equivalent provision in respect of Unregistered Community Design, which is worded identically to Art.8(1). It was held that this exclusion applies only if the functional purpose could not be achieved in any other way (i.e. the section does not apply simply because a design serves a functional purpose – it must be the only way of achieving that purpose) (*Landor & Hawa International Ltd* v. *Azure Designs Ltd* [2006] All ER (D) 17). This is a considerably narrower approach than had been applied under previous registered design law in the UK, where a very similarly worded exclusion had been held to mean that features were excluded from design protection if 'attributable to or caused or prompted by function' (*Amp Inc.* v. *Utilux Pty Ltd* [1972] RPC 103).

This narrow approach to the scope of the exclusion was approved by the High Court in relation to registered Community design (*Procter & Gamble* v. *Reckitt Benckiser* (above)). The new design regime is therefore more generous to the designer than the previous law, and will exclude from protection only features which would effectively prevent competitors from making products having the same function.

Features necessary for interconnection

In addition to the exclusion of features solely determined by technical function, features which are necessary for the interconnection of the product to another are excluded from the protection of the design – the so-called 'must fit' exception. Once again, this is a narrow exclusion: the features must need to be reproduced in their exact form and dimensions to permit the product to be mechanically connected to or placed 'in, around or against' another product so that either product may perform its function (Art.8(2)). However, modular products (i.e. designs intended to allow multiple assembly or connection of mutually interchangeable products) are excluded from the exception (Art.8(3)). Thus, features of such products which are necessary to enable the modules to interconnect can nevertheless be protected by a registered Community design.

Spare parts

The question of use of design right to monopolise the downstream market in spare parts has always caused considerable difficulty for policy makers. Clearly, in the era of planned obsolescence manufacturers of many classes of products have a lucrative market in supplying components to repair their goods as they break down, and there is a difficult issue as to where the public interest lies between incentivising development by allowing the monopoly to extend into that market, and permitting competition to the benefit of consumers, as products will cost far less to repair if there are alternative sources of supply. The right to repair a product which had been lawfully bought from the rightholder was at one stage seen under UK law as preventing the rightholder from derogating from the grant of rights implicit in the sale of the original (*British Leyland Motor Corp. Ltd* v. *Armstrong Patents Co. Ltd* [1986] AC 577) – a curious importation of a legal principle from land law into intellectual property.

The issue has been subject to extensive debate and lobbying, with the result that the Community Designs regime effectively ducked the issue. As part of the transitional provisions for the new regime, design protection is excluded from any design 'which constitutes a component part of a complex product used . . . for the purpose of repair of that complex product so as to restore its original appearance' (Art.110). To date, no permanent provision has been proposed on the subject.

Policy and morality

Designs contrary to public policy or morality, assessed on an EU-wide basis, cannot be protected by a registered Community design. Once again, the lack of case law to date makes it difficult to assess what kind of designs may be excluded by this. The only guidance available is that from the Green Paper preceding the legislation, which suggested that any design incorporating a swastika with a clear intention of provoking the public would be excluded. This implies that designs offensive on political and religious grounds are likely to be excluded; there is no guidance as to what might be considered immoral.

State insignia

Various State emblems and flags cannot be registered unless the appropriate authority has consented.

Ownership

First ownership

The rights to a Community design vest in the designer (or joint designers) unless the designer is an employee who made the design in the execution of his or her duties or following the employer's instructions. If so, the rights vest in the designer's employer (Art.14). The designer has the right, similar to that of an inventor of a patented invention, to be cited in the register.

Note that the commissioner of a design does *not* automatically get the right to apply for registration of the design – that must be specifically provided for in the commissioning contract. It may of course be possible to argue that there is an implied term to this effect, but that argument will depend upon meeting the usual stringent criteria for terms to be implied, under *Liverpool City Council* v. *Irwin* [1977] AC 239. It is far safer to make express provision.

Once a design has been registered, the person whose name appears in the Register as the proprietor is presumed to be entitled to the design.

Transactions

Any transfer of title must therefore be recorded in order to take legal effect (Art.28). Any claim to entitlement to a design which has been registered by another must be brought within three years of publication of the registration, unless it can be shown that the registered proprietor was acting in bad faith (Art.15).

Licences and mortgages must also be registered in order to be effective as against third parties (unless actual knowledge of the transaction can be shown) (Art.33).

Only insolvency proceedings in the Member State in which the debtor has its main interests can apply to Community registered designs (Art.30). Similarly, the property laws of the Member State in which the proprietor has its seat or domicile will govern the right (Art.27).

Infringement

Acts which infringe

The registered Community design is an absolute monopoly, i.e. it protects the owner against independent development as well as unauthorised copying. Application to any product of a design which does not give an informed user a different overall impression will infringe. Once again, the informed user is taken to be aware of the degree of freedom which was available to the designer (Art.9).

Similarly, any subsequent use, offer for sale or import, export or stocking of such a product for sale will also infringe (Art.19(1)). In principle, therefore, consumers who buy what proves to have been an infringing item could themselves infringe by using the product, save that acts done privately and for non-commercial purposes do not infringe (Art.20(1)). A commercial purchaser of infringing products which proceeds to use them in its business without passing them on would, nevertheless, infringe.

There are no secondary or contributory infringing acts, i.e. acts which require knowledge of the existence of the design in order to infringe.

Assessing overall impression

The crucial question of what constitutes a different overall impression was considered at length in *Procter & Gamble Co.* v. *Reckitt Benckiser* (above). The test does not derive from any pre-existing national design law, and therefore falls to be worked out by pure statutory interpretation.

The Court of Appeal held that the assessment should be done with the relevant design at hand, rather than merely recollected in the way that confusion is assessed in trade mark cases. The test to be applied is whether the overall impressions of the registration and alleged infringement are different, but does not require them to be *clearly* different. Difference alone is enough. Thus, the impression of a poor quality or cheap imitation of a registered design is not the same as the impression of the registration itself.

A new design which is markedly different from anything that has gone before is likely to have a greater overall visual impact than if it is 'surrounded by kindred prior art'. The overall impression created by such a design will be more significant, so the room for differences which do not create a substantially different overall impression is greater. Protection for a striking novel product will therefore be correspondingly greater than for a product which is incrementally different from the prior art. But it is not sufficient to ask 'is the alleged infringement closer to the registered design or to the prior art?' The test remains, 'is the overall impression different?' This 'is almost the equivalent to asking whether they are the same – the difference is nuanced, probably, involving a question of onus and no more'. The comparison between the two designs has to be carried out at the same level of detail, which must be sufficient not only to identify the important features but also to characterise the impression which they give. But in doing this comparison the informed user is taken to know where shapes are, to some extent, required to be the way they are by reason of function and will discount features constrained by the product's functional requirements.

Defences

It is permitted to use a registered design:

(a) for experimental purposes;
(b) to reproduce it for teaching or citation (presumably in the context of discussion of design developments or the like) provided this is fair, acknowledges the source and does not unduly prejudice the normal exploitation of the design; or
(c) on a ship or aircraft temporarily in a Member State, including importation of spare parts for or repair of such a vehicle (Art.20(2)).

Further, if an alleged infringer can demonstrate that before the date of filing of the application (or earlier priority) it has made in good faith commercial use of the design within the EC or serious and effective preparations to that end, then that use can continue notwithstanding the registration of the design (Art.22). The right is personal and not transferable save as part of the business to which it relates. Since any publication of such a prior use would invalidate the design, this defence can in practice only relate to private use or preparations of the design. Initial design sketches and product ideas are unlikely to be sufficient to engage the defence. In patent law, the courts have been reluctant to find 'serious and effective preparations' were being made at any stage earlier than the tooling and pre-launch activities for a defined product.

Enforcement and remedies

Designated courts

The Intellectual Property Court of the Chancery Division and the Patents County Court have been designated as the Community Design Courts for the United Kingdom, along with the Scottish Court of Session and the High Court in Northern Ireland. The Community Design Courts have exclusive jurisdiction over actions for infringement and, in the course of infringement proceeding, the validity of Community designs. Absent an infringement action, invalidity actions must be brought at OHIM. Any person can bring such a challenge as there are no qualifying criteria required to give *locus standi*.

Pan-European actions

The Community Design Courts have the power, if their jurisdiction is based on the domicile of the parties rather than merely a local act of infringement, to grant a pan-European injunction. This is a consequence of the unitary character of these two new Community Designs. Once one Community Design Court in any Member State is seized of jurisdiction for the purpose of deciding infringement and/or validity of a design, any other Member State's court in which an action between the same parties is brought must stay it, save for the grant of any interim relief in its territory. In practice, this can be a very effective tactic since a certain 'domino effect' can arise when one court has granted an interim injunction, so that considerable pressure is applied to the alleged infringer to withdraw from the market or settle before the court actually seized of the issue reaches its final decision.

The right to sue

An infringement action can be brought by the proprietor or an exclusive licensee as of right, and by a non-exclusive licensee if given the right to do so by their licence. To confer this right the licence must be in writing and signed by the parties. If the proprietor brings an action, any licensee has the right to join the proceedings for the purpose of claiming damages (Art.32(4)). A transferee of the right whose name is not yet on the register may in principle bring the action as equitable owner, provided that its title is made good in the course of the proceedings.

Remedies

In addition to the grant of an interim or permanent injunction, the courts can award damages or an account of profits for the infringing activities, delivery up of infringing products, dies or tools predominantly used to manufacture the infringing goods, and costs. Further, the court may order the infringer to recall products already on the market and to inform its distributors of the decision against it.

Threats actions

The action

Provisions permitting a person unjustifiably threatened with legal action for infringement of a registered Community design rights were not initially provided for in the Community design regime. However, in the UK they have been introduced by the Community Design Regulations 2005, SI 2005/2339, bringing the regime for protection of consumers and traders from Community rightholders making unjustified threats of litigation into line with that applicable to the national design rights.

An action to restrain someone from making groundless threats of proceedings for infringement of a registered Community design can be brought by any person aggrieved, not only the person threatened. Thus for instance threats made against retailers may be actionable by the manufacturer or central distributor of the product concerned since if customers hear of claims for infringement they may be dissuaded from purchasing 'infringing' products from the distributor. The rationale is that litigation, even if wholly unmeritorious, takes sufficient time and money that many businesses may choose to change supplier rather than risk becoming embroiled. A groundless threat may therefore be a powerful marketing tool.

No action can be brought to restrain threats of infringement proceedings against someone who is making or importing a product. Otherwise, it is very unwise to make any such threats except in the course of genuine 'without prejudice' communications (*Unilever plc* v. *Procter & Gamble* [2000] FSR 344). As ever, simply marking correspondence 'without prejudice' will not establish this protection if in fact no genuine settlement discussions are in contemplation (*Kooltrade Ltd* v. *XTS Ltd* [2001] FSR 13).

Actionable threats

Mere notification of the existence of a Community design does not amount to a threat falling within this provision, but almost anything more than notification does even if no one is named as the proposed defendant and there is no direct reference to proceedings. For instance, a notification via eBay's VeRO system for the protection of intellectual property that certain products infringed (leading to eBay removing the accused listings) constitutes a threat to bring infringement proceedings, since a reasonable person in eBay's position would understand that it could be subject to future infringement proceedings if it failed to take down the allegedly infringing sales pages (*Quads 4 Kids* v. *Campbell* [2006] All ER (D) 162 (Oct)).

Accordingly, 'cease and desist' letters and letters before action need to be drafted with extreme care. References in letters to 'protecting interests' or 'not allowing' actions have both been held to be actionable threats of litigation (*Rosedale Assoc. Manufacturers Ltd* v. *Airfix Products Ltd* [1956] RPC 360; *Kurtz* v. *Spence* (1888) 5 RPC 161). A threat may arise from the cumulative effect of a series of individually non-threatening letters (*Willis & Bates Ltd* v. *Tilley Lamp Co.* (1944) 61 RPC 8). A mere general warning to all the world not to infringe a given design lest enforcement action be taken is not an actionable threat, however (*Johnson* v. *Edge* (1892) 9 RPC 142).

The threats action can be brought against any person making the threat – including a solicitor writing on behalf of a client.

Defences and remedies

A threats action is based upon threats being a wrong against the subject of them because they are groundless. Thus the only effective defence is to prove that they were good, i.e. by showing that the acts in question did (or would) constitute an infringement.

It is not a defence that no design registration exists, or that it is owned by someone other than the person making the threats so that in fact there is no possibility of an infringement action being launched.

The remedies available if an allegation of groundless threats is successful are a declaration to the effect that the threats are unjustifiable, an injunction against the continuance of the threats; and such damages, if any, as the claimant has sustained by reason of the threats. This is of course subject to the existing case law on when damages will be recoverable. In particular, the claimant will need to demonstrate that any losses flowed from the threat itself and not from any other causes, such as the subsequent issue of proceedings (*Carflow Products (UK) Ltd* v. *Linwood Securities (Birmingham) Ltd* [1998] FSR 691).

5.3 UNREGISTERED COMMUNITY DESIGNS

Designs capable of qualifying for registration

The substantive requirements for a design to attract unregistered Community design protection are the same as those for registration of a registered Community design (discussed at **5.2**), i.e. that it meets the definitions of 'design' and 'product', is new and of individual character and does not fall within any of the exclusions. The date on which novelty is judged is the date on which the design is first made available to the public (Art.5(1)(a)). This means the date on which it is published, exhibited or used in trade in such a way that the event could reasonably have become known to the relevant sector of commerce in the normal course of business (Art.11(1)).

The objective of this automatic but short-lived right is to protect designs in fast-moving industries such as fashion, where the shelf-life of the design may be such as not to warrant application for registration.

An issue may arise, however, as to the extent to which an unregistered Community design protects parts of products, since there is no registration to which to refer to establish what the product or design is. It is arguable that the effect of first marketing a new design is to bring into effect a bundle of separate unregistered Community designs relating to the various elements making up the whole, as has been successfully argued in relation to UK unregistered design right (*A Fulton Co. Ltd* v. *Totes Isotoner (UK) Ltd* [2004] RPC 301), but there is no authority so far.

Duration

Unregistered Community design protection applies automatically for three years from the date of the first sale or marketing of the design in the EU (Art.11). Thus, from the point of view of a potential Community design owner, the unregistered Community design is clearly a good thing insofar as it gives a short-term Community-wide right at no cost.

It will however be the subject of considerable debate as to when a particular design was first sold or marketed in the EU, if the design in fact originates elsewhere. Prior publication outside the EU could arguably invalidate the right, and the regional court of Frankfurt-am-Main has concluded in one case that it does (GRUR-RR (2005) No.1). This does not appear to be the intention of the legislature, since the date for assessing novelty is not tied to the date upon which the protection first takes effect. Thus, a design could in principle be first disclosed in Australia, setting the date upon which novelty is to be judged, but not be first marketed in the EU until a year or more later. Unregistered Community design right, coming into existence only at that later date of first marketing, would not commence for a considerable time after the design was first made public. Global trade through websites complicates the possibilities yet further: would an offer for sale on an Australian website with an international shipping option constitute first marketing in the EU? In view of the German court's decision, the ECJ may at some stage need to confirm the correct operation of this provision.

Infringement – need to prove copying

The test for infringement of an unregistered Community design is the same as that for infringement of the registered Community design.

The disadvantage of relying only on the unregistered Community design is that the monopoly is partial rather than absolute. In addition to meeting the 'same overall impression' test, it is necessary to show copying from the rightholder's design in order to establish liability for infringement (Art.19(2)).

Copying will not be inferred from mere similarity if the alleged infringement results from an independent work of creation by a designer who may reasonably be thought not to be familiar with the design made available to the public by the holder. This looks like a definition of independent creation, but additional questions will arise as to whether or not the designer may reasonably thought not to be familiar with the design. For instance, geographical circulations of products may be relevant. If the rightholder in fact sells only in the Scandinavian Member States, would a designer located in Slovenia or Cyprus reasonably be thought not to be familiar with it? Once again, this point will have to await clarification through case law.

The provision appears to set up a presumption that copying *will* be inferred where the designs are similar and the designer may reasonably be thought to be familiar with the rightholder's design, but this is not an inference that the English courts have readily drawn in copyright cases in the past. It remains to be seen what evidence as to the market profile of the design or of the alleged infringer's knowledge of it through other channels may be required to prove that copying has taken place on the balance of probabilities.

Ownership

The rules as to ownership of an unregistered Community design are the same as those for a registered Community design – the designer or his or her employer will be the default first owner. Assignment or invalidity can only be for the entire Community, though licensing can be on a territorial basis.

Complications can, however, arise as to the property law which applies to the right if it is in joint ownership. Unless the joint owners designate a particular Member State's law for this purpose, the default law will be that of Spain. Similarly, if the holder of an Unregistered Community Design is not an EU entity, Spanish law will apply.

Enforcement and remedies

Actions for infringement can be brought by:

(a) the holder of the right;
(b) the exclusive licensee if the holder fails to take action after an appropriate period of notice; or
(c) a non-exclusive licensee with the holder's permission.

In each case, since there is no register to establish ownership the action will be complicated (in comparison with enforcement of the registered Community design) by the need to bring evidence to show both subsistence of the right and title to it.

The Community Design Courts have exclusive jurisdiction over both the infringement and validity of an unregistered Community design. Unlike registered Community design, a validity challenge must be brought in the courts of the Member State where the holder of the right is domiciled, under the normal rules of jurisdiction under the Brussels Convention. OHIM's Invalidity Division has no jurisdiction.

The remedies for infringement are the same as those available for infringement of a registered Community design.

5.4 NATIONAL REGISTERED DESIGNS

Introduction

In parallel with the introduction of the Community registered design, the Designs Directive (Directive 98/71/EC of the European Parliament and of the Council of 13 October 1998 on the legal protection of designs) was passed to harmonise the laws of Member States in relation to design rights registered with the central industrial property offices of Member States, the Benelux Design Office and design rights registered under the Community-wide scheme.

The Designs Directive therefore introduced into all national registered design laws a new definition of design which is identical to that governing Community Designs: the appearance of the whole or any part of a product, including such aspects as texture and materials in addition to the more traditional features of shape, colour and contours. It also covers features of items not previously regarded as products, such as graphic symbols and typographic typefaces.

The Designs Directive was implemented in the UK by amendment of the Registered Designs Act (RDA) 1949. The implementation, which was done by statutory instrument through the positive procedure, was challenged as falling outside the powers granted to the Secretary of State under the European Communities Act 1972, s.2. The challenge succeeded at first instance on the grounds that since the Directive left choices as to how to deal with the validity of existing registrations, neither of the options was a 'Community obligation' as such so that either could only be implemented by primary legislation. On appeal, the challenge was rejected (*Oakley Inc.* v. *H. Young (Operations) Ltd & Anr* [2005] EWCA Civ 1191), thereby eliminating a concern that the UK's implementation of numerous copyright Directives may have been unconstitutional.

The new law applies to both infringement and validity of any design registered on or after 9 December 2001. It also applies to infringement of any pre-existing registrations. The old law of validity continues to apply to pre-existing registrations.

Registrability under the new law

Criteria for registration

To be eligible for protection the design has to be both new and of individual character, both of which are defined as for Community designs. Where a design is part of a complex product (i.e. one which is composed of multiple replaceable components) it is registrable only if in normal use it remains visible and the appearance of the visible part is new and of individual character.

The exclusions to registrability which apply in respect of Community registered design also apply to national registrations. The only difference is in respect of the exclusion for reasons of public policy or morality, where a UK-only test will be applied by the UKIPO, potentially in contrast to the EU-wide test to be applied by OHIM.

Any disclosure by the proprietor to the public in the 12 months prior to the priority date is ignored for the purposes of assessing novelty and individual character.

The right granted by the registration can be renewed up to a total of 25 years and is infringed by any design which does not produce a different overall impression on the informed user. The defences to infringement for acts done privately for non-commercial purposes or acts done for experimental purposes apply, as in respect of the Community registered designs.

Main changes from the previous UK registered designs law

The most important difference from the old law is that there is no longer a requirement for a design to have 'eye appeal' in order to be registrable. Thus, aesthetically 'functional' designs can now be registered (provided that the design is not dictated solely by function). The case law on validity of registered designs under the previous regime is no longer relevant to any design registered on or after 9 December 2001.

Further, when registering a design, it is no longer necessary to do so in respect of an article. Although a product needs to be identified, it does not need to meet the criteria (discussed below) established for this requirement under the old law. Similarly, the right accorded to the owner of a registered design is no longer limited to preventing the use of the design in respect of the article covered by the registration.

Finally, the prior art to be considered is global (within the criteria explained in connection with the registered Community design) rather than UK-only.

Registration

Registration takes place through the Designs Section of the UKIPO in Newport.

Ownership

The principal difference between the harmonised UK registered design and the Community-wide rights is the law on ownership of rights. This aspect was not addressed in the Designs Directive.

By RDA 1949, s.2 the author of the design is the original proprietor, subject to two exceptions. If a design is created pursuant to a paid commission, the commissioner is the original proprietor. In any other case, if the designer is an employee and creates the design in the course of his or her employment then the employer will be the proprietor.

The author is the person who creates the design – conceiving it and giving it visible expression – or, where the design is computer generated, the person by whom the arrangements necessary for the creation of the design are made (for example, setting up the parameters for the program to apply). The same person will own any UK unregistered design right in the design; ownership should therefore normally be in the same hands.

Providing for the commissioner to take precedence as regards ownership over the designer or their employer (if any) neatly avoids the problem common in copyright commissioning arrangements, that the commissioner may not end up with ownership if (for instance) a design agency presented with a commission in fact engages a freelance designer to carry it out.

There is no express provision for joint authorship and hence joint ownership, but neither is there any indication that it would not be accepted were a factual situation to arise in which two people jointly and indistinguishably contributed to a final design.

Since a registered design is a form of property, it can be assigned, mortgaged, inherited or pass to a trustee in bankruptcy by operation of law. In all such cases, the new proprietor must register their title in order to become entitled to enforce the right and to avoid the risk that the former owner may grant later assignments or licences while still registered as proprietor. If so, a later assignee who registers their title before the earlier assignee will get good title provided that they had no notice of the earlier assignment.

By CDPA 1988, s.224 any subsequent assignment of the registration is presumed also to assign the unregistered design right in the design, if any. Similarly, an assignment of the unregistered design right will presumptively assign the registration unless expressed not to (RDA 1949, s.19(3B)). If the two rights are transferred into separate legal ownership, the title to the registered design cannot be registered – which will prevent the new owner from taking any enforcement action, effectively assigning title further or granting licences.

Licences should also be registered in order to give notice of the licensee's rights to any future assignee of the registration, making such assignment subject to the licensee's prior rights.

Enforcement and remedies

General

The registered proprietor of a national registered design has the right to sue for infringement. An exclusive licensee also has the statutory right to bring proceedings.

Proceedings must be brought in the Intellectual Property Court of the Chancery Division, the Patents County Court, the Scottish Court of Session or the High Court in Northern Ireland, which have exclusive jurisdiction over registered designs.

Since the UK registered design right is an absolute monopoly it is not necessary to show copying.

The remedies available are the same as for infringement of a registered or unregistered Community design.

Threats actions

The threats provisions recently introduced in respect of Community designs, discussed above, are identical to those under RDA 1949.

Validity of pre-existing UK registered designs

Preservation of the old law

The substantive requirements for registrability which were in force before 9 December 2001 still apply to designs registered before that date. Thus, they form the grounds upon which any future challenge to the validity of such a design must be brought.

The principal requirements were that the design had to have 'eye-appeal' and be new. Designs also had to relate to features of shape, configuration, pattern or ornament to be applied to an article by an industrial process, and not fall into any of the exceptions.

Eye appeal

The most important criterion was that features constituting the design must 'appeal to and be judged by the eye of the customer' (not the designer). Eye appeal does not mean that the design had to have artistic merit. Provided that aesthetic considerations are taken into account by prospective purchasers to some degree, however small, then the design was registrable.

This did not, however, restrict registrability to those cases where the eye appeal is immediately apparent to the customer purchasing the article. For example, a design of a toy included inside a hollow chocolate egg might be registrable even though the customer did not see it at all before purchasing. It is simply that the design could not be registered if the appearance of the article is completely immaterial in the eyes of those acquiring or using articles of that description – such as, for example, the electric terminals used in a washing machine (*Amp* v. *Utilux* [1972] RPC 103).

Even if the features have a predominantly functional purpose, where their particular dimensions and shape had been chosen so as to produce a LEGO brick which, taken as a whole, was an attractive object, the design of the brick was found to be registrable (*Interlego AG* v. *Tyco Industries Inc* [1989] AC 217).

Novelty

To be registrable under the old law a design also had to be novel. Novelty in this context meant that the design must not previously have been published – but with an important restriction: only prior publications in the UK, rather than anywhere in the world, were relevant. Thus, a registration could validly be obtained for a design which had already been commercialised abroad, as long as it had not been either registered or published in the UK in respect of the same or any other article, at the date of the application for registration. Publication for these purposes could include drawings, written descriptions (if they clearly and unambiguously directed the reader how to produce the design) or use, as long as such use had been visible to the public, even if only by an article being on display to visitors to a private house. Confidential disclosure by the proprietor, or by a recipient in breach of confidence, did not destroy the novelty of the application.

Where there is a prior publication in respect of a very similar design, the design could still be novel if it differed from that design in more than:

(a) immaterial details; or
(b) variants commonly used in the trade.

The question of whether the two designs were indeed very similar to start with was purely to be judged by the eye looking at the two designs as a whole, both when the two were side by side and also looking at them separately and from a small distance (*Allen West & Co.* v. *British Westinghouse Electrical & Manufacturing Co.* (1916) 33 RPC 157). The novelty has to be sufficient to be appreciable in such a comparison.

IMMATERIAL DIFFERENCES

A detail is immaterial only if it is of no importance to the prospective purchaser. For example, the sort of variations which any skilled workman might make between different examples of the same product are insufficient to confer novelty (*Simmons* v. *Mathieson & Co.* (1911) 28 RPC 486). Thus, the number of previous designs in the same field may make a difference since in such a field there may be a very large number of minor variations with which consumers are familiar, such that purchasers are only likely to notice more striking changes (*Le May* v. *Welch* (1885) 28 ChD 24).

VARIANTS COMMONLY USED IN THE TRADE

Variants commonly used in the trade might be anything which is in occasional but not universal use in the trade for the relevant class of articles. For example, running shoes sometimes but not invariably may have spikes to improve grip, so a design consisting solely of adding spikes to an old design of running shoe was not sufficiently novel to be registrable (*Phillips* v. *Harbro Rubber Co.* (1920) 37 RPC 233). A mere change of colour was unlikely to be enough to make a design novel. On the other hand, if there was only one prior instance of a particular variant being used, or only one manufacturer or supplier supplying that variant in the UK, then adding such a variant to a pre-existing design could be enough to confer novelty (*Re Britvic's Application* [1960] RPC 201).

Where only part of the overall design was novel, the design application had to state which aspect this was claimed to be.

Other requirements

To be registrable, a design had to relate to a feature of shape, configuration, pattern or ornament, or all four features. Generally, 'shape and configuration' relate to three-dimensional aspects of a design while 'pattern or ornament' relate to two dimensional features, such as surface decoration or a textile design.

An 'article' meant something made and sold separately on the market, and delivered to the customer as a finished product. This could range from a sheet of wallpaper to a pre-fabricated building; this was generally not an issue, but became problematic when spare parts were concerned. The question was considered from an economic point of view: did a market exist for the article separate from that for which it is primarily manufactured?

This is of particular significance to spare parts, since parts which have no reality as articles of commerce apart from their forming part of a complete item cannot be said to be made and sold separately, and so cannot be considered as 'articles'. For example, an extreme example was an application for a design registration in respect of an icon on a computer screen. The application was rejected for several reasons, including that it was not capable of being sold in isolation.

The spare parts dispute has been hardest fought in the motor industry. For instance, Ford applied to register designs for, amongst other car spare parts, door panels which are sold either as a part of the car for which it was designed to fit, or as a spare part to that particular car. Although they are indeed made and sold separately from the car to which they relate, the application was rejected on the grounds that they were in reality a mere adjunct to that car as a whole. Thus, they were not 'articles' and the design for them could not be registered. By way of contrast, many steering wheels or wing mirrors can be fitted to a variety of different cars by way of customisation and, therefore, can be said to be made and sold separately, and so can be considered 'articles' (*Ford Motor Co. Ltd's Application* [1994] RPC 545).

Application by an industrial process

The requirement for application by an industrial process normally goes without saying, particularly since 'industrial process' includes hand application, as long as this is carried out as part of an industrial arrangement. For example, a design used on mass-produced hand-painted china would qualify even though the design was applied to the article by hand in every instance.

A complete building operation, which must necessarily be tailored in each case to the circumstances of the site, does not constitute an industrial process; thus, a design for a petrol station was considered unregistrable (*Re Collier & Co's Application* (1937) 54 RPC 253).

Excluded articles

Designs for certain types of articles were expressly excluded from registration by the Registered Designs Rules 1989, SI 1989/1105, r.26:

(a) works of sculpture;
(b) wall plaques, medals and medallions; and

(c) printed matter primarily of a literary or artistic character.

However, these may have intellectual property protection under copyright as discussed below.

Exceptions to registrability

(A) METHOD OR PRINCIPLE OF CONSTRUCTION

A design was not registrable if it constituted a method or principle of construction. This requirement rarely had any effect; it was designed to prevent monopolies arising from these rights in industrial techniques which would more appropriately be patented. For example, a design for a basket woven in a certain way has been held not to be registrable as, in a very early case, was an application which attempted to cover the way a bicycle's spokes relate to the rim and hub – unless the applicant agreed to restrict the effect of the registration solely to the particular arrangement of spokes shown in the drawing and not to include all possible arrangements (*Pugh* v. *Riley Cycle Co. Ltd* (1912) 29 RPC 196).

(B) FUNCTION

Where the design relates to features of shape or configuration, those features must not be dictated *solely* by the function which the article has to perform. Thus, a shape is excluded if it possesses no features beyond those which are necessary to enable the article to fulfil its function. However features which are functional could still be validly registered if their particular proportions and/or dimensions were selected to give the article some individuality apart from the purely fundamental version of the same product.

(C) MUST MATCH

This exception related again to the debate over the degree of protection which ought to be provided for motor vehicle spare parts (although of course it also applies to parts intended for inclusion in any other larger whole). Features of shape or configuration of an article were excluded by s.1(1)(b) of RDA 1949 if they were dependent upon ('must match') the appearance of another article of which the article is intended by the author of the design to perform an integral part. The effect is that some vehicle parts, such as body panels, were excluded from registered design protection, even if held to be 'articles', since there was no design freedom involved (per the Divisional Court in *Ford Motor Co. Ltd's Design Application* [1994] RPC 545): they can only be sold to match the overall shape of the vehicle for which they are intended and are not interchangeable, either upon the same vehicle or for use with other models.

5.5 UNREGISTERED DESIGN RIGHT

Introduction

Design right (confusingly so-called in the Act) was created in 1988 by CDPA 1988 as part of the reorganisation arising out of the debate over intellectual property protection for spare parts. It applies only to original designs created on or after 1 August 1989. Designs created before then, but not eligible for registration, may have some protection under copyright, as discussed below.

Design right was introduced to rationalise the system of protection for what are essentially industrial drawings. Up until CDPA 1988, *any* drawing, of no matter how utilitarian a function, qualified for copyright and the accompanying protection for, potentially, over 100 years. This protection had been conceived for works of artistic intent and value, and was considered disproportionate for everyday design drawings. Registration, on the other hand, was available only for designs which had eye appeal. Thus, abolishing copyright for industrial drawings would have left no protection at all for more functional works, which may nevertheless involve considerable creativity and effort. Design right was intended to fill that gap, protecting the investment in designs for purely utilitarian items, such as the internal elements of a machine.

This right is exceptional in that it is a right peculiar to UK law. All of the other statutory rights discussed in this Handbook have counterparts (although these may differ in some respects) in the laws of most other countries. Unregistered designs, however, are not protected by a special right in most countries, New Zealand being an isolated exception. Elsewhere, unregistered designs (as defined in CDPA 1988) either continue to be protected by copyright or are unprotected. Thus, there are no international reciprocating provisions to rely upon where a design originates in another country: to qualify for protection, the design must have some connection with the UK.

The right, which arises automatically, is similar to copyright in that it does not confer a monopoly against the world in general, only protection from copying. The unregistered design right lasts in practice for only about 10 years. Further, as with the registered rights but unlike copyright, caution is necessary in asserting the right since it is possible to bring an action for unfounded threats.

Protected designs

Design right subsists in a *design*, created on or after 1 August 1989 and *recorded* in some manner. The design must be *original*, must *qualify* by connection with the UK and must not fall within the scope of any *exception*. Each of these requirements is considered in turn below.

Definition of a 'design'

A design is any aspect of the *shape or configuration* (whether internal or external) of the whole or any substantial part of *an article*. Thus, it is principally concerned with the three-dimensional character of objects or aspects of objects. Unregistered designs can be protected even if they relate only to a part of an article which is never sold separately from the whole.

No distinction is made between aesthetic and functional design.

The right only comes into existence when either the design is recorded in a design document, or an article has been made to that design, even if the design is not made public at that time. Clearly, it would be impossible for normal trade to take place if rights could be asserted in a design which as yet existed only in the designer's head.

Originality

In order to be protected, the design must be original, in the sense of being the creator's own work, not copied from an existing work. A design can be protected even if in fact an identical design already exists, provided the later design was created independently.

Further, it must not be 'commonplace in the design field in question at the time of its creation'. Thus, complete trivia of the trade will not gain protection just by being newly incorporated into a design.

'Not being commonplace' is not the same as being entirely novel, but it must have something about it to 'excite . . . peculiar attention in those in the relevant art' (*Ocular Sciences* v. *Aspect Vision Care Ltd* [1997] RPC 289). It may be that no more than a few prior examples will result in a design being regarded as commonplace. A combination of individually commonplace features could in theory produce a design which was not commonplace, but a 'run of the mill' combination of well-known features is likely to result in a commonplace design. However, it is important to consider the design at the right level of generality – most functional articles will share some essential features such that possession of those features could be said to be commonplace. The originality of a particular implementation may lie in the exact orientation or proportion of a feature (such as legs on a stool) which in itself is essential and therefore commonplace.

The 'design field in question' is to be considered broadly. So different categories of clothing would all fall within a single 'clothing' category (*Lambretta Clothing Co. Ltd* v. *Teddy Smith (UK) Ltd* [2004] EWCA 886). The fact that a prior design is old does not exclude it from consideration if in fact it would be considered by present day designers, for instance as when vintage clothing is considered as a source of ideas. Nevertheless, a design must be being used in the same field of activity to be commonplace – transposition of common designs from rock art into jewellery did not preclude design right from arising (*Sales* v. *Stromberg* [2005] EWHC 1624 (Ch)).

There is still some ambiguity, however, as to whether the design field is to be considered worldwide, or only as regards what is known in the UK. The statute is silent. Park J in *A Fulton Co. Ltd* v. *Totes Isotoner (UK) Ltd* [2003] RPC 499 concluded that only UK designs should be taken into account but the correctness of this has been questioned although the issue itself was not appealed.

Qualification by connection with the UK

As mentioned above, due to the relative international uniqueness of the UK's design right law, protection is only available to certain classes of design, decided by reference either to:

(a) the *nationality* of the designer, his or her commissioner or employer; or
(b) the *country* in which the design was first marketed.

The Qualifying Countries include the UK and the rest of the EU plus New Zealand and the Channel Islands.

The design will qualify by the first route if the designer, or their commissioner or employer (if applicable), is an individual who is a citizen of, or habitually resident in, a Qualifying Country. If the commissioner or employer is a corporate body, then it must either be formed under the law of a Qualifying Country, or have substantial business activities within a Qualifying Country.

The designer is the *creator* of the design or, in the case of computer generated works (e.g. the output of CAD equipment), the designer is the person by whom the arrangements necessary for the creation of the design are undertaken. Note that the designer need not necessarily be the person who actually records the design; that could be recorded by the machine itself, for example, or by a draughtsman working under the designer's instructions.

If the design does not qualify for protection by any of the above criteria, it may still qualify for protection if the first marketing of articles made to the design took place in a Qualifying Country. For this to qualify the design for protection in the UK, the first marketing would have to be done by a person/organisation who is exclusively authorised to put the articles on the market in the EU; and that person/organisation would have to qualify under the nationality requirements set out above in respect of designers, commissioners or employers.

Exceptions

(A) A METHOD OR PRINCIPLE OF CONSTRUCTION (CDPA 1988, S.213(3)(a))

This is included principally to prevent overlap with cases where patent protection would be available.

(B) SURFACE DECORATION (CDPA 1988, S.213(3)(c))

Purely two-dimensional features on a surface may be protected by copyright, but are likely to be excluded from design right. Three-dimensional surface features (bumps and dips) included purely for their decorative effect would not qualify for protection, but if in addition they serve a functional purpose the exception will not apply. Thus, ribbing on a vacuum-cleaner handle was found not to be excluded since it also served the functional applications of strengthening the handle and improving the user's grip (*Dyson* v. *Qualtex* [2006] EWCA Civ 166).

(C) MUST FIT (CDPA 1988, S.213(3)(b)(i))

This exception relates to features of shape or configuration which enable the article to be connected to, or placed in, around or against, another article so that either article may perform its function. For example, no protection could be obtained for the components of line-isolating transformers for telephone lines since the two parts had to be connected to each other to form the whole (*Electronic Techniques (Anglia) Ltd* v. *Critchley Components Ltd* [1997] FSR 401). The shape cannot be protected if it 'must fit' even if it also performs some other function such as appearing attractive. However, the exclusion is narrow: it does not apply unless the design is the only way of achieving the functional purpose (*Landor & Hawa International Ltd* v. *Azure Designs Ltd* [2006] All ER (D) 17).

(D) MUST MATCH (CDPA 1988, S.213(3)(b)(ii))

This is similar to the previous exception. It covers features of shape or configuration which are dependent upon the appearance of another article of which the article is intended by the designer to form an integral part. The exception does not apply where spare parts are concerned unless the spare parts manufacturer can demonstrate that there is a real practical need to copy a feature of the original article because of the way the original had been designed (*Dyson* v. *Qualtex* [2006] EWCA Civ 166). Evidence that non-matching spares have been sold will tend to undermine this. The nature of the product will be significant. For example, a car door panel must match the outline and any decorative features present on the rest of the vehicle in a seamless fashion. Other components, such as steering wheel or exhaust pipe, will not be excluded since there is clearly much scope for variation without necessarily duplicating the features of the original part, yet still matching the car. Components of a vacuum cleaner, on the other hand, may preferably match but may well be acceptable even if they do not.

Ownership, duration and dealings

First ownership

The first owner of design right in a design is determined according to a strict order of priority as follows:

(a) if the design qualifies for protection by reference to first marketing, the *first marketer* owns the design right; otherwise
(b) if it qualifies by reference to nationality, then
    (i) if the design was commissioned, the *commissioner* owns the right; otherwise,
    (ii) if it was created in the course of employment, the *employer* owns the right; or
    (iii) if neither of the above, the *designer* owns the right.

Term of protection

Design right comes into existence as soon as the design is recorded (or first marketed, if this is how the design 'qualifies'). The right has a maximum possible period of protection of 15 years from the end of the calendar year in which the design is recorded. However, once articles made to the design are marketed, then the right expires 10 years from the end of the calendar year when those articles were first marketed *unless* the 15-year long-stop term runs out first.

In addition, any person is entitled to obtain a licence of the design right, as of right, during the final five years of the design right's term. If necessary, the prospective licensee can bring proceedings to settle the terms, including royalty to be paid, of such a licence.

As a result of these provisions, the total period of exclusivity for a design which is being exploited commercially is a maximum of five years.

Transactions

Design right can be assigned in whole or in part. An assignment must be in writing signed by or on behalf of the assignor. This can also cover design rights which have not yet come into existence. For instance, if a design has been commissioned, the commissioner could assign its rights in the design before it is produced, and once the designer has produced that design the design right would belong to the commissioner's assignee. It may also be licensed, exclusively or otherwise.

Infringement

Primary infringement

An unregistered design right is primarily infringed by anyone who, without the permission of the design right owner copies the design for commercial purposes to produce articles wholly or substantially to the design. The infringement need not be deliberate – a copy infringes, whether or not the copyist knows that the design right subsists. It is also primary infringement to authorise anyone else to make such copies.

Genuinely independent creation of a similar design does not infringe, and nor does substantially reproducing a design for private purposes.

Secondary infringement: dealing in infringing articles

Certain other commercial activities are also prohibited with respect to articles incorporating a protected design: these are generally referred to as secondary infringement. Knowledge that the article in question is an infringing article is required before a party can be liable for secondary infringement, since they often could not reasonably be expected to know or have cause to investigate the circumstances of design and manufacture. As a result, the protection available against these activities is weaker than it is against primary infringement by manufacture of copies: it is always difficult, and sometimes impossible, to prove what someone else did or did not know.

It is secondary infringement of an unregistered design right, if without the permission of the design right owner, someone: imports into the UK; or possesses for commercial purposes; or sells, hires (or offers so to do) in the course of a business an article which is, and which the infringer knows or has reason to believe is, an infringing article.

An article is an infringing article if its making to that design was an infringement of design right, or would have been if it had been made in the UK. This covers the case where the articles were made by completely unauthorised manufacturers or by licensees whose licences do not cover the UK. Alternatively, it is an infringing article if its making in the UK would have been a breach of an exclusive licence agreement relating to the design. Thus, if the design right owner grants someone else an exclusive licence to manufacture articles to the design in the UK, but then goes ahead and manufactures them themselves, the resulting products will still be infringing articles.

Substantiality

Both primary and secondary infringement require that the alleged infringement comprises articles exactly or substantially to the design. Since design right subsists in individual *aspects* of shape or configuration of an article, for any given article, a bundle of design rights may protect various aspects of the shape and/or configuration. Each of these may be separately infringed, or not. This gives the rightholder a greater degree of freedom in formulating any allegation of infringement, and care should be taken to specify which aspects are protected and which have been infringed rather than relying upon an allegation of infringement of rights in the article as a whole.

What amounts to a substantial copy is considered through the eyes of the person to whom the design is directed, i.e. the consumer (*C & H Engineering* v. *Kluznik (F) and Son Ltd* [1992] FSR 421). If the design of the accused product looks substantially the same to the likely purchaser, then it is a substantial copy. Features which are commonplace in the design field in question at the time of creation of the design (and therefore are not protected by design right) are disregarded.

Enforcement and remedies

Either the design right owner or their exclusive licensee can sue over any infringement of the right.

The same categories of remedies apply for infringement of design right as for the infringement of registered and unregistered Community designs.

Recovery of damages for infringement of design right may be limited, however, since only commercial activities will infringe, and damages cannot be awarded for any period of time when the infringer did not know and had no reason to believe any design right subsisted – that is, until notified of the right by the right owner. An account of profits may still be available for that period. Further, if a secondary infringer can show that it acquired the infringing articles innocently (without knowing they were infringing articles) then the damages are limited to a reasonable royalty (CDPA 1988, s.233).

Conversely, the design right owner may have a right to additional damages if the infringement was particularly flagrant or resulted in great enrichment of the infringer (CDPA 1988, s.229).

Overlap with copyright

Unregistered design right and copyright may both subsist in the same article. However, to avoid double recovery of damages for any infringement, insofar as an act would be an infringement of copyright in that work, it will not be an infringement of the unregistered design right, and vice versa (CDPA 1988, s.236). It is not an infringement of the copyright in the design for anything other than an artistic work to make an article to the design: in such circumstances design right will be the right infringed, if either.

For example, consider the design drawings for an artistic sculpture (not industrially exploited). Reproduction of the sculpture (itself being an artistic work) will amount to copyright infringement. Whilst design right may well also subsist in the sculpture it is not infringed by reproduction and the term of protection is thus determined according to the more favourable copyright rules.

On the other hand, if the article in question was a telephone handset (not itself an artistic work), the copyright exclusion bites such that reproduction of the handset would amount to design right infringement but not to copyright infringement.

There is, however, no rule that if copyright is excluded design right must subsist or vice versa – it is possible for a design to fall between two stools and not be entitled to any protection at all.

Threats

The threats provisions in respect of unregistered design right are identical to those relating to registered designs.

5.6 PROTECTION OF DESIGNS BY COPYRIGHT

Introduction

Until the passing of CDPA 1988, copyright was the principal protection available for industrial designs. Making an article in accordance with a design drawing was an infringement of copyright in the drawing. A copy of an article made without seeing any design drawing for it was nevertheless an indirect copy of any design drawing for that document, and therefore an infringement of the copyright in the drawing. Thus, spare exhausts for a car were held to infringe copyright in the design drawing underlying the original exhausts (*British Leyland Motor Corp Ltd* v. *Armstrong Patents Co. Ltd* (above)).

Copyright protection for designs was largely removed by CDPA 1988, which introduced unregistered design right precisely in order to separate the forms of protection for industrial designs from the protection accorded by copyright to artistic works. For instance, drawings or diagrams of or preparatory to industrial designs are likely to be protected as either artistic or literary copyright works, since there is no requirement of artistic quality (*Anacon Corp. Ltd* v. *Environmental Research Technology Ltd* [1994] FSR 659). Using them to reproduce articles according to the design will not infringe that copyright.

The separation was not complete, however. Copyright remains effective protection for designs in two important categories.

Since UK unregistered design right does not protect surface decorations, copyright remains available as a form of protection (alongside Community designs and national registered designs, if the design qualifies) for any purely decorative features applied to the surface of an article. This includes three-dimensional features provided they are included for purely decorative purposes.

In addition, any three-dimensional objects or structures which fall within the definition of artistic works, such as buildings, sculptures and works of artistic craftsmanship, remain protected by copyright rather than design right. Many works of artistic craftsmanship are nominally functional items (such as bowls, vases and couture clothing) which could otherwise qualify as design items. Where, however, they are made by an artist-craftsman with the intent to produce an artistic piece, copyright protection will apply rather than any design right.

Limitation of copyright in respect of designs

Three-dimensional copies

The protection afforded by copyright is in all cases moderated by the effect of CDPA 1988, s.51, the core of the scheme for separation of protection of industrial designs from copyright protection.

Section 51(1) provides that it is not an infringement of any copyright in a design document or model recording or embodying a design for anything other than an artistic work or a typeface to make an article to the design or to copy an article made to the design.

A design document is any record of a design: it may be in written, drawn or photographic form, hard copy or electronic. By 'model' must be meant any three-dimensional mock-up, prototype or other illustration of a proposed design (there is no special definition in the Act). In both cases, the document or model is a design for something – it is not itself the intended end product, and must be intended by its author to be used for the creation of such a product. 'Design' in this context is defined as for unregistered design right, i.e. an aspect of shape or configuration of an article (s.51(3)). There will therefore be some designs which are excluded from protection under design right exceptions, but are also excluded from copyright protection under s.51, leaving no protection at all.

Thus, by s.51 the document retains its copyright but that copyright can no longer be used to prevent the making of an article, unless that design was for an artistic work (such as a building or sculpture) or a typeface. Nor can the copyright be used to prevent the making of design drawings for similar articles, by copying a sample of the original. However, design documents for an artistic work, which will remain protected by copyright, are themselves to be treated as copyright works.

Industrial exploitation of artistic works

Where an object is protected by copyright as a work of artistic craftsmanship or otherwise, such that s.51 does not apply, the extent of copyright protection is nonetheless limited under CDPA 1988 if the work is industrially exploited. By CDPA 1988, s.52, if a copyright work is reproduced by or under licence from the copyright holder in the form of articles made by an industrial process and subsequently marketed (whether in the UK or abroad) then the copyright ceases to be enforceable after 25 years. An 'article' here is an object having some function other than merely carrying the design, whether the same kind of article as the copyright holder has produced or others. An industrial process is defined as the production of more than 50 copies (whether mechanically or by hand) or if the goods are made by machine in lengths or pieces. If the work is a set of 50 or more pieces then each set counts as a single copy.

The limitation to 25 years is intended to align the copyright protection given to industrially exploited works with that available to registered designs.

The limitation of the copyright period under s.52 does *not* apply if the work is of a 'primarily literary or artistic character'. This is defined to include book jackets, calendars, certificates, postcards and greeting cards, dress-making patterns, maps, playing cards and more functional materials such as labels, trade advertisements and coupons. However, even though a work falls within the excluded categories it will only get the benefit of the exemption from the limitation if it is also marketed as an article primarily of a literary or artistic character. In *Fearns (trading as Autopaint International)* v. *Anglo-Dutch Paint and Chemical Co. Ltd* [2007] EWHC 955 (Ch) the benefit of the exemption was withheld from a printed label including a logo which was initially pasted and later lithographed onto tins of paint. The court concluded that the articles being marketed were paint tins which did not fall within the category of printed matter.

Further, some articles such as printed wallpapers apparently falling within the exempted list have traditionally been treated otherwise for the purpose of registration of designs (*Lamson Industries Ltd's Application* [1978] RPC 1) and are therefore unlikely to get the benefit of this exemption.

Works of a primarily literary or artistic character, which include sculptures and wall plaques, medals and medallions, are also excluded from registrability under the registered designs regime. The test for whether or not a three-dimensional object is classed as a sculpture is not clear, but may be whether it is intended for use to create replicas (as in a mould from which further copies may be cast) or not. If the object is intended for use in its own right as a decoration, then it is likely to class as a sculpture and so the restriction on copyright will not apply.

Nor does the limitation apply to reproductions of the artistic work other than in the form of further articles.

Two-dimensional articles and surface decoration

Copyright protection remains most significant in respect of designs for surface decoration of all kinds.

The effect of s.51 in the context of surface decoration remains problematic. If the design drawing shows both the shape and configuration of the article and also proposed surface decoration, the exclusion of protection may bite only on the shape and configuration. Copying the surface decoration either on to the same article or onto another could infringe the copyright (per Mance LJ in *Lambretta Clothing Co. Ltd* v. *Teddy Smith (UK) Ltd*). However the Court of Appeal in *Lambretta* was unfortunately split on this point, with Jacob LJ arguing that it was impossible to separate the surface decoration from the rest of the design drawing, so that s.51 prevented copyright in any elements from being infringed.

This objection is understandable in the context of that case, where the surface decoration consisted only of coloured stripes to be placed on the body and sleeves of track suits, but seems illogical where any more complex surface decoration is concerned, or decoration whose artistic quality is less dependent upon the integration with the shape and configuration of the design in question. The scope of the exclusion will ultimately have to be clarified by the House of Lords. In the interim, Mance LJ's approach has been preferred at first instance in *The Flashing Badge Co. Ltd* v. *Groves* [2007] EWHC 1372, a case relating to graphics on a flashing badge, suggesting that a surface decoration which can readily be identified and separated from its particular substrate on an article, and could be applied to other articles, is not excluded from copyright by the effect of s.51.

Co-existence with registered design

It is possible for a design to have been registered for a product but copyright also to subsist in the design. In these circumstances, the proprietor of the registration is likely also to be the owner of the copyright and is assumed to intend to deal with both rights consistently. Thus, where a licence has been granted or assignment given under the registration by the registered proprietor, any act of the licensee or assignee which would otherwise be an infringement of copyright is taken to have been licensed or assigned along with the registration (CDPA 1988, s.53).

Ownership, infringement and enforcement

The rules governing ownership, infringement and enforcement of copyright in designs are the same as those for any other category of copyright, discussed in **Chapter 2**.

CHAPTER 6

Confidential information

Lorna Brazell

6.1 INTRODUCTION

Trade secrets and other confidential commercial information

Trade secrets are a particular case (i.e. material warranting particularly strong protection) of the broader category of confidential commercially valuable information. This is an important category, encompassing many things which fall outside the areas protectable by the intellectual property rights. Classic examples of information which may be protected by confidentiality include:

(a) minor (that is, unpatentable) innovations to a product or process;
(b) commercial details such as business plans and customer lists; and
(c) the 'know how' which may be necessary to maximise the efficiency of any kind of industrial or commercial operation.

Whether any particular example of these will qualify as a true trade secret in practice, is a question of fact and degree. Any kind of confidential information may have value to a business, however. Thus, it may be worth taking steps to ensure that the information is not disclosed or made available to competitors to use.

Although the category is broad, it is not all-inclusive. In particular, merely describing or labelling something as confidential does not mean that it actually is, or that a court will recognise it as such even if an express contractual obligation to keep it confidential is imposed. One person's trade secret is another person's general background knowledge, or may seem to the recipient to be too trivial to warrant secrecy. The information must genuinely have the quality of confidentiality for any protection to be available.

Confidentiality and privacy

The rise of the celebrity culture has caused a separate body of case law to evolve looking at the extent to which personal information may be protected either by the law of confidentiality or under the Human Rights Act (HRA) 1998 by way of a claim to privacy.

For many celebrities, information about their personal lives has commercial value and is exploited for that value, causing the law of confidence to stretch, sometimes uncomfortably, between the realms of family and the rights of the individual, and commercial law. This is unfortunate since the issues raised in the two contexts can be fundamentally different and the tensions that gives rise to are causing difficulties in the development of the law. In particular the decision of the House of Lords in *Douglas* v. *Hello!* [2007] UKHL 21, addressing the very specific and unusual set of circumstances surrounding a celebrity wedding, arguably diverges from principles established in the previous 50 years in respect of commercial confidentiality. However, their Lordships expressed their decision to be based upon the existing principles and it is probable that these will continue to be used in the assessment of when the law of confidentiality will provide protection for information in the future.

Data protection

The laws on data protection also provide some constraints on the use of information, specifically what use an organisation can make of personal data about identifiable individuals which it holds for whatever reason. Although much personal data may qualify as confidential, the principles of data protection cover non-confidential information as well and are framed for a different purpose from the principles governing the law of breach of confidence. This chapter therefore does not cover data protection or the related issues of employee monitoring at work and privacy in electronic communications.

6.2 COMMERCIAL INFORMATION: WHAT CAN BE PROTECTED

Contractual definitions

Even under the law of confidence prior to the introduction of HRA 1998, the question of what information could be protected by an action for breach of confidence was surprisingly problematic. Particularly in the transactional side of legal practice, a tension existed between the contract drafter's instinct to define confidential information by a list comprising every possible form of information which might have some value, and the courts' approach in reviewing the question once an alleged breach had taken place.

Comprehensive definitions do serve one purpose: to put the contracting parties on notice that information falling within them may be considered by one party or the other to be confidential, thereby ensuring that a reasonable person standing in the shoes of the recipient would realise that it might be confidential. Such awareness is a critical issue in the legal test to determine if the information would in practice be protected. But this definitional approach cannot render protectable information which, by virtue of its triviality or its widespread public availability, is not in fact confidential as the courts understand the term.

A pointer to a more principle-based approach can be obtained from European law governing transactions involving confidential information. The Technology Transfer Block Exemption Regulation (TTBE) (Commission Regulation (EC) No.772/2004 of 27 April 2004 on the application of Art.81(3) of the Treaty to categories of technology transfer agreements), discussed in **Chapter 8**, covers licences of know-how, which it defines as 'a package of non-patented practical information, resulting from experience and testing, which is secret, substantial and identified' (Art.1(1)(i)). For this purpose:

(a) 'secret' means that the information 'is not generally known or easily accessible';
(b) 'substantial' means that the information 'is significant and useful for the production of the contract products'; and
(c) 'identified' means that the information 'is described in a sufficiently comprehensive manner so as to make it possible to verify that it fulfils the criteria of secrecy and substantiality' (TTBE, Art.1(1)(i)(i)–(iii)).

These definitions provide a valuable guide to characterising information, whether technical or purely commercial, as truly confidential or otherwise. The information needs to be both significant and useful: there are materiality and utility standards to be considered. Further, the information needs to be identified in enough detail for it to be possible to verify that it is secret and substantial. In contrast, a comprehensive list of types of information will almost certainly include within the definition numerous items of information which on a common sense view are neither secret nor substantial.

In practice, the receiving party can more realistically be expected to recognise as confidential and handle accordingly identified information, if it is not in principle also expected to treat every other piece of information which may come its way as such. Further, use of an all-encompassing definition risks undermining the disclosing party's right to enforce any obligation of confidence, by appearing to attempt to abuse the fundamental equitable basis of the right. The risk can be allayed by incorporating disclaimers to exclude the most obviously non-confidential material, such as information already in the public domain, or already in the recipient's possession, or subsequently acquired from a third party without breach of confidence. Nevertheless, a more thoughtful approach to defining what information is considered to be confidential in the first place can only enhance the likelihood of it being accepted as such if a dispute later arises.

An accurate definition is particularly important in the context of pre-licensing or acquisition discussions or other negotiations where there is a real possibility that the parties may not conclude any agreement and revert to the status of competitors. In such circumstances the truly confidential information needs to be ring-fenced in the hands of the recipient to the extent of limiting disclosure beyond the negotiating team (and any named recipients necessary to carry out any technical evaluation), restricting transfer of the information onto the recipient's computer network and providing a workable mechanism for the return of all records of the information at the end of the discussions.

Legal definitions

Issues as to confidentiality arise in a wide range of contexts, with the result that there is no over-riding legal test, applicable in all circumstances, to determine whether information can be protected as confidential. For information to be 'of a confidential nature', one test requires that it should be 'some product of the human brain which suffices to confer a confidential nature upon the information' (Megarry J in *Coco* v. *A.N. Clark (Engineers) Ltd* [1969] RPC 41). To be protected, the information had also to have been communicated in circumstances of confidence, creating an equitable duty to respect that confidence on the part of the recipient.

Megarry J's test, which made sense in the context of a commercial dispute over technical information, was accepted as the appropriate approach for nearly 20 years. However, in the decision of the Court of Appeal in the *Spycatcher* litigation (*AG* v. *Guardian Newspapers (No.2)* [1988] 3 All ER 545), neither intellectual input nor communication in circumstances of confidentiality was considered necessary for obligations of confidentiality to apply. *Spycatcher* related to a former civil servant's memoir of his career in counter-espionage. Publication was clearly in breach of the author's obligations under the Official Secrets Act, but took place abroad. The case concerned the Government's attempts to prevent a third party, the *Guardian* newspaper, subsequently publishing extracts in the UK. Lord Goff's analysis, when *Spycatcher* reached the House of Lords (*AG* v. *Guardian Newspapers Ltd (No.2)* [1990] 1 AC 109), was that information can be subject to an equitable obligation of confidence even where there has been no communication from a confider to a confidant.

This analysis appeared to be accepted in principle in subsequent cases. Thus, in order to be protectable under the classic principles of the law of confidence, information must:

(a) be of a truly confidential nature; and
(b) originate or be disclosed in circumstances such that the recipient is placed under an obligation to keep it confidential.

It is evident from this formulation that there will be a range of material which can legitimately be classified as confidential. Some may warrant only temporary protection, or protection from use in a limited class of applications, while other may be protectable indefinitely against all the world. The more complex the information, the more likely it is to embody some product of the human mind which is capable of being truly confidential, but many complex processes and formulae are in the public domain through patent documents and so will no longer be protected in confidence.

Trade secrets

At the top end of the scale, the Court of Appeal (*Lansing Linde Ltd* v. *Kerr* [1991] 1 All ER 418) has roughly defined a trade secret as information:

(a) which is used in the trade or business;
(b) whose dissemination is limited or discouraged by the owner; and
(c) which if disclosed to a competitor would cause real or significant harm to the owner.

The approach shares the essential principles with the European Commission's definition in the TTBE even though it does not tally precisely with it. The key issues are utility, secrecy and substantiality – the potential to cause real or significant harm through disclosure. This definition covers technical secrets, but many other kinds and elements of information, such as plans for discontinuance of old products and introduction of new ones, may fall within it as well.

These definitions are helpful in that they give an indication as to the level of importance of the information: if a business would suffer only embarrassment, or trivial or transient harm as a result of its disclosure, then it cannot be a trade secret as such. However, in order to enforce confidentiality over it, the information must be sufficiently defined to amount to a specific trade secret. A general proposal to 'open a second branch' or 'consider diversifying into home furnishings' is not likely to be protectable; detailed costings, sales projections and negotiations with potential suppliers for such a project are very likely to be.

The requirement of 'use in the trade or business' should be interpreted broadly. Clearly, research work into technologies which have not yet been patented and are still further from being developed into commercial products, would merit protection as trade secrets for as long as they remain on the development path. Their disclosure would certainly cause real harm, by giving a competitor a clear insight into planned future products and potentially enabling them to prepare to launch before the originator had finished work, without much of the cost.

Limited disclosure by the person in possession of the information may not immediately result in it losing its confidential status if public access to the information is in fact limited. It will, however, undermine the prospects of asserting trade secrecy in the future by undermining the credibility of the argument that the owner discouraged its dissemination. Circulation of information to a large group of shareholders, for instance, is likely to prevent a subsequent claim of confidentiality from succeeding.

Other confidential information: the 'necessary quality of confidence'

PRINCIPLES

Information may be of a truly confidential nature if it has 'the necessary quality of confidence . . . something that is not public property and public knowledge' (Lord Greene MR in *Saltman Engineering Co. Ltd* v. *Campbell Engineering Co. Ltd* [1948] 65 RPC 203). This sets the threshold for confidentiality very low. But there is still a threshold, and the test for what information qualifies has objective as well as subjective elements. It is necessary but not sufficient that the possessor of the information considers it to be confidential; it must in addition not in fact be publicly available *in the relevant commercial sector*, and there must be some advantage to the possessor from the information remaining secret. Further, these issues must be judged in the light of the practice of the industry concerned (*Thomas Marshall* v. *Guinle* [1978] WLR 116). Information may be common knowledge in one industry and unheard of in another; its use in the latter could then be protected by the law of confidence.

Information need not be either complex or voluminous to be confidential. Conversely, an extensive compilation of non-confidential items of information will not necessarily acquire the character of confidentiality. The circumstances of compilation, or the criteria used for selection and compilation, must amount to a mental or physical process sufficient to confer that additional level of value. Genuine preparations to publish the information commercially, or sell or license it, will support a claim that it is truly confidential, since otherwise how could it have commercial value?

Describing a document as confidential, even where care is taken to maintain the secrecy of the contents, will not turn a piece of information which is not inherently capable of being confidential into confidential information. A summary of a publicly available document, even if marked 'confidential', cannot be protected from use or disclosure if in fact its contents add nothing (such as opinion or commentary) to the public version which is widely consulted. Similarly, requiring employees to enter into an undertaking as to the confidentiality of their employers' business information will not render the day-to-day trivia of the business protectable if it has no technical or commercial value to start with. This mistake is commonly made: the sense of outrage provoked by, for instance, a departing employee setting up in competition, leads otherwise rational businesspeople to attempt to prevent the use of information which is commonly known, simply because it was being used in their business and the departing employee learned it there. This can be counter-productive, leading the court to the view that there is little or nothing worth protecting, when a more selective approach might have inculcated the opposite view (*Faccenda Chicken* v. *Fowler*, discussed at **6.4**).

The issue is one of fact and judgement in every case. In many cases (the formula for Coca-Cola, for example) the value of the information, and its confidentiality, is easy to recognise. Characteristically, however, disputes arise about allegedly confidential information which is only one step away from the public domain. It is these marginal cases which are difficult to categorise.

INFORMATION DERIVED FROM PUBLIC SOURCES

There does not have to be anything secret about the starting materials, for information derived from them to be confidential. Where the starting elements are commonplace, however, the resulting information will normally need some degree of distinctiveness for it to be recognised as confidential. There has to have been some input of the human mind which, going beyond the simple assemblage of items of public knowledge, transforms the total into something of greater value (*Saltman Engineering* v. *Campbell* (above)). For example, an initial idea for an all-night night club with separate areas for socialising and dancing was held not to be sufficiently distinctive to be protectable, even when implementation of the idea resulted in the distinctive London club 'Ministry of Sound' (*De Maudsley* v. *Palumbo* [1996] FSR 447). The commercial success of Ministry of Sound derives not from the high level concept, but from the details of implementation: interior decoration, quality of DJs, door policy leading to an atmosphere of exclusivity and the like. These details, the product of thought, market knowledge and judgement, could certainly have been protected by confidentiality, but the general concept could not.

Where information is already in the public domain, it is unlikely (although not necessarily impossible (*Schering Chemicals* v. *Falkman Ltd* [1982] QB 1)) to be possible to enforce an obligation of confidentiality over it. It is possible to impose a contractual condition in a contract for hire that the product will not be reverse engineered(*KS Paul (Printing Machinery) Ltd* v. *Southern Instruments (Communications) Ltd* [1964] RPC 118). But in a recent case where the claimant argued that the defendant distributor breached a contractual obligation of confidence by analysing the components of the claimant's product and producing its own version, the court held that there could have been no breach of confidence since the key information was in the public domain in the form of a patent application filed by the claimant. The decision was upheld by the Court of Appeal, although Jacob LJ giving the leading judgment declined to comment upon the extent to which information in the public domain could nonetheless be confidential, commenting that it is a difficult legal point (*EPI Environmental Technologies Inc. & Anr* v. *Symphony Plastic Technologies Plc* [2006] EWCA Civ 3).

The crucial distinction here is as to exactly what information is in the public domain. The fact that information may be obtainable from the public domain by for instance measuring or analysing a product publicly available does not make that information itself automatically public: effort would be required for an interested person to obtain it, whereas someone privy to (for instance) engineering drawings need make no such effort. In these circumstances, a recipient of the information should not be allowed, by virtue of their breach of confidence, to get a head-start or 'springboard' over the rest of the population in using the information. If, on the other hand, the information publicly available is sufficient so that no additional work is needed by other interested parties, such as should be the case where a patent application has been published, then the recipient of confidential information gets no springboard and accordingly will not be restrained from using it.

The springboard argument is applied even if the confidential information is later published: the recipient may still be restrained even after the public in general are free to use the information – at least for the period for which the headstart they have obtained might have produced an unfair commercial advantage.

The same test can be applied where a partial disclosure of the information has taken place, by whatever means, to evaluate whether the information has by that disclosure lost the 'necessary quality of confidence'. If the information disclosed is sufficient for the public to implement the product or commercial development, then the confidentiality may well have been lost. However, disclosure only to a limited number of people, or of only a portion of the information such that to reconstitute the whole would still take material effort, will not destroy the confidentiality of the package of information as a whole. Once again, it will be a question of fact and degree how wide the disclosure can have been before confidentiality is lost. Publication on a website might suffice – but not if it was a subscription-only website with a limited number of users and was in fact only accessed by one or two people before being removed. In such circumstances it is clearly still arguable that the interested public at large has not obtained effective access.

Of course, disclosure to any number of recipients, each subject to an obligation of confidentiality, will not cause the confidentiality to be lost.

Derivative information

Information developed through application of confidential information, but which no longer comprises much of the original information itself, is a particularly difficult category. Since an action for breach of confidence is normally based in equity, it is apparent that the conscience of a person who has used confidential information to derive a new formula or develop a new business plan may still be tainted even though their end product contains none of the original information.

Use of such derivative material will breach the confidentiality of the original material if the derived material can be said to be a disguised embodiment of the original. However, even if the original information is still confidential, it will not always be true to say that the derived material is an embodiment of it; there will be a point of remoteness where the relationship is too tenuous to support such a claim. For example, in *Ocular Sciences Ltd* v. *Aspect Vision* [1997] RPC 269 Laddie J considered the design and manufacture of contact lenses by a company established by a group of former employees of a competitor. Whilst it was certainly the case that details of the former employer's designs were confidential, the new designs had moved beyond merely disguising the original information: they did not incorporate any confidential details from them and were not produced using any process which was exclusive to the former employer in the sense of being more than a variant on known techniques used by a number of competitors in the field. The claim therefore failed.

6.3 PRIVATE PERSONAL INFORMATION AND ECHR ART.8

Privacy and free speech

The competing interests of respect for privacy and the right of freedom of expression are enshrined in Arts.8 and 10 of the European Convention for the Protection of Human Rights and Fundamental Freedoms (ECHR). This requires a balance to be struck every time publication of private personal information is proposed. The ECHR has been incorporated into law in many of the countries of continental western Europe for half a century. In England and Wales, however, the existing equitable cause of action in breach of confidence is considered to be flexible enough to meet society's need for protection from its own interest in others' private affairs. In the circumstances, Parliament has never deemed it necessary to introduce any specific provision on privacy.

The incorporation of the ECHR into English law by way of the Human Rights Act (HRA) 1998 was controversial in that the ECHR is a creature more of international or civil law systems, relying upon the brief statement of a series of principles, rather than a detailed set of directions leaving only limited room for interpretation by the courts in accordance with the style of the English legislative tradition. Concerns were voiced as to how these principles might be brought to bear on a whole range of areas of law, such as employment and prisoners' rights as well as issues such as free speech. The judiciary themselves warned that litigants should be slow to assert human rights in every possible action, lest the court system be weighed down with creative, but fundamentally unmeritorious, claims bolstered by allegations of human rights issues.

Although HRA 1998 did not of itself bring about the immediate step-change in jurisprudence that some may have looked for, it is now having an impact in conjunction with the evolving law of human rights set out by the European Court of Human Rights in Strasbourg, whose interpretations of the ECHR are to be taken into account in any interpretation of HRA 1998. That Court is itself taking a position more supportive of the principle of privacy, as can be concluded from its ruling that national law must protect a public figure (Princess Caroline of Monaco) against publication of photographs taken of her in public, but going about her private life rather than her official duties (decision of 24 June 2004 in ECHR Case No.59320/00, *Von Hannover* v. *Germany*). The Court held that a State must if necessary adopt measures designed to secure respect for private life even in the sphere of relations of individuals between themselves. Accordingly, national courts, being public authorities bound under Art.6 of the Convention to ensure compliance, are required, as Lord Nicholls put it in *Campbell* v. *MGN* [2004] 2 WLR 1232, to interpret the relevant national law 'to ensure that the State complies with its positive obligation under the Convention to protect private life'.

In *Campbell* v. *MGN* (above), English law took a significant step closer to the protection of privacy as such. Even though the House was split as regards the appropriate outcome on the facts of that particular case, their Lordships unanimously acknowledged that the values of privacy and free speech set out in the Convention now form part of the cause of action for breach of confidence ('better encapsulated now as misuse of private information' according to Lord Nicholls' judgment). The judgment expressly denies that this involves recognition of a high level principle of privacy, even though Lord Nicholls appeared to recognise that 'the right to control the use of one's own image' is now a requirement under the ECHR. The scope of any actual image right was not discussed further in that decision, and was expressly disclaimed by the House in *Douglas* v. *Hello!* [2007] UKHL 21, but the implications of the *Douglas* decision appear in practice to point in a very similar direction, if not beyond – to the control of information about events one participates in. Image rights in some jurisdictions are capable of being the subject of economic transactions well beyond the former applicability of the equitable duty of confidence. It remains to be seen, however, how much further this will be developed in English law through future cases.

What private information is to be protected?

In line with *Von Hannover*, and as suggested *obiter* even before HRA 1998 in *Hellewell* v. *Chief Constable* [1995] 1 WLR 804, even disclosure of photographs taken at a distance of someone engaged in a private act in a public place could now be actionable as a breach of confidence. More pointedly, even details of a person's identity can be protected if the consequences of a breach of that confidence would be sufficiently damaging. In *Venables and Thompson* v. *News Group Newspapers Ltd and Others* [2001] Fam 430 an injunction was granted against publication of the whereabouts and new identities of the recently released Bulger murderers, in view of the real risk that publication could well result in the death of one or both of the applicants. Thus, in apparent contrast with Jacob LJ's difficulty in assessing whether commercial confidential information could be protected if in the public domain, purely personal information obtained from the public domain appears to be accepted to be protectable in some circumstances.

The test is whether the person proposing to disclose the information is in a situation where he or she knows or ought to know that the other person can reasonably expect his or her privacy to be protected (*A* v. *B* [2003] QB 195, affirmed in *Campbell*). If that test is satisfied, then the threat of disclosure can found an action for breach of confidence unless the intrusion can be justified, for instance by reference to the public interest.

If the information is obviously private, then the person concerned can reasonably expect their privacy to be respected. It is only if the information is not obviously private, in the sense that some sectors of society might consider it so but others might not, that it is necessary to go on to consider further. The question here is whether a reasonable person of ordinary sensibilities would find the disclosure of such information *about themselves* offensive (*Campbell* v. *MGN* (above)). It may also be pertinent to take into account the particular circumstances: only a drug addict can meaningfully assess whether publication of information about their treatment would be offensive, since no one else is in a position to know what impact publication might have on a person in that situation (*P* v. *D* [2000] 2 NZLR 591, considered in *Campbell*). This differs from the test of the US and Australian courts, that publication would be 'highly offensive' to a person of ordinary susceptibilities.

The effect would appear to be less certainty rather than more. Formerly, recipients of information could at least ask themselves 'have I been told or given other reason to imagine that this information should be treated as confidential?' If it was possible confidently to answer 'no', then recipients were in a reasonable position to assert that the information, by being now in their possession with no obligation of confidentiality, was no longer confidential even if it once had been – or still was, in other people's hands. The recipients must now ask themselves 'does the person to whom this information relates have a reasonable expectation of privacy in these circumstances?' Although there are obviously circumstances in which this question can confidently be answered either 'yes' or 'no', there is a broad spectrum of uncertainty which is bound to lead to further disputes in the future. Since the personal circumstances of the subject of the information are relevant, it may be 'no' if the person is in any way in the public eye – and it may vary according to how great their celebrity currently is, or has been.

One issue arising is whether private information necessarily relates to a single individual – personal relationships, for instance, necessarily relate to both participants. However, the motivation for potential readers may indicate whose private life is actually of interest and hence the true subject of a disclosure. Where one participant is unknown and the other is a high profile individual, the fact of shared experience will not prevent the details of the relationship remaining the private information of the latter. Further, if the information proposed to be disclosed would not contribute to a debate of general interest, that factor weighs against publication (*McKennitt* v. *Ash* [2006] EMLR 178).

Confidentiality, privacy and commercial value

Exclusives and confidentiality

The question of value was central to the reasoning of the majority (Lords Hoffmann and Brown, Baroness Hale) of the House of Lords in *Douglas* v. *Hello!*. They held that even though the details of the Douglases' wedding were being made public by the exclusive publication in *OK!* of a set of authorised photographs, the residual information (in effect, all other photographic information about the appearance of the wedding apart from the exact details shown in the official photographs) still represented protectable confidential information since *OK!* had been prepared to pay £1m for the exclusivity. Their Lordships further held that the confidentiality was owed to both the Douglases and *OK!* such that the latter were entitled to enforce it, despite having had no presence at all at the wedding. The intrusion into the Douglases' privacy, a cause of action 'shoehorned' (in the words of the Court of Appeal) into the action for breach of confidence, takes economic second place to the breach of a contractually-created obligation of confidence by which the consciences of both *Hello!* and the photographer who took the pictures were held to have been bound despite not being parties to it. In effect, once *OK!* was known to have exclusive rights to photographs of the wedding, an obligation arose of such force that all the world was subject to it.

This radical view was not supported by Lords Nicholls and Walker, who agreed with the Court of Appeal ([2005] EWCA Civ 595) in taking the view that the actual information (the bride's dress, the look of the room and the cake) *was* entirely made public through the publication of the official photographs. Consequently, in the minority's view the action of *Hello!* in publishing unofficial photographs could not breach confidence.

What information remained confidential?

The difference between their Lordships' analyses might have come down to the level of detail at which the information is considered. If 'information about the bride's dress' is considered to be 'was it white, yellow or red?' then clearly the totality of that information was made public by the publication of a single official photograph. If the pertinent information is considered to be 'did the embroidery cover the back of the dress as well as the front?' then the official photograph taken from the front did not publish the information at all. To a dedicated follower of fashion, of course, a hundred details still more minute – the nature of the fabric, the fine details of an embroidered pattern, and so on – may be just as important. A judgement could be made as to whether such fine details are in fact capable of protection by confidentiality or are treated as mere trivia and therefore not capable of protection.

This was not, however, the basis for the majority's decision, which accepted the reasoning of Lindsay J at first instance that the information contained in the unauthorised photographs was confidential simply because those photographs were not publicly available prior to the publication of the relevant issue of *Hello!*, and thereafter focussed solely on the willingness of *OK!* to pay for the exclusive right to photographs. Per Lord Hoffmann at para.120 of the Lords' Opinion:

> I see no reason why there should not be an obligation of confidence for the purpose of enabling someone to be the only source of publication if that is something worth paying for. Why should a newspaper not be entitled to impose confidentiality on its journalists, sub-editors and so forth to whom it communicates information about some scoop which it intends to publish the next day? That does not of course prevent publication by someone who receives the information otherwise than under an obligation of confidence. And I say nothing about cases in which there is a public interest in communicating the information to others or the public at large. But otherwise it is simply information of commercial value.

The effect of this reasoning is that information formerly not protectable in confidence as being too trivial or 'mere tittle-tattle' (even though in any age of possible commercial value to gossip columnists) may now be able to found an action for breach provided that the claimant can satisfy the court that some commercial value may have attached to it.

The special status of photographs

The decision in *Douglas* v. *Hello!* may also reflect the recognition of a special status for personal information in the form of unauthorised photographs. In

Theakston v. *MGN* [2002] EWHC 137, QB, the judge accepted that even though the fact that Mr Theakston had been to a brothel and the details as to what he did there were not to be restrained from publication in the form of verbal description, the publication of photographs taken there without his consent 'could still constitute an intrusion into his private and personal life and would do so in a particularly humiliating and damaging way'. Likewise, the majority in the House of Lords in *Campbell* v. *MGN* (above) distinguished between photographs as an instrument of invasion of privacy and all other means. In that case Lords Hope and Carswell and Baroness Hale seem to have felt that the unauthorised photographs, even though in no way objectionable in themselves (given that thousands of photographs of Ms Campbell in similar street scenes have been published), tipped the balance of her action against the *Daily Mirror* in her favour. They recognised the probable impact on her ability to continue with her therapy at Narcotics Anonymous because of her feeling, reasonable in the circumstances, that her attendance was now subject to secret, public scrutiny.

The distinction was relied upon again by the Court of Appeal in *Douglas*. Photographs:

> enable the person viewing the photograph to act as a spectator, in some circumstances voyeur would be the more appropriate noun, of whatever it is the photograph depicts. As a means of invading privacy, a photograph is particularly intrusive.
>
> . . .
>
> Insofar as a photograph does more than convey information and intrudes on privacy by enabling the viewer to focus on intimate personal detail, there will be a fresh intrusion of privacy when each additional viewer sees the photograph and even when one who has seen a previous publication of the photograph, is confronted by a fresh publication of it. To take an example, if a film star were photographed, with the aid of a telephoto lens, lying naked by her private swimming pool, we question whether widespread publication of the photograph by a popular newspaper would provide a defence to a legal challenge to repeated publication on the ground that the information was in the public domain. There is thus a further important potential distinction between the law relating to private information and that relating to other types of confidential information.

The House of Lords in *Douglas* did not expressly refer to any distinction between verbal and photographic disclosure. Nevertheless, their Lordships' assessment in the light of the sum that *OK!* were prepared to pay to have the only photographic record is consistent with an analysis that personal or private information in photographic form may be protected as confidential in circumstances where a mere verbal description would not.

6.4 CIRCUMSTANCES GIVING RISE TO AN OBLIGATION OF CONFIDENCE

Legal test

The reasonable man

Where the circumstances of disclosure are a factor in assessing whether the information is confidential, a good guideline is whether the circumstances were such that a reasonable man standing in the shoes of the recipient of the information would have realised, upon reasonable grounds, that the information was being given in confidence (*Coco* v. *A.N. Clark (Engineers) Ltd* (above)). This adds a helpful element of objectivity (most people can if necessary put themselves in the shoes of the 'reasonable man') but is not definitive. It is necessary to maintain a flexible approach, because of the range of different circumstances in which breach of confidence may be alleged.

Disclosure by recipient

The position of a third party, to whom confidential information is brought by the recipient with a view to dissemination or publication, is difficult. Provided that the third party knows the information to be confidential, they are under an obligation in good conscience not to publish it. If there is a real risk that the information is confidential, for example because of its nature, then even if the recipient does not know that it in fact is either genuine or confidential, caution should be used before publishing (*Sir Elton John* v. *Countess Joulebine & Others* (2001) (QBD, 26 January 2001)). But once the information has been disclosed to the public, then a third party cannot be required to treat it as though it still were confidential.

Use of the information by the third-party recipient may be permitted unless the third party is under some fiduciary obligation to the discloser. Merely taking advantage of another's unsolicited breach of confidence does not amount to any dishonesty or other unconscionable behaviour which would make the third party liable (*Satnam Investments Ltd* v. *Dunlop Heywards & Co. & Others* (TLR, 31 December 1998)).

Where the information has become public as a result of the recipient's own disclosure (as, for example, Peter Wright's publication of his memoirs, *Spycatcher*) it is obvious that the information itself, having worldwide notoriety, can no longer be judged confidential (*AG* v. *Guardian Newspapers (No.2)* (above)). This does not undermine the originator's right as against the recipient – if it could, then all any recipient of confidential information would need to do to be relieved of the obligation of confidentiality would be to publish – but it will affect the remedies available: the owner will only be able to get damages rather than an injunction.

Contractual obligations

If it is expressly written into a contract of employment, or mutual confidentiality or non-disclosure agreement, or stated at the point of hand-over of the material, that particular material is to be treated as confidential, then no reasonable recipient could be left in any doubt as to its intended confidentiality (*Dunford & Elliot Ltd* v. *Johnson & Firth Brown* [1978] FSR 143). An express requirement not to disclose information may be supplemented by an implied term not to use it either (*Thomas Marshall (Exports) Ltd* v. *Guinle* [1979] 1 Ch 227). Even putting up a sign stating that what can be seen in a given area is private can, sometimes, be enough to impose a requirement of confidentiality (*Shelley Films Ltd* v. *Rex Features Ltd* [1994] EMLR 134). But in many situations the information will not be handed over in such a formalised context; for example it may simply be picked up in the course of conversation, or observed on a visit. In such intermediate situations difficult issues can arise.

Practical issues

Where no express requirement of confidentiality has been imposed, then uncertainty may arise as to whether or not the recipient was placed under any obligation of confidence. For example, if the information is common knowledge in the trade, or is treated by the discloser as though it were common knowledge, then it is reasonable for the recipient to assume that they are not being put under any obligation to keep it confidential. Alternatively, the context may be such as to disarm the recipients from any feeling of confidentiality (the ideas allegedly later used for the development of the 'Ministry of Sound' were discussed at a dinner party, such that no-one present had any inkling they were being told in secret). Nor is merely encrypting information enough to give rise to an inference that it is intended to be confidential, if in reality the encrypted information will be legitimately accessible over a long period in a public place, such that anyone with the relevant skills could access and decrypt it (*Mars UK Ltd* v. *Teknowledge Ltd* [2000] FSR 138).

Once again, the conservative approach is more likely to be effective. If all material handed to a visitor is labelled 'confidential', including for instance the directions to the car park, then a reasonable person could quite easily doubt whether that or any of the labelling was intended to be taken at face value and a court is likely to treat all of the claim to confidentiality with scepticism. It is preferable to be selective and apply the label only to material which has some genuine claim to confidentiality.

The holder of confidential information must maintain a high standard of caution, however. Discussion in a public place, for example, or reviewing material on a laptop on public transport raises a risk of being overheard or overseen which could damage the confidentiality of the information. Even information picked up from a police telephone tap is not confidential, on the grounds that 'anyone who utters confidential information must accept the risk of any unknown overhearing that is inherent in the circumstances of the communication' (*Malone* v. *Commissioner of Police of the Metropolis (No.2)* [1979] 2 All ER 620). A private telephone tap, on the other hand, does not necessarily have the same confidentiality-destroying effect (*Francome* v. *Mirror Group Newspapers* [1984] 2 All ER 408).

Regardless of whether an obligation of confidence may be implied because of the special relationship of the parties, it will almost always be advisable in the commercial context to draw up a contract and state expressly what information is to be kept secret, how long the duty is to last, and what limits are placed on the use and subsequent disclosure of such information.

Common situations

Employer–employee: during employment

The relationship of employer and employee is considered to be that of master and servant. Such a relationship implies as a matter of common law a duty of loyalty on the part of the employee, as well as a duty of good faith. The latter obligation of fidelity in itself obliges the employee to respect the confidentiality of their employer's affairs (*Robs* v. *Green* (1895) 2 QB 315), whether or not the contract of employment includes (as they almost invariably do) an express clause binding the employee to keep confidential all information about their employer's business to which they gain access through the course of their employment. The value of including a covenant on confidentiality in an employment contract is that it raises the presumption that the employee was aware what they were handling included confidential information, and that the employer considered it confidential. It will not, however, render confidential information which does not have the necessary characteristics.

A breach of the employee's obligation of confidentiality during the employment may justify dismissal. The court will consider whether the information can easily be isolated from other information which the employee is free to use or disclose; if not, then breach may be treated more leniently.

If a contract of employment already in effect contains no confidentiality clause, it is possible to impose an express obligation of confidence by way of a separate covenant of confidentiality. For any covenant to be enforceable, consideration must pass, even if the covenant is made by deed (*Mitchell* v. *Reynolds* [1711] 10 Mod Rep 130). This may be difficult since the contract is already in effect. The employer can try to argue that the consideration is the disclosure of the information itself, or introduce the new restrictions as part of the new terms and conditions accompanying a promotion. It is not, however, possible to introduce it as part of a salary review making the review conditional upon accepting the additional terms. This may be in breach of the employer's own common law obligation of trust and confidence towards the employee. Still less can an employer tell employees they have to accept a new covenant or be sacked: this can found a claim for unfair dismissal regardless of whether the restrictions sought to be introduced are enforceable or even business critical (*Willow Oak Developments Ltd* v. *Silverwood* [2006] EWCA Civ 660). Such a statement is bound to undermine the employer/employee relationship.

The precise extent of the employee's duty depends upon:

(a) the nature of the particular relationship;
(b) the nature of the information; and
(c) when use or disclosure takes place or is threatened to take place.

THE RELATIONSHIP

The relationship is defined by what the employee is employed to do. Some roles will involve handling confidential information on a day-to-day basis, while others may bring the employee in contact with such information rarely or never. Employees accustomed to handling confidential materials can be expected to be more sensitive to the possibility that information to which they are privy may be confidential. The obligation to keep their employer's business confidential becomes more onerous the more senior the employee's role within the organisation (*Balston* v. *Headline Filters* [1990] FSR 385). At a certain level of seniority, employees may be expected to understand issues such as confidentiality without express direction.

CATEGORIES OF INFORMATION

The way the employee can be required to treat the information depends on its degree of uniqueness and secrecy.

Information available to employees in the course of their employment will fall into one of three legal categories as regards its confidentiality. The first is the mundane trivia of the business, which is not confidential and cannot be made so. Secondly, there is information which does have a confidential aspect, must be kept confidential during employment and may be capable of limited protection even after the employment ends. Finally, there are truly confidential trade secrets: information which is protectable both while the employees remain in employment and indefinitely afterwards. If it is truly confidential, in the sense of a trade secret or other substantial and valuable know-how, then an employee can be expected to handle it more carefully than if it is merely information which competitors could obtain through, for example, employing a competent consultant, or collating information from public sources. It is not essential for the employer to impress the confidentiality upon an employee if the employee is in fact aware.

The mundane aspects of a business can never be regarded as confidential in the true sense, and accordingly employees cannot realistically be required to keep them secret even while they remain employed. This will include all information about the business or industry which is available to the public, either generally or on demand. It will also cover custom and practice in the trade.

Information which has some confidential element can be required to be kept secret from third parties while the employee remains employed. However, its confidentiality may either not be enforceable afterwards at all, or only for a limited period.

Information in this category includes information such as pricing policies and differentials, customers, technology and know-how, and even the names and addresses of other employees to whom the departing colleague may wish to offer future employment. Business policy is unlikely to be protectable, and business methods will need to be broken down into categories of information in order to separate out those which are peculiar to the business in question from those which apply in a variety of different trades or industries. It is also difficult to stop a business method becoming part of the employees' own skill and knowledge, which every employee has the right to take with them upon changing employers.

Even information which falls into the category of confidential and protectable during employment may be disclosed by an employee in certain circumstances by virtue of the Employment Rights Act 1996, s.103 (as amended). If the employee believes that the information tends to show that a person has failed or is likely to fail to comply with a legal obligation, then s.103 permits disclosure, and if the employer's response is dismissal, it is automatically unfair. The legal obligation in question is not limited to public obligations, such as health and safety requirements; it can also cover breach of contract.

In considering disclosures of this kind the court must balance competing interests: those of the employer, in keeping confidential information confidential, and those of the public in bringing the information to light. This is discussed further in the context of the public interest defence at **6.7** below.

To qualify for protection, such a disclosure must be made in good faith, not with the motive of revenge against the employer over some grievance.

PREPARATIONS TO COMPETE AFTER LEAVING EMPLOYMENT

The employee is required by common law to act in good faith and not put him or herself in a position where the duty to the employer may conflict with his or her own interests. However, preparations while employed to set up in competition after departure do not automatically breach this obligation (*Laughton & Hawley* v. *Bapp Industrial Supplies Ltd* [1986] IRLR 245). The precise point where preparations end and activities amounting to competition, with the resulting inequitable use of confidential information, may be hard to define; and may depend upon whether the employee has the status of a director, with the accompanying fiduciary duties, or is merely an employee bound by no more than contractual obligations (*Helmet Integrated Systems Ltd* v. *Tunnard* [2006] EWCA Civ 1735).

Nevertheless, if found to have used confidential information for a competing prospective business while still employed, an employee may be injuncted from using information after termination through breach earlier, to prevent them from gaining a 'springboard' advantage.

Employer–employee: after employment ends

CONTRACTUAL ISSUES

The obligation of confidentiality imposed by the employment relationship can continue in effect after the termination of the contract, to varying extents (as discussed below), although it may cease to be effective if the termination results from the employee accepting a repudiatory breach of contract (*General Billposting Co. Ltd* v. *Atkinson* [1909] AC 118).

In addition to express clauses imposing confidentiality during the employment, contracts of employment often add a post-termination restrictive covenant intended to prevent the employee from either setting up in competition or working for a competitor, for a certain period of time after leaving the employment. This is frequently backed up by having the employee sign such a covenant upon departure. As a matter of law such a reinforcement of the position is unnecessary, but evidentially it can be very useful to demonstrate that the employee realised at the critical point in time that their obligations of confidentiality remained.

As a general rule, a restrictive covenant is more likely to be found reasonable, and therefore enforceable, if it is appropriately limited to a particular geographical area, duration and activities. Restrictive covenants of this type will be held valid only for a period of a year, or two at most. It is important to recognise the competing public interest in employees' freedom to change jobs and to continue to develop their knowledge and expertise for their own, and future employers' benefit. Attempts to impose draconian restrictions on the use of all information are unlikely to be effective since they may be in restraint of trade – and also reveal a degree of paranoia on the part of an employer as to its own ability to compete successfully in the market.

To be effective, the covenant needs to identify the precise information which is said to be protected. This may go wider than trade secrets, strictly defined, but may still not be enforceable if the restrictions imposed on the employee, especially regarding future employment, are unreasonable in view of the extent of use of the information in the public domain and the damage likely to be caused by its disclosure. As ever, these questions need to be considered on a case-by-case basis.

COMMON LAW

The extent of the employee's duty of good faith and fidelity after the employment has ended varies according to the kind of employment. A company has less right to expect continuing confidentiality from an employee whose duties did not include handling valuable confidential information, as the employee will not be expected to have the same kind of sensitivity to the material as an employee whose job regularly involved access to secrets.

This is particularly relevant in the context of information carried away in the heads of departing employees. It is impossible for an employee not to learn a certain amount about their employer's business in the course of their employment. The increasing experience of skilled workers, wherever gained, is likely to augment their existing level of skill in their particular occupation. Information which becomes part of the employee's own skill and knowledge set cannot be required to be kept confidential once the employee has left that employer. Complex or voluminous information is less likely to be absorbed in the course of ordinary duties by the employee; but this also will depend upon the particular employees, their existing professional skills and qualifications and the nature of the job held. To a skilled chemist, highly complex formulae or reaction conditions are simply the kind of information they work with day-to-day and therefore cannot be assumed to be confidential solely on the basis of their technical nature (*Ocular Sciences Ltd* v. *Aspect Vision* [1997] RPC 269).

Any evidence of dishonesty or surreptitious behaviour by the ex-employee, however, will be persuasive that the information really was confidential, and that the employee realised this. If it can be shown that the employee had consciously memorised or copied the information, rather than simply picking it up over time, this will indicate that the information has not simply become part of the employee's general background knowledge. In most cases, this will not be easy to prove unless the employee has actually told another person what he or she is doing.

CASE STUDY: FACCENDA CHICKEN V. FOWLER [1987] 1 CH 117

Faccenda Chicken Ltd was a breeder, slaughterer and distributor of fresh chickens to butchers and caterers, and Mr Fowler was for several years their sales manager. While working for Faccenda, Mr Fowler came up with the idea of distributing chickens by refrigerated vans to a wide area across the Midlands. Each salesman had an area to cover and visited customers at least once a week carrying sufficient produce for each customer's standing order; however, customers were free to take more or less than their usual quantity on any given occasion. Faccenda also charged different prices to different customers.

In December 1980, following an accusation of theft (of which he was later acquitted) Mr Fowler resigned and subsequently set up his own company to distribute fresh chickens in competition with Faccenda. He placed a newspaper advertisement for salesmen and recruited five former Faccenda salesmen – with their detailed knowledge of Faccenda's customers, routes and delivery schedules. Faccenda Chicken sued Fowler, his company and their other former employees for breach of confidence in this information.

The judge was not impressed by the details of the allegedly confidential information. As to the details of delivery routes and schedules, he found that these were clearly not capable of being business secrets in their own rights since they could be observed by anyone who wished to do so simply by following Faccenda's vans. The method of selling from refrigerated vans was part of Mr Fowler's own skill and knowledge, which he could not be prevented from taking away with him. The pricing information was, perhaps, more sensitive, but here it counted against Faccenda Chicken that their claim of confidentiality was to the entire package of information taken as a whole. Given the inclusion of the trivia of delivery routes and so on, the court considered that the inclusion of such items in the package threw light on the claim of confidentiality for the whole, and held the whole to be non-confidential.

Faccenda Chicken remains the leading case but contrasts strongly with the Court of Appeal's decision in *AG* v. *Barker & Anr* [1990] 3 All ER 257, where a very wide confidentiality clause was upheld and enforced through a worldwide injunction despite there being no finding as to whether the particular information which was to be disclosed, concerning the operation of the Royal Household, was of a confidential nature or not. The Court stated that the fact the Royal Family was concerned was irrelevant, but it is difficult to see any other basis on which such a divergent result could be reached.

Independent contractors

The obligations of confidentiality undertaken by an independent contractor are purely a matter of the contract for services without any of the additional obligations of fidelity arising in an employment relationship. It is therefore essential in drafting such contracts to include an obligation of confidentiality from the outset.

The principle in *General Billposting* (above) (i.e. that the obligations of an employment contract will not survive a repudiatory breach) does not apply to the relationship of independent contractor (*Campbell* v. *Frisbee* [2002] EWHC 328).

Potential licensees and collaborators

Information concerning new techniques and products is frequently disclosed in the context of negotiations, where the inventor for example requires additional backing in order to exploit their idea and seeks a development partner or licensee. Although the negotiations may be centrally concerned with one particular invention or idea, discussions may cover a variety of matters not directly connected with the principal subject-matter. It will be a question of fact whether such extraneous material is also confidential between the parties, but generally the courts are prepared to find a broad obligation of confidence in these circumstances.

In *Seager* v. *Copydex* [1967] 2 All ER 415, Mr Seager was in negotiations with Copydex over a possible licensing arrangement for a carpet grip he had invented, known as the 'Klent'. In the course of the negotiation Mr Seager disclosed to Mr Preston of Copydex another carpet grip, but Copydex said that they wanted the original Klent and no more was said. After the negotiations broke down, Copydex applied for a patent for a carpet grip virtually identical to Mr Seager's alternative design, and began marketing it. Mr Preston was named as the inventor, although he had no technical background. The court found that even if it was true that no one at Copydex remembered having heard Mr Seager's explanation, the coincidence between the two grips could only be explained by their having unconsciously used the information he had given them. Given the context of the negotiations over the Klent, it was found to have been given in confidence.

Collaborators and venture partners

A collaboration in the capital markets may involve several parties jointly contributing expertise to formulate financing arrangements and the structure and timing for a deal. The resulting plan may be portable, in the sense that a different consortium of participants can equally well execute it. Although the details of the proposal clearly qualify as confidential information, the individual collaborators have no specific rights in that information. The relationship has no fiduciary aspects, so that a party who pulls out has no right either to obstruct the remaining collaborators from proceeding with the deal or to share in any of the resulting profits (*Murray* v. *Yorkshire Fund Managers Ltd & Anr* (TLR, 18 December 1997). The only way to protect the time and skill invested in formulating such a plan is to execute an express agreement that the deal will proceed with all contributors or not at all.

A similar situation arises at the beginning of a proposed acquisition, where ultimately it may be expected that all of the target's commercial secrets will be disclosed for evaluation. In the light of the possibility that the transaction may not ultimately complete, or not with this particular buyer, the parties may not initially feel the need to enter a full agreement setting out all aspects of the preliminary collaboration. Nevertheless, in the nature of such transactions information is disclosed progressively, such that it can easily transpire that significant information is disclosed while the details of the contract are still under discussion.

Although the equitable duty of confidence would certainly provide some protection, drawing up a confidentiality agreement will help to prove that even the early discussions were understood by both sides to be confidential, which will materially assist if it is necessary to apply for an injunction to prevent misuse or further disclosure. It will thereby act as a deterrent to the recipient against any such disclosure or use, as well as helping the discloser to define what confidential information is being disclosed as the process evolves. This will also assist in any application to injunct further use, provided the definition of the scope of the discussions is sufficiently detailed to back up the claim that the information which passed was truly confidential.

6.5 DURATION

Secrecy maintained

Confidential information can remain confidential indefinitely: for as long as it is kept truly confidential and continues to have value. The European Commission's previous Technology Transfer Block Exemption Regulation (Regulation (EC) No.240/96) allowed an upper limit of five years for any licence of pure know-how, on the assumption that confidentiality could not be maintained for longer than this. This limit has been deleted from the current Regulation.

Disclosure under terms of confidentiality

In order to be exploited fully, however, commercial confidential information often needs to be disclosed. It can be disclosed to an unlimited number of people without losing its confidential character, as long as each and every one of them receives it on terms of confidentiality (*HRH Prince of Wales* v. *Associated Newspapers Ltd* [2007] 2 All ER 139).

Disclosure for a specific, limited purpose will not destroy the confidentiality of information for all other purposes. Thus, disclosure for the purpose of negotiations will not entitle the recipient to use the information other than in the course of those negotiations. Information supplied to professional advisers (e.g. solicitors, accountants and bankers) is received by them subject to strict terms of confidence and only for use in advising the client. Similarly information supplied to officials under any sort of statutory requirement can only be used for the purposes envisaged by the statute. Finally, contractors and sub-contractors who receive information to enable them to carry out their contract will usually also be subject to an obligation of confidence, limiting them from using the information for other purposes.

Expiry of confidentiality

Where disclosure takes place under a contract which provides a time limit, and that has expired and the information become public, confidentiality cannot be reimposed. However, until the information does in fact become public or lose its commercial value by obsolescence it is arguable that a parallel equitable duty of confidence may remain in effect. The point at which this ceases to be effective will be a question of fact in each case.

Thus, in faster-moving industries, a secret may be protectable only for a shorter time since thereafter its value diminishes whether disclosed or not.

An obligation to keep information confidential which is imposed for reasons of public policy will last until that reason ceases to apply.

In employee contracts, a reasonable estimate for the duration of the obligation of confidence after termination of the contract in respect of confidential information (other than trade secrets) is that it may last for a similar period to any restrictive covenant in the same contract.

Once information has ceased to be confidential, it is unlikely to be possible to stop the use of material which has been derived from it, even if it is reasonable on the facts to treat it as a camouflaged embodiment of the original.

6.6 DEALING IN CONFIDENTIAL INFORMATION

Trade secrets, not being legally a property right like the other intellectual property rights, cannot be assigned from one exclusive owner to another in the way that those can. Instead, the best that can be done is for the owner to agree to disclose the secret and all supporting information and materials to the proposed 'transferee', and simultaneously to agree not thereafter to use the information themselves nor to disclose it to any third parties. Thereafter, the new owner's remedy for any leak of the information from the former owner is to sue for breach of contract. It may also be useful to have the right to call upon the former owner to lend their name and assistance in any subsequent action against third parties.

6.7 ENFORCEMENT AND REMEDIES

Breach

An obligation of confidentiality can be breached by either:

(a) using the information outside any permitted purpose; or
(b) disclosing it to others.

Use of confidential information other than for the purposes for which it has been disclosed breaches confidentiality, even where it is not inevitable that through its use the information will be disclosed to any third party. Nevertheless, in order to put the receiving party on notice of this any confidentiality clause should expressly forbid both use and disclosure, whenever either is mentioned.

Who can sue

The action for breach of confidence may be brought by any person to whom an obligation of confidence is owed, and only by such a person (*Fraser* v. *Evans* [1969] 1 QB 349).

Prior to the decision of the House of Lords in *Douglas* v. *Hello!* (above) that person would have been considered to be the party whom the information concerned or in whose possession it was confidential prior to the disclosure. In *Douglas* v. *Hello!*, however, Lord Hoffmann took a broader approach. He treated the obligation of confidence imposed by the Douglases over their wedding arrangements as having been for the benefit of *OK!* as well as the Douglases themselves, even though *OK!* neither participated in the security arrangements for the wedding nor even in the production of the confidential information in the form of the official photographs: the official photographer was hired by the Douglases. *OK!*'s only connection with the wedding was through its contractual arrangement with the Douglases for exclusive access to and publication of photographs selected by the Douglases. Lord Hoffmann observed (para.117):

> The point of which one should never lose sight is that OK! had paid £1m for the benefit of the obligation of confidence imposed upon all those present at the wedding in respect of *any* photographs of the wedding. That was quite clear. Unless there is some conceptual or policy reason why they should not have the benefit of that obligation, I cannot see why they were not entitled to enforce it. And in my opinion there are no such reasons. Provided that one keeps one's eye firmly on the money and why it was paid, the case is, as Lindsay J held, quite straightforward.

Effectively, therefore, the wedding guests owed not only an obligation to the Douglases based upon the personal and private nature of the event to which they were invited, but a further obligation of confidence based solely upon the fact that a third party had paid for the exclusive right to publish photographs. None of the guests had any relationship with *OK!* which could have been abused by their taking of photographs in breach of the ban so as to taint their consciences. Nevertheless, the mere fact that they were on notice that the exclusive contract existed seems to have been enough to bring them within the scope of the law of confidence. The same analysis has also been applied by Lord Hoffmann in *Campbell* to explain the obligation of confidentiality in the classic case of *Prince Albert* v. *Strange* (1849) 2 De G & Sm 293, although he declined to find that by threatening to publish unofficial photographs *Hello!* had interfered in any actionable way with *OK!*'s contractual rights.

Alternative causes of action

The alternative cause of action upon which *OK!* relied (of unlawful interference with contractual relations) was unanimously rejected by the House of Lords. Lord Hoffmann analysed the history of the economic torts and concluded that there are only two such. To be found liable for the first, inducing breach of contract, the defendant must be an accessory to an actionable wrong (breach of contract) committed by another, and to have intended to cause a breach of contract (even if not necessarily intending to cause loss to the parties to the contract). No breach of contract took place in the *Douglas* case since the Douglases had performed their obligation not to permit any other photographer entry; it still has not been established how Mr Thorpe in fact gained access.

The second, causing loss by unlawful means, does not require an associated cause of action in contract. The defendant is liable (if at all) as a primary tortfeasor. But the tort requires that the means used to cause loss be:

(a) intrinsically unlawful; and
(b) of such a nature as to affect the third party's freedom to deal with the claimant.

It also requires intention to cause loss to the claimant. Intention to cause loss includes the case where no specific 'harm' is meant, so will include an action taken not to do the claimant personally damage but simply to maximise the defendant's business. This intention was present in the *Douglas* case in that *Hello!*'s expressed purpose was to fulfil their readers' desire to know about the wedding, and it was apparent that to do so they would necessarily spoil the exclusivity of *OK!*'s feature. But their Lordships agreed that *Hello!* had not done anything which restricted the Douglases' freedom to deal with *OK!* nor used unlawful means – although the photographer had trespassed, it was not at *Hello!*'s instigation.

These actions are therefore rarely effective as an alternative to establishing a breach of confidence as such.

Remedies

Civil actions: preliminary relief

The preferred remedy in civil proceedings will generally be an injunction to prevent the unauthorised further disclosure and/or use of the confidential information. This can be obtained at the outset of proceedings on an interim basis if the owner can establish sufficiently clearly:

(a) the confidential nature of the information;
(b) the existence of a breach or threatened breach of confidence;
(c) that the information is still confidential save for the defendant's use/proposed use of it; and
(d) the likelihood of irreparable damage to the owner's business if the release of the information, or its use, is not stopped before the case gets to trial.

In deciding whether to grant an injunction at an early stage, the court will try to assess on which side the greater potential damage falls, and whether each side can adequately be compensated financially. If an injunction would effectively close the recipient's business until trial, then this factor will tend to reduce the likelihood of an injunction being granted, since the damage may not be capable of being remedied. Additional factors may include considering whether the owner is genuinely interested in control of the information or is primarily concerned with reaping a due reward, or has brought the case oppressively. In such instances, even if the other factors point to the grant of an injunction, the court may refuse it and award damages alone.

Where personal private information is concerned, damages after trial are rarely likely to be an adequate remedy in view of the injury suffered, nor by way of possible deterrent to any newspaper or magazine with a large circulation. The refusal of a preliminary injunction could, therefore, be inconsistent with the court's duty as a public authority, under Art.6 of the Convention, to provide mechanisms for a proper respect to be paid to the right to a private life.

Once an injunction has been ordered, the majority of cases for breach of confidence tend to settle.

A further form of preliminary relief which may be appropriate if the owner has a very strong case will be the search order, discussed in detail in **Chapter 2** in the context of copyright cases. This may enable the owner to act rapidly, allowing recovery of copies of any confidential documents or other materials, pending a hearing between the parties. The same cautions as to the extent of search and the care which needs to be taken in carrying it out apply as there described. Alternatively, if the defendant is a reputable undertaking, then an order for detention, preservation, delivery up or inspection of documents or materials can be sought.

Civil actions: relief after trial

Damages can be awarded for breach of confidence, either instead of or in addition to a permanent injunction. In deciding whether a permanent injunction should be granted, the court will assess the nature of the information, and the nature and extent of the disclosure or use of the information by the defendants. As ever, if the disclosure or use can be quantified and hence compensated in monetary terms then damages may be considered sufficient. If the use made of the information is only limited, then similarly damages may be considered adequate and the imposition of an injunction unwarranted.

In principle if an injunction is granted, orders for delivery up or destruction of materials obtained or made in breach of confidence are also available.

Where the obligation of confidentiality arises from a contract, then the measure of the damages to be awarded will be that which will put the owner in the position they would have been in had the contract been carried out correctly – often the owner's loss of profits up to trial arising from the disclosure and wrongful use of the information. If the claimant would have licensed the information, then the loss will be the licence fees which could have been obtained.

In theory, if the duty of confidentiality arises outside the contractual context, damages can also be awarded to cover future losses, but in practice these will be next to impossible to quantify.

An alternative to damages is an account of profits. This may be appropriate where the owner has not suffered much loss itself, but believes that the defendant has made substantial sums by virtue of using the information.

Defences

The principal defence to an allegation of breach of confidence is to demonstrate that the information was not in fact confidential, or was not obtained through any breach.

Where the information concerned relates to a person's misconduct, then as a matter of public policy, the discloser of 'iniquity' to the light cannot be prevented from making it public or required to pay compensation. Examples include the following.

1. The disclosure by an employee of accounts showing that his employer had been involved in fraud (*Gartside* v. *Outram* (1857) 26 IJ Ch (NS) 113).

2. The disclosure of price-fixing agreements contrary to the Restrictive Trade Practices Act (*Initial Services* v. *Outterill* [1968] 1 QB 396).
3. Use by a firm of solicitors of papers relating to the affairs of a former partner, in bringing proceedings against him for breach of his duty to the partnership.

This rule has now been relaxed somewhat so that it is a defence to show that there was some just cause or excuse for disclosure (*Lion Laboratories* v. *Daily Express* [1985] QB 526). That case concerned the leaking of internal memoranda of the manufacturer showing that the breathalyser used as a basis for criminal prosecutions was often inaccurate. The fact of the inaccuracy was hardly iniquitous, but since the result was injustices perpetrated upon potentially innocent citizens, the disclosure was found to be justified. As with all public interest defences, it is necessary to demonstrate a genuine public interest in the disclosure rather than merely that the information would be of interest to the public (and therefore likely to sell newspapers). As famously put by Griffiths LJ in *Lion Laboratories*:

> there is a world of difference between what is in the public interest and what is of interest to the public.

Further, the disclosure must be made to someone with a proper interest in receiving the information.

Pre-emptive defence: application for declaratory relief

Where a dispute seems likely to arise, the recipient of supposedly confidential information should remember the possibility of applying to court pre-emptively for a declaration, either that the information is not confidential, or that the proposed disclosure or use would not breach any contractual or other obligation. This can, in the right circumstances, be an effective means of avoiding a drawn out and costly legal proceeding.

There are, however, no grounds for obtaining damages for unjustified threats of proceedings for breach of confidence, in contrast to the position in respect of patents, trade marks and designs.

Criminal sanctions

Confidential information is in an anomalous position compared to the intellectual property rights properly so called, in that there are no criminal provisions specifically applicable, and it has fallen outside the scope of the general criminal law. It cannot be stolen, since it does not fall within the definition of 'property'. The confidentiality of information only affects the owner's right under civil law to control the time and means of its publication or use; it does not affect its nature. Thus, an Oxford undergraduate who 'borrowed' a proof copy of an examination paper, read it but returned the actual piece of paper on which it was written, was acquitted since the University had not been permanently deprived of any property (*Oxford University* v. *Moss* [1979] Crim LR 119). (It would have been different if any tangible property had been kept.) It has been argued that borrowing of this kind does permanently deprive the owner of some of the economic value of the information and therefore should be capable of being treated as theft, but so far without success.

Other possibilities include charges under the 1906 Prevention of Corruption Act. This has been used in the situation where attempts were made by bribery or other corruption to obtain disclosure of another's trade secrets. It could, for example, apply if an offer of alternative employment were made specifically for the purpose of obtaining the secrets the departing employee could bring with them. As always, however, where there are reasonable alternative explanations which could explain the offer (as, for example, the employee's own skill and knowledge) it will be very difficult to prove the suspected ulterior motive.

6.8 PRACTICAL STEPS TO KEEP INFORMATION CONFIDENTIAL

Restricting access to confidential information plays an important role in establishing and maintaining its confidentiality. This may include, depending upon the level of secrecy warranted by the nature of the information:

(a) limiting the number of copies made and the persons who may have access to them;
(b) making sure that those employees who do handle the information are aware that it is not to be distributed except to other authorised employees;
(c) stamping each page on which confidential material appears as 'confidential';
(d) distributing copies on a numbered, signed-for basis and keeping copies under lock and key when not in use.

Confidential information in electronic form should at least be kept in access-restricted files, preferably with passwords or other restrictions which are regularly changed and automatically constrained to be difficult to guess (i.e. not common words or names). Highly sensitive information should be stored on a standalone workstation, which may be kept in an access-restricted room and not linked to the internet, rather than on a shared network. It may also help to encrypt it. Transmission of information over the internet increases the risk of its being intercepted and leaking into the public domain, so should be prohibited where information of the status of a trade secret is concerned.

Ultimately, unless the holder is able to show when attempting to assert confidentiality that it has made genuine attempts to keep the information confidential then the claim is that much less likely to succeed. Labelling alone is not necessarily sufficient, particularly in view of the common tendency to exaggerate what information is to be treated as confidential. It is a balancing exercise in each case: just how much value the business puts on retaining exclusivity over the information, is illustrated by how much effort it is prepared to put into keeping it truly confidential. If the owner appears to have thought that the information does not merit the effort to keep it secure, then the level of protection a court will be prepared to give it may well be proportionately low.

CHAPTER 7

Intellectual property and commercial and corporate transactions

Sally Shorthose

7.1 INTRODUCTION

Transaction drivers

In this chapter, consideration will be given to the means by which the value in intellectual property can be leveraged and exploited.

Patents have long been seen as valuable (or invaluable) assets of a business, to be developed, protected and exploited. In the last couple of decades, the value of trade marks has finally become recognised in the accounts of brand-driven companies. Increasingly companies are moving towards exploitation of their intellectual property (notably patents but other types of intellectual property also) using ever more diverse models of collaboration and external sources of technology: not only by incorporating these inventions or rights into their own processes or products and services but also by licensing them out to third parties. The quid pro quo of such licensing out is that a collaboration may also result in a licensing-in of technology which will fill an otherwise unfilled hole in a portfolio or may provide a platform or springboard to greater things.

The process of licensing in and out is most traditionally prevalent in hi-tech industries such as pharmaceuticals and biotech, where big pharmaceutical companies have needed to back-fill their intellectual property portfolio by licensing in technology, or indeed by acquiring technology-rich companies. But, increasingly, international firms in all industries will seek to find partners throughout the world either to develop technology together with that third party or otherwise to operate through them, thereby exploiting to the maximum the relevant technology. As firms are increasingly open to novel models of innovation based on collaboration and external sourcing of technology, expertise and knowledge, they are exploiting their patents, and other intellectual property in a wider variety of ways.

Licensing is an important channel for disseminating knowledge and facilitating the cross fertilisation of ideas; a well-operating (i.e. one where the benefits are enjoyed by both licenser and licensee) technology market can improve the innovation and development processes by facilitating exchanges of patented inventions (whether by assignment or licensing). Another advantage of an open and commercial technology market is that the new inventions are most likely to end up in the hands of those most well-suited to commercialise them.

Issues to consider

The transactions identified above are frequently complex, and could well form the subject of a handbook in their own right. Within the confines of a single chapter, it is not possible to address them in any great detail and instead, this chapter will focus on the key issues which must be considered and the key categories of agreement in which intellectual property issues are likely to be prominent.

In order to establish a good platform for exploitation of intellectual property, the owner (or indeed the purchaser or licensee of intellectual property) will need to determine the following.

1. *Ownership.* This is not always straightforward, as employees, contractors or collaborators may all have a call on the intellectual property which is the subject of the transaction. Before embarking on a transaction, whether a sale, acquisition or collaboration, it is essential to identify all the applicable intellectual property rights, to establish who owns these and then to secure them.
2. *Assignment or licence?* There are advantages and disadvantages in each route, and the choice will be dependent on many factors.
3. *Exclusive, sole or non-exclusive licence?* Assuming licensing is the route to follow there are decisions to be made about whether the licence should be exclusive, sole or non-exclusive.
4. *What type of agreement?* How far down the technology food chain is it intended that the licence will operate? It could be research only, research and development, manufacturing, supply and distribution, franchising or a fully fledged joint venture.
5. *What should be included?* What particular clauses should be included in order to maximise the benefit of the exploitation?

Each of the above is considered below.

7.2 OWNERSHIP ISSUES

Employees

General principles

Much significant intellectual property will be created by individuals who are also employees. This intellectual property could be a patentable invention, whether related to a new product or manufacturing process, valuable know-how which must be kept confidential, copyright in creative material or software, designs or trade marks.

The general rule in the UK is that the employer owns the fruits of the work of its employee. The relevant UK statutes, discussed in the separate sections on each category of right, each give an employer automatic ownership in patents (with qualification – see below), copyright, database rights, unregistered designs and registered designs in works created by its employees. However, the operation of obtaining ownership is not the same in relation to all rights, and TMA 1994 is silent on the subject, so they must be considered in turn. The regime relating to the ownership of patents and employees is particularly complex and is worthy of particular consideration.

Ideally, the situation will be clarified from the moment the employee's employment commences, by including unequivocal language in the employment contract to ensure that intellectual property rights arising from work done by an employee during the course of employment automatically belong to the employer. Disputes can arise regarding ownership of rights which are created outside of office hours, or using the employee's own resources, or where the invention was created outside the scope of the employee's normal duties.

Patents

The principles as to which patentable inventions will belong automatically to the employer are discussed in more detail in **Chapter 4**. Note, however, that PA 1977, s.42(2) renders unenforceable any term in an employment contract which 'diminishes the employee's rights in inventions . . . made by him . . ., or in or under patents for those inventions or applications for such patents'. Whereas the rule in relation to most intellectual property rights is that such rights are automatically vested in the employer, with patents, the outcome can be determined by the seniority of the employee and the extent to which the employee is employed to make inventions. Section 39 of PA 1977 (which goes into significant detail on this issue) and ss.40 and 41 provide that an employee is entitled to compensation for inventions 'of outstanding benefit'. Although the clause in the employee's contract can make express provision relating to the ownership of patentable inventions, this right to compensation cannot be overturned.

Trade marks

Trade marks created by an employee are not dealt with by TMA 1994. However, an employer may notify the Trade Mark Registry that a pending application has been wrongfully applied for by an employee trying to appropriate the employer's brand, and the Registry can reject that application, either on the basis of bad faith, or on the basis that the employer has already built up goodwill in the brand. Once again, the ideal solution would be to ensure that the issue is dealt with unequivocally in the employment contract.

Copyright

Section 11(1) of CDPA 1988 provides that the author or creator of a work is the first owner in copyright in it. However, s.11(2) provides that in the absence of any agreement to the contrary, copyright created in literary, dramatic, musical, artistic and film works by an employee vests in his or her employer. Other works, such as sound recordings, films or broadcasts are not covered by s.11(2) and an express assignment of such rights (in writing, to comply with the provisions of CDPA 1988, and to include an assignment of future copyright in works) should be included in an employment contract.

Once again, disputes can arise out of the difficulty of assessing whether the work was created during the employee's employment and appropriate wording – especially in relation to the employee's job description – should be introduced to clarify any uncertainty in this regard.

In addition to copyright, 'moral rights' arise in favour of most creators of copyright. These rights (such as the rights of 'paternity' and 'integrity') have very limited commercial value and are non-assignable, so they cannot be transferred to the employer, but an employee can in writing waive these rights and therefore relieve the employer from the burden of asserting them. Such a waiver is recommended.

Designs

The rules regarding ownership of UK designs follow closely those relating to copyright – RDA 1949 provides that the employer is entitled to apply for and then own a registered design created by its employee, and CDPA 1988 provides that, subject to the right of any commissioner, the employer is the first owner of any unregistered design right in designs made by an employee in the course of his or her employment. As with provisions regarding copyright and patents, it is important adequately to set out the scope of the employee's duties and responsibilities so that it will be clear whether the design was indeed created during the course of the employee's employment.

Similarly, rights in Community designs will vest in the employer if the design is created by an employee in the course of employment.

Confidential information and know-how

Know-how is not strictly an intellectual property right as such because there is no 'property' per se to own. It is advisable to make express provision for protection of the employer's confidential information, both during and after the term of employment. There are limits to the information which can be protected after employment, as seen in *Faccenda Chicken Limited* v. *Fowler; Fowler* v. *Faccenda Chicken* [1986] 1 All ER 617 (see **6.4**)) where it was held that confidential information concerning an employer's business acquired by an employee in the course of his service could be used after his employment had ceased, unless the information was classed as a trade secret. Unfortunately for the employer, a customer list was held not to comprise a trade secret in the circumstances of that case, and the ex-employee was entitled to use the same.

Once again, the seniority of the employee may affect the type of information which will qualify as a trade secret. The employee in the *Faccenda* case was not senior. If an employee is senior and therefore more likely to be privy to trade secrets, or is directly involved in research and development activities, the information he or she acquires is much more likely to be treated as a trade secret (*SBJ Stephenson Ltd* v. *Mandy* [2000] FSR 286).

A word of warning, however: provisions which would have the effect of preventing such employees from earning their living after termination, or attempting to force them to treat as confidential material which would not normally enjoy the quality of a trade secret will generally be seen as too restrictive and unenforceable.

Domain names

Domain names are again not strictly intellectual property rights, but tend to be dealt with under the intellectual property auspices. A domain name may be registered by an employee in his own name but there are clear procedures (such as the Uniform Dispute Resolution Procedure, discussed in **Chapter 10**) which an aggrieved employer can take, to resolve a dispute regarding a registration by an employer. It is likely that if the registration has been carried out in bad faith or has for example involved the employer's trade mark, then the employer will be able to succeed in reversing that registration.

Drafting suggestions

In summary, the following drafting suggestions should be kept in mind when a contract of employment is drawn up.

1. Clarify the job title to ensure that the scope of the employee's responsibilities is unequivocal, so that both the employer and the employee can be clear whether intellectual property has been created during the course of the employee's employment. Although it is tempting to ignore an

employment contract once completed, the description of duties should be kept up to date.

2. Definitions: include careful and appropriate definitions to deal with the following:
   - 'confidential information';
   - 'inventions'; and
   - 'intellectual property rights'.
3. Intellectual property provisions:
   - compulsory disclosure of inventions (regardless of when or how made);
   - further assurance clause regarding securing patent protection;
   - assignment of copyright (including future works);
   - waiver of moral rights;
   - appointment of the employer as attorney;
   - non-imperilment of intellectual property rights.
4. Confidentiality:
   - cover period of employment and afterwards;
   - disclosure provisions;
   - exclusion on usual terms of public domain information.
5. Restrictions should be adapted to the particular circumstances of the employee and (in order for the restrictions to be enforceable) it should be ensured that they are not overly wide in terms of time, location and subject matter.

Contractors and consultants

It is a common misconception that intellectual property created by a contractor or consultant will be owned by the business or person who has employed that contractor or consultant. This is far from the norm (as opposed to the situation relating to employees, where the norm is for the employer to own the inventions of its employee where the same is made in the course of his or her employment), as will be demonstrated below.

Copyright

Copyright in commissioned works will be owned by the creating contractors, even if those contractors have been expressly commissioned to carry out the creation of those works. Many a business has discovered to its cost that it has no rights to a website or computer program, creation of which has been commissioned by that business and carried out by a consultant, since the contract establishing the commission did not provide for the assignment of the copyright in the commissioned material to the commissioner. In addition to computer programmers, this can affect freelance photographers, designers and portrait artists, all of whom will be the author of a work and therefore, in the absence of contractual provision to the contrary, the owners of copyright in that work.

If it is not intended that the contractor should own the work, then an assignment should be included in the contract for services/terms of engagement, dealing with the assignment of future works. If, for whatever reason, it is not intended that the copyright should be assigned, clearly the commissioner is going to require a licence to use the work. The scope of this licence must be wide enough to cover any use the commissioner needs to make of the work, and any other terms such as rights to assign that licence, or to sub-license it, should be spelled out, together with any financial terms relating to such use.

From time to time, a court may imply terms into the terms of a contract for the purposes for business efficacy, i.e. when it is reasonable and equitable so to do and where the terms are obvious, capable of clear expression and do not contradict any express terms. If therefore the terms of engagement are silent as to copyright, the court can in principle imply a licence or even an assignment of that copyright, to the commissioner. The nature and terms of such implied licence or assignment will often be determined by the value of the contract – the higher the price paid, the more likely an assignment will be implied, or the wider the terms of any implied licence. The effect on the contractor will also be taken into account; a consequential loss of capacity to enforce the copyright against infringers, to license others, or to use the work himself in subsequent assignments affect the scope of any implied licence to the commissioner. The court will also try to interpret the intention of the parties in relation to the scope of the licence. For example in *Andre Durand* v. *Marlo Molino* (unreported, 30 July 1999) the copyright in the commissioned portrait of the owner of the commissioning chain of restaurants remained with the artist and the implied licence was limited to the declared use – hanging the original in the restaurant and reproducing it in menus.

As was seen in the case of *Robin Ray* v. *Classic FM plc* [1998] FSR 622, the courts will imply only the minimum necessary to effect the business efficacy and a full assignment is most rare. This was a particularly instructive case in the area of copyright created by contractors. Nine propositions were set out as to the terms to be implied in any commission of copyright work:

(1) the Contractor is entitled to retain the copyright in default of some express or implied term to the contrary effect;
(2) the contract itself may expressly provide as to who shall be entitled to the copyright in work produced pursuant to the contract. Thus under a standard form Royal Institute of British Architects ('RIBA') contract between an

architect and his client, there is an express proviso that the copyright shall remain vested in the architect;

(3) the mere fact that the contractor has been commissioned is insufficient to entitle the Client to the copyright. Where Parliament intended the act of commissioning alone to vest copyright in the Client e.g. in the case of unregistered design rights and registered designs, the legislation expressly so provides . . . In all other cases the Client has to establish the entitlement under some express or implied term of the contract;

(4) the law governing the implication of terms in a contract has been firmly established . . . in *Liverpool City Council v. Irwin* [1977] AC 239 . . .

(5) where (as in the present case) it is necessary to imply the grant of some right to fill a lacuna in the contract and the question arises how this lacuna is to be filled, guidance is again to be found in *Liverpool* . . . in deciding which of various alternatives should constitute the contents of the term to be implied, the choice must be that which does not exceed what is necessary in the circumstances . . .;

(6) accordingly if it is necessary to imply some grant of rights in respect of a copyright work, and the need could be satisfied by the grant of a licence or an assignment of the copyright, the implication will be the grant of a licence only;

(7) circumstances may exist when the necessity for an assignment of copyright may be established . . . these circumstances are, however, only likely to arise if the Client needs in addition to the right to use the copyright works the right to exclude the Contractor from using the work and the ability to enforce the copyright against third parties . . .;

(8) if necessity requires only the grant of a licence, the ambit of the licence must be the minimum which is required to secure to the Client the entitlement which the parties to contract must have intended to confer upon him . . .

(9) the licence accordingly is to be limited to what is in the joint contemplation of the parties at the date of the contract and does not extend to enable the Client to take advantage of a new unexpected profitable opportunity . . .

Moral rights cannot be assigned to the commissioner of work, but the contractor can agree to waive such rights.

Designs and databases

In contrast to the position on copyright, even where a designer is an employee, the commissioner of the design will be the person entitled (by RDA 1949, s.2(1A) and CDPA 1988, s.215(2)) to any subsequent registered design or unregistered design rights in the design. Under Art.4 of the Database Directive 96/9/EC (Directive 96/9/EC of the European Parliament and of the Council of 11 March 1996 on the legal protection of databases), the commissioner of a database will be the maker/author of the database and therefore the owner thereof and as such will be the only person entitled to reproduce, adapt or distribute the same.

Trade marks

Trade marks are most likely to become a problem with contractors if a logo or brand is developed by a third party and inadequate contractual provision was made to secure assignment of all relevant rights (including copyright in a trade mark) to the commissioner. The terms of engagement should deal with this explicitly, as well as clarifying the scope of any licence to the commissioner's trade mark which is necessary to give effect to the commission.

Patents

There is no assumption that, in the absence of any contractual provision to the contrary, patents or patentable inventions will vest in the commissioner. It is therefore essential to provide for full disclosure of all inventions to the commissioner by the contractor. The commissioner will want to include a provision that it is entitled to the full, absolute and exclusive benefit of every work, invention, improvement or discovery arising out of the commission, and that all intellectual property rights will be assigned in the commissioner to the extent that the law does not vest them automatically. In the light of such a clause, the contractor will then hold the same on trust for the commissioner pending formal assignment. Since the obtaining of patents involves various administrative steps, the commissioner will want the contractor to provide a further assurance that it will co-operate in the securing of any protection that may be available to the commissioner in relation to such intellectual property.

Confidential information and know-how

There is no assumption that valuable know-how will be owned by the commissioner of the work. Know-how is not an intellectual property right as such, but know-how can be included within reports which may benefit from copyright – which copyright can be assigned to the commissioner, but will not necessarily provide protection for the information unless the report is the only possible source of it. It is therefore essential in the terms of engagement with a contractor to set out clearly what information is to be treated as confidential and any further restrictions to be applied to its use (or lack thereof).

Existing intellectual property of the contractor

To the extent that existing intellectual property owned by or created by the contractor will be necessary to complete the commission or indeed to enable the commissioner to use or exploit any fruits of the commission, then a licence to use the same must be agreed up front, with clarity as to scope (exclusive, sole, non-exclusive, territorial restrictions, field of use) and any financial terms. The commissioner would normally expect such a licence to include a warranty that the contractor has no other such rights which would affect the ability of the commissioning party to exploit fully the developed technology.

Collaborators

Finally within this ownership section, it is necessary to consider intellectual property issues arising out of arrangements with collaborators. Ideally, the relevant collaboration agreement, whether a research and development agreement, joint venture (commercial or corporate), marketing and distribution arrangement or otherwise, will set out clearly which party has what rights to what technology. The areas to watch are competition law (which is dealt with in detail in **Chapter 8**) and the law which will determine ownership of intellectual property within the collaboration if the agreement is silent on this point.

Background intellectual property and foreground intellectual property

The terms 'background intellectual property' and 'foreground intellectual property' are frequently used and it is important that the meaning and scope of these terms is understood.

'Background intellectual property' comprises intellectual property which is created by a party prior to or outside the scope of the collaboration, and over which normally the other party will gain no rights except for a licence to use or exploit the same for the purpose of the collaboration, or to the extent necessary to use or exploit the foreground intellectual property. It is normal for the licensor of that background intellectual property to give full disclosure of the background intellectual property, subject to the normal confidentiality undertakings.

Foreground intellectual property will comprise the intellectual property created during the course of the collaboration. The intellectual property clause will be key as it sets out the ownership of the foreground intellectual property, the use each party can make of it and any obligations each party will have in relation to disclosure and maintenance/enforcement of such intellectual property rights. In determining ownership, consideration will be made of the respective contributions made to the collaboration and the respective business/scientific interests the parties have. Whilst ownership of background intellectual property will normally remain untouched, the foreground intellectual property can vest in the party responsible for the relevant invention, or the intellectual property can be owned jointly and equally. Section 36 of PA 1977 sets out the position of a patent as to what, in relation to that patent, each owner can and cannot do without the consent of the other. The provisions of s.36 can however be overridden by agreement (*Young* v. *Wilson*

(1955) 72 RPC 31), for example, where only one of the parties is in a position to work the invention. If the provisions of s.36 are to be expressly overridden, then the following should be specifically addressed.

1. Whether the ownership is as tenants in common or as joint tenants (in equal undivided shares). If a joint tenancy, on the death of the co-owner, the surviving owner acquires the remaining share. It is more common to see provision for tenancy in common, which provides that each co-owner's share shall remain discrete.
2. Allocation of responsibility for renewal fees, suing infringers, and resisting revocation.
3. Compulsory licensing provisions.
4. How any income in respect of the patent should be shared.

Co-ownership

Co-ownership of intellectual property is not generally the best route for dealing with intellectual property in a collaboration. More commonly, provision is made for intellectual property to be owned by one party, with provision for licensing to the other. The ownership can be determined by fields of use – one party takes one field of use and the other all others, or one party can take one field of use, the other another, and all other intellectual foreground intellectual property will be jointly owned (subject to the provisos above).

If ownership by one party is agreed, then provision should be made for:

1. assignment of rights as they arise;
2. a structure for notification of inventions or improvements;
3. provision for co-operation from the other party in relation to prosecution and maintenance of patents;
4. payment of costs (these are normally borne by the assignee);
5. a step-in right for the assignor to file patents in territories where the assignee has failed to file;
6. a step-in right for the assignor to take action against infringers if the assignee fails to take steps; and
7. grant back of licence to exploit rights.

Co-ownership of confidential information can also give rise to problems as co-owners of confidential information have wider rights than co-owners of patents and if such freedom is not intended by parties to collaboration, contractual restrictions should be imposed. In *Murray* v. *Yorkshire Fund Managers Ltd & Another* [1998] FSR 372, CA, the court held that in the absence of any agreement to the contrary, where confidential information belonged to a team for the purpose of facilitating a project and one of the team could be excluded from the project, he could not, after his exclusion, prevent the others from using the information as they wished, including disclosure to a third party.

7.3 ASSIGNMENT OR LICENCE?

If an owner of intellectual property decides that its best option for exploiting that intellectual property will be with the co-operation of a third party, it will need to determine whether assignment or licensing is the better route. Licensing, for patents at least, is certainly the most common route for commercialisation, but in certain circumstances, assignment may be preferable. The nature of the intellectual property being exploited will also affect whether a licence or assignment will be more appropriate. It is not possible for example to assign know-how as such – not least because a person or entity cannot 'unknow' something. When in other circumstances an assignment would be the most appropriate route for commercialisation (for example if a company wants to pass on its interest in a business to a third party), what will normally happen in practice is that an exclusive right to valuable know-how will be offered, in exchange from an undertaking from the licensor that it will make no further use of that know-how after the date of the licence.

The following should be taken into consideration in making the decision whether to license or assign.

What is licensing?

Licensing is the grant by the licensor of exploitation rights over intellectual property to a licensee, without surrendering ownership.

Usually the licence will be contained in a legal document in which will be set out the terms upon which the exploitation rights are granted, including performance obligations that a licensee must comply with, as well as maintenance and prosecution obligations on the licensor. Failure to comply with those obligations may lead to the termination of the licence, or a reduction in the scope of the rights from an exclusive arrangement to a sole or non-exclusive arrangement, or, in the case of serious breach, the reversion of exploitation rights back to the licensor.

The key difference between a licence and an assignment is that a licence can normally be terminated. This revocability can provide the licensor with comfort that if the relationship with the licensee or prevailing circumstances change, or if the licensee does not perform, then all is not lost. This can provide a powerful tool in maintaining the efficient exploitation of intellectual property.

What is assignment?

In contrast to a licence, an assignment is normally irrevocable and involves the sale and transfer of ownership of the relevant intellectual property by the assignor to the assignee. The previous owner will have no continuing right or interest in that property. An assignment of intellectual property may be more appropriate if the assignee is better placed to exploit the intellectual property, if the assignor needs an up front payment or if the assignor does not want to be involved in a particular business and finds that the most lucrative and efficient way of commercialising the relevant technology is to divest the relevant business and its assets.

There may be considerable capital value in any patent that is to be assigned – research and development costs (including the costs of creating other inventions which were not patentable), prosecution costs (which may be very substantial, particularly if the patent application was opposed), potentially legal costs if there have been infringements or alleged infringements, either of the patent in question or third party patents, and other costs in maintenance. If these costs are substantial, the receipt of a capital lump sum can be extremely advantageous and attractive to an assignor: he can recoup some of his investment costs and raise capital for future projects whilst leaving the exploitation of the intellectual property to someone else. This is particularly likely if the assignor's strengths are in creation of inventions rather than exploitation of the same, or if a territorial assignment is proposed. The assignor may have no presence in the assigned territory and is advised to hand over exploitation to a local entity. The raising of capital by assignment of intellectual property can be a simpler method than other means such as issuing shares (resulting in a dilution of the assignor's equity) or raising debt capital, as some investors and lenders do not recognise the full value of intellectual property and are likely to discount heavily its value.

Royalties

The requirement or desire for a royalty stream can affect the intellectual property owner's decision as to which route to commercialisation it should follow.

A royalty is normally a payment on the sales of products made or created with the benefit of the patent (or other intellectual property). The royalty will be fixed at a certain percentage per product, and the amount on which the percentage is to be calculated needs to be specified with care. This could be cost, gross sales price, net sales price, or arm's length price even on transfers within a group, for example.

If the intellectual property right owner has a medium or long-term strategy for earning revenue through the payment of royalties, licensing is the most common, and most prudent route to commercialisation. If it is a patent which is being licensed, then royalties are typically (though not necessarily) paid over the unexpired term of a patent (as may be extended by a Supplementary Protection Certificate in life sciences). The licensor therefore has the prospect of deriving revenue from its intellectual property for the life of that intellectual property.

Licensing is preferable to an assignment in this scenario for a number of reasons.

1. In a licence, the failure to pay royalties will be a breach of the licence agreement, and would entitle the licensor to terminate the license. This is an important contractual provision: the licensee will be deterred from breaching the royalty payment obligation, since its breach may result in the loss of the licensed rights. Such a protection could not be achieved by way of assignment, when non-payment of consideration would simply result in the assignment not taking place.
2. The licensor will be able to police the exploitation of the intellectual property by the inclusion of various performance obligations.

There are however downsides to very long licences. The intellectual property owner runs the risk that over that long period there may be:

1. a technical failure;
2. market failure or significant change in market conditions including the entry into the market of a competing product which erodes the royalties that might otherwise have been paid or which renders the choice of the licensee inappropriate or ineffective;
3. regulatory failure (or again, a change in prevailing regulatory conditions) which means sales of the licensed products are far lower than anticipated.

As far as possible, flexibility should be built into the licence to make provision for unexpected changes of circumstance. Such provisions include:

(a) amendment of royalty rates;
(b) a change of the type of licence – e.g. from exclusive to sole or non-exclusive status so that the licensor can limit his financial damage; or
(c) the reference of any resultant dispute to an independent arbiter who can decide the most equitable solution to the problem.

Lump sum payment

Given the uncertainty that can arise from the reliance on royalty payments in a long-term licence, the intellectual property owner may prefer to receive a lump sum payment, at the outset, receiving all the value of the licence in this way on one single occasion only. Clearly the disadvantage of this route is that if the products created using the intellectual property are a huge success (or at least more successful than the scenario anticipated in valuing the price of the unexpired term of the patent value of the assigned intellectual property), then the owner does not share in the financial upside of that success. By the same token, the owner will have the security of being protected from an unexpected failure as long as the owner has complied with the terms of any warranties in the assignment, and provided that there are no clawback provisions in the assignment dealing with the effects of such failure. The licensee's assumption of risk will be factored into the lump sum price, as will a discount for the licensor's having the immediate benefit of a sum of money which, if paid otherwise as royalties, would have comprised over time a greater financial amount.

More rarely, a licence may be subject to payment of a series of lump sums rather than royalties. In such cases, the series of payments will generally, though not always, be regarded by the payer as a lump sum purchase price for the intellectual property and as such on final payment the licensee/person making those payments will seek a permanent and irrevocable assignment of the relevant intellectual property, and will seek to be released from the other terms of the licence.

Where the lump sum payment relates to a shorter period than, say, the unexpired period of the patent, then assignment would be inappropriate, and a licence for the period that relates to the actual lump sum payment would be the better route to commercialisation.

If the licence is a part of a research and/or development agreement, further sums (known as milestone payments) may be made on the achievement of certain goals.

Alternatively, lump sum and royalties may be combined with, for example, a lump sum payable by way of a disclosure fee for the provision of know-how relevant to the licensed products and royalties payable on an on-going basis against other intellectual property used in their manufacture or marketing.

Performance obligations

An intellectual property licence typically contains performance obligations upon both the licensor and the licensee, but inevitably these are more onerous for the licensee. Typically, such performance obligations will comprise two types: pre-market entry development milestones, and post-market entry sales targets.

Pre-market entry milestones

Pre-market entry milestones require a licensee to achieve or meet certain agreed milestones. Milestones may include:

(a) undertaking a trial or validation of the product;
(b) producing a prototype;

(c) producing a pilot plant (or batch of product);
(d) meeting regulatory requirements;
(e) progressing through clinical trial phases; and so on.

On achievement of these milestones, the licence will continue and the licensee earns the right further to exploit and develop the intellectual property. On the other hand, if the licensee fails to achieve or meet those milestones, the licensor may terminate the licence. The advantage of milestone provisions is that the licensee is obliged to develop the intellectual property, that is, he cannot become an inactive rights holder, resulting in no commercialisation, and no financial benefits going back to the licensor. Without milestone provisions a licensee may, for any number of valid commercial reasons, decide not to progress the development of the intellectual property, with the result that there is never a market entry, no sales or exploitation and thus no royalties for the licensor.

Post-market entry milestones

Other performance obligations will come into play once market entry has occurred. These will normally comprise a requirement on the licensee to achieve minimum sales of products and services through which the licensed intellectual property is exploited. Sales targets, supported by minimum sales requirements, mean that the licensor is guaranteed an income stream. Failure to achieve minimum sales targets can result in the down-grading of a licence from an exclusive position to a sole or non-exclusive one, so that the licensor can either exercise the invention itself or introduce new licensees into the market. Alternatively, if the licensee fails to make the minimum sales figures, he can be obliged to pay the royalties that would have been payable, had the minimum sales been achieved. Such performance obligations are, as with the pre-market milestones, crucial in ensuring the commitment of the licensee to the exploitation of the intellectual property.

Another possible sanction for failure to make minimum sales is termination of the licence, with the reversion back to the licensor of any intellectual property rights. Then the licensor has the security of knowing that if it has appointed the wrong licensee, the licensor will have the opportunity of recouping its control of the intellectual property and then being able to license the intellectual property to another entity that does have the capability to meet these performance obligations.

By contrast, it would be most unusual to see such performance obligations included in an assignment. Not unexpectedly, an assignee, having purchased the intellectual property, will consider that performance obligations such as these are inappropriate. Since an assignment of a patent or other intellectual property is normally absolute and irrevocable, termination for failure to meet performance obligations is simply not possible.

Conclusion

Neither licensing nor assignment will invariably be the most prudent, commercially attractive or suitable route to commercialisation. The decision as to which route will be followed will be assessed on the facts and prevailing circumstances of the relevant transaction. On each occasion an assessment of the advantages and disadvantages of assignment versus licensing needs to be made, balancing the benefits of securing a royalty stream, as against the benefits of receiving a once only lump sum, with all other implications, such as retained control as opposed to transferred risk, to reach a conclusion whether on a particular occasion, a licence or an assignment is to be the preferred course.

7.4 TYPES OF LICENCE

Exclusive, non-exclusive or sole licence

Exclusive licence

If a licensor chooses to grant an exclusive licence, it will be giving the licensee the 'exclusive' right to exploit the licensed subject matter (which may be patented technology, a trade mark or a copyright work). Crucially, in granting an exclusive licence, a licensor gives away its own right to exploit the subject matter in competition with the licensee. The licence is to the exclusion of all others, including the owner of the subject matter. Therefore a licensor must think very carefully before granting an exclusive licence.

It is possible to limit the scope of the exclusivity, for example by reference to time, field of use or geographical location. Rather than granting an exclusive licence of unlimited duration throughout all of the world, the licensor may prefer to grant the licence for a fixed period of time and restricted to a particular country or region. For example, a patentee may grant a sole licence to a third party to manufacture and sell patented technology for a period of five years in the EU. It could not grant anyone else a licence to manufacture or sell the technology in the EU during the period of the sole licence. However, it could grant licences in other territories during the five-year period or in the EU, once the five-year licence had expired.

The licence can also be limited as to the mode of exploitation permitted. For example, as discussed in **Chapter 2**, copyright is a 'bundle of rights'. A licensor may grant an exclusive licence to publish a particular book but retain, or license to a third party, the right to make adaptations and translations of the book.

Licensors will often be able to charge a higher fee or royalty for an exclusive licence than a non-exclusive licence. This is because a licensee should be willing to pay more for a licence if they will acquire rights to the exclusion of all others, including the licensor. This will be an issue for the licensor to consider when deciding what type of licence to grant.

Non-exclusive licence

A non-exclusive licence grants the licensee the right to exploit the subject matter pursuant to the terms of the licence agreement which may be limited geographically, temporally and/or to certain acts. In the case of a non-exclusive licence, the licensor does not exclude itself from also exploiting the subject matter in the same way as the licensee is permitted to do under the licence. The licensor also retains the right to grant licences of exactly the same rights on the same or similar (or any other) terms to third parties.

Sole licence

A variation on a non-exclusive licence is a sole licence. A sole licence is where a licensor grants rights to a licensee and agrees not to grant any other licences on the same or similar terms. A sole licence is not granted to the exclusion of the licensor, so the licensor would be free to exploit the subject matter of the licence in competition with the licensee (during the licence period only, within the EU because of competition laws).

7.5 LICENSING CONTEXTS

Licensing agreements are commonly used in the following contexts:

(a) research and development;
(b) manufacturing;
(c) supply and distribution;
(d) franchising; and
(e) joint ventures.

The outlines below should be considered in conjunction with **Chapter 8** dealing with competition law, but some of the main issues to look out for are included in this chapter.

Research and development (R&D)

Intellectual property ownership

Research and development (R&D) agreements are used in the context of collaborations where the parties are likely to be creating intellectual property. The parties may each bring their own intellectual property to the collaboration ('background intellectual property') and will intend to create new intellectual property through a combination of each party's background intellectual property and further research. It is important to be clear from the outset who will own what. All parties to the agreement should agree to obtain assignments from employees and contractors of intellectual property created in pursuance of the collaboration.

As mentioned above, background intellectual property should be clearly defined so that each party knows what the other is bringing to the collaboration. The agreement will usually provide for reciprocal licences so each party can use the background intellectual property of the other party or parties. The parties will also need to agree on who will own intellectual property created in the course of the R&D project ('foreground intellectual property'). The owner may be one of the parties, the parties jointly or a separate holding company in which the parties own shares. The non-owning party will then usually be granted a licence to use the foreground intellectual property depending on the contribution they have made to it.

Competition law can place significant constraints on how collaborators can deal with intellectual property that is developed during collaboration. Because the essence of intellectual property is about restrictions and monopolies, by the same token, it (and particularly the means by which it is exploited) can impose restrictions which would breach competition law. Article 81(1) of the EC Treaty prohibits restrictions or agreements 'that may affect trade between member states and have the object or effect of preventing, restricting or distorting competition within the common market'. In addition to the EU competition law issues, domestic UK competition laws should be considered. An agreement which would at first sight create an unlawful restriction, may however be exempt because the benefits of imposing that restriction outweigh the negative effect on competition. This, and the possible exemption routes, is discussed in more detail in **Chapter 8**. In practice, unfortunately, few research and development agreements between large companies fall within the R&D block exemption (R&DBE) because the joint market shares will cause the agreement to fall outside the exemption.

Typical clauses

Clauses typically found in an R&D development agreement will include the following.

DEFINITION OF THE WORK PROGRAMME OR PROJECT

The work programme definition will determine the scope of the collaboration – will it be research only, will it proceed to development or will it go as far as dealing with the exploitation of the outcome of the research and development programme? The latter is unusual; it is more common to see provision for a process for getting to the exploitation stage on the basis of good faith negotiations.

This definition (which will create the 'engine room' for the agreement) must be as clearly defined as possible from the beginning, whilst having sufficient flexibility (through change control mechanisms) for the work programme it relates to, to develop, grow and transform as the research project evolves. The results emerging from the programme may be unexpectedly good or bad, and the project needs to be able to be refocussed (probably through the means of a jointly managed steering committee) to reflect the outcome of the research.

It is important to be clear on the aim of the R&D project. What are the common and individual goals which the parties are setting out to achieve? It is also important to clearly identify the role of each party in the collaboration and what is expected from them.

The work programme will of course set out the details of the project:

(a) the milestones and the contributions (in kind or in cash) to be made by each party;
(b) the procedure for determining whether or not milestones have been achieved;
(c) sanctions or consequences of non-achievement of milestones;
(d) details of the personnel who will carry out the R&D (including academic supervisors and students in academic collaborations);
(e) choice of a project manager; and
(f) change control procedures.

Although it may be tempting to leave this to a schedule to be drafted by the technical people heading the project on both sides, the result may be that it does not get done, leaving an agreement without a core, and thus void for uncertainty. It is advisable to treat this as a key clause alongside the provisions on payments and ownership of foreground intellectual property.

MANAGEMENT AND REPORTING

In order to monitor the progress of the project, efficient management and reporting procedures must be set out clearly. This will include production of regular written reports, and if required, regular face to face meetings to discuss progress.

FINANCIAL PROVISIONS

Each party needs to be clear about its financial commitment and potential income from royalties. The programme must be adequately funded from the outset, but if the costs change substantially from expectation, as with unexpected scientific results, change control procedures must be established so that the parties are clear about their respective rights and responsibilities.

Will each party be responsible for its own costs or will one party bear the costs while the other party provides the research facility and resources? If the collaboration is being publicly funded, the R&D agreement must meet any requirements stipulated by the funding body.

The financial provisions will vary considerably – an R&D arrangement between two equally sized and well-funded companies will look very different from an academic collaboration which is funded by a commercial organisation. In both instances, costs and expenses will need to be controlled and predictable, but the payment of milestone payments will be more straightforward in the latter than the former scenario.

INTELLECTUAL PROPERTY OWNERSHIP

These provisions are likely to be key to the agreement as the purpose is to develop valuable, exploitable intellectual property.

In summary, provision should be made for:

(a) written assignments of intellectual property from employees and contractors;
(b) disclosure of background intellectual property contributed by each party (and licence therefor);
(e) division of foreground intellectual property (as discussed above);
(f) responsibility for prosecution, maintenance and enforcement of patents (or other registrable intellectual property);
(g) terms of licences for the exploitation of intellectual property (whether background, or foreground); should these be exclusive or non-exclusive (beware of competition law issues!), subject to royalty payment or royalty free, worldwide or limited to a particular territory or field of use, terminable or irrevocable?

Warranties

As well as a warranty that each party is entitled to enter into the agreement, it would be expected that each party would warrant that:

(a) it has authority to enter into the agreement;
(b) use of their respective background intellectual property will not infringe the rights of third parties;
(c) they have provided full disclosure of relevant matters; and
(d) the foreground technology will not to their knowledge infringe third-party rights.

Supply and distribution

Supply and distribution distinguished from agency

A supply and distribution agreement is appropriate where it is intended that one party (the distributor) will buy products from a manufacturer or supplier for its own account. The distributor takes title to those goods and resells them to its own customers.

This is to be contrasted to an agency arrangement where (in the most common circumstances) an agent is appointed who is authorised to negotiate and enter into contracts of sale on the principal's behalf. Such an agreement envisages that the agent holds stock, invoices the customer and fulfils orders, but the agent will normally have more control over pricing, marketing strategy and choice of customers than a supplier would be able to exercise through a distributor, and most importantly, the contract for the sale of goods is between the customer and the principal, not the agent. Whereas an agent will normally be paid on a commission basis, a distributor makes its profit on the difference between the supply price at which it purchases goods and the price at which they are resold to its customers.

Typical clauses

The distribution agreement will set out the obligations of each party, and specific terms are are likely to include the following.

(A) TYPE/SCOPE OF DISTRIBUTORSHIP

This may be:

(a) *exclusive* (only the distributor will be permitted to sell the goods within the territory covered by the agreement – not even the supplier itself may resell in the territory – and normally the distributor will undertake not to sell the goods of a competitor of the supplier);
(b) *sole* (the supplier can resell goods in the territory but no third party distributor will be appointed);
(c) *non-exclusive* (both parties can buy from and sell to third parties and other distributors can be appointed in the territory); or
(d) *selective* (the appointment of distributors is restricted to those who fulfil a set of pre-determined qualitative criteria).

The *territory* will be defined – this may have competion law implications.

(B) DISTRIBUTOR'S OBLIGATIONS

These will include sales and promotional commitments, after sales support, reporting details, maintenance of a satisfactory sales force, stock control, conformity with legislation, and will be closely linked to any minimum purchase targets and exclusive purchasing provisions.

(C) MINIMUM PURCHASE TARGETS/EXCLUSIVE PURCHASING PROVISIONS

These are most likely to be included in exclusive and sole distributorships (see **7.5** on the likely scope and effect of these). They are included to give the supplier comfort that the appointment of the distributor was justified, that it will not sit on its hands and the supplier is guaranteed a return or a sanction for breach.

Again, in a sole or exclusive arrangement, the supplier may require that the distributor purchases exclusively from the supplier, and will not sell the goods of its competitors.

These terms must comply with competition laws, and long term exclusive or quasi-exclusive purchasing arrangements can create problems. Tying, whereby the purchase of one product is conditional on the purchase of another product, should only be included after careful consideration of competition law.

(D) SUPPLIER'S OBLIGATIONS

The Sale of Goods Act 1979 implies various terms into a sale of goods, and the supplier might wish to exclude these from the agreement to the greatest extent permitted by law. It is not possible to exclude the warranty that the supplier has the capacity to sell the goods, i.e. that it owns them. Further obligations may be implied by industry-specific legislation such as toys, medicines, cosmetics and food.

Undertakings regarding the quality of goods will be included, as will conditions regarding timely supply of goods and spare parts. In some cases, support, such as training of staff and supply of promotional materials, will be provided for, and agreement to replace defective goods.

The distributor will want appropriate restrictions placed on the supplier to give effect to the scope of the distributorship, i.e. not to resell to a third party in a sole or exclusive relationship.

(E) TITLE, PAYMENT AND INSURANCE

Distribution agreements frequently include retention of title provisions, providing that the title to the goods will not transfer until full payment has been made to the supplier. The practical effect of such clauses varies by jurisdiction.

Payment provisions should be clear in relation to time of payment, currency (including a mechanism for dealing with currency fluctuations) and method, e.g. bank transfer, cheque etc., together with interest provisions in case of late payment.

(F) INTELLECTUAL PROPERTY PROVISIONS

Express provisions relating to the licence of the supplier's intellectual property (which licence may be implied into the agreement anyway) should be included, dealing with the scope of the licence, ownership of the intellectual property, obligation to use trade marks (to avoid revocation for non-use), help with registration and maintenance, prohibitions on the use of confusingly similar trade marks, and how to deal with litigation.

(G) PRODUCT LIABILITY

EU law provides that the manufacturer will always be liable for damage or injury caused by a defect in goods it has produced. Consequently, the distributor must not be allowed to admit liability for the products to customers without the express permission of the manufacturer. Notwithstanding the strict liability imposition on manufacturers (Consumer Protection Act 1987), a distributor will be held liable if it is the importer of goods from outside the EU, if it holds itself out as producer by adding its name and/or trade mark to the goods or fails to identify to the affected party, who supplied the goods.

Section 2 of the Unfair Contract Terms Act 1977 provides that liability cannot be excluded for death or personal injury caused by negligence and all other exclusions for negligence must be reasonable.

A distributor may wish to protect itself by seeking an indemnity for product liability claims. The scope of this indemnity will vary according to the type of goods supplied, the value of them and the involvement of the distributor in their packaging and physical distribution, for example.

(H) CONDITIONS OF SALE (OR PURCHASE)

Frequently the supplier will append its standard terms and conditions of sale to the agreement. Less usually, the distributor wins the 'battle of the forms' and its terms and conditions of purchase are appended.

(I) TERMINATION

What breaches will give rise to a right to terminate? What is the effect of termination? Normally, the distributor will be given the right to sell out goods that it has already bought, and any intellectual property provisions will be extended accordingly.

Many of the proposed clauses relevant to the supply and distribution agreement will also apply to manufacturing, franchising and joint ventures.

Manufacturing

Manufacturing agreements are used when one party enters an agreement with another party whereby the second party is to manufacture a product to the first party's specifications. To do so, the manufacturer will need a licence from the product owner under any intellectual property used in manufacturing the first party's products.

Key terms to decide include the price that the licensor will pay to the manufacturer and the basis on which this is to be calculated.

Will the licensor be under an obligation to purchase a certain number of units from the manufacturer each month, quarter or year, and to make a compensatory payment if such purchase obligation is not achieved?

It may be important to the licensor to know that the manufacturer will not be servicing any of the licensor's competitors. However, a licensor should be prepared to pay a premium for this exclusivity. If the agreement is not exclusive (in the sense that the manufacturer will be free to manufacture products for other parties in the same market) it will be especially important to have confidentiality undertakings from the manufacturer. The last thing a licensor will want is for details of the manufacturing process of its products to be leaked to a competitor.

Inevitably some products will not conform to the product specification. The parties must consider who will bear the cost of non-conforming products (usually the manufacturer) and how long the licensor will have to reject non-conforming products. Latent defects may need to be considered separately as the licensor may not discover these defects until after the rejection period has ended.

Another concern will be who should bear the cost of product recalls. This will usually be the manufacturer but it is advisable to state this clearly, together with any consultation and payment provisions, in the manufacturing agreement.

Franchising

A franchise agreement is a specific type of licensing agreement whereby:

(a) the licensor (franchisor) grants a licence to use a name (usually a registered trade mark or portfolio of registered trade marks);
(b) the franchisor has some control over the franchisee;

(c) the franchisor provides set up and ongoing assistance to the franchisee; and
(d) the franchisee pays a fee to the franchisor.

Where an ordinary licensor may have very little control over the licensee's business, a franchisor plays an integral part in the franchisee's business by providing, for example, staff training, handbooks and guides, advertising on behalf of all franchisees and demonstrating a tried and proven business format. Well-known franchises include McDonald's, The Body Shop and Threshers.

Franchising remains self-regulated in the UK. This is in stark contrast to the heavily regulated US franchise market. However, the British Franchise Association requires members to comply with the European Code of Ethics for Franchising (the Franchising Code). The Franchising Code contains requirements that the franchisor operate a pilot operation before launching the franchise, owns all relevant brand names and trade marks and provides initial and ongoing training.

Joint ventures

Joint ventures (JVs) are sometimes established when two or more parties with a common interest decide to work together in furtherance of a particular goal. Common structures for a JV are a limited liability company or partnership, as a partnership (or limited partnership) or a contractual co-operation agreement.

The relationship between the JV partners and between them and the JV company are governed by the memorandum and articles of association. There should also be a separate JV or shareholders' agreement. As for R&D agreements discussed above, it is important to agree at the outset of the relationship what each party's background intellectual property is and who will own any foreground intellectual property. The parties may also share know-how and confidential information under strict terms of confidentiality.

Many of the proposed clauses relating to an R&D agreement will apply equally to joint ventures, but there is not space in this chapter for an in-depth analysis of the various agreements required.

7.6 DUE DILIGENCE

The need for due diligence

Having made a decision to acquire a business, a company will be concerned to ensure that the acquisition/collaboration will be a success, not just in terms of the acquisition and negotiation process itself, but more importantly, the long-term integration of the new business. The buyers and sellers may take various forms; for example, a seller may be a company seeking a merger or acquisition, divesting a product line, or a division, licensing a technology, promoting an initial public offering, or an entrepreneur seeking venture investment.

The importance of due diligence in any of these scenarios cannot be overstated. Unfortunately the process is often an afterthought and a hastily organised exercise after the business transaction has been agreed. In a hi-tech or bioscience industry, the web of intellectual property rights can take significant time to untangle and understand, but it is in exactly this type of business that intellectual property is likely to be of vital importance and value. It is therefore important to start the analysis early enough to determine whether the target (or indeed the target when acquired by the buyer), has freedom to operate in its intended field.

A properly conducted and timed due diligence provides a potential investor, purchaser or licensee with detailed information about the target that may affect pricing or other key elements of the transaction. The consequences of mismanaging or ignoring the due diligence can be severe. Without proper prior investigation into an entity's assets, an investor may find for example that, after the deal is concluded, it does not have the ownership of the sought-after intellectual property or that such assets have been transferred or encumbered by third party interests or litigation.

A thorough due diligence requires more than compiling a list of the target's assets, however; it should include an assessment of the strength of a target in the marketplace and requires a continuing focus on the essential nature of the transaction. Every transaction has its unique issues, whether due to a particular technology, the geographic market, the level of the competition and the litigious nature of the industry. The due diligence team must assess how the unique aspects may ultimately affect the resultant corporate structure and its place in the market. A lack of understanding of the marketplace and the lack of strategy and understanding for dealing with third party rights often leads to a mismatch in the valuations put forward by the parties or a mismatch in expectation.

Every company, especially early stage companies hoping to secure capital or partner with a large international company, should prepare early on for due diligence. A buyer that is aware of the areas upon which due diligence focusses and the types of problems that arise during due diligence will be better prepared to avoid, or if timely discovered, solve problems.

Failure to plan, manage and execute a full, focussed and effective due diligence can, and has, resulted in high profile disasters where acquisition targets fail to meet their assumed potential. This is particularly true in the case of intellectual property rich acquisitions and collaborations, as failure to identify problems or omissions can go to the heart of the *raison d'être* of the transaction.

For the purposes of this chapter 'the buyer' means the potential purchaser of a business, or whichever entity wishes to carry out due diligence. 'The target' is the company that the buyer wishes to own, to which it wishes to license technology or in which it wishes to invest.

The aims of due diligence

Due diligence is about assessing and managing risk and its purposes therefore are:

(a) to value the investment;
(b) to protect against the principle of 'caveat emptor', or the buyer beware;
(c) to determine whether the investment is sound;
(d) to assist with negotiations so that the buyer is armed with the information to determine the risks and rewards of the transaction and to renegotiate terms where appropriate;
(e) to secure satisfactory warranty and indemnity protection; and
(f) to enable the buyer of a business to plan its post-completion integration.

Intellectual property and due diligence

Intellectual property due diligence is carried out to determine ownership, freedom to operate, and the technical and commercial value of the intellectual property. In doing so, the commercial terms of assignments, licences and other contracts will be reviewed.

The level of importance and scope of the due diligence will depend on the shape and nature of the transaction. The factors that will affect the criticality of the intellectual property due diligence will include:

(a) the significance of the technology, patents or trade mark(s) to be acquired as part of the bundle of assets or licensed in or out;
(b) whether the technology is owned by the target or licensee, and if so, on what terms; and
(c) where and how the buyer wishes to exploit such technology and trade marks.

Due diligence must be tailored to the needs of particular transactions since a business's dependence on technology and branding can vary dramatically. It is, however, safe to assume that (despite what is sometimes asserted!) all businesses will have computer software on which they rely and for which they may need licences. They will own some trade marks (whether registered or unregistered) and will have confidential information and trade secrets which will need protection or may lose value on transfer of the relevant business or company. They may well also have patents or patent applications, design right (registered or unregistered) or database right.

Essential intellectual property checks

First, a search should be made at the UKIPO in order to determine the existence of any patents, registered trade marks and registered designs, and any applications for these items which have been filed. Depending on the territorial scope of the transaction, equivalent searches of other registries, including the EPO, should be carried out. It is also possible to determine whether any assignments have been obtained, where these have been recorded, and whether any licensees or security interests have been listed on the appropriate register.

Secondly, the lawyer on the due diligence team responsible for assessing the value and security of the target's intellectual property must ensure that proper expert input is given to the intellectual property questionnaire that will be sent to the target. This questionnaire can often take a rather generic format but as early as possible (perhaps after an initial review of the searches of the public register, and after a discussion with the commercial cognoscenti) the intellectual property section of questions must be reviewed to ensure that the questions deal fully with items of particular interest and value to the buyer's team in this specific transaction.

For example, time may be limited so there is little point in spending significant time and effort (and, frequently, money) determining to the tiniest detail the provenance or security of an intellectual property right which is not of commercial or strategic significance to the buyer.

Good management of the questionnaire process such as following up diligently any anomalies or omissions in replies, or any reluctance to provide copies of third-party agreements will, when used in conjunction with public searches, provide a solid base for the buyer's evaluation.

All of the target's intellectual property should be identified and catalogued, including current patent and trade mark applications. This should include dates of application, publication and information on maintenance payments and territorial coverage.

Additionally, the buyer will need to know whether the target owns or has valid rights to its intellectual property and whether the target can exploit or use its intellectual property in accordance with its business plan without infringing a third party's intellectual property rights.

Ownership

On the issue of ownership, a target should be able to provide documentation that demonstrates that it either owns or has the appropriate valid rights to the intellectual property. Ownership verification requires meticulously analysing any assignments and licence agreements as well as cross referencing the national patent and/or trade mark office registers. It cannot be stressed too highly that everything should be independently verified. Any ambiguities or uncertainty in this area will be a signal to potential investors or partners of increased risks.

For many companies the chain of title to ownership to the relevant intellectual property is something that is often overlooked. Failure to obtain valid assignments from inventors and entities involved in the development of the intellectual property is common. Individuals and entities commonly involved in the development of a biotech company's intellectual property include the founders, directors, employees, consultants, students, associated universities and grant funding bodies. It cannot be stressed enough that this is something that needs to be clarified way in advance so that the necessary unencumbered rights can be transferred to the purchaser or potential licensee.

One important aspect to consider, for example, is the way that intellectual property developed within academic institutes is treated. University policy on ownership of intellectual policy differs from university to university throughout the world. Therefore, it is important to review all policies and guidelines of the target relating to the protection or use of all types of intellectual property.

Another factor to consider is the issue of joint ownership of intellectual property. The rights of joint owners to deal with intellectual property differs from country to country. For example the joint owners of a patent in the UK may themselves use the invention without reference to each other, but they cannot license the patent to a third party or assign the patent without the consent of the other. In the US, on the other hand, the joint owner can license the patent or assign without the consent of the other party. Therefore if there are instances of joint ownership, the seller needs to ensure that the relevant consents have been obtained where appropriate and the buyer needs to scrutinise the patents and agreements, taking into account the different laws of each country to ensure that there are the rights to use the patents in question.

Sufficiency

The due diligence process should demonstrate whether the target has sufficient intellectual property to make, use and sell its inventions without infringing the intellectual property rights of third parties. Key patents should first be analysed to determine if they sufficiently cover the product lines of interest. As emphasised above, independent verification is key as it is not uncommon to find that the listed patent portfolio does *not* cover the main product lines.

The due diligence should then turn to the identification of any third party rights that may adversely affect the ability to commercialise the key product(s) or pipeline. Since the value of a patent is directly related to the owner's ability to use the patent, part of the due diligence process should include an evaluation of third party patents to determine the patent holder's freedom to operate in the market. For patents, the buyer or potential licensee should consider obtaining a 'freedom to operate' opinion which is designed to identify other patents covering similar technology and analyse situations where either the target may infringe a third party's rights or the seller has a valid claim of infringement against a third party. Either circumstance may seriously influence the decision of the buyer of the value of the target.

For trade marks the buyer might consider having a search conducted to determine what other parties have registered or are using the same or similar marks for other goods and services.

Through this analysis, the buyer can assess the strength of the intellectual property and whether this is in line with its overall strategy and fits in with the proposed deal.

Right-specific checklists

Trade marks

If the target is an owner of product or service brands with substantial market recognition, much of its value may be in its trade mark portfolio. The due diligence will focus on an investigation of registered trade marks, jurisdictions of registration, and maintenance and possible infringement of the trade marks.

In order to determine this, the buyer will need to elicit from the target (preferably) or elsewhere:

(a) details of any unregistered trade marks, logos, devices, names which are used in connection with the target or its products together with details of any intention to register such unregistered trade marks where relevant;
(b) a list of all the target's trade marks that have been issued or applied for (including graphical representation where appropriate);
(c) trade mark registration numbers or application numbers;
(d) the class and specification of goods or services for which a mark is registered or for which a trade mark application has been made;
(e) country of registration;
(f) date of applications;
(g) date of issue and the date of expiry or next renewal date (as relevant);
(h) the name of the owner of the trade mark registration or trade mark application, where different from the target at the date of registration or application;
(i) details of any threatened or current challenges to validity or scope of any of the trade mark registrations or applications (including any risk of invalidity due to non-use) together with opinions (if any) which have been obtained;
(j) details of prior owners, if any;
(k) details of licensed trade marks (whether licensed in or out);
(l) details of co-existence or other third party agreements relating to the use of any trade mark; and

(m) whether assignments have been properly recorded, so that an accurate chain of title exists.

From the results of these searches or answers to these questions, the buyer will have a further series of questions:

1. If the trade mark is not protected in all the countries that would normally have been anticipated, the buyer should ask 'why not'?
2. Where the trade mark is not registered by the target, has a third party registered it, or applied to do so? Such a situation could devalue the brand.
3. Have all required maintenance fees been paid, or are any of the registered trade marks or applications likely to fail? Loss of a brand could prove expensive.
4. Before using any trade marks (whether registered or not), did the target carry out trade mark searches to establish that it would have free use of that trade mark in the classes in which it intended to use that mark?
5. Is the target using the trade mark in the same form and for the same products and services (classes) for which it is registered? If not, it runs the risk of either encroaching on the intellectual property rights of a third party and/or losing its right in due course to use the trade mark for the registered products and services.
6. Has the trade mark been in use? Failure to use a trade mark for period of time creates the presumption that the trade mark has been abandoned and may make it vulnerable to being struck off the register.
7. Has the target taken any steps to monitor and enforce its trade marks and prevent misuse? If not, it will have weakened any case it may have had for trade mark infringement and possibly passing off.
8. Does it have a process for identifying suitable trade marks and clearing use of these by products, territory and use?
9. Has the target received any notification, whether formal or otherwise, that the use of the trade marks infringes the rights of a third party? Trade mark litigation could prove to be time consuming and costly; if such an action is lost, a valuable asset may have been lost.

Domain names

The buyer will need to obtain a list of all registered domain names (and applications therefor) in the name of the target, plus any of its subsidiaries, business or trade marks, in all jurisdictions, and then check that these registrations are owned by the target or its affiliates or licensees. Ideally, homophonic words, or cleverly mis-spelt words should be checked too, again to check for possible instances of trade mark infringement or passing off. Action may be needed to challenge registrations held by third parties which infringe the target's proprietary names.

It may be possible to outsource these searches.

Patents

Depending on the nature of the target's business, patents can be of crucial importance to the value and viability of the business. In such cases, careful due diligence will be key. The buyer will need to establish that patents, on the basis of whose claims products will be sold, are valid and adequately maintained (i.e. all fees and formalities are up to date), licences in and out are commercially acceptable and do not restrict the buyer's own ambitions for such products. Ownership must be established and verified and where possible the key technical claims should be checked.

The buyer will need to establish whether there are any disputes regarding either the target's own patents, whether regarding validity or infringement of third party patents. Has the target had to take action to assert its rights to its own patents? Patent litigation is notoriously time-consuming, expensive and a drain on resources; the buyer will want to make sure that purchasing the target will not result in such activity having to be undertaken.

Much of the above can be determined by searches of public registries, but for key patents, the buyer will want to undertake an analysis of the target's systems to ensure that, for example, they searched appropriately and analysed competitors' patents before filing their own, and also if they have processes to secure appropriate patent protection for any new products in order to avoid a loss of rights.

The following details of all patents or patent applications owned or licensed in by the target should be found:

(a) application number and date of filing;
(b) publication number and date of publication;
(c) details of any priority documents;
(d) priority date(s);
(e) title of patent or patent application;
(f) technology or product covered by patent or patent application;
(g) proprietor;
(h) inventor, together with an indication as to whether the inventor is an employee of the target;
(i) countries in which patent is registered or in which patent protection has been applied for;
(j) details of any opposition or (in the US) interference proceedings together with copies of any opinions received on the merits of such opposition or interference proceedings;
(k) whether there are any reasons to suggest the patent or patent application may be invalid; and
(l) details of any revocation or invalidity proceedings either threatened or ongoing.

Where the patent is subject to a licence, then details of any relevant agreements should be sought. Ideally a copy should be obtained, but a detailed summary at the very least should be provided, together with a description of:

(a) the rights licensed in or out;
(b) details of any field of use restrictions or other restrictions on the way in which such rights can be used;
(c) whether the target is aware of any breaches of the licence agreement; and
(d) details of royalties payable.

In life science transactions, supplementary protection certificates may be relevant – details of all of these should be obtained.

Following the collection and analysis of the above information, patent attorneys and clients should work closely together to identify goals and commercial priorities and to establish whether the state of the target's patent portfolio, including licences thereof and thereto justify investment or acquisition.

Copyright

Copyright is an unregistered right, which comes into effect immediately as soon as something which can be protected is 'fixed', for example on paper, or in electronic records. Thus, the process for carrying out due diligence on copyright material necessarily differs from those rights where there are external registers and finite items for examination.

The target will not be able to list all copyrighted material, but a list of commercially important work, such as software, databases, operating manuals and research data should be requested, together with details of authorship. Since copyright in a commissioned work (such as a software program or website) does not automatically belong to the commissioner, a review of any commissioning contracts will be essential in order to determine whether the target will be free to use all copyright material post-completion. Is there a non-transferable licence in place perhaps, or was an assignment ever completed? Are any licences to software broad enough for the buyer's requirements post-completion?

Once again, an assessment must be made of any copyright infringement by the target (infringing third party programs using material without permission or exceeding the terms of any licence in). Does the target monitor use of its copyright material and does it enforce its rights against such infringement?

To the extent that important copyright material is found the following should be established:

(a) a description of the copyright work;
(b) details of the product or area of business to which the copyright relates;

(c) the identity of the author of copyright, including details as to whether the author is an employee or an independent contractor;
(d) copies of any assignments of copyright including the parties to any such assignment and date of execution of such assignment;
(e) the date of creation of the copyright work;
(f) any evidence supporting the originality of the creation and hence the existence of copyright;
(g) whether the target is aware of anything suggesting the copyright might not be enforceable or is invalid including details of any threatened or actual challenges to the existence of copyright; and
(h) if the target has rights or activities in the US, details of any registrations of copyright.

Furthermore, details of material licences-in or licences-out of copyright should be obtained – either ideally a copy of the same or at least a detailed summary of the important terms of that agreement, together with details of any known or alleged breaches thereof.

Trade secrets and confidential information

The value of the target's trade secrets and confidential information will be driven very much by the discipline (or otherwise) that the target has used in protecting these. As with copyright, trade secrets and confidential information are unregistered rights and are protected either by non-disclosure (ideal but uncommercial in most cases!) or contract (confidentiality agreements). The target's remedy for loss of confidential information would normally be an injunction to prevent further disclosure, but in some circumstances may be limited to damages.

Due diligence to be carried out in this area will include an investigation into the target's practices and procedures in relation to the protection of trade secrets. For example, is adequate cover given in employees' contracts of employment by way of non-disclosure agreement? Does the target habitually enter into non-disclosure agreements with suppliers, customers and collaborators? Is there an e-mail policy preventing the wholesale electronic dissemination of trade secrets?

If the answer to the above is negative, the value of the target's trade secrets and confidential information may be severely diminished as the information may have lost its very essence of confidentiality.

Summary

The key points are planning, focus, analysis and probing in order for the due diligence team to derive the information that they need to assess the viability of the relevant transaction in order to do the following.

1. Identify the intellectual property assets used by the business.
2. Identify whether the business owns or has rights to the intellectual property assets it requires.
3. Ensure that all the intellectual property assets are properly assigned, notified, transferred or dealt with during the transaction.
4. Identify any material issues relating to any of the intellectual property, for example conflicting third party rights, litigation, or employee ownership issues.
5. Verify or support listing particulars.
6. Enable a seller to know:

   (a) the risks of giving any particular warranty;
   (b) what must be disclosed in a disclosure letter;
   (c) the risks of giving any indemnity;
   (d) what measures need to be taken before a deal can be concluded.

7. Enable a buyer to know:

   (a) which warranties and indemnities it requires;
   (b) the risks it runs in acquiring the intellectual property assets (or the business);
   (c) whether a deal should be structured differently to minimise any particular risk (for example an asset sale rather than a share sale).

Careful planning and focus, using correctly briefed and knowledgeable teams, should achieve all of the above.

CHAPTER 8

Intellectual property and competition law

Jeremy Robinson

8.1 INTRODUCTION

The evolution of competition law

The owner of an intellectual property right may, for the duration of that right, prevent another party making unauthorised use of that which is protected by that right. In this way, the law protects the owner from third parties, who may seek to profit from the owner's ingenuity. Conversely, the owner has the option of exploiting the right, for example, by granting a licence of it to a third party.

At several points, these rights appear to clash with responsibilities that businesses have in EU and national law to ensure that competition in the European internal market is not distorted (EC Treaty, Art.3(1)(g)). The challenge is to understand at what point, in a given situation, these rights become circumscribed. This is hardly straightforward in theory, and is yet more complex in practice as competition law has developed since the EC Treaty came into force in 1958, so the boundary between acceptable and unacceptable use of intellectual property has moved.

Where once the Commission and Community courts applied competition law in a way often described as 'formalistic' or 'legalistic', it now applies the rules using its more sophisticated understanding of economic theory. The result in competition law has been a more tolerant approach towards intellectual property, and a greater willingness to regard intellectual property and competition law as two approaches to resolving the same question of consumer welfare and efficient allocation of resources.

Contexts in which issues arise

When considering the question 'what is the practical effect of competition law on intellectual property?' this chapter's exposition suggests three approaches.

First, there are a series of effects relating to the processes by which the 'things' protected by intellectual property are created. These relate to transactions where undertakings (whether competitors or not) collaborate in research and development (R&D) and might in the process agree on how any rights created should be exploited.

The second set of effects relates to transactions regulating how intellectual property should be exploited through licensing. Many transactions are relevant:

(a) corporate or structural transactions where businesses are created or acquired, and intellectual property are managed as a necessary adjunct of that transaction;
(b) licensing of 'technology' (defined by the Technology Transfer Block Exemption Regulation (TTBE)) to include patents, know-how and software copyright), including the complexities introduced by standardisation;
(c) licensing of non-technology intellectual property rights, such as copyright and trade marks. Included here are risks of licensing on terms that are abusive of dominant market positions.

The third set of effects is on the distribution and sale of products that are the subject of intellectual property licences (for example, a drug that is protected by a patent). Here the effects relate to restrictive agreements for distribution, abuses of dominance and infringement of the EC Treaty rules on free movement of goods.

To apply the rules to best practical and commercial effect, it is important to pay close attention to the type of transaction in which intellectual property is relevant, to understand the type of intellectual property at issue, and to analyse the relationship between the undertakings in question and their position in relevant markets. The competition/intellectual property law overlap is too large for more than outline treatment in a short chapter. This chapter provides a practical overview of the relevant competition law and then provides a method of negotiating the maze of legal rules and principles and guidance concerning the clash of competition law and intellectual property.

8.2 THE CLASH OF INTELLECTUAL PROPERTY AND COMPETITION LAW

Intellectual property

The first essential function of an intellectual property right is the ability to prevent exploitation, by others, of the thing protected by that right. Second, intellectual property allows its holder to profit from that right, for example, by putting on to the market a product exclusively incorporating an invention covered by a patent; or alternatively, to license a third party to make and market that product, in return for a royalty paid to the intellectual property-holder.

The essence of intellectual property is a monopoly, granted by law, for a limited time. Its purpose is simple: the prospect of obtaining a monopoly right (and the profits that can accrue from exploiting it) is intended to be a powerful incentive to invent or create. Since invention and creation may increase competition (which benefits the economy through improving consumer welfare and economic efficiency), intellectual property is essential to a healthy economy.

One of the many complexities of intellectual property and competition law, is that Community competition law establishes a system in operation, as far as possible, on a consistent basis throughout the Community. Intellectual property rights, however, are protected by the national laws of Member States, as well as by Community laws (e.g. the CTM), and the scope of intellectual property laws can vary between Member States. This complexity becomes particularly relevant when applying the EC Treaty rules on free movement of goods to products protected by national laws of different scope.

Competition law

Competition law in essence aims to promote consumer welfare and the efficient allocation of resources. In the European Union, a further objective is the creation and maintenance of a single market. This latter feature of European Union law does not apply in UK law. Community and UK competition law attach to several different types of transactions in the economy, aiming to penalise and deter activity that reduces competition. Thus, there is a system prohibiting restrictive agreements, abuses of dominant positions and anti-competitive mergers.

Tension between competition law and intellectual property

The exercise of intellectual property can at times be anti-competitive. Enforcement of rights may prevent competitors producing certain goods or services. A licence agreement can contain restrictions that prevent, restrict or distort competition, even if the overall purpose (e.g. making available technology for exploitation that might otherwise not be released) is acceptable. Alternatively, intellectual property can contribute to an undertaking holding a dominant position in a market, such that whether and on what terms the undertaking chooses to license its intellectual property, can be anti-competitive. Also, the distribution of products subject to intellectual property can include conditions that impose onerous barriers to trade between Member States.

It is important to note what the tension between intellectual property and competition law is *not*. It is commonly supposed that the core of the matter is that intellectual property rights are monopoly rights, and competition law frowns on monopolies. This is wrong. Competition law frowns on abuses of market power and restrictions on competition that might increase market power. An intellectual property right does not, of itself, create market power (although there may be cases where this is so). However, it might, in conjunction with other things, contribute to a position of market power. A licence of an intellectual property right does not infringe competition law on restrictive agreements unless it contains restrictions that have the object or effect of restricting competition.

Historically, the European Commission treated intellectual property and intellectual property licences as suspicious, but this approach has given way to a positive appraisal of the benefits of intellectual property. As the Commission states in its Guidelines on the application of the EC Treaty, Art.81 to technology transfer agreements (TTBE Guidelines) at para.7:

> . . . Nor does [the fact that intellectual property rights grant exclusive rights of exploitation] imply that there is an inherent conflict between intellectual property rights and the Community competition rules. Indeed, both bodies of law share the same basic objective of promoting consumer welfare and an efficient allocation of resources. Innovation constitutes an essential and dynamic component of an open and competitive market economy. Intellectual property rights promote dynamic competition by encouraging undertakings to invest in developing new or improved products and processes. So does competition by putting pressure on undertakings to innovate. Therefore, both intellectual property rights and competition are necessary to promote innovation and ensure a competitive exploitation thereof.

8.3 THE STRUCTURE OF EU AND UK COMPETITION LAW

The discussion below describes the competition law that may be applied to intellectual property.

EC Treaty articles establishing competition law

Community competition law derives from the EC Treaty. Article 2 begins:

> The Community shall have as its task, by establishing a common market and an economic and monetary union and by implementing common policies or activities referred to in Articles 3 and 4, to promote throughout the Community a harmonious, balanced and sustainable development of economic activities . . .

Article 3(1) states that for the purposes set out in Art.2, the activities of the Community shall include, as provided in this Treaty:

> (g) a system ensuring that competition in the internal market is not distorted.

These foundation principles have created a system which contains the following elements:

(a) a prohibition on barriers to trade;
(b) a prohibition on restrictive agreements;
(c) a prohibition on abuses of dominant positions;
(d) a system for appraising mergers; and
(e) a system for controlling State subsidies (State aid).

In the UK, the competition law framework includes prohibition of restrictive agreements and abuses of dominant positions, and a system for appraising mergers.

EC prohibition on restrictive agreements

Article 81 states:

> 1. The following shall be prohibited as incompatible with the common market: all agreements between undertakings, decisions by associations of undertakings and concerted practices which may affect trade between Member States and which have as their object or effect the prevention, restriction or distortion of competition within the common market, and in particular those which:
>
>   (a) directly or indirectly fix purchase or selling prices or any other trading conditions;
>   (b) limit or control production, markets, technical development or investment;
>   (c) share markets or sources of supply;
>   (d) apply dissimilar conditions to equivalent transactions with other trading parties, thereby placing them at a competitive disadvantage;
>   (e) make the conclusion of contracts subject to acceptance by other parties of supplementary obligations which, by their nature or according to commercial usage, have no connection with the subject of such contracts.
>
> 2. Any agreements or decisions prohibited pursuant to this Article shall be automatically void.
>
> 3. The provisions of paragraph 1 may, however, be declared inapplicable in the case of:
>
>   – any agreement or category of agreements between undertakings;
>   – any decision or category of decisions by associations of undertakings;
>   – any concerted practice or category of concerted practices;
>
>   which contributes to improving the production or distribution of goods or to promoting technical or economic progress, while allowing consumers a fair share of the resulting benefit, and which does not:

(a) impose on the undertakings concerned restrictions which are not indispensable to the attainment of these objectives;
(b) afford such undertakings the possibility of eliminating competition in respect of a substantial part of the products in question.

What is an agreement?

'Agreement' and 'concerted practice' include most forms of co-ordination or agreements between undertakings. No legally binding or written contract is required: a so-called 'gentlemen's agreement' is sufficient (Cases 209/78 etc., *Van Landewyck* v. *Commission* [1980] ECR 3125). Similarly, several separate contracts may be found, together, to form a single agreement (*BP Kemi* [1979] OJ L 286/32). A 'concerted practice' can be found where undertakings co-ordinate their behaviour in a way that 'knowingly substitutes practical cooperation between them for the risks of competition' (Case 48/69 *ICI Ltd* v. *Commission* [1972] ECR 619).

To be caught by Art.81(1), an agreement or concerted practice must exist between at least two undertakings. A parent company and its wholly controlled subsidiaries are usually considered to form a 'single economic entity' and, as a result, are treated as a single undertaking for this purpose (Case C-73/95 *Viho Europe* v. *Commission* [1996] ECR I-5457). Consequently, many intra-group transactions will fall outside Art.81(1).

Affecting trade between Member States

'Affecting trade between Member States' has broad application. If an agreement 'may have an influence, direct or indirect, actual or potential, on the pattern of trade between Member States, such as might prejudice the aim of a single market', the criterion will be met (Case 42/84 *Remia* v. *Commission* [1985] ECR 2545). In practice, an effect on trade will generally be found where an agreement includes terms which relate to imports or exports, extends to more than one Member State or covers the whole of the territory of a single Member State (since this may have the effect of partitioning that state from the rest of the common market) (Case 8/72 *Cementhandelaren* v. *Commission* [1972] ECR 977). For these purposes, most if not all economic activity will qualify as 'trade'.

The Commission's Guidelines on the Effect on Trade Concept contained in Arts.81 and 82 of the Treaty (OJ C 101/07, 27 April 2004) suggests that there is unlikely to be an effect on trade between Member States if the combined market share of the parties in the relevant market does not exceed 5 per cent and the parties' combined turnover in products incorporating the licensed technology does not exceed €40 million, whether the agreement be horizontal, vertical or a licence.

Conversely, some agreements may by their nature be capable of affecting trade between Member States, for example, because they concern imports or exports or cover several Member States. For these, there is a rebuttable presumption that the effects on trade are appreciable if the above thresholds are exceeded.

How much effect on competition?

In principle, any agreement that may reduce competition between the parties or restrict the ability of third parties to compete, may be caught by Art.81(1). The distinction between 'preventing', 'restricting' and 'distorting' competition is not significant. The essence of the assessment is a comparison between the level of competition in the relevant market with and without the agreement.

An agreement falls outside Art.81(1) if it does not *appreciably* affect competition (Case 5/69 *Völk* v. *Vervaecke* [1969] ECR 295), that is normally where, for an agreement between actual or potential competitors, the combined share of the relevant market is 10 per cent or less; or between non-competitors, 15 per cent or less. If there is doubt about whether the parties are competitors, the lower 10 per cent threshold is used (Commission Notice on agreements of minor importance which do not appreciably restrict competition under Article 81(1) of the Treaty establishing the European Community (OJ C 368/07, 22 December 2001)). These '*de minimis*' provisions do not apply if the agreement contains serious or 'hardcore' restrictions of competition, such as price-fixing, limiting output or sales and allocation of markets between customers.

Consequences of infringing Art.81(1)

There is a fine distinction between falling outside Art.81(1), and falling within it but meeting the criteria for exemption under Art.81(3). At one level, the distinction has no practical relevance – the result is still that the agreement is 'allowed'. At another level, however, the distinction does matter: an apparent restriction that in fact falls outside Art.81(1) does not carry the risk that the Art.81(3) criteria will fail to be met, for instance because the restriction goes beyond what is necessary to achieve the pro-competitive objective. The risk is substantial.

1. If an agreement falls within Art.81(1) and it does not qualify for exemption under Art.81(3), its anti-competitive aspects are void and will not be enforced by national courts in the EU. The whole of the agreement might become unenforceable.
2. The Commission may impose fines of up to 10 per cent of worldwide turnover on undertakings for breach of Art.81(1) (Modernisation

Regulation (Council Regulation (EC) No.1/2003 of 16 December 2002 on the implementation of the rules on competition laid down in Articles 81 and 82 of the Treaty), Art.23(2)). Fines are, however, typically imposed only in the most serious cases.

3. The Commission may, by decision, order infringing undertakings to take such action as necessary to terminate the infringement (Modernisation Regulation, Art.7). The Commission can, however, accept legally binding commitments from undertakings to modify their behaviour in a defined way to overcome identified competition concerns, allowing the Commission to close the file without adopting an infringement decision (Modernisation Regulation, Art.9);
4. It is possible for third parties injured as a result of a breach of Art.81(1) to sue the offending undertakings for damages. Such an action can be brought in the English courts (*Crehan* v. *Inntrepreneur Pub Company CPC* [2004] EWCA 637).

Competition Act 1998 prohibitions

UK competition law derives from the Competition Act (CA) 1998 and the Enterprise Act (EA) 2002. The Chapter I and Chapter II prohibitions in CA 1998 mirror the Treaty prohibitions in Arts.81 and 82. The principal difference between EU and UK competition law in the area of restrictive agreements and abuses of dominance is that EU law applies where the restriction may affect trade between Member States of the EU, whereas UK law applies where the restriction may affect trade within the UK.

An agreement has been found to affect trade between Member States where it covers merely the whole of one Member State, as this would reinforce the compartmentalisation of national markets, contrary to the EC Treaty (Case 8/72 *Cementhandelaren* v. *Commission* [1972] ECR 977).

Both the UK and EU competition law may apply to the same agreement. Rather than proceeding with two investigations, the authorities decide, through detailed procedural rules and practice, which one is better placed to investigate. Other than that, the body of procedural rules is designed to achieve consistency in the application of competition law (i.e. in the investigation and penalising of infringements), whilst CA 1998, s.60 is designed to ensure that, subject to any 'relevant differences' in the provisions, the substance of the both sets of law develop consistently.

Restrictive agreements – the exemption regime

The exemption system for restrictive agreements is described below. There is no equivalent for abuses of dominance or mergers.

The block exemptions

If an agreement contains restrictions that fall within the EC Treaty, Art.81(1) or the Chapter I prohibition, there are two routes by which it might be exempt: a block exemption, and the 'general' exemption of Art.81(3) itself. Since 1 May 2004, there has been no system for formally notifying and obtaining individual exemption for agreements falling within Art.81(1) or the Chapter I prohibition. However, the exemption criteria of Art.81(3) and CA 1998, s.9 are still relevant: an agreement within Art.81(1) or s.9 will be exempt from the prohibition if the criteria are met, no prior decision to that effect being necessary (Modernisation Regulation, Art.1). In an action to enforce an agreement, the UK courts have power to declare that the criteria in Art.81(3) are met.

Block exemptions define classes of agreement that can generally be expected to meet the exemption criteria of Art.81(3), and they are enacted in EC law by Regulation. The UK also has power under CA 1998, s.6 to introduce block exemptions, but for most purposes, and to minimise the differences between EU and UK law, these will be few (the only one so far being the Competition Act 1998 (Public Transport Ticketing Schemes Block Exemption) Order 2001 (as amended), SI 2001/319). Instead, EU block exemptions take effect in UK law (i.e. as exemptions from the Chapter I prohibition) applied by CA 1998, s.10 as parallel exemptions.

The three block exemptions of principal interest to matters of intellectual property are:

(a) the R&D block exemption (created by Commission Regulation (EC) No.2659/2000 of 29 November 2000 on the application of Article 81(3) of the Treaty to categories of research and development agreements) (R&DBE);
(b) the Technology Transfer block exemption (TTBE); and
(c) the Vertical Restraints block exemption (created by Commission Regulation (EC) No.2790/1999 of 22 December 1999 on the application of Article 81(3) of the Treaty to categories of vertical agreements and concerted practices) (VRBE).

The Specialisation block exemption (Commission Regulation (EC) No.2658/2000 of 29 November 2000 on the application of Article 81(3) of the Treaty to categories of specialisation agreements) might also occasionally be relevant. However, this is outside the scope of this chapter.

Each block exemption defines the type of agreement that it covers.

1. *Vertical agreement:* one entered into between two or more undertakings each of which operates, for the purposes of the agreement, at a different level of the production or distribution chain, and relating to the conditions under which the parties may purchase, sell or resell certain goods or services (VRBE, Art.2(1)).

2. *Technology transfer agreement:* a patent licensing agreement, a know-how licensing agreement, a software copyright licensing agreement or a mixed patent, know-how or software copyright licensing agreement. Provisions which relate to the sale and purchase of products or which relate to the licensing of other intellectual property rights or the assignment of intellectual property rights may be covered, provided that those provisions do not constitute the primary object of the agreement and are directly related to the technology, or a combination thereof where part of the risk associated with the exploitation of the technology remains with the assignor (Art.1(1)(b), TTBE). This definition is discussed further at **8.5** below.
3. *Research and development:* the acquisition of know-how relating to products or processes and the carrying out of theoretical analysis, systematic study or experimentation, including experimental production, technical testing of products or processes, the establishment of the necessary facilities and the obtaining of intellectual property rights for the results (R&DBE, Art.2(4)).

Next, the block exemptions define market share boundaries within which one or other of the parties to the agreement must fall, if the block exemption is to apply. These vary between block exemptions.

The block exemptions each define a list of 'black-listed' clauses, the appearance of any of which will prevent the block exemption applying: these are often termed 'hardcore' restraints of competition, and include price fixing and market sharing.

Other than the hardcore restraints, it is often plain that a restriction falls outside the conditions of either general or block exemption not because the type of restriction is itself objectionable, but due to its extent, as discussed below.

The definition of relevant markets

To apply competition law properly, whether to restrictive agreements, dominant positions or mergers, it is necessary to define relevant markets. The ECJ established that whether an agreement fell within the prohibition, or met the conditions for exemption, depended on an analysis of market context (Case C-234/89 *Delimitis* v. *Henninger Bräu AG* [1991] ECR I-935).

The Commission 'Notice on the definition of the relevant market for the purposes of Community competition law' [1997] C372/03, describes market definition as (para.2):

> a tool to identify and define the boundaries of competition between firms. It serves to establish the framework within which competition policy is applied . . . The main purpose of market definition is to identify in a systematic way the competitive constraints that the undertakings involved face.

Defined markets have both a product and a geographic element:

> The objective of defining a market in both its product and geographic dimension is to identify those actual competitors of the undertakings involved that are capable of constraining those undertakings' behaviour and of preventing them from behaving independently of effective competitive pressure.

From the definition of a market it is possible to calculate market shares, and these are used to provide meaningful information regarding whether and in what degree, undertakings have 'market power'. Market power means the ability to price above cost, and finds legal expression in the EU law concept of 'dominance', which is discussed below.

The process of defining a market involves identifying the competitive constraints on an undertaking, which consist principally of demand substitutability (i.e. the range of products which consumers would regard as substitutes for each other) and supply substitutability (i.e. the ability of suppliers to switch to the relevant products and to market them in the short term). Potential competition is also relevant to consider as a constraint on an undertaking's behaviour, but this is taken into account after the market has been defined. The most important is demand substitutability: it is considered the most immediate and effective disciplinary force on the suppliers of a given product, in particular on their pricing decisions.

INTELLECTUAL PROPERTY MARKET DEFINITION

Defining markets is not easy, particularly when the markets involve intellectual property, as distinct from products produced or marketed under intellectual property. In the TTBE Guidelines, the Commission distinguishes 'technology' and 'product' markets. Technology markets consist of (para.22):

> licensed technology and its substitutes – i.e. other technologies which are regarded by the licensees as interchangeable with or substitutable for the licensed technology, by reason of the technologies' characteristics, their royalties and their intended use.

The process for defining relevant technology markets is the same as for other product markets. But there are two practical problems. The first is that, whilst a technology is being developed, it is extremely difficult to predict what market will be identified as relevant by a court or competition authority in the future.

The second problem is that it is not easy to assign market shares to the undertakings possessing technology. The Commission suggests two approaches to calculating market shares. The preferred method is to calculate shares from sales of products incorporating the licensed technology on downstream product markets. In practice, applying the market share caps in block exemptions can be fraught with uncertainty.

However, market share is not the only indicator of the market power that might be conferred by ownership of intellectual property. For technology licences, the Commission considers that outside the safe harbour of market share ceilings provided by the TTBE, 'market share may not always be a good indication of the relative strength of available technologies' (TTBE Guidelines, para. 24). The Commission would instead consider the number of independently-controlled technologies available, besides the technologies controlled by the parties to the agreement, that are substitutes for the licensed technology at a comparable cost.

EC prohibition on abuses of dominance

Article 82 states:

> Any abuse by one or more undertakings of a dominant position within the common market or in a substantial part of it shall be prohibited as incompatible with the common market insofar as it may affect trade between Member States.
>
> Such abuse may, in particular, consist in:
>
> (a) directly or indirectly imposing unfair purchase or selling prices or other unfair trading conditions;
> (b) limiting production, markets or technical development to the prejudice of consumers;
> (c) applying dissimilar conditions to equivalent transactions with other trading parties, thereby placing them at a competitive disadvantage;
> (d) making the conclusion of contracts subject to acceptance by other parties of supplementary obligations which, by their nature or according to commercial usage, have no connection with the subject of such contracts.

To determine whether an abuse contrary to Art.82 has occurred, it is necessary to consider whether an undertaking:

(a) holds a dominant position in a substantial part of the EU;
(b) has abused that dominant position; and
(c) has, as a result, affected trade between Member States.

A dominant position

Dominance, for a defined product and geographic market, is:

> a position of economic strength enjoyed by an undertaking which enables it to hinder the maintenance of effective competition on the relevant market by allowing it to behave to an appreciable extent independently of its competitors and customers and ultimately of consumers.
>
> Case 322/81 *Michelin* v. *Commission* [1983] ECR 3461

Variations on this definition have been used in other cases, e.g. Case 85/76 *Hoffman-La Roche* v. *Commission* [1979] ECR 461.

The test for dominance is *not* whether there is a complete absence of competition to the dominant firm. It is whether the competition is effective in constraining the behaviour of the dominant firm.

An undertaking might be found dominant in a defined market if various conditions are met: these are not precise conditions, and the assessment of dominance involves evaluating these in the precise market context. Amongst these conditions, market share can be very significant. At one extreme, a share below 40 per cent is unlikely to confer dominance unless other conditions are present. At the other extreme, even very high market shares above 50 per cent are not conclusive evidence of dominance. It might be possible to rebut an allegation of dominance, for example, if there is good evidence that the high market shares are unstable, or if market entry/supply-side substitution is possible, which would defeat any attempt by the undertaking to charge supra-competitive prices.

However, high market shares, together with other conditions, can create a position of market dominance. Intellectual property can contribute to a dominant position by conferring a technology advantage on an undertaking and a barrier to the entry of a competitor, although it should be stressed that the existence of an intellectual property right *in itself* will not confer the dominant position.

A dominant position can be held solely or, exceptionally, collectively. This derives from the text of Art.82 – the prohibition is on the abuse *by one or more* undertakings. A position of collective dominance requires that the allegedly dominant undertakings be able to reach a common understanding about the terms of co-ordination, such that:

- those firms can monitor whether the terms of co-ordination are adhered to;
- there is a deterrent to deviating from that common understanding; and
- outsiders, including current and future competitors outside the common understanding, would not be able to jeopardise the results coming from that coordination (Case T-342/99 *Airtours* v. *Commission* [2002] ECR II-2585).

Abuse

Dominance itself is not unlawful. Abuse, by a dominant undertaking, is. Legally, a dominant undertaking has a 'special responsibility' not to damage competition. This does not prevent it meeting a challenge posed by a competitor, such as lowering its prices or innovating, but in this area, great care is needed to avoid the situation where 'meeting competition' becomes abusive.

Abuses that are relevant to intellectual property exploitation are discussed in **8.5**.

EC merger control

The EC Merger Regulation (Council Regulation (EC) No.139/2004 of 20 January 2004 on the control of concentrations between undertakings) (ECMR) regulates 'concentrations' (including mergers, acquisitions and full-function joint ventures) with a 'Community dimension'. Since research often takes place through the vehicle of a joint venture, the ECMR may be important for intellectual property development.

When the European Commission clears a concentration under the ECMR, it also clears 'ancillary restraints', that is, restrictions on competition accepted between the parties, for example, some form of supply arrangement or intellectual property licence, that are 'directly related and necessary' to the implementation of the concentration. It is a question of fact, to be adjudged by the parties when transacting, whether a particular restriction or restrictions are actually 'directly related and necessary'. If they are not, or to the extent that they are not, they might not be enforceable in national courts under national law.

UK merger control

UK mergers are regulated by Part 3 of the Enterprise Act 2002. Ancillary restraints are in essence treated in the same way as under the ECMR.

8.4 COMPETITION LAW AND TRANSACTIONS RESULTING IN THE CREATION OF INTELLECTUAL PROPERTY

This section is concerned primarily with R&D, i.e. situations where undertakings collaborate in R&D, where the results can be protected by intellectual property rights. Together, the undertakings might achieve what individually they could not, whether owing to lack of money or lack of expertise. Through R&D, the parties might be able to bring products to market earlier.

There are two contexts to examine: first, where there is a transaction falling within the EU or UK merger control rules; second, where the transaction does not fall within merger control rules. In the latter case, Art.81(1) and (3) and the national equivalents might apply.

Merger control – EU

The ECMR will apply to the establishment of a 'full function joint venture' (JV) by two or more parties, where there is a 'Community dimension'. There are several elements to define.

Control

First, there is the creation of an entity, for example, a limited company, which is jointly controlled by two or more of its shareholders. 'Control' comprises a range of rights that the shareholders might have that enable them to exercise 'decisive influence' on the JV entity, including voting rights at general meeting or on boards. As a minimum a shareholder, albeit with a trivial or a non-voting shareholding, may be considered to 'control' the JV entity if it has a right of veto over one or more matters of strategic importance, such as its budget or business plan, the appointment or removal of its senior management, or its strategic investments.

The practical advice with joint control is that advisers must pay close attention to the documents incorporating the JV, such as the shareholders' agreement, often in conjunction with the constitutional documents (such as articles of association for a UK company) of that entity, to establish whether there is likely to be joint control. In cases of genuine doubt, it is advisable to seek (on a non-binding basis) the opinion of Commission officials about whether they consider the JV to be jointly controlled.

Full-function

Second, the entity must be 'full-function', that is, it is 'performing on a lasting basis all the functions of an autonomous economic entity' (ECMR, Art.3(4)). As a minimum, the JV entity must have a management dedicated to its day-to-day operations and access to sufficient resources including finance, staff and assets to conduct its business activities within the area provided for. Importantly, a JV will not be full function if it takes over only one aspect of its parents' activities.

The practical implication is that a JV which has only R&D as its objective will not be considered full function, as it would be taking over only one aspect of its parents' operations. But if a JV for example would also carry out (or be responsible for carrying out) the downstream production of the products resulting from the R&D, that might constitute full-functionality. It is therefore important to look carefully at the proposed operations of the JV.

Community dimension

Community dimension is a measure of whether a transaction is large enough to be reviewed, and is established by the relevant undertakings meeting one of two sets of turnover tests. The details are beyond the scope of this chapter.

If the ECMR applies, national merger control rules will not normally apply but the creation of the JV will need administrative approval from the European Commission, which will investigate whether the creation of the JV (and thereby the possible reduction of competition between the parents in the area(s) in which the JV will be active) would significantly impede effective competition in the common market or in a substantial part of it.

Directly related and necessary restraints

A clearance decision by the European Commission will also cover 'ancillary restraints', that is, restrictions on competition agreed between the parties that are 'directly related and necessary' to the concentration. The Commission has issued a 'Notice on restrictions directly related and necessary to concentrations' (2005/C56/03). The question is an objective one (that is, it is not determined merely by the undertakings regarding restrictions as directly related and necessary). However, in common with the application of the rules on restrictive agreements, it remains for the undertakings and their advisers to assess whether any such restrictions are 'directly related and necessary', which is a question of fact on which the Commission no longer opines in its decisions.

Whether a particular restraint is directly related and necessary depends on an assessment under the principles of Arts.81 and 82. Of relevance here is the question of licence agreements granted as part of the transaction. The Commission regards licences, which are granted by the parent undertakings to the JV, as directly related and necessary, regardless of whether or not the licence is exclusive, and whether or not it is limited in time. The licence may be restricted to a particular field of use, which corresponds to the activities of the joint venture.

If the JV grants licences to its parents, or cross-licences, these will also be ancillary under similar principles. The Commission treats intellectual property in broadly the same fashion. Licences of patents and know-how would be ancillary even if not limited in time, whether simple or exclusive, whether or not limited to certain fields of use. Similar principles apply to licences of trade marks, business names, design rights, copyrights or similar rights.

In the following cases restrictions will not be treated as ancillary.

1. Territorial limitations on manufacture reflecting the territory of the transferred activity.
2. Restrictions that go beyond otherwise permitted levels, such as those which protect the licensor rather than the licensee.
3. Licence agreements between the JV's parents.

UK merger control

The Office of Fair Trading's approach to ancillary restraints follows that of the Commission: by CA 1998, Sched.1, mergers incorporating ancillary restraints are excluded from the Act's effect.

Non-merger control – the R&D block exemption

When the R&D block exemption applies

The discussion below defines R&D agreements and distinguishes them from technology transfer agreements and vertical agreements, before applying the R&DBE particularly in the context of clauses relating to intellectual property.

It is important to analyse precisely the nature and purpose of the agreement because this will determine which block exemption might be relevant. The classification, primarily between the TTBE and R&DBE, depends on the 'primary object' of the agreement: an agreement can contain elements of both types, but the primary object is determinative.

The Commission defines research and development in the R&DBE as (Art.2(4)):

> the acquisition of know-how relating to products or processes and the carrying out of theoretical analysis, systematic study or experimentation, including experimental production, technical testing of products or processes, the establishment of the necessary facilities and the obtaining of intellectual property rights for the results.

Research and development agreements encompass both pro- and anti-competitive aspects. A recent formulation of the Commission's work in balancing these stated:

> Cooperation in R&D may reduce duplicative, unnecessary costs, lead to significant cross fertilisation of ideas and experience and thus result in products and technologies being developed more rapidly than would otherwise be the case. As a general rule, R&D cooperation tends to increase overall R&D activities . . . Through R&D cooperation there is a likelihood that overall R&D by SMEs will increase and that they will be able to compete more vigorously with stronger market players.
>
> Under certain circumstances, however, R&D agreements may cause competition problems such as restrictive effects on prices, output, innovation or variety or quality of products.
>
> (Commission Notice – Guidelines on the applicability of Article 81 of the EC Treaty to horizontal cooperation agreements (Horizontal Guidelines) (2001/C3/02), paras.40–2)

The table below compares the 'primary object' for the application of each block exemption.

R&DBE	TTBE
Conditions under which the undertakings pursue:	Technology transfer agreements entered into between two undertakings permitting the production of contract products. Technology transfer is:
joint research and development of products or processes and joint exploitation of the results of that research and development	patent licensing agreement
joint exploitation of the results of the research and development of products or processes jointly carried out pursuant to a prior agreement between the same parties	know-how licensing agreement
joint research and development of products or processes excluding joint exploitation of the results	software copyright licence agreement

Thus, as a broad rule of thumb, the R&DBE will apply to cooperation through which intellectual property rights relating to new products or processes will be created; the TTBE will apply to the manner in which those intellectual property rights are exploited through licensing to third parties. The Commission attempts to guide undertakings and advisers in choosing which block exemption to apply.

Where undertakings establish a production JV (rather than a full-function JV) and license the JV to exploit technology, which is used in the production of the products produced by the JV, the R&DBE will apply. It will also apply to licensing between the parties and by the parties to a joint entity in the context of a R&D agreement, including the conditions for licensing the fruits of the R&D agreement to third parties.

Third party licences are covered by the TTBE:

> since third party licensees are not party to the research and development agreement, the individual licence agreement concluded with third parties is not covered [by the R&DBE]. (TTBE Guidelines, para.60.)

There is further guidance in the TTBE Guidelines on when the VRBE might apply; whereas the TTBE regulates agreements between licensor and licensee of technology, including obligations imposed on the licensee to regulate the way in which it sells the licensed product, the VRBE regulates agreements between a licensee and buyers (further down the distribution chain).

Effect of the R&D block exemption

Agreements within the scope of the R&DBE are exempted from the Art.81 prohibition for the duration of the research and development. If the parties jointly exploit the results, the exemption can continue to apply for up to seven years from when the contract products were first put on to the market within the common market. If the parties are competitors, this exemption (both during and after the research and development) applies only where the combined shares of the parties do not exceed 25 per cent of the relevant market (Art.4).

'No challenge' versus 'termination on challenge'

The block exemption does not provide exemption for 'no challenge clauses', but may exempt, depending on circumstances, 'termination on challenge' clauses – that is, clauses that permit one party to terminate an agreement (for example, a licence) if the validity of the intellectual property underpinning that licence is challenged by the other party. The distinction between no-challenge clauses and termination-on-challenge clauses is a fine one. Practically, it might make little difference: an agreement by which one party can terminate for the other's challenge might act to discourage such challenge. Nevertheless, the Commission states that the two are distinct. The problem with no-challenge clauses is that they may contribute to keeping in place invalid intellectual property rights, which can discourage further innovation.

The principles are the same whether the agreement is properly characterised as R&D or technology transfer, but the application is different because the role of intellectual property is slightly different in each agreement. To qualify under the R&DBE, an R&D agreement must not prohibit a challenge, after completion of the R&D, to (Art.5(1)(b)):

(a) the validity of intellectual property rights which the parties hold in the common market and which are relevant to the R&D; or
(b) the validity of intellectual property which the parties hold in the common market and which protect the results of the R&D.

If an agreement should contain a no-challenge clause, the R&DBE implies that exemption will not be available. Although the R&DBE does not distinguish, as in other block exemptions, between 'hardcore' and merely 'excluded' (but not hardcore) restrictions, the proper meaning of the prohibition on no-challenge clauses can be ascertained from the TTBE, by analogy. There, a no-challenge clause is an 'excluded' provision: unlike a hardcore restraint, it will not automatically cause the whole agreement to fail, without the possibility of severance. In practice, however, whether an offending no-challenge clause can be severed will depend upon the terms of the agreement and the interpretation given by national courts.

Nevertheless, the prohibition of no-challenge clauses is 'without prejudice to the possibility to provide for termination of the research and development agreement in the event of one of the parties challenging the validity of such intellectual property rights' (Art.5(1)(b)). The distinction is justified, not in the R&DBE Guidelines, but in the TTBE Guidelines, which argue that a termination-on-challenge clause justifies lighter treatment, in effect by balancing the interests of licensor and licensee – and in particular, not forcing a licensor to continue dealing with a licensee that challenges the very basis of the licence (TTBE Guidelines, para.113). Applied to R&D agreements, if one party to the joint R&D challenges the intellectual property which have been developed as a result of that R&D, this implies a serious breakdown in goodwill between the parties, making it reasonable to allow for termination in that case.

Prohibited restrictions

Agreements will not be exempt under the R&DBE if they contain the type of restrictions that are in other block exemptions referred to as 'hardcore' restraints, which would not be exempt under Art.81(3), such as the limitation of output or sales and the fixing of prices when selling the contract product to third parties. In particular, Art.5(1)(a) of the R&DBE excludes from the exemption:

> the restriction of the freedom of the participating undertakings to carry out research and development independently or in cooperation with third parties in a field unconnected with that to which the research and development relates or, after its completion, in the field to which it relates or in a connected field.

This might be termed an extension of the general principle in Art.81(3) that to be exempt, an agreement must not contain restrictions that are not indispensable to achieving the agreement's objectives. It is plain that a restriction on each party's ability to do research in unconnected fields goes beyond what is necessary either to achieve the object of the joint research or to maintain necessary levels of goodwill between the parties.

Conclusions

Competition law can apply to transactions that might result in the creation of intellectual property. These transactions might be structural, in which case merger control rules might apply, perhaps alongside Art.81 for ancillary restraints or JVs having the object or effect of coordinating the competitive behaviour of parents. The transactions might also be collaborative, in which case the general principles of Art.81 and the relevant block exemptions will be relevant.

8.5 COMPETITION LAW AND THE EXPLOITATION OF INTELLECTUAL PROPERTY

The discussion below relates to transactions where the principal purpose is the exploitation of intellectual property. The approach adopted here is to distinguish technology and non-technology licensing, although it will be seen that many of the principles of the former can be applied directly or by analogy to the latter.

This will be of particular relevance to agreements to exploit involving manufacturing products or providing services based on licensed technology.

The application of Art.81 to technology licensing

As discussed above, the test for applying Art.81(1) to a licence is whether the licence, or any of its clauses, has as its object or effect, the prevention, restriction or distortion of competition. Some restrictions (for example, price fixing clauses) are regarded as inherently anti-competitive and are considered to be 'restrictions by object'. If found, then it is not necessary to prove that there has been an anti-competitive effect (Cases 56 and 58/64 *Consten and Grundig* v. *Commission* [1966] ECR 299). If an agreement does not have an anti-competitive object, it is necessary to examine whether it has an anti-competitive effect.

Two classes of restrictions will be examined: those that might, on the whole, fall outside Art.81(1), and those which, if they do fall within Art.81(1) might benefit from exemption, either under the TTBE or by meeting the Art.81(3) conditions of exemption.

Restrictions commonly falling outside Art.81(1)

According to para.155 of the TTBE Guidelines, the following types of common obligations generally do not restrict competition and therefore do not fall under Art.81(1), whether the agreement is between competitors or non-competitors:

(a) confidentiality obligations;
(b) obligations on licensees not to sub-license;
(c) obligations not to use the licensed technology after the expiry of the agreement, provided that the licensed technology remains valid and in force;
(d) obligations to assist the licensor in enforcing the licensed intellectual property rights;
(e) obligations to pay minimum royalties or to produce a minimum quantity of products incorporating the licensed technology; and

(f) obligations to use the licensor's trade mark or indicate the name of the licensor on the product.

Restrictions falling within Art.81(1) – application of the TTBE

For a licence which contains restrictions falling within the Art.81(1) prohibition nonetheless to fall within the TTBE, and thus be block-exempt from Art.81(1), certain formal requirements must be met. Thus, to assess whether the exemption will avail either directly or by analogy, the TTBE requires businesses to undertake careful analysis of licences.

WHAT IS 'TECHNOLOGY TRANSFER'?

First, the licence must concern 'technology transfer': patent licences, know-how licences, software copyright licences and any combination of these. This apparent simplicity belies the complex definitions of those terms.

'Patent' is defined in TTBE, Art.1(1)(h) to include patents, patent applications, utility models, applications for registration of utility models, designs, topographies of semiconductor products, supplementary protection certificates for medicinal products or other products to which such supplementary protection certificate may be obtained and plant breeder's certificates.

'Know-how' means a package of non-patented practical information, resulting from experience and testing, which is secret, substantial and identified (TTBE, Art.1(1)(i)). This means that, for a know-how licence to come within the TTBE it must cover know-how that is:

1. Secret, in the sense of not generally known or easily accessible. This may require that it is confidential and supplied under an obligation of confidentiality.
2. Substantial, in the sense that it is significant and useful for the production of the products or services covered by the licence or the application of the process covered by the licence. In other words, the information must significantly contribute to or facilitate the production of the contract products. Where the licence relates to process technologies, the know-how should be useful in the sense that it can reasonably be expected at the date of conclusion of the agreement to be capable of significantly improving the competitive position of the licensee, for example by reducing his production costs.
3. Identified, in that the know-how must be described in a sufficiently comprehensive manner to make it possible to verify the fulfilment of the two criteria above.

In addition, licences of other intellectual property, such as trade marks, are covered by the TTBE if these other intellectual property licences are not the *primary object* of the agreement and are directly related to the production of the products or services being produced under the agreement. Such provisions are covered only to the extent that they are contained in a licence of patent, software copyright and/or know-how rights and they serve to enable the licensee better to exploit the licensed technology (TTBE Guidelines, para.50). The judgement of the 'primary object' of an agreement is subtle.

Further, assignments of patents, know-how, software copyright (or a combination) fall within the TTBE where the assignor retains part of the risk associated with the exploitation of the technology. In particular this covers the situation where the sum payable in consideration of the assignment depends on the turnover obtained by the assignee for products made using the assigned technology, the quantity of such products produced or the number of operations carried out using the technology.

RIGHTS TO MANUFACTURE

The TTBE applies only where the licensee is actually manufacturing a product using the licensed technology, or is providing the licensed service. It will apply even if the licensee must carry out further development work before there is a product or process that can be commercially exploited, provided that an end product has been identified. It also applies to agreements by which the licensee undertakes to produce exclusively for the licensor, certain products on the basis of the licensed technology – effectively contract manufacturing arrangements. Further, the TTBE covers obligations on the licensee to impose restrictions on its resellers, provided these are compatible with the VRBE.

The TTBE will not apply to pure sales licences, or licences where other intellectual property rights are licensed but where these rights are not merely ancillary to the patent, software copyright or know-how licence. However, where copyright is licensed for reproducing or distributing the protected work (i.e. producing copies for resale), the TTBE principles will apply by analogy because it is similar to technology licensing (TTBE Guidelines, para.51).

Also, the TTBE will not apply to agreements whose *primary object* is sub-licensing, but it will apply by analogy to master licensing agreements where production of products or provision of services using the licensed technology is the primary object. Finally, the TTBE does not apply where the primary object is providing R&D services, not production of goods using licensed technology – there, the R&D block exemption applies.

MULTI-PARTY AGREEMENTS

Although the TTBE formally applies to agreements only if they are between two parties, if there are more than two parties, the TTBE can still apply by analogy (TTBE Guidelines, para.40). It will not apply to agreements to form technology pools, where the owners of different intellectual property pool these for licensing to third parties as a package of technology.

DURATION

If the TTBE applies, the exemption will last for the lifetime of the patent or software copyright (i.e. until it has lapsed, expired or been declared invalid) or, for know-how, as long as it remains secret. If the know-how becomes public owing to the licensee's actions, the exemption will nonetheless last for the duration of the agreement.

Competitors and non-competitors

How the TTBE applies will differ according to whether the parties to an agreement are competitors on the technology or product markets. Competitors on the technology market are parties which could license competing technologies to third parties. Competitors on the product market either sell competing products (actual competitors) or would realistically enter the market by supply-side substitution if market conditions warranted (potential competitors). To assess whether parties are competitors, the question needs to be asked *in the absence* of the licence – would they be considered competitors without the licence?

MARKET SHARE CAPS

One difference in application is the market share cap, above which in general the TTBE will not apply (although Art.81(3) still might). For agreements between competitors, the combined share must not exceed 20 per cent of the relevant technology and/or product market(s). For non-competitors, the individual share must not exceed 30 per cent. If after the agreement has been signed the market shares expand and breach the caps, the exemption will continue to apply for two calendar years following that in which the cap was breached (TTBE, Art.8(2)).

HARDCORE RESTRAINTS

A further difference is in the definition of 'hardcore' restraints, the presence of which will invalidate the use of the TTBE or even Art.81(3), not merely for the clauses themselves, but for the entire agreement. The consequence of including hardcore restraints is that the whole agreement is likely to be void and competition authorities and third parties might seek public (fines) and private (damages) remedies from the parties. The following is an overview of the hardcore restraints: for their detailed application, refer to the text of the TTBE and its Guidelines.

For agreements between competitors, these include:

(a) restrictions on a party's ability to determine its sale price;
(b) limitations of output (except those on the licensee in a non-reciprocal agreement or only imposed on one licensee in a reciprocal agreement);
(c) the allocation of markets or customers (with certain exceptions); and
(d) restrictions on the licensee's ability to exploit its own technology or restrictions on either party's ability to carry out independent research and development, unless such a restriction is indispensable to prevent the disclosure of the licensed know-how to third parties.

For agreements between non-competitors, hardcore restraints include:

(a) restrictions on a party's ability to determine its sale price, excepting recommended resale prices and maximum resale price obligations (provided these do not amount to fixed or minimum resale prices as a result of pressure from or incentives offered by any of the parties);
(b) restrictions of the territory into which, or the customers to whom, the licensee may sell the contract products or services (with exceptions); and
(c) the restriction of active or passive sales to end-users by members of a selective distribution system operating at the retail level of trade, without prejudice to the possibility of prohibiting a member of the system from operating out of an unauthorised place of establishment.

EXCLUDED RESTRICTIONS

There are three excluded restrictions within the TTBE. Unlike hardcore restrictions, these restrictions can (subject to national law) be severed from the agreement: consequently, the benefit of the TTBE would be lost only for that clause, allowing the rest to be enforced. These are first, any direct or indirect obligation on the licensee to grant (or second, to assign) an exclusive licence to the licensor to use the licensee's own severable improvements or his own new applications of the licensed technology will not benefit from exemption. Severable improvements are those that can be exploited without using the licensed technology. Non-exclusive licences of severable improvements or new applications (including those that are not reciprocal) are permitted. Thirdly, there is, in common with the R&D block exemption discussed above, a prohibition on no-challenge clauses, although it is permissible to use a termination on challenge clause.

Other common provisions are permitted up to the market share thresholds (in addition to those discussed in the previous section).

RESTRICTIONS PERMITTED UP TO THE MARKET SHARE CAPS

Certain restrictions in licences that fall within Art.81(1) will be permitted where the market share caps are not exceeded. If these caps are exceeded, Art.81(3) might still apply. Restrictions within this category are:

(a) *tying* (such as a licensor making the licensing of one technology conditional upon the licensee taking a licence for another technology or purchasing a product from the licensor);
(b) *bundling* (where two technologies or a technology and a product are bundled together and are not sold separately);
(c) *non-compete clauses*, provided they do not limit the licensee's ability to exploit his own technology or his ability to carry out independent research and development, unless indispensable to prevent the disclosure of the licensed know-how to third parties; or
(d) *royalties* – unless the setting of royalty rates is designed to achieve one of the blacklisted restrictions, such as an obligation, in an agreement between competitors, making royalties payable on products that do not incorporate the licensed technology. In that case, the TTBE will not apply.

Standardisation agreements

Technology licences between licensors and licensees can, and in the electronics industry in particular often do, take place in the context of a standardisation agreement. These raise special complexities.

Establishing a technical standard can be pro- or anti-competitive. On the one hand, where undertakings agree to develop and sell products that conform only to a particular standard, competition will be restricted, in that each undertaking will have agreed not to diverge from the agreed standard. Such a restriction will fall within Art.81(1).

On the other hand, where undertakings may freely diverge from that standard, the Horizontal Guidelines note that competition is not restricted and Art.81(1) will not apply. Moreover, if a standards agreement does engage Art.81(1), it might be exempt under Art.81(3) if there are adequate countervailing benefits. For example, the standard must be set in a transparent and non-discriminatory manner, it should not limit innovation, and the necessary information to apply the standard must be made available to anyone wishing to enter the market.

Furthermore, to meet the requirement of 'indispensability', the agreement on standards must not go beyond what is needed to achieve the specific level of standardisation. Finally, to ensure that competition is not eliminated, third parties must be able to access the standard on fair, reasonable and non-discriminatory (FRAND) terms; i.e. licences on such terms must be available to all-comers. By contrast, if the standard is not open in this way, the benefit of Art.81(3) exemption might be lost.

How far access to a standard is necessary for market participation will depend on several factors. The competitive importance of the benefits accruing from access to the standard or the standard setting procedure is relevant. Further, the availability of alternative standards is material. For standards permitting interoperability this will be determined by the market share of the parties using the standard. It is also necessary to assess whether there are barriers to establishing a competing standard.

A standard's effects on competition between the parties with access to it will depend, first, on whether the parties are actual or potential competitors. If they are not, the standard can have no restrictive effect on competition between them. If the parties are actual or potential competitors, the standard may reduce the ability of parties using the standard to compete, by reducing product diversity and reducing the scope and incentive for innovation. The extent of these restrictive effects will in general depend on the market shares of the parties; whether the parties agree to use the standard exclusively; whether the parties agree to share innovations relating to the standard; and the depth of the standard. If full design specifications are standardised as opposed to mere functional specifications, product differentiation and further improvements may be foreclosed.

In addition, the market power associated with ownership of a standard may enable the owner to impose additional anti-competitive terms and conditions, for example tying, on licensees of the standard.

While seeking to limit the anti-competitive effects that may flow from standardisation, competition law must also take account of the potential advantages of standardisation. In the European Union, these may include eliminating barriers to trade between Member States. In addition, standardisation may permit private firms to capture the benefits of network effects in marketing, rationalisation of productions, economies of scale, R&D efficiencies and others, whilst at the same time offering consumers benefits in interoperability and substitutability of products, and known product qualities. Where a standard actually or potentially offers such advantages, these must be weighed against any potentially anti-competitive effects.

Arrangements for patent licensing in the context of standardisation agreements should therefore:

(a) be based on objective verification of which patents are essential;
(b) not restrict the terms of licences (other than requiring FRAND terms);
(c) ensure licensees are not required to pay for patents they do not need; and
(d) not require licensees to pay unreasonably high royalties, at least insofar as this would restrict competition in downstream markets.

Technology licensing and abuse of dominance

As discussed above, it is a pre-condition to a finding that an undertaking has abused a dominant position contrary to Art.82 that the undertaking be found to enjoy a dominant position in a defined product and geographic market. For technology licensing, the concepts of dominance and abuse are intractable.

First, an intellectual property right does not, *of itself*, constitute a market that could be defined for competition law purposes (Cases C-241 and 242/91 *RTE* v. *Commission* ('*Magill*') [1995] ECR I-743), although this may be true in some instances. Instead, an intellectual property right can form part of a broader technology market.

Second, where significant intellectual property is created and pooled and used in standards, the delineation between technologies and undertakings that compete, and those that complement each other, can be difficult to find.

Third, the types of abuse that are commonly alleged (such as refusal to supply, excessive pricing and discriminatory pricing) might be straightforward to understand in principle, but fraught with difficulty and controversy in application. When an undertaking might be forced under competition law to grant a licence of intellectual property, and on what terms, is a vexed question.

Forms of abuse

EXCESSIVE PRICING

It is abusive for a dominant company to charge prices that are unfairly high compared to the 'economic value' of the products or services being supplied. To establish abuse, the comparators are the prices for comparable goods or services (Case 226/84 *British Leyland* v. *Commission* [1986] ECR 3263) or the costs of production of the relevant goods or services (Case 27/76 *United Brands* v. *Commission* [1978] ECR 207). In a case about copyright royalties, referred to the ECJ on the question of 'unfair trading conditions' contrary to Art.82(a), an abuse was found where royalties were higher in one Member State than in another, taking account of relevant differences:

> When an undertaking holding a dominant position imposes scales of fees for its services which are appreciably higher than those charged in other Member States and where a comparison of the fee levels has been made on a consistent basis, that difference must be regarded as indicative of an abuse of a dominant position. In such a case it is for the undertaking in question to justify the difference by reference to objective dissimilarities between the situation in the Member State concerned and the situation prevailing in all the other Member States.
>
> (Joined Cases 110/88, 241/88, 242/88 Lucazeau v. SACEM [1989] ECR 2811)

However, identifying the point at which a price becomes abusively high is extremely difficult. The case law on excessive pricing is still thin.

DISCRIMINATORY PRICING

Discriminatory pricing can be abusive, as a form of 'applying dissimilar conditions to equivalent transactions with other trading parties, thereby placing them at a competitive disadvantage' (Art.82(c)). For instance, a dominant company charging distributors different prices for particular goods delivered to the same place, according to the country where the distributor is intending to resell them, has been condemned (Case 27/76 *United Brands* v. *Commission* [1978] ECR 207).

Where the discrimination is less artificial, or objectively justified, a price difference might be permitted. If not, and the pricing significantly affects the purchaser's ability to compete in a neighbouring or downstream market on which it competes with the dominant firm, it may be objectionable. There is some overlap with excessive pricing – a price that is excessive compared to comparables might also be discriminatory within Art.82(c).

REFUSAL TO LICENSE

A non-dominant undertaking can lawfully choose its trading partners – to supply, or not to supply. A dominant undertaking might not be so free. A refusal to supply, or a refusal to grant access to *essential facilities*, without objective justification, can be abusive under two headings of Art.82: limiting production, markets or technical development (Art.82(b)) or applying dissimilar conditions to equivalent transactions (Art.82(c)). This includes a refusal to supply except on terms that are unacceptable to the buyer (known as *constructive* refusal to supply).

However, before a refusal to license intellectual property can be abusive, more conditions must be met. To understand how these conditions arise, it is worth summarising the principal recent cases.

Principal cases

MAGILL – EXCEPTIONAL CIRCUMSTANCES

In *Magill* (above), the ECJ found that the exercise of an exclusive right by its owner may, in exceptional circumstances, involve abusive conduct which may justify the imposition of a compulsory licence. The case involved a refusal to supply information which, since only available from the single source in the form of listings of forthcoming television programmes produced by the owner, was in effect protected by copyright: no one could publish the information without copying these listings. For an intellectual property holder, there is some comfort that there would be no compulsory licensing of intellectual property *unless* there were exceptional circumstances, but what these were precisely, was not known. The elements in *Magill* were that the refusal to supply prevented a new product (a weekly rather than daily TV guide) appearing. This was a product which the intellectual property holder did not offer, and for which there was potential demand.

BRONNER – TEST OF 'INDISPENSABILITY'

Oscar Bronner claimed that Mediaprint, which owned the only national newspaper home delivery network in Austria, abused its dominant position by refusing access to Bronner. The ECJ ruled that, unlike *Magill*, the refusal of the service would not eliminate all competition in the daily newspaper market. To show that the creation of an alternative delivery system was not realistic and that access to the existing system was indispensable, it was not enough to argue that it was unviable because of the small circulation of the daily newspaper or newspapers to be distributed. It would be necessary to show that it was not economically viable to create a second home-delivery scheme for the distribution of daily newspapers with a circulation comparable to that of the daily newspapers distributed by the existing scheme (Case C-7/97 *Oscar Bronner GmbH & Co. KG* v. *Mediaprint Zeitungs- und Zeitschriftenverlag GmbH & Co. KG and Others* [1998] ECR I-7791).

IMS – INDISPENSABILITY IN INTELLECTUAL PROPERTY LICENSING

IMS refused to license its copyright in its '1860 brick structure' by which Germany was divided into 1,860 sales areas, which had become standard in the German pharmaceutical industry. The ECJ ruled that a refusal by a dominant undertaking to grant an intellectual property licence constitutes an abuse only where the product or service at issue is indispensable to an undertaking to carry out business in the relevant market (following the *Oscar Bronner* case) and the following conditions are fulfilled:

(a) the undertaking requesting the licence intends to offer new products or services not offered by the copyright owner and for which there is potential consumer demand (that is, where such undertaking does not intend to limit itself essentially to duplicating the goods or services already offered on the relevant downstream market by the copyright owner);
(b) the refusal is not justified by objective considerations; and
(c) the refusal has the effect of reserving a downstream market to the copyright owner by eliminating all competition on that market (Case C-418/01 *IMS Health GmbH & Co. OHG and NDC Health GmbH & Co. KG* (29 April 2004) [2004] ECR I-5039.

INTEL – MAY BE ABUSE EVEN IF NEW PRODUCT NOT ENTIRELY EXCLUDED

In *Intel Corp.* v. *Via Technologies and Anr* [2002] All ER(D) 346, the UK Court of Appeal held in a preliminary judgment that there was an arguable case that a refusal to grant a patent licence could constitute abuse of a dominant position. The court found that the circumstances in *Magill* and *IMS* were not necessarily the only circumstances which might amount to abuse. Thus there could in principle be an abuse even if the dominant party's actions did not entirely exclude a new product.

MICROSOFT – WERE THE *IMS* CONDITIONS NECESSARY OR MERELY SUFFICIENT?

These are weighty conditions to meet. Following *IMS*, one might conclude that it would be only in rare cases that a court will order an intellectual property holder to grant a licence. However, the case law is not yet settled. The Commission decided that Microsoft had abused its dominant position in PC operating systems by deliberately restricting interoperability between Windows PCs and non-Microsoft work group servers (which the Commission found formed part of a wider objective of excluding competitors from the market for work group server operating systems). Where Microsoft had disclosed interface information, it did so selectively or discriminatorily; in other cases, it did not disclose at all. As a remedy, the Commission ordered Microsoft to disclose to competitors, within 120 days, complete and accurate interface information required for their products to be able to interoperate fully with the Windows operating system. To the extent interface information was protected by intellectual property in the EEA, Microsoft could charge a reasonable licence fee.

Microsoft appealed this decision. The Court of First Instance upheld the Commission's decision that Microsoft had abused its dominant position and that exceptional circumstances did exist to justify the Commission's decision that withholding IP protected information constituted such an abuse. Microsoft was therefore ordered to disclose 'interoperability information' to its competitors by the compulsory licensing of its IP rights (Case T-201/04 *Microsoft Corporation* v. *Commission* [2007] 17/9/2007).

Non-technology licensing – trade marks and copyright

Does Art.81(1) apply?

The case law on copyright and related rights may sometimes be helpful. For film performance rights, the ECJ has indicated that the grant of exclusive rights to show a film in a particular territory need not in itself restrict competition (Case 262/81 *Coditel SA* v. *Cine Vog Films SA (No.2)* [1982] ECR 3381), although the Court in that case also suggested that an exclusive licence could infringe Art.81(1) where it created artificial and unjustifiable barriers and restricted competition.

In a case concerning film purchases by German television stations, involving exclusive licences to broadcast a large number of films in the MGM/UA film library for a period of 15 years, the Commission found that Art.81 did apply to the exclusivity, and the licensee was obliged to exclude licences which had to be granted for its films to other broadcasting organisations, before the Commission would grant an exemption under Art.81(3) (Commission Decision 89/536 [1989] OJ L 284/36). The Commission has also in several cases decided that a ban on exports of goods produced under copyright licence, such as books, cassettes, tape recordings and records, was contrary to Art.81 and not permissible.

Finally, it has also found that terms prohibiting the licensee from challenging the validity of copyright are not permissible and that terms requiring the payment of royalties on products which are not protected by the licensed copyright are not permitted. Given the more recent evolution in approach represented by the TTBE and VRBE, many of these points will have to be re-examined.

If a licence contains potentially prohibited terms, it is useful to consider whether it may be block exempt.

Which block exemption?

The TTBE does not apply directly to licences of copyright (other than software copyright) and neighbouring rights, database rights and trade marks, if they are not ancillary to patent, software copyright and know-how licences, and/or may involve pure sales licences. However, the TTBE and its Guidelines guide the analysis of restrictions in licences of non-technology intellectual property. This particularly applies to those arrangements which involve more than just resale of the licensed product, software, database or content, since the TTBE does not apply to pure sales licences but requires manufacturing using the licensed technology or the use of licensed processes.

The VRBE (see **8.6**) applies only to those agreements containing intellectual property licences to the buyer, where these are not the primary objective of the agreement, but support other provisions relating to the supply of goods and services.

Applying the correct block exemption – TTBE or VRBE – is essential, as they differ in important respects.

Where the agreement is primarily for the licensing of copyright other than software and the licence is for the reproduction of the protected work (i.e. the production of copies for resale), the principles of the TTBE can be applied by analogy.

Where a licence covers rights in performances or other neighbouring rights, the TTBE and Guidelines will not apply even by analogy.

Differences in effect

Complete bans on active sales outside the licensee's territory or customer group are allowed by the TTBE, and the licensee can be prohibited from even passive (responses to unsolicited orders) sales into the territory or customer group of the licensor or other licensees, but there, only where this territory or customer group has been exclusively reserved to the licensor or exclusively allotted to another licensee. In this case the restriction can last for only two years from the first marketing of the licensed product in the territory or customer group by the protected licensee.

However, under the VRBE, it is not possible to restrict passive sales outside the distributor's territory, and restrictions on active sales are permissible only for the exclusive territories or customer groups of the supplier or other distributors.

8.6 COMPETITION LAW AND TRANSACTIONS INVOLVING SALE/DISTRIBUTION OF PRODUCTS PROTECTED BY INTELLECTUAL PROPERTY

The discussion below is relevant to transactions involving the sale of products protected by intellectual property. These will generally include sales arrangements, franchise agreements and distribution agreements, including agreements for the purchase, sale and resale of services. The two areas under discussion are vertical agreements in EC competition law and the application of the rules on free movement.

Vertical agreements

Article 2(1) of the VRBE defines a vertical agreement as one in which two or more undertakings operate 'for the purposes of the agreement, at a different level of the production or distribution chain' and the agreement contains 'conditions under which the parties may purchase, sell or resell certain goods or services'. This means that an agreement between a manufacturer and a wholesaler, or a wholesaler and a retailer, or involving all three, will be 'vertical' in nature.

It is a commonplace that vertical agreements are generally less restrictive of competition than horizontal agreements, and the VRBE and its Guidelines set out the conditions under which a vertical agreement will be exempt from Art.81(1), by application of the general exemption criteria of Art.81(3) or by application of VRBE.

Vertical agreements within the scope of the VRBE

To be within the scope of the VRBE, the agreement must meet several criteria.

OPERATE AT DIFFERENT LEVELS

First, the parties must operate at different levels of the market – an agreement between two wholesalers or between two distributors operating as such for the purpose of the agreement will not be covered. These will need to be assessed under Art.81(3), with the assistance of the Horizontal Guidelines, and where applicable, block exemptions for specialisation or the R&D block exemption.

If a vertical agreement falls within the TTBE, R&DBE or the Specialisation Block Exemption, then the VRBE does not apply, as it will not apply 'to vertical agreements the subject matter of which is regulated by other block exemption regulations': for example, a patent licence permitting manufacturing and distribution of products using these rights might be covered by the TTBE but not the VRBE.

AGREEMENTS BETWEEN COMPETITORS

Second, by Art.2(4), the VRBE will apply to agreements between parties that are actual or potential competitors only if the agreement is non-reciprocal and either:

(a) the buyer's annual turnover does not exceed €100 million; or
(b) the supplier is a manufacturer and a distributor of goods, while the buyer is a distributor and does not manufacture goods or services that compete with the contract goods or services; or
(c) the supplier is a provider of services at several different levels of trade, while the buyer does not provide competing services at the level of trade where it purchases the contract services.

In all other cases, the VRBE will not apply to agreements between parties which are actual or potential competitors, even if they are at different levels of the production/distribution chain for the purpose of the agreement.

MARKET SHARE CAPS

Third, the relevant parties must not exceed the market share cap of 30 per cent. This will refer to the supplier's market share, in general, and the buyer's market share if the agreement contains 'exclusive supply obligations'. These are 'any direct or indirect obligation causing the supplier to sell the goods or services specified in the agreement only to one buyer inside the Community for the purposes of a specific use or for resale' (Art.1(c)). As with the TTBE, discussed above, the exemption can still apply for two calendar years after the year in which the cap was breached, provided that the share remains below 35 per cent. Once it exceeds 35 per cent the exemption can continue for only one year (although the two extensions cannot be combined; by Art.9(2)(e) the maximum period for application after the 30 per cent barrier is two years).

HARDCORE RESTRICTIONS

Fourth, the agreement must not contain any hardcore restrictions. These are restrictions:

(a) on the buyer's ability to determine its sale price, with the exception of recommended resale prices and maximum resale price obligations (provided that these do not amount to fixed or minimum resale prices as a result of pressure from or incentives offered by the supplier);
(b) of the territory into which, or the customers to whom, the buyer may sell the contract goods or services apart from restrictions on active sales to territories or customer groups that the supplier has exclusively reserved to itself or allocated exclusively to another buyer;
(c) on sales to end-users by wholesalers;
(d) on resale to unauthorised distributors by members of a selective distribution network;
(e) of the buyer's ability to sell components, supplied for the purposes of incorporation, to customers who would use them to manufacture the same type of goods as those produced by the supplier;
(f) of active or passive sales to end-users by members of a selective distribution system operating at the retail level of trade, without prejudice to the possibility of prohibiting a member of the system from operating out of an unauthorised place of establishment;
(g) on cross-supplies between members of a selective distribution system; and
(h) preventing a supplier of spare parts that are used by the buyer for incorporation into its own product from selling them as spare parts to end-users or to independent repairers or service providers.

INTELLECTUAL PROPERTY CRITERIA

By Art.2(3), the VRBE applies to:

> vertical agreements containing provisions which relate to the assignment to the buyer or use by the buyer of intellectual property rights, provided that those provisions do not constitute the primary object of such agreements and are directly related to the use, sale or resale of goods or services by the buyer or its customers.

In other words, the intellectual property provisions must be ancillary to the main objects of the agreement, which is the purchase or distribution of goods or services. The Guidelines elaborate on the necessary conditions for applying the VRBE to agreements relating to intellectual property.

1. The intellectual property provisions must form part of a vertical agreement, i.e. an agreement with conditions under which the parties may purchase, sell or resell certain goods or services. This means that agreements where one party provides another with a master copy and licenses the other to produce and distribute copies will not come under the block exemption, nor will trade mark licensing agreements for the purpose of merchandising, sponsorship contracts or copyright licences such as broadcasting contracts concerning the right to record and/or broadcast (or presumably webcast) an event.
2. The intellectual property must be assigned to, or for use by, the buyer. Consequently, the VRBE does not apply to agreements where intellectual property is provided by the buyer to the supplier. In particular, subcontracting involving the transfer of know-how to a subcontractor to enable the subcontractor to manufacture products is not covered by the VRBE. However, vertical agreements under which the buyer provides only specifications to the supplier which describe the goods or services to be supplied can be exempted.
3. The intellectual property provisions must be directly related to the use, sale or resale of goods or services by the buyer or his customers. According to the Guidelines, the goods or services for use or resale are usually supplied by the licensor but may also be purchased by the licensee from a third party supplier. The intellectual property provisions will normally concern the marketing of goods or services. For example, in a franchise agreement, the franchisor sells to the franchisee goods for resale, and in addition licenses the franchisee to use its trade mark and know-how to market the goods.
4. The intellectual property provisions, in relation to the contract goods or services, must not contain restrictions of competition having the same object or effect as vertical restraints which are not exempted under the Block Exemption. This means that they cannot include any hardcore restrictions or the various non-compete provisions excluded from the VRBE.

Trade marks and software copyright

A trade mark licence to a distributor may be related to the distribution of the licensor's products in a particular territory. If it is an exclusive licence, the agreement amounts to exclusive distribution.

Agreements under which hard copies of software are supplied for resale and where the reseller does not acquire a licence to any rights over the software but has the right only to resell the hard copies, are agreements for the supply of goods for resale under the VRBE. Under this form of distribution, the licence of the software takes place only between the copyright owner and the user of software. This may take the form of a shrink-wrap licence, i.e. a set of conditions included in the package of the hard copy which the end-user is deemed to accept by opening the package. Buyers of hardware incorporating software protected by copyright may be obliged by the copyright holder not to infringe the copyright, for example not to make copies and resell the software or not to make copies and use the software in combination with other hardware, and these restrictions will be covered by the Block Exemption.

Non-exempt restrictions in the VRBE

Any restrictions that go beyond what is necessary to achieve objectives that are compatible with Art.81(3) are excluded by the VRBE.

Unlike the more serious hardcore restraints (discussed above), these are potentially severable (depending on national law) although the English courts may not consider exclusivity and non-compete provisions that go beyond what is covered by the VRBE to be capable of severance (*James E McCabe Ltd* v. *Scottish Courage Ltd* [2006] EWHC 538). The provisions include:

(a) certain 'non-compete' obligations. By VRBE, Art.1(b) these are any:

> direct or indirect obligation causing the buyer not to manufacture, purchase, sell or resell goods or services which compete with the contract goods or services, or any direct or indirect obligation on the buyer to purchase from the supplier or from another undertaking designated by the supplier more than 80% of the buyer's total purchases of the contract goods or services and their substitutes on the relevant market, calculated on the basis of the value of its purchases in the preceding calendar year;

(b) any post-term restrictions on competition; and
(c) restrictions on a selective distributor selling specific competitor brands.

Licences to end-users

Licences to end-users may in some cases fall within Art.81(1), although the lack of relevant guidance from the Commission or the ECJ hampers the application of plain rules. Limitations restricting the use of copyright material or a database to a particular physical site or to a particular computer platform or CPU will arguably fall outside Art.81(1) in many cases, as would other restrictions designed to control the number of users of the subject matter of the copyright or database rights. However, Art.81(1) might well apply to a restriction which merely limited the use to a particular manufacturer's hardware platform if, for example, the licensor were thereby attempting to tie the use of his own hardware, without an objective justification. Restrictions on copying or sub-licensing may also fall outside Art.81(1) in many cases.

On the other hand, a restriction on the use of competing products, or on the user himself competing with the licensor, is likely to fall within Art.81(1), and could be difficult to justify under Art.81(3).

Parallel imports and the EC prohibition on barriers to trade

The rules on restrictive agreements, deriving from Art.81, and the free market rules, deriving from Arts.28–30 of the EC Treaty, relate to each other in complex ways.

EC competition law differs from UK or other national competition law in that its objective is not merely the promotion of consumer welfare and economic efficiency. It is also to create and maintain a single market, functioning as though it were a national market, on a Community-wide scale.

This objective explains some hardcore restraints provisions of the block exemptions: for example, the prohibition in the VRBE of provisions that purport to prevent passive sales outside an exclusive territory. Absolute territorial protection clauses are regarded as serious restraints of competition, whose presence constitutes a restriction by 'object' which cannot be exempted.

The free movement rules of the Treaty are set out in Arts.28–30.

Article 28:

> Quantitative restrictions on imports and all measures having equivalent effect shall be prohibited between Member States.

Article 29:

> Quantitative restrictions on exports and all measures having equivalent effect shall be prohibited between Member States.

Article 30:

> The provisions of Articles 28 and 29 shall not preclude prohibitions or restrictions on imports, exports or goods in transit justified on grounds of . . . the protection of industrial and commercial property. Such prohibitions or restrictions shall not, however, constitute a means of arbitrary discrimination or a disguised restriction on trade between Member States.

For these purposes industrial property can be read as intellectual property other than copyright and its neighbouring rights. These rules, applied by extensive case law, impose further limits on the restrictions and controls that owners of intellectual property can impose on trade in products protected by intellectual property.

To determine where intellectual property stopped and competition law began, the ECJ has devised a distinction between the 'existence' and the 'exercise' of intellectual property. The existence of intellectual property, subject (originally) only to national laws, is protected from the application of the competition rules, whereas the exercise of intellectual property can be circumscribed by the competition rules (*Consten and Grundig* (above)).

The more recent approach has been to justify the exercise of intellectual property to protect its 'specific subject matter' which comprises the 'core rights' of particular intellectual property. Whilst the core rights differ in detail as between patents, trade marks and copyright, they always include:

(a) the right to put the product into circulation on the market in the Community for the first time (whether directly or through licensees); and
(b) the right to prevent infringements of the right by third parties unconnected with the proprietor of that right.

Thus, an intellectual property holder can exercise its rights to prevent others putting on the market a product incorporating the intellectual property. Once a product has been put on the market for the first time in the Community by the intellectual property holder or with its consent, however, the intellectual property holder can no longer sue for infringement to prevent the importation of that product into another Member State by a parallel trader. The rights are described as having been 'exhausted'.

A special set of exhaustion of rights arguments concern the problem of the parallel importer who repackages goods legitimately bought under a particular trade mark and resells them elsewhere, under either the same trade mark or a different trade mark also used for the same goods by the company which first placed it onto the market. Particularly where potentially dangerous goods such as pharmaceuticals are concerned, the trade mark owner may have legitimate reasons for opposing the resale of repackaged goods. This is discussed in more detail in **Chapter 3**.

Whilst agreements which aim to hinder parallel trade in principle have the restriction of competition as their object or effect, it cannot be presumed that parallel trade in pharmaceuticals has a detrimental effect on the prices paid by consumers. Therefore it does not automatically follow that an agreement intended to limit parallel trade has the object of restricting competition. An economic analysis is required to determine this (Case T-168/01 *GlaxoSmithKline Services Unlimited* v. *Commission*, CFI decision 09.06, [2006] All ER (D) 132 (Sep)).

Non-EU parallel imports

Where parallel imports originate from outside the European Union, EU law permits a trade mark holder to prevent their resale in the UK unless they enter the UK after a sale has already taken place within another EU country (in which case the EU principle of free movement of goods applies exactly as for parallel imports originating within the EU). The ECJ rejected the arguments for international exhaustion of trade marks, on the grounds that it was necessary for coherence of the Customs Union for all Member States to take consistent positions on this in order for the internal market to function properly (*Silhouette International Schmied Gmbh & Co. KG* v. *Hartlauer Handelsgesellshaft Gmbh* [1998] 2 CMLR 953). The same approach may now be taken in respect of products protected by copyright, on the same grounds given the harmonising intent of the Copyright Directive, although there has been no case to date.

Patents, however, are not yet subject to any harmonisation at EU level. The exhaustion of rights through a sale outside the EU therefore remains subject only to national law. The English courts have treated such goods as subject to an implied licence that they may be exported from the country of first sale and imported into the UK unless the patentee can show that such a licence was effectively and invariably excluded (*Roussel-Uclaf SA* v. *Hockley International Ltd* [1996] RPC 441). This may be difficult to achieve in practice since even labelling each individual product with a prohibition on import may not be effective to exclude a licence in favour of a broker who buys without notice of the term and sells on to a third party without the label being brought to its attention.

CHAPTER 9

Taxation and intellectual property

Mathew Oliver and Ingrid Toth

9.1 INTRODUCTION

Overview

The previous chapters in this Handbook have discussed the nature of intellectual property and the related commercial considerations. However, this book would not be complete without a discussion of the UK taxation issues arising from the holding of, and transactions involving, intellectual property. This requires consideration of the income tax, capital gains tax, corporation tax, value added tax (VAT) and withholding tax regimes.

The aim of this chapter is to give an overview of the UK taxation laws relevant to common intellectual property transactions. A full review of the law in this area requires an understanding of most of the UK tax system and how it applies to intellectual property. This could be the subject of a book in its own right and it is impossible to provide a detailed analysis in only one chapter. Therefore, we have chosen to discuss areas which we feel, in our experience, would benefit the majority of readers with limited knowledge in this area.

While this chapter introduces relevant tax issues, it is not comprehensive nor a substitute for professional tax advice.

The chapter is divided into three parts:

(a) direct taxes (corporation tax for companies; income tax and capital gains tax for individuals);
(b) withholding taxes; and
(c) VAT.

As there is no longer stamp duty in the UK on intellectual property, the stamp duty regime will not be covered. It is also beyond the scope of this chapter to discuss inheritance tax.

Sources

The UK tax laws relating to intellectual property can be found in a number of sources: UK legislation, case law, EU legislation, Her Majesty's Revenue and Customs (HMRC) guidance, concessions and practices. The key UK statutory sources referred to in this chapter are:

(a) Income and Corporation Taxes Act (ICTA) 1988;
(b) Value Added Tax Act (VATA) 1994;
(c) Income Tax (Trading and Other Income) Act (ITTOIA) 2005;
(d) Taxation of Chargeable Gains Act (TCGA) 1992;
(e) Capital Allowances Act (CAA) 2001;
(f) Income Tax Act (ITA) 2007;
(g) various Finance Acts, e.g. Finance Act (FA) 2000, Finance Act (FA) 2002 and Finance Act (FA) 2003.

This chapter is written as of 1 June 2007 and takes account of the changes made by the Budget on 21 March 2007.

9.2 DIRECT TAXES

UK tax laws comprise three main types of direct taxes: corporation tax, income tax, and capital gains tax. Corporation tax applies to UK companies on their profits or capital gains, while the other two apply mainly to individuals. The rules that apply to a given taxpayer depend on the legal status of that taxpayer.

While each tax regime has its own particular rules, there is some overlap. For example, many of the rules for calculating a capital gain apply equally to capital gains tax and corporation tax.

Where a corporation holds intellectual property, then the precise corporation tax rules that apply to the income and gains derived from that asset differ depending on whether that asset was 'acquired or created' before 1 April 2002 (in which case the rules are similar to the income tax/capital gains tax rules) or on or after that date (when a new set of rules came into force). We refer to the two regimes in this chapter as the 'post-April 2002' corporation tax regime and the 'pre-April 2002' or 'old' corporation tax regime.

Income tax liability

The income tax regime is applicable for taxpayers other than UK companies. This includes individuals and trusts. It can also apply in certain circumstances to certain non-resident companies.

As a partnership is not a separate legal entity under the Partnership Act 1890, each partner must account for the tax on his or her share of partnership profits (ICTA 1988, s.111). The income tax or corporation tax regime will apply depending on the status of the partner concerned. Limited partnerships and limited liability partnerships are generally treated in the same way as partnerships for tax purposes.

JURISDICTION TO INCOME TAX

The UK has jurisdiction to apply income tax to an individual's worldwide trading profits if that person is a *resident* of the UK (ITTOIA 2005, s.6(1)). Further, UK income tax is payable by a *non-resident* on trading profits if they arise from a trade carried on wholly or in part in the UK (ITTOIA 2005, s.6(2)).

The same rules apply to income derived from professions and vacations (ITTOIA 2005, s.6(3)).

In respect of savings and investment (non-trading) income, an individual is subject to UK income tax on:

(a) worldwide income if he or she is a resident of the UK (ITTOIA 2005, s.368(1)); and
(b) income sourced from the UK (ITTOIA 2005, s.368(2)) if it arises to a non-resident – although generally speaking, UK source investment income accruing to a non-resident taxpayer is only taxable to the extent of tax deducted at source.

RESIDENCE

There is no legislative guidance as to whether an individual is a resident of the UK. Accordingly, the generally accepted meaning is adopted and has been interpreted in various cases.

Taxpayers have been held to be residents of the UK in the following circumstances:

- spending three to four months each year in the UK, having a bank account in the UK and storing personal effects in the UK (*Reid* v. *IRC* (1926) 10 TC 673);
- working abroad but visiting the 'family home' in the UK where the taxpayer's spouse and children live (*Re Young* (1875) 1 TC 57 and *Thomson* v. *Bensted (Surveyor of Taxes)* (1918) 7 TC 137);
- annually renting a house in Scotland for two months and holding a lease of a shooting box there (notwithstanding that the taxpayer is resident of another country) (*Cooper (Surveyor of Taxes)* v. *Cadwalader* (1904) 5 TC 101); and
- living in a yacht anchored in UK waters (*Bayard Brown* v. *Burt* (1911) 5 TC 667).

The following factors indicate non-residence:

- staying in UK hotels while occasionally visiting the UK (*IRC* v. *Zorab* (1926) 11 TC 289 and *IRC* v. *Combe* (1932) 17 TC 405); and
- temporary visits to the UK (*Withers* v. *Wynyard* (1938) 21 TC 724).

Therefore, regular physical presence as well as having some 'ties' to the UK is required to establish residency. As a guide, an individual who is physically present in the UK for at least 183 days (ignoring date of arrival and departure) will be regarded as a resident of the UK (*HMRC Residence Guide* IR 20, para.1.2). However, recent case law (*Robert Gaines-Cooper* v. *HMRC* [2007] STC (SCD) 23) suggests that it can be dangerous to take too literal an interpretation of such guidance.

Income tax and 'old' corporation tax regimes

As stated above, the precise corporation tax rules that apply to the income and gains derived from intellectual property assets differ depending on whether that asset was 'acquired or created' before 1 April 2002 or on or after that date. First, we will consider the old corporation tax rules (for intellectual property acquired or created before 1 April 2002) and the income tax and CGT rules, which in many cases are similar.

The first part of any direct tax analysis under these rules is whether income or expenditure is on income account (i.e. subject to income tax or corresponding corporation tax rules) or on capital account (subject to CGT/corporation tax on chargeable gains).

The income/capital distinction

Under the pre-April 2002 regime for corporation tax, and apart from certain specific exceptions considered below (e.g. sale of patent rights), receipts are included as income and expenditures are allowed as income deductions to the extent that such items are not capital in nature. Capital gains tax and corporation tax on chargeable gains do not apply to items charged to tax as income.

So the question to be asked is, when is a receipt or outgoing income or capital in nature?

More often than not, this is an issue that presents 'almost insoluble conundrums' (Lord Upjohn in *Strick* v. *Regent Oil Co. Ltd* (1965) 43 TC 1) and 'indeed in many cases it is almost true to say that the spin of a coin would decide the matter almost as satisfactorily as would an attempt to find reasons' (*IRC* v. *British Salmson Aero Engines Ltd* (1938) 22 TC 29 at 43).

Part of the reason for these observations is the tax legislation does not provide a definition of 'income' or 'capital'. Accordingly, these concepts must be interpreted in accordance with their ordinary meaning by having regard to case law.

CASE LAW ON RECEIPTS

The most recent leading authority on this topic, *Inland Revenue Commissioners* v. *John Lewis Properties plc* [2003] STC 117 provides the following list of considerations in determining whether a receipt is income or capital in nature:

(a) if the payment is for the disposal of an asset which has an enduring or long-lasting quality then the payment is more likely than not to be capital;
(b) if the payment is of a single lump sum for the once and all disposal of a particular asset, it is more likely to be a capital payment; if the payment is one of a series of recurring payments made at frequent intervals, it is likely to be income in the hands of the payee;
(c) if the disposal of the asset is accompanied by a transfer of risk in relation to it, this suggests that the sum paid for the asset is capital.

These considerations must then be applied to the facts.

The following receipts were held to be income in the context of intellectual property:

- payment on disposal of an author's copyright (*MacKenzie* v. *Arnold (Inspector of Taxes)* (1952) 33 TC 363);
- lump sum payments for advice from time to time as to improvements and modifications in manufacture and design of aircraft engines (*Jeffrey* v. *Rolls-Royce Ltd* (1962) 40 TC 443);
- payment (comprising lump sum and royalty) for a non-exclusive licence to manufacture (*Rustproof Metal Window Co Ltd* v. *IRC* [1947] 2 All ER 454);
- lump sum received for sale of patents by a company whose sole business was the exploitation of patents as part of its trade and the profits on the sale were made in the course of that business (*Rees Roturbo Development Syndicate Ltd* v. *Ducker* (1928) 13 TC 366);
- lump sum consideration for information consisting of secret processes and formulae (*Coalite & Chemical Products Ltd* v. *Treeby (HM Inspector of Taxes)* (1971) 48 TC 171);
- patent royalties derived by a trading company (*IRC* v. *Tootal Broadhurst Lee Co Ltd* (1949) 29 TC 352; *IRC* v. *Desoutter Bros Ltd* (1946) 29 TC 155; *IRC* v. *Rolls-Royce Ltd (No. 2)* (1944) 29 TC 137; *IRC* v. *Anglo American Asphalt Co Ltd* (1941) 29 TC 7); and
- lump sum paid to the inventor of an interrupter gear for aircraft machine guns used in World War I (*Constantinesco* v. *Rex* (1927) 11 TC 730) as it was a payment for the right to use the invention over time.

The following receipts were held to be capital in the context of intellectual property:

- an amount payable in instalments for the exclusive grant of a licence to construct, use and sell engines (*IRC* v. *British Salmson Aero Engines Ltd* (1938) 22 TC 29);
- payment on disposal of copyright by a dramatist not carrying on the profession of an author (*Withers* v. *Nethersole* (1948) 28 TC 501);
- lump sum for a licence to use of patented invention for five years (*Desoutter Bros Ltd* v. *JE Hanger & Co. Ltd and Artificial Limb Makers Ltd* [1936] 1 All ER 535);
- lump sum derived from the disposal of Japanese patent rights which forms part of a company's business (*Collins (Inspector of Taxes)* v. *Firth Brearley Stainless Steel Syndicate Ltd* (1925) 9 TC 520);
- lump sum payments in respect of exclusive licences to foreign companies in various countries in which the taxpayer covenanted to keep out of such countries (*Murray (HM Inspector of Taxes)* v. *Imperial Chemical Industries Ltd* (1967) 44 TC 175); and
- lump sum payment for taxpayer agreeing not to establish another tyre soling plant which was effectively an exclusive covenant not to compete (*Margerison* v. *Tyresoles Ltd* (1942) 25 TC 59).

CASE LAW ON EXPENDITURE

Expenditure will be classified as capital if it has an enduring benefit and brings into existence an asset for use in the trade (*British Insulated and Helsby Cables* v. *Atherton* [1926] AC 205, HL). For example, a sum paid for the acquisition of a business was held to be capital in nature (*Triage Services Ltd* v. *HMRC* Sp C 519 [2006] SCD 85).

Having regard to the case law, HMRC offers the following guidance to indicate capital expenditure:

(a) expenditure on an intangible benefit or advantage (for example, trading agreements, licences or other) in which the identifiable asset is sufficiently substantial and enduring (*Business Income Manual* BIM35505);
(b) expenditure that secures a permanent commercial advantage such as the closing down of a potentially damaging competitor (*Business Income Manual* BIM35510);
(c) expenditure incurred in connection with the acquisition, alteration, enhancement or defence of the fundamental structure of a business (*Business Income Manual* BIM35525);
(d) a payment that secures an enduring benefit to the business in terms of a change in organisation or structure is likely to be capital (*Business Income Manual* BIM35545) as distinct from one that has the effect of preserving the existing business, its goodwill or assets (which would be on revenue account: *Business Income Manual* BIM35540).

(Note that the *Business Income Manual* is one of HMRC's manuals for its staff, and these offer a useful guide as to how HMRC will interpret the law.)

Classification of income

Once it is determined that a receipt is income in nature, it is necessary to determine the manner in which it is taxed.

Historically, income was charged to tax under the so-called 'scheduler system' which applied for both corporation tax purposes and income tax purposes. The scheduler system remains intact for corporation tax purposes. However, the rules have been restated and amended for income tax purposes such that the old schedules no longer remain valid for income tax.

The schedules do however remain valid for corporation tax purposes and, in many cases, the new income tax rules are the same as the old scheduler rules with changes only in respect of terminology.

Under the old scheduler system, income was taxable if it fell within one of the heads of charge. These include:

- Schedule A – rents or other receipts from UK land;
- Schedule D Case I – profits of any trade carried on in the UK or elsewhere;
- Schedule D Case II – profits of any profession or vocation;
- Schedule D Case III – interest, annuities and other annual payments (including loan relationship profits for companies);
- Schedule D Case IV– dividends and other income from securities outside UK;
- Schedule D Case V – income from other possessions abroad;
- Schedule D Case VI – other annual profits or gains; and
- Schedule F – dividends and distributions.

Income tax is now calculated under ITTOIA 2005 and the Income Tax (Earnings and Pensions) Act 2003. The Income Tax (Earnings and Pensions) Act 2003 is not of general significance for earnings from intellectual property and we do not consider it further here. However, it should be noted that in certain circumstances charges under the 2003 Act may arise in intellectual property related contexts (e.g. where it is not clear whether income arises from intellectual property or from an employment).

Further rules relating to the calculation of income tax and reliefs available (e.g. utilisation of losses) as well as the main charging provisions for income tax are contained in ITA 2007. We do not, generally, consider these details in this chapter.

Under ITTOIA 2005, income is classified into:

(a) trading income;
(b) property income;

(c) savings and investment income; and
(d) other miscellaneous income.

Property income is not relevant for intellectual property purposes as it refers to land only. Similarly, savings and investment income covers financial investments such as income from shares, securities, insurance contracts and unit trusts.

As the rules on trading income take precedence over the rules on miscellaneous income we start by discussing how the rules on trading income work and how they could be applied to intellectual property.

Trade profits

Income tax is charged on the profits of a trade, profession or vocation (ITTOIA 2005, s.5; ICTA 1988, s.18).

The profits of a trade must be calculated in accordance with generally accepted accounting practice but are subject to any tax adjustments (ITTOIA 2005, ss.25 and 26; FA 1998, s.42).

Therefore, the starting point is to use the profit before tax as disclosed in the accounts and adjust it for tax. Some income may be excluded (as it is not chargeable) and/or an expense may not be allowable as a deduction. For example, depreciation will not be allowed as a deduction for tax purposes (ITTOIA 2005, s.33; ICTA 1988, s.74(1)(f)), although expenditure 'capitalised' in accounts may be deferred revenue expenditure which could be deducted when amortised under generally accepted accounting principles (GAAP). Instead, capital allowances relief may be available for capital expenditure. Also, capital receipts are not chargeable to income tax and should not be included in calculating the profits of a trade, unless there is a specific rule to the contrary (ITTOIA 2005, s.96(1); ICTA 1988, s.18 and BIM14060).

What is a 'trade'?

In some cases, determining whether profits are derived from a trade is quite obvious and in other cases it can be quite difficult. This is because no statutory definition for 'trade' is provided in the legislation and hence the term must be interpreted in accordance with its ordinary meaning for both income tax and corporation tax purposes.

The Final Report of the 1954 Royal Commission on the taxation of profits and income summarised the most important considerations in determining whether a taxpayer has engaged in trade (termed 'badges of trade').

The main factors to look at to indicate whether a transaction is trading in nature are as follows (*Marson (Inspector of Taxes)* v. *Morton* (1986) 59 TC 381 at 393):

(a) *frequency of transaction* – a taxpayer repeatedly entering into the same transaction (as distinct from a one-off transaction) would be indicative of an adventure in the nature of trade;
(b) *relationship to the taxpayer's trade* – a transaction relating to the trade which the taxpayer already carries on suggests that activity as being in the course of trade;
(c) *subject matter* – a transaction in a commodity of a kind which is normally the subject matter of trade would be suggestive of a trade activity; e.g. a bulk purchase of whisky or toilet paper is essentially a subject matter of trade, not of enjoyment;
(d) *supplementary work* – work done to repair or improve the item suggests the transaction as being in the nature of trade; and
(e) *profit motive* and *intention* – a purchase made with a view to resell at a profit or with the intention to resell in the short term indicates that the transaction was not by way of investment.

In *Ransom (Inspector of Taxes)* v. *Higgs* [1974] 3 All ER 949 Lord Reid observed that the term 'trade' is used to:

> denote operations of a commercial character by which the trader provides to customers for reward some kind of goods or services.

Intellectual property receipts regarded as trading income

Certain receipts from intellectual property transactions are specifically treated as trading income such as receipts from the disposal of know-how in the course of trade (ITTOIA 2005, ss.193–5; ICTA 1988, s.531).

The term 'know-how' is defined as any industrial information or techniques likely to assist in:

(a) manufacturing or processing goods or materials;
(b) working a source of mineral deposits (including searching for, discovering or testing mineral deposits or obtaining access to them); or
(c) carrying out any agricultural, forestry or fishing operations (ITTOIA 2005, s.192).

Where the trade is also disposed of, the receipt is treated as a capital payment for goodwill although in certain circumstances this may be disapplied.

Relief for trading expenditure

Expenditure is deductible against trading profits for tax purposes if it is incurred wholly and exclusively for the purposes of trade (ITTOIA 2005, s.34(1); ICTA 1988, s.74(1)(a)) and is of an income nature.

If expenditure is incurred for more than one reason, one of which is a non-business reason, then strictly the entire expenditure is not deductible. However, where an identifiable part of the expense can be attributed as being wholly and exclusively for the purposes of trade, then HMRC will not disallow that part.

Certain expenditure in respect of intellectual property transactions that are in the course of trade is specifically treated as deductible from trading profits:

(a) expenses incurred (and fees paid for corporation tax purposes) for the purposes of obtaining the grant of a patent or extension of term of a patent or in connection with an abandoned or rejected application in each case for the purposes of trade (ITTOIA 2005, s.89(1); ICTA 1988, s.83);
(b) expenses incurred for the purposes of the registration of a registered design or a trade mark (or extension or renewal thereof) for the purposes of trade (ITTOIA 2005, s.89(1), 90(1); ICTA 1988, s.83);
(c) expenditure incurred in respect of relevant telecommunication rights irrespective of whether capital in nature (see above).

Copyright

Copyright royalties received by an individual are chargeable to tax where their activities constitute a profession (ITTOIA 2005, s.5; ITCA, s.18(1)(a)(ii)) or not (ITTOIA 2005, s.579).

Copyright income of professional authors etc is normally taxable as profits from a profession (*Purchase* v. *Stainer's Executors* (1951) 32 TC 367; *Carson* v. *Cheyney's Executor* (1958) 38 TC 240). One effect of the income falling within Schedule D Case II rather than Schedule D Case I is that the principle in *Sharkey* v. *Wernher* [1956] AC 58 (whereby appropriations of trading stock by the trader have to be brought into account for tax purposes at market value) does not apply (*Mason* v. *Innes* (1967) 44 TC 326). HMRC do not generally seek a market value capital gains charge in these circumstances.

Post-cessation receipts (e.g. after the death of the author) are taxed under ICTA 1988, ss.103–110 as Schedule D Case VI income unless the author is not a UK tax resident and the copyright is not UK sourced. Additionally, capital sums received by an author's personal representatives on assignment of copyright is subject to capital gains tax rather than being taxed under the post cessation receipts rules. It is possible to elect to carry back post cessation receipts to be taxed as if received on the day of cessation.

Royalties from acquired copyright, by contrast, are taxable under Schedule D Case III (or potentially, Schedule D Case I where the taxpayer is trading).

Lump sums received from granting rights in connection with an author's work are generally assessable under Schedule D Case II (e.g. *Billam* v. *Griffith* (1941) 23 TC 757). However, in certain circumstances (e.g. where the author is no longer carrying on the profession of author), the receipt may be treated as capital (e.g. *Nethersole* v. *Withers* (1948) 28 TC 501, *Beare* v. *Carter* (1940) 23 TC 353).

Other literary exploits (carried on other than by professional authors) have, however, been held not to have arisen from a profession. Such activities may be taxed under Schedule D Case VI (e.g. *Hobbs* v. *Hussey* (1942) 24 TC 153) unless capital in nature (*Earl Haig's Trustees* v. *IRC* (1939) 22 TC 725). In practice, casual authors such as someone publishing an autobiography are taxed under Schedule D Case VI. Such authors are taxed under the capital gains rules on assignment.

Professional authors and artists

Payments receivable after 5 April 2001 for copyrights, designs and other artists' receipts are subject to averaging rules. The rules have been repealed for corporation tax purposes but still apply for income tax purposes. The rules apply where profits from a taxpayer's trade, profession or vocation are derived wholly or mainly from designs or from literary, dramatic, musical or artistic works.

A claim for averaging can be made where the relevant tax profits of two consecutive years are different by 75 per cent or less of the higher profits or where one of the consecutive tax years has relevant profits and the other does not.

Where the difference is 70 per cent or less, the two years' profits are simply averaged. If the difference is between 70 and 75 per cent the adjusted profits are calculated in accordance with the following formula (which is added to the lower of the two profits and subtracted from the higher profits):

$$(D \times 3) - (P \times 0.75)$$

where:

D is the difference between the relevant profits for the two tax years; and

P is the relevant profits of the tax year of which those profits are higher.

The formula cannot apply to the year in which the taxpayer starts or ceases to carry on the trade, profession or vocation or, the qualifying trade, profession or vocation.

An averaging claim can be made in relation to a year which was the later year on a previous claim, however a claim cannot be made if one has already been made for a later year.

The claim must, generally, be made no later than two years after the end of the later tax year.

There are specific rules dealing with deduction of tax at source from copyright royalties.

Other miscellaneous income rules

If a person is not carrying on a trade, profession or vocation in respect of his or her intellectual property rights then he or she could be taxed under these rules. For income tax purposes these are classified as:

- ITTOIA 2005, Part 5, Chapter 2 – receipts from intellectual property;
- ITTOIA 2005, Part 5, Chapter 3 – receipts from films and sound recordings;
- ITTOIA 2005, Part 5, Chapter 4 – certain telecommunications rights;
- ITTOIA 2005, Part 5, Chapter 7 – other annual payments;
- ITTOIA 2005, Part 5, Chapter 8 – other income.

For corporation tax purposes (on pre-April 2002 intellectual property) these rules are mainly covered by Schedule D Case III or Schedule D Case VI.

There are further rules for income from trusts. Whilst intellectual property rights could be held under trust, it is outside the scope of this chapter to discuss how trusts are taxed in the UK.

Income from intellectual property derived from a non-trading activity

This income is chargeable to income tax on the amount of income arising in the tax year (ITTOIA 2005, s.579(1)).

The term 'intellectual property' is defined in ITTOIA 2005, s.579(2) as:

(a) any patent, trade mark, registered design, copyright, design right, performer's right or plant breeder's right or any right under UK law which is similar to these;
(b) any rights under the law of any territory outside the UK which correspond, or are similar, to rights within paragraph (a); and
(c) any idea, information or technique not protected by a right within paragraph (a) or (b).

There is no direct equivalent for corporation tax purposes. However non-trading royalty income from a pre-April 2002 UK source is taxable under Schedule D Case III (non-UK source income comes under Schedule D Case V).

SPREADING, DEDUCTIONS AND RELIEFS

Where the income relates to patent royalties the recipient can, if the royalties have a UK source, spread the income for tax purposes over up to six years (depending on the length of the licence) under ICTA 1988, s.527.

Expenses wholly and exclusively incurred for the purposes of generating the income are deductible for income tax purposes unless:

(a) they would not have been deductible for trading purposes if there had been a trade (e.g. capital payments); or
(b) they are relievable for other tax purposes.

Additionally relief is given under ITTOIA 2005, s.600 in respect of certain expenses relating to patents.

The chargeability of intellectual property royalties is limited by the exception in ITTOIA 2005, s.727 (for income tax purposes) or ICTA 1988, s.347A (for corporation tax on pre-April 2002 intellectual property) which exempts annual payments made by an individual resident in the United Kingdom who is not making the payment for commercial purposes linked to a trade, profession or vocation regardless of the recipient's status. The exemption does not apply in certain circumstances where the individual has sold the right to receive the annual payments for non taxable consideration.

Non-trading income from the disposal of know-how

Tax is charged on the amount of profits arising in a year on the disposal of know-how or for giving or fulfilling an undertaking in connection with such a disposal which restricts any person's activities (whether or not enforceable) (ITTOIA 2005, ss.583–6, ICTA 1988, s.531(4)).

'Know-how' for this purpose has the same meaning as defined on page 277.

This tax charge does not apply (ITTOIA 2005, s.584) where:

(a) the disposal is taxed as trading income;
(b) the consideration is taxed under ITTOIA 2005, s.579 (charge to tax on royalties etc.), or where a balancing charge is bought into account for capital allowances in respect of know-how;
(c) where the consideration is treated as a capital receipt for goodwill on the disposal of a trade;
(d) where the disposal is by way of sale between firms under common control.

The old corporation tax charge was under Schedule D Case VI.

A deduction is allowed for expenditure wholly and exclusively incurred in the acquisition or disposal of know-how (so long as only taken into account once).

Non-trading income from the sale of patent rights

Tax is charged on any non-trading profits from the sale of the whole or part of any patent rights. For non-residents, the tax is charged only on the sale of UK patent rights. Under the old corporation tax rules the profits are taxed under Schedule D Case VI (ITA 2007, s.910; ITTOIA 2005, ss.587(1) and 589; ICTA 1988 s.524(1) and (3)).

The term 'patent rights' means the right to do or authorise the doing of anything which, but for the right, would be an infringement of a patent (ITTOIA 2005, s.587(4); ICTA 1988, s.533).

Licences are treated as sales. The grantor of a licence is treated as making a part sale unless the licence is exclusive and for the remaining period of the rights, in which case it is treated as the sale of the whole of those rights.

The profit brought into charge is the difference between any capital sum comprised in the proceeds of sale less any deductible costs (ITTOIA 2005, s.588(1); ICTA 1988, s.524(1), (3) and (7)).

SPREADING, DEDUCTIONS AND RELIEFS

The deductible costs are the capital costs of the rights sold (less amounts met by certain other persons, e.g. public bodies) and, for income tax purposes, incidental expenses incurred by the seller in connection with the sale of the patent rights (ITTOIA 2005, s.588(2); ICTA 1988, s.524(1), (3) and (7)).

Relief may be available under ITTOIA 2005, s.600 against patent income for expenses incurred by an individual in respect of devising an invention for which a patent has been granted including the patent application and maintenance expenses (as well as expenses for extensions and rejected or abandoned patent applications). This relief is given in respect of patent income in the year of the expense and to the extent it cannot be so used is available for carry forward against future patent income.

Under ICTA 1988, s.526 a company obtains an allowance where, otherwise than for a trading purpose it pays fees or incurs expenditure on obtaining or maintaining a patent registration (or in connection with an extension or rejected or abandoned application).

Under spreading rules, the seller (if UK tax resident) must spread the profits over six years for tax purposes unless he elects to tax it all in the year of receipt (ITTOIA 2005, s.590; ICTA 1988 s.524(1) and (2)).

Non-residents selling UK patent rights will be taxed in the year of receipt unless they elect to spread the income over six years (ITTOIA 2005, s.591; ICTA 1988, s.524(6)).

Any election under ss.590 or 591 must be made on or before the first anniversary of the self-assessment filing date for the year of receipt. A corporation tax election under ICTA 1988, s.524 must be made within two years of the end of the relevant accounting period. If any election is made and the recipient subsequently dies (or if the recipient is a company, is wound up), any remaining tax is assessed in the year in which the seller dies (or is wound up). By election the seller's personal representatives may treat the income as accruing from the tax year of receipt to the tax year of death.

Where non-residents are charged to tax under these rules, the person paying the consideration may have to deduct tax at source (see **9.3**).

Non-trading income in connection with films and sound recordings

There are special rules for income in connection with films, recordings and certain telecommunications rights (ITTOIA 2005, Part 5, chap.3). These rules are outside the scope of this chapter.

Annual payments not otherwise charged elsewhere in ITTOIA 2005 (ITTOIA 2005, s.683; ICTA 1988, s.18(1), Schedule D Case VI))

In order to fall within these provisions, the income needs to be an annual payment. Broadly speaking this includes any royalties that are not taxed under any other provisions. Specifically, annual payments will be construed under the old case law that applies for the purposes of Schedule D Case VI.

In particular, an 'annual payment' is one which is payable under a legal obligation and is capable of recurring over a period of more than 12 months (*Moss Empires Ltd* v. *IRC* (1937) 21 TC 264). The payments must be of pure income profit to the recipient taxable under Schedule D Case III on the gross amount received (*IRC* v. *London Corporation (as conservators of Epping Forest)* (1953) 34 TC 293). The amounts must be income receipts (and not capital) of the recipient (*Campbell* v. *IRC* (1970) 45 TC 427).

Exemptions from this charge to tax include:

(a) certain annual payments by individuals made otherwise than in respect of a trade, profession or vocation (ITTOIA 2005, s.727; ICTA 1988 s.347A); and
(b) exemptions under the EC Interest and Royalties Directive (see **9.3**).

Income not charged to tax by any other provision of ITTOIA 2005 (ITTOIA 2005, s.687)

Section 687 acts as a sweeper to catch any item of income that is not caught by any other income tax provision. There is no equivalent for corporation tax. It does not apply to annual payments or to any income that would be chargeable to tax under another provision but for an exemption.

Reliefs

Annual payments and royalties which are not deductible under any of the heads of charge may be deducted from an individual's total taxable income where tax has been deducted at source under ITA 2007, s.900(2) or s.903(5) (ITA 2007, s.448). Before ITA 2007 such payments were referred to as 'charges on income'. A deduction is made in the tax year in which the annual payment/royalty is paid.

Additionally intellectual property expenditure may be included in capital allowance claims and expenditure on creating intellectual property may, for companies, be included in a claim for research and development (R&D) relief.

Capital gains tax

Capital gains tax applies to all unincorporated taxpayers resident or ordinarily resident in the UK in the year of the disposal (TCGA 1992, s.2(1)).

In the case of a corporate taxpayer, the capital gain is included in profits chargeable to corporation tax (TCGA 1992, s.1(2)).

Jurisdiction to capital gains tax and residence

An individual resident or ordinarily resident in the UK, is liable to capital gains tax on any chargeable gains (TCGA 1992, s.2).

If an individual is non-resident, then the individual will only be liable to tax if carrying on a trade in the UK through a branch or agency where the UK asset has been used for the purposes of such trade, branch or agency (TCGA 1992, s.10(1)).

An individual with a non-UK domicile is only liable to capital gains tax on disposals of assets situated in the UK or remittances to the UK of gains from non-UK assets sold at a profit (TCGA 1992, s.12).

The rules as to when a company is within the charge to corporation tax on its chargeable gains are set out under the discussion of 'Corporation tax' below.

The rules as to whether an intellectual property asset is a UK asset or a non-UK asset are summarised below (TCGA 1992, s.275).

Asset type	UK asset if:
Goodwill	Trade, business or profession carried on in the UK
Patents, trade marks and registered designs	Registered in UK
Rights or licences to use a patent, trade mark or registered design	Rights are exercisable in the UK
Copyright, design right, franchises	Rights are exercisable in the UK
Rights or licence to use in the copyright, work or design in which the design right subsists	Rights are exercisable in the UK

Capital gains

Where an asset is disposed of by an individual, the individual will be chargeable to capital gains tax. Similarly a company within the charge to corporation tax will be liable for corporation tax on chargeable gains.

A capital gain is subject to tax at the taxpayer's top marginal rate of tax (TCGA 1992, s.4).

A chargeable gain or capital loss is calculated as the proceeds received on disposal (consideration) less the base cost (cost of the asset, expenditure wholly and exclusively incurred for the purpose of enhancing the value of the asset, costs incidental to the acquisition and costs incidental to making the disposal) (TCGA 1992, ss.37 and 38). Individuals have an annual exemption for capital gains tax purposes (£9,200 for 2007/08).

The consideration will be deemed to be the market value (as distinct from the actual amount received) where the transaction is between connected parties or not at arm's length (TCGA 1992, ss.17 and 18).

Gains are not chargeable to capital gains tax (or corporation tax on chargeable gains) if they are subject to tax as income (TCGA 1992, s.37).

Indexation

For a corporate taxpayer, the base cost can be increased by indexation (i.e. the base cost is increased in line with the retail price index) from the date of acquisition until the date of sale.

In the case of an unincorporated taxpayer, indexation applies from the date of acquisition up to 6 April 1998. From that time, taper relief applies.

Taper relief

Taper relief applies to individuals, trustees and personal representatives from 6 April 1998. It is not available to companies.

The effect of taper relief is to reduce the capital gain by a specific percentage depending on the type of asset (business asset or non-business asset) and the period in which that asset has been held by the taxpayer.

For example, if an individual held a business asset for at least two complete years before selling the asset, only 25 per cent of the gain would be chargeable to the individual as compared to 60 per cent if the asset was a non-business asset and held for 10 years (TCGA 1992, s.2A). Special rules apply where an asset has had both business and non-business use. More information on taper relief (including a table showing the different rates) can be found in Help Sheet IR 279 'Taper Relief' available on the HMRC website (**www.hmrc.gov.uk**).

Corporation tax

The corporation tax regime operates to tax companies.

A 'company' is defined as any body corporate or unincorporated association, but does not include a partnership, a local authority or local authority association (ICTA 1988, s.832).

The charge to corporation tax arises in respect of a company's accounting period. The rate applicable depends on the amount of profits chargeable to corporation tax derived by the company for a given accounting period.

An 'accounting period' is dictated by the period to which the accounts are made up but cannot be longer than 12 months. Therefore if accounts are made up for a 16-month period there will be two separate accounting periods: one for the first 12 months and the other for the remaining four months.

The amount on which corporation tax is chargeable is the sum of income computed under the various schedules/cases and chargeable gains computed in accordance with the rules in TCGA 1992.

Where the company makes a loss, there are various rules as to how this can be utilised depending on the type of loss. For example, a capital loss can be carried forward to reduce a future capital gain.

Jurisdiction to corporation tax and residence

Whether a company is subject to corporation tax in the UK will be governed by whether or not it is resident in the UK, as follows:

1. If it is a UK resident, the company is subject to UK corporation tax on all of its profits and gains regardless of the source of the profits/gains or whether they are remitted to the UK (ICTA 1988, s.6(1), TCGA 1992, s.2(1)).
2. If it is non-UK resident but carries on a trade through a permanent establishment in the UK, the company is subject to UK corporation tax on all its profits arising from its trade through that establishment (ICTA 1988, s.11(1), (2) and (2A)) and chargeable gains on assets situated in the UK and used for the trade or permanent establishment (TCGA 1992, s.10B(1)).

3. If it is non-UK resident, the company is subject to UK corporation tax on certain UK source income (generally where tax is deducted at source).

RESIDENT

The definition of 'resident' has evolved over time through case law and legislation.

In a nutshell, a company is a resident of the UK if it:

(a) is incorporated in the UK (FA 1988, s.66); or
(b) has its central management and control in the UK (*De Beers Consolidated Mines Ltd* v. *Howe* (1906) 5 TC 198).

In respect of determining the location of a company's central management and control, HMRC (*International Tax Handbook* ITH 323) suggests that this requires consideration of two questions:

1. Where and by whom (according to the constitution of the company and the law of the land) ought this company be managed and controlled?
2. Exceptionally, if the people lawfully charged with management and control do not exercise it, who does?

Therefore, it is necessary to consider where the active decision making takes place or, in other words, 'where the real heart of the company is' (*International Tax Handbook* ITH 328).

It is necessary to consider the 'highest level of control of the business of a company' (*Statement of Practice* SP 1/90). Such management and control may be exercised by a chairman or a managing director.

For example, a company operating business in South Africa was held to be a UK resident as the majority of directors resided in the UK (*De Beers Consolidated Mines Ltd* v. *Howe* (above)). Also, a New Zealand company with New Zealand directors was held to be a resident of the UK as overall control lay with the separate London board of directors (*New Zealand Shipping Co Ltd* v. *Thew* (1922) 8 TC 208).

Where a company is resident in both the UK and elsewhere (e.g. because it is incorporated in the UK but managed and controlled in another jurisdiction) it is necessary to consider whether there is a tie breaker clause in the relevant double tax treaty. Most treaties use the place of 'effective management' to determine where the company is resident. This is a similar concept to the UK 'central management and control' test. Treaty non-resident companies are not resident for UK tax purposes (FA 1994, s.249).

PERMANENT ESTABLISHMENT

A company will have a 'permanent establishment' in the UK if it has a fixed place of business in the UK through which its business is wholly or partly carried on or its agent (other than an independent agent acting in the ordinary course of its business) has and habitually exercises their authority to do business on its behalf (FA 2003, s.148(1)). A 'fixed place of business' includes a branch, office, factory, workshop, place of management or a building site (FA 2003, s.148(2)).

Profits chargeable to corporation tax

Corporation tax applies to the profits of a company.

The term 'profit' is defined as follows.

1. For a resident company, profit is income and chargeable gains adjusted for tax purposes (ICTA 1988, s.6(4)(a)).
2. For a non-resident company with a permanent establishment in the UK, profit is trading income arising directly or indirectly through, or income from property or rights used or held by or for, the permanent establishment and chargeable gains subject to corporation tax (ICTA 1988, s.11(2A)).

However, profits do not include dividends or other qualifying distributions received from a UK resident company. In practice, the starting point is to take the accounting profit before tax and make tax adjustments on account of, say, income that should not be included and/or expenditure not deductible for tax purposes.

INCOME PROFITS

Income is taxed in accordance with specific rules depending on which category applies to the amount. The heads of charge are set out above.

However, in the context of intellectual property, as and from 1 April 2002, there is a standalone regime for intellectual property which calculates taxable profits from intellectual property transactions. This will be considered in detail below. Such profits or losses are then assigned to one of the Schedules or Cases depending on the use to which the intellectual property is put (e.g. intellectual property held for the purpose of a trade is taxed under Schedule D Case I).

Properly categorising the income is relevant in applying various rules, for example, those relating to losses.

CAPITAL PROFITS

In addition to income receipts, profits includes capital gains chargeable under TCGA 1992 (TCGA 1992, s.8(1) and ICTA 1988, ss.6(4)(a) and 11(2A)(c)). Chargeable gains are calculated in accordance with the capital gains tax rules.

ALLOWABLE EXPENDITURE

Expenditure that is allowed for tax purposes to reduce profits is determined in accordance with specific charging provisions.

So, as stated above, any disbursement or expense of an income nature wholly and exclusively laid out or expended for the purposes of trade is deductible against profits of that trade for corporation tax purposes in the same manner as for income tax (ICTA 1988, s.74(1)(a)).

Additionally there are specific rules outside the charging schedules which allow tax deductions against total profits, for example:

(a) research and development expenditure;
(b) capital allowances;
(c) relief for accounting losses on loan relationships and derivative contracts; and
(d) charges on income (note that as loan relationships now have their own regime for corporation tax purposes, charges on income in the corporation tax context are now mainly limited to donations to charities).

Pre-April 2002 regime for taxation of intellectual property

As a result of the introduction of a new regime for intellectual property taxation, two separate tax regimes exist for intellectual property held by a company – the post-April 2002 regime and the pre-April 2002 regime.

The pre-April 2002 regime will apply to intellectual property acquired prior to 1 April 2002 which remains in the ownership of the company or related parties on or after 1 April 2002.

However, royalties derived from intellectual property held prior to 1 April 2002 and received after that date will be taxed in accordance with the post-April 2002 regime.

Broadly, the tax rules discussed under 'Corporation tax' above constitute the pre-April 2002 regime.

Post-April 2002 corporation tax regime for taxation of intellectual property

The post-April 2002 regime in FA 2002, Sched.29 provides a much broader base for taxation of intellectual property and relief in respect of intellectual property expenditure.

It is a self-contained regime for the taxation of expenditure and receipts in respect of intangible fixed assets which is based on the accounting treatment of such assets, thereby eliminating the need to make capital and income distinctions.

It applies to intangible fixed assets that are:

(a) created by the company on or after 1 April 2002;
(b) acquired by the company on or after 1 April 2002 from an unrelated party; or
(c) acquired by the company on or after 1 April 2002 from a related party and either:
    (i) the asset was a chargeable intangible asset within Sched.29 immediately before acquisition;
    (ii) the seller acquired the asset on or after 1 April 2002 from a person who was not related to the seller or the acquiring company; or
    (iii) the asset was created on or after 1 April 2002.

Intangible fixed asset

An intangible fixed asset is 'an intangible asset acquired or created by the company for use on a continuing basis in the course of the company's activities' (Sched.29, para.3(1)).

The term 'intangible asset' adopts the meaning used in generally accepted accounting practice in accounts of UK companies that are intended to give a true and fair view (Sched.29, paras.2(1) and 5 and ICTA 1988, s.832(1) and FA 2004, s.50(2)).

More particularly, if the company has adopted:

(a) Financial Reporting Standard (FRS) 10, then 'intangible assets' are defined as 'non-financial fixed assets that do not have physical substance but are identifiable and are controlled by the entity through custody and legal rights' (FRS 10, para.2); assets are identifiable if they are capable of being disposed of or settled separately without disposing of a business of the entity; or
(b) International Financial Reporting Standards (IFRS), then 'intangible assets' are identifiable non-monetary assets without physical substance. Assets are identifiable if they are separable or arise from contractual or other legal rights (regardless of whether those rights are separable from the entity) (International Accounting Standard 38, paras.8 and 12).

Intangible assets include any intellectual property, which means:

(a) any patent, trade mark, registered design, copyright or design right, plant breeders' rights or rights under the Plant Varieties Act 1997, s.7;
(b) any right under the law of a country or territory outside the UK corresponding to, or similar to, a right within paragraph (a);
(c) any information or technique not protected by a right within paragraph (a) or (b) but having industrial, commercial or other economic value; or
(d) any licence or other right in respect of anything within paragraphs (a) to (c) inclusive such as a licence to exploit a patent or copyright material.

The rules also apply to goodwill in the same manner as they apply to intangible fixed assets (Sched.29, para.4(1)).

It is not necessary for the intangible asset to be included in the company's balance sheet for it to be regarded as a fixed asset (Sched.29, para.3(3)).

The regime does not apply to an asset where that asset is held:

(a) for a purpose that is not a business or other commercial purpose; or
(b) for the purpose of activities which are not subject to UK corporation tax (Sched.29, para.77).

Even though an asset may fall into the definition, some are expressly excluded from the definition such as:

(a) rights in relation to tangible movable property (Sched.29, para.73);
(b) rights enjoyed by virtue of an estate, interest or right in or over land (Sched.29, para.73);
(c) oil licences (Sched.29, para.74);
(d) financial assets (Sched.29, para.75);
(e) rights or interests in a company, trust or partnership (Sched.29, para.76) such as shares, interest in a partnership or rights under a trust;
(f) intangible fixed assets (except as regards royalties):
    (i) held by an insurance company for the purposes of its life assurance business other than computer software (Sched.29, para.78);
    (ii) held for the purposes of any mutual trade or business (Sched.29, para.79);
    (iii) to the extent that they represent expenditure on the production or acquisition of a film or master version of a sound recording (Sched.29, paras.80A and 80B); or
    (iv) to the extent that they represent expenditure by the company on computer software that falls to be treated for accounting purposes as part of the costs of the related hardware (Sched.29, para.81); and
(g) intangible fixed assets to the extent they represent:
    (i) expenditure by the company on research and development (Sched.29, para.82); or
    (ii) capital expenditure on computer software where an election has been made by the company for expenditure to be excluded from Sched.29 (Sched.29, para.83).

The excluded assets definition also extends to options or rights to acquire or dispose of excluded assets (Sched.29, para.72(1)).

Where an asset is excluded in part, it is treated as a separate asset representing so much of the asset as is excluded, with apportionment being made as necessary on a just and reasonable basis (Sched.29, para.72(3)–(5)).

Royalties and other credits

The post-April 2002 regime has an accounting focus. It treats all costs (debits) on the acquisition and development of intangible fixed assets for tax on the same basis as for accounting and treats all royalties and disposal proceeds (credits) as income receipts.

A credit can arise as follows:

(a) an accounting gain/royalty receipt recognised in the company's profit and loss account (Sched.29, paras.14 and 14A);
(b) an accounting gain in respect of the revaluation of an intangible fixed asset (Sched.29, para.15). In this case, the amount taxable is the lower of the amount corresponding for tax purposes to the increase in value and the debits previously brought into account. No asset would be brought into account if the asset is depreciated for tax purposes on a fixed 4 per cent basis (see below);
(c) an accounting gain in respect of negative goodwill written back following a business acquisition, that is, when the fair value of the assets less liabilities acquired exceed the price paid for a business (Sched.29, para.16);
(d) an accounting gain in respect of the reversal of previous accounting losses which led to deductible debits (Sched.29, para.17); and
(e) an accounting gain in respect of realisation of intangible fixed assets (Sched.29, paras.18–24). A 'realisation' means an asset ceases to be recognised in the company's balance sheet because it has been sold or there is a reduction in the accounting value of the asset as the result of a transaction (as per UK GAAP). Assets with no balance sheet value are deemed to have one for tax purposes.

In respect of the realisation of assets, where any debits have previously been claimed on the asset then either a credit (proceeds of realisation in excess of the tax written down value of the asset) or a debit (tax written down value of an asset exceeds the proceeds of realisation) will arise. If there are no proceeds of realisation then a debit equal to the tax written down value of the asset will be brought into account (Sched.29, para.20(2)(c)).

Debits

Debits are brought into account for tax purposes in respect of expenditure on intangible fixed assets when recognised for accounting purposes.

For example, debits can arise:

(a) where expenditure is recognised in the profit and loss account (Sched.29, para.8(1));
(b) where an accounting loss arises from capitalised expenditure because of amortisation or an impairment review (Sched.29, para.9(1));
(c) on the realisation of an intangible asset (Sched.29, para.20(2));
(d) on reversals of previous accounting gains (Sched.29, para.12).

Alternatively, a company may elect to write down an intangible fixed asset for tax purposes at a fixed 4 per cent per annum instead of the accounting rate of amortisation. An irrevocable election must be made in writing to HMRC within two years of the end of the accounting period in which the asset is created or acquired in relation to the whole amount capitalised for accounting (Sched.29, para.10(3)). The election will take effect with respect to all capitalised expenditure in respect of that asset (Sched.29, para.10(4)).

Where transfers of intangible assets take place between related parties, the transfer is treated as taking place at market value (Sched.29, para.92).

Taxation of credits and debits

The manner in which debits and credits are brought into account will depend on the use to which the intellectual property is put.

Trading assets will give rise to trading (Schedule D Case I) credits/debits. Assets held for a property business are taxed as profits/losses of that business under Schedule A. Non-trading assets give rise to non-trading profits/losses taxable under Schedule D Case VI.

If there is a non-trading loss then the taxpayer is entitled to deduct the non-trading loss against total profits of the relevant accounting period, surrender it by group relief or carry it forward to relieve in future periods.

Date of acquisition

Broadly speaking, an intangible asset is regarded as created or acquired after commencement to the extent that expenditure on its creation or acquisition was incurred on or after 1 April 2002 (Sched.29, para.120(2)) (*Corporate Intangibles Research and Development Manual* CIRD 11670).

If part of the expenditure was incurred pre and some post, the asset is treated as being two separate assets with apportionment being on a just and reasonable basis (Sched.29, para.120(3)).

Internally generated goodwill is treated as created before 1 April 2002 if the business was carried on before that date.

Reliefs

Business asset rollover relief

In the context of CGT, an individual taxpayer can defer a capital gain made (and hence tax liability otherwise arising) in respect of the disposal of an asset used in the course of trade where the taxpayer acquires a replacement asset which is also used in the course of trade (see TCGA 1992, ss.152–7). However, CGT rollover relief is not available in respect of intellectual property (other than goodwill) and we do not therefore consider this further.

A similar relief is available under the post-April 2002 corporation tax regime for intangible fixed assets including intellectual property (FA 2002, Sched.29, Part 7).

CONDITIONS

The following conditions must be satisfied for rollover relief for intangible fixed assets to apply.

1. The old asset disposed of was a chargeable intangible asset of the company both at the time of disposal and, either, throughout the period of its ownership by the company or for a substantial part of such period. If the asset was not held for the entire period of ownership, it is deemed to be two assets, one representing the asset for which rollover relief is available and the other the asset for which it is not.
2. The proceeds of realisation exceed the cost (or proportionate amount if part disposal) of the asset.
3. The expenditure on the new asset must be incurred in the period beginning 12 months before and ending three years after the realisation of the old asset (or as such period may be extended by HMRC).
4. The new expenditure must be capitalised by the company for accounting purposes.
5. The new assets must be chargeable intangible assets in relation to the company immediately after the expenditure is incurred.

EFFECT OF THE ROLLOVER

The effect of the rollover relief is to rollover or defer the gain to a later time (date of disposal of the new asset) by reducing the base cost of the new asset by the amount of the gain deferred. A gain arising on the new asset will include the 'rolled over' gain. Additionally, under the chargeable intangible assets regime, the amount of expenditure incurred on the new asset for the purposes of amortisation is reduced by the gain rolled over.

Where not all of the proceeds of sale of the original asset are reinvested, only a proportion of the gain is rolled over.

In some circumstances it is possible to make rollover claims within a group of companies.

Group relief

There are a number of 'group' reliefs for corporation tax purposes, including (in the context of intellectual property ownership):

(a) relief for trading losses and other amounts eligible for tax relief by way of surrender between members of the same 75 per cent group (and in certain circumstances to and from members of a consortium and a 'consortium company');
(b) CGT relief on transfers of assets intra-group;
(c) relief on transfers of intangible fixed assets intra-group.

All three of these reliefs will be of interest where intellectual property is held within a group.

The definition of group varies between the loss relief rules and the capital gains/intangible fixed assets rules.

For loss relief, companies are in the same group if one is a 75 per cent subsidiary of the other or both are 75 per cent subsidiaries of a third company. The 75 per cent test needs to be met in terms of ownership of ordinary share capital, entitlements to profits on a winding up and entitlement to profits each year. It used to be the case that for group relief to apply both companies had to be within the charge to corporation tax. However, following the decision in Case C-446/03 *Marks & Spencer plc* v. *David Halsey (Insp of Taxes)* it is now possible to group relieve losses cross-border within the EU in certain limited situations.

For capital gains/intangible fixed assets, assets transferred within a group are transferred at no gain/no loss (for capital gains purposes) or on a tax neutral basis (for chargeable intangible assets). For chargeable gains purposes, transferor and transferee both need to be within the charge to corporation tax as regards the asset. For intangible fixed assets, the asset needs to fall within the new UK corporation tax rules for both transferor and transferee. A group is defined (for both these sets of rules) by reference to a 'principal company' (which cannot be a 75 per cent subsidiary of another company by ownership of ordinary share capital). A principal company and its 75 per cent subsidiaries, and their 75 per cent subsidiaries (by ownership of ordinary share capital) form a group, provided that the group does not include any company which is not an 'effective 51 per cent subsidiary' of the principal company. Broadly speaking, an 'effective 51 per cent subsidiary' is defined to include any company in respect of which the principal company is directly or indirectly entitled to more than 50 per cent of profits per annum and more than 50 per cent of assets on a winding up.

A trap to watch for both capital gains and intangible fixed assets group relief is crystallising a 'degrouping' charge following an intra-group transfer of assets. This can happen when assets are transferred intra-group and the transferee leaves the group (without the transferor leaving with it) within six years following the transfer. The transferee is deemed as a result of the de-grouping to have sold and re-acquired the asset at its market value at the date of the intra-group transfer.

Although outside the scope of this book, it is worth noting that there are further reliefs from the capital gains and intangible fixed asset rules for certain corporate reorganisations.

R&D reliefs

There are two types of relief for income expenditure on R&D (ignoring specific reliefs for, e.g. vaccines). These are:

- *R&D relief for small and medium sized companies (SMEs).* R&D tax relief is available as a 150 per cent (rising to 175 per cent in 2008) tax deduction for an SME which incurs revenue expenditure on R&D. Loss-making SMEs can choose to surrender their R&D losses for a 16 per cent cash payment.
- *R&D relief for large companies.* R&D tax relief is available as a 125 per cent (rising to 130 per cent in 2008) tax deduction for large companies which incur revenue expenditure on R&D. Large companies cannot surrender the allowances for cash.

The rules are contained in FA 2000, Sched.20 and FA 2002, Sched.12.

SMES

The European Commission's SME definition is used for R&D tax purposes. An SME is a company (together with any 25 per cent (or more) subsidiary), which has less than 250 employees and either an annual turnover of up to €40 million, or a balance sheet of not more than €43 million. A company must satisfy the SME criteria over two consecutive financial years. The SME must also be independent (25 per cent or more joint ownership) of one or more large companies.

Pursuant to the Finance Bill 2007, the SME definition is to be extended to companies with less than 500 employees, turnover of less than €50 million and a balance sheet of less than €100 million. This change will take effect from a day to be nominated by Treasury order. Larger SMEs (more than 250 employees) will not be able to claim both R&D and vaccine relief on the same expenditure.

What are qualifying R&D activities and what expenses qualify?

QUALIFYING R&D ACTIVITIES

R&D is defined as 'activities that fall to be treated as research and development in accordance with generally accepted accounting practice' (i.e. UK GAAP) (ITA 2007, s.1006(2)).

The Department for Business, Enterprise and Regulatory Reform (BERR) guidelines (available at **www.berr.gov.uk**) provide detailed information on the definition of R&D, including examples. These guidelines were given legal force from 1 April 2004 under the Research and Development (Prescribed Activities) Regulations 2004, SI 2004/712.

According to the BERR's guidelines, R&D for tax purposes takes place when a project seeks to achieve (but may not achieve) an advance in science and technology. R&D includes direct activities (such as experimental testing, or planning) that contribute to achieving the advance by attempting to resolve elements of scientific, technological or system uncertainty associated with the project. Other activities, such as student research and maintaining R&D equipment (including computers) that are essential to the undertaking of the R&D project, can also qualify indirectly as R&D.

A product does not become an advance simply because it has been created using science/technology, and activities of a routine nature or involving the use of routine methods are not R&D. Further, R&D does not include activities such as market research, general data collection, product standardisation or the promotion of the sale of the end product.

The end result should achieve an extension or increase in the overall knowledge and capability of a particular scientific/technological field, by the standard of a 'competent professional working in the [relevant] field'.

R&D ends for a project when the knowledge is in a usable or readily deducible form for a competent professional working in the field.

Not all R&D activities attract the R&D tax relief, which is restricted to qualifying expenditure on R&D activities.

WHAT R&D EXPENSES QUALIFY?

The expenditure must be of a non-capital nature and directly attributable to the R&D project. This means that the R&D work must be related to a trade carried on/to be carried on by the company and directly undertaken by the company, or on its behalf.

At present, qualifying expenditure for R&D purposes generally includes spending on employing staff directly and actively engaged in carrying out R&D activities and (in certain circumstances), subcontracted R&D carried out on behalf of the company. The rules differ between SMEs and large companies (see below).

Benefits in kind paid to employees are not qualifying costs, and support staff (e.g. secretaries) are not treated as directly engaged in R&D.

There are anti-avoidance provisions within the R&D tax credit legislation (FA 2000, Sched.20, para.21) to prevent companies making artificially inflated claims for relief.

EXTRA REQUIREMENTS FOR SMES IN RESPECT OF QUALIFYING R&D EXPENDITURE

For an SMEs' expenditure to qualify the following requirements must be satisfied:

1. any intellectual property rights arising or flowing from the R&D work to which the expenditure is attributable must vest (in part at least) in the SME claiming the R&D relief;
2. the expenditure must not be subsidised. Grants so received are deducted from qualifying expenditure, thus reducing the R&D relief available. However, FA 2003 (Sched.31, para.15) introduced a right for an SME, under certain conditions, to claim at the large company rate of relief (see below) for qualifying R&D expenditure that has been subsidised.

R&D relief is also available for expenditure in the form of contributions made to qualifying scientific research associations, charities and universities for independent R&D work related to the company's trade.

Operation of the R&D tax relief

The relief only applies to companies. A claim for relief can be made if the company has incurred at least £10,000 on qualifying R&D expenditure in a 12-month accounting period.

The relief must be claimed by the company for the relevant accounting period in which the expenditure was incurred. A claim can be withdrawn at any time up to the first anniversary of the filing date of the tax return.

More details are available from HMRC's *Corporate Intangibles Research and Development Manual.*

R&D RELIEF FOR SMES

A trading SME may deduct 150 per cent of its qualifying R&D expenditure for a 12-month accounting period when it calculates its taxable profits/losses if the expense is incurred wholly and exclusively for its trade. The deduction can be set against the profits of the SME and therefore creates an enhanced trading loss for the accounting period.

A non-trading SME which intends to carry out a trade derived from the R&D can make an election to use the 150 per cent deduction to create a deemed trading loss for the accounting period. This election must be made within two years from the end of the accounting period to which the election relates.

An SME's trading loss in the accounting period (enhanced or deemed by the R&D relief) can be surrendered to HMRC in return for a (tax free) cash payment equal to 16 per cent of the amount surrendered (which according to HMRC, could amount to £24 for every £100 of the actual R&D expenditure). The amount that can be surrendered to HMRC for the accounting period is subject to a maximum of either:

(a) 150 per cent of the qualifying R&D expenditure; or
(b) the amount of the SME's unrelieved losses.

Once surrendered, the remainder amount of the unrelieved losses (for either a trading or non-trading SME) can be carried forward.

The tax credit is restricted to an amount equal to the total of the company's PAYE/NIC liabilities for the accounting period if this amount is lower than the 16 per cent credit. In this case, the balance of the surrenderable loss that could *not* be used for the tax credit can be carried forward.

The tax credit will first be offset against any corporation tax liability of the SME before any excess being paid by HMRC.

R&D RELIEF FOR LARGE COMPANIES

Large companies can deduct 125 per cent of their qualifying R&D expenditure for the 12-month accounting period when calculating their taxable profits, if the expense is incurred wholly and exclusively for the purposes of its trade or proposed trade. The expense is deducted in the period in which it is incurred or, if later, the first trading period.

Large companies cannot surrender a trading loss in return for a cash payment from HMRC. Therefore, unlike SMEs, large companies would not be entitled to a tax credit. Instead, the loss would be relieved in accordance with the tax loss rules (e.g. carried forward).

Unlike SMEs, large companies cannot make a pre-trading election.

SUBCONTRACTOR/GROUP TREATMENT

There are additional rules to determine whether R&D relief is available where work is subcontracted or carried on throughout a group.

Capital allowances

A deduction for capital expenditure is available to reduce profits for corporation tax (under the pre-April 2002 regime) and for income tax purposes.

Generally, expenditure must be classified as capital and must be incurred on specified assets. Specific rules provide for expenditure on R&D, know-how and patents to be relieved.

The quantum of capital allowance that can be claimed by a taxpayer is provided at a specified rate for each tax year and depends on the type of capital asset and the type of entity incurring the expenditure.

(a) Acquisition of know-how

Where a taxpayer incurs expenditure for the purpose of acquiring know-how from an unconnected person, a capital allowance deduction may be available if the know-how is used in a trade (CAA 2001, s.454(1)).

'Know-how' is defined as 'any industrial information or techniques likely to assist in manufacturing or processing goods or material; working a source of mineral deposits; or carrying out any agricultural, forestry or fishing operations' (CAA 2001, s.452(2)).

HMRC takes the view that this definition does not extend to commercial know-how (such as market research, customer lists and sales techniques) because this is not 'industrial information or techniques likely to assist in the manufacture of goods or materials' (*Capital Allowances Manual* CA70030).

The rate of allowance depends on the tax year in which the relief is sought. Where relief is sought, the allowance is:

(a) all years (except year in which (b) applies) – 25 per cent of the excess of available qualifying expenditure (AQE) for the pool of assets subject to capital allowance deduction over total disposal value (TDV); and
(b) final tax year (e.g. when trade discontinued) – amount by which the AQE exceeds the TDV (CAA 2001, ss.458(1), (6); 457(4), (5)). If the TDV exceeds AQE then an assessable balancing charge will arise to the taxpayer (CAA 2001, ss.457(3); 458(5)).

Broadly speaking AQE is capital expenditure on know-how that is incurred for the purposes of the trade and TDV is the net proceeds of sale (which consists of capital sums).

(b) Acquisition of patent rights

A capital allowance deduction is available for capital expenditure incurred to acquire *patent rights* for the purpose of a trade within the charge to UK tax (CAA 2001, s.468(1)) or for patent rights which give rise to UK taxable income (CAA 2001, s.469).

Patent rights are defined as rights to do or authorise the doing of anything which would, but for that right, be an infringement of a patent (CAA 2001, s.464(2)).

There is a separate pool of expenditure for each trade and a pool for non-trading expenditure. The writing down allowance available is 25 per cent of the excess of the AQE over total disposal receipts (TDR) (CAA 2001, s.472) each tax year with similar rules for balancing charges/allowances as know-how.

(c) R&D allowances

Capital allowances of 100 per cent are available for capital expenditure incurred on R&D or providing facilities for R&D provided that the R&D is for a trade or a trade is subsequently commenced which is connected with the R&D. R&D is defined in ICTA 1988, s.837 such that it bears the same general meaning as for the R&D tax credit regime.

(d) Plant & machinery (including software)

Plant (including computer software and expenditure incurred in acquiring the right to use or otherwise deal with computer software) and machinery are subject to capital allowance deductions at 25 per cent (on a reducing balance basis) reducing to 20 per cent from 2008.

'Software' is not defined in the legislation and therefore its ordinary meaning is used.

Anti-avoidance rules

Historical approach

In the context of intellectual property, there would, in the absence of rules to the contrary, be significant scope for tax planning as its nature means that it is easy to move across borders.

As Lord Tomlin said in *IRC* v. *Duke of Westminster* (1936) 19 TC 490 at 520:

> Every man is entitled if he can to order his affairs so that the tax attaching under the appropriate Acts is less than it otherwise would be.

Based upon this dictum, taxpayers and their advisers have sought to mitigate taxes through devising transactions or structures for the ownership of assets which seek to minimise taxes payable.

The new approach

It used to be the generally held position (on the basis of the *Duke of Westminster* case) that one could take a literal interpretation of tax legislation and devise schemes which circumvented that legislation. However, modern jurisprudence following a line of cases including *Ramsay (WT) Ltd* v. *IRC* [1982] AC 300, *Furniss* v. *Dawson* [1984] STC 153 and more recently *Barclays Mercantile Business Finance* v. *Mawson* [2005] STC 1 have taken a more purposive interpretation of tax legislation. As Lord Nicholls says in *Barclays Mercantile Business Finance* v. *Mawson*:

> The essence of the new approach was to give the statutory provision a purposive construction in order to determine the nature of the transaction to which it was intended to apply and then to decide whether the actual transaction (which might involve considering the overall effect of a number of elements intended to operate together) answered to the statutory description.

For example, in *Furniss* (above), the court held that where there was:

(a) preordained (or predetermined) series of transactions; and
(b) steps were inserted which have no commercial (business) purpose apart from the avoidance of a liability to tax,

then the inserted steps are disregarded for tax purposes.

The courts are not prepared to take a blinkered look at each transaction but will consider the tax avoidance scheme as a whole.

Tax planning in respect of intellectual property should therefore always consider whether what is planned falls within the relevant legislation after taking a purposive interpretation of such legislation.

Further specific anti-avoidance rules have been developed to catch the more obvious schemes that have been devised (e.g. ICTA 1988, s.775A which catches transfers of rights to receive annual payments for non-taxable consideration).

For example, without anti-avoidance rules it would be possible for individuals and companies to hold intellectual property offshore (e.g. in a wholly owned subsidiary) and to roll up income offshore without paying UK tax.

There are therefore a raft of anti-avoidance rules designed to prevent such practices. The two main types of rules which could apply in these circumstances to counter tax avoidance are:

(a) rules which impose an arm's length price on any transaction (transfer pricing rules); and
(b) rules which deem income of a company to accrue to its shareholders (generically referred to as 'assets held offshore' below).

Transfer pricing

Where transactions take place between related, associated or connected companies, there is an incentive for profits to be 'moved' from a company with a relatively high tax rate to another company with a relatively low tax rate. This could be achieved, for example in the context of a patent licence, by an 'inflated' royalty being charged by a licensor in a low tax jurisdiction to a licensee resident in a high tax jurisdiction (thus stripping taxable profits out of the high tax jurisdiction).

The transfer pricing regime seeks to prevent this type of practice by requiring an arm's length price to be paid (in our case an arm's length royalty to be paid by the licensee). This is a general rule which is similar to the specific rules which impose market value prices on transactions between connected persons (e.g. for capital gains tax, TCGA 1992, s.17 and for chargeable intangible assets, FA 2002, Sched.29, para.92).

Many countries have a transfer pricing regime although the precise mechanics vary from country to country.

Transfer pricing rules

The UK's transfer pricing rules are in ICTA 1988, Sched.28AA.

Broadly, the provisions seek to adjust the tax return of a person who obtains a potential UK tax advantage from its non-arm's length dealing with another person. The tax return is adjusted as though the transaction had been at arm's length.

The provisions apply to 'advantaged' persons which includes companies, partnerships, and individuals. To be 'advantaged', the UK taxpayer must *control* the other or be under control of the same person. 'Control' means voting control or control by virtue of powers conferred by the articles of association or other document regulating the powers of a company whereby the company's affairs are conducted in accordance with the wishes of the controller (ICTA 1988, s.840). In the context of a partnership, control means the right to a share of more than one half of its assets or income. The definition is extended in certain circumstances (e.g. to include rights held by connected persons, rights which will be acquired in the future or persons who own 40 per cent or more of the shares in a company where there is another such 40 per cent or more shareholder).

Where the provisions apply, penalties may be assessed to the extent of tax lost due to fraud or negligent conduct. However, where the taxpayer makes an honest and reasonable attempt to comply with the legislation, HMRC will not impose a penalty (HMRC Tax Bulletin 38 (December 1998)).

VALUATION

In practice, determining the arm's length value, particularly one that is acceptable to the revenue authorities of both countries, is a difficult exercise. This is particularly the case for intangible assets such as intellectual property which are often unique to the company or group concerned.

The OECD Transfer Pricing Guidelines describe valuation methods which are generally acceptable to tax authorities around the globe and which have been accepted by HMRC. The methods are divided into transaction-based methods and profit methods.

TRANSACTION-BASED METHODS

Comparable uncontrolled prices method

The comparable uncontrolled prices (CUP) method compares 'the price for property or services transferred in a controlled transaction to the price charged for property or services transferred in a comparable uncontrolled transaction in comparable circumstances'.

Although this is generally the best pricing method, it is often not practical. In the context of intellectual property there is usually no CUP and, if there is, it is often confidential. In practice, this method is rarely used even though all OECD member countries recognise that the CUP method provides the most direct comparison and encourage its use.

Resale price method

The resale price method is 'based on the price at which a product that has been purchased from an associated enterprise is resold to an independent enterprise. The resale price is reduced by the resale price margin. What is left after subtracting the resale price margin can be regarded, after adjustment for other costs associated with the purchase of the product (e.g. customs duties), as an arm's length price'.

Cost plus method

The cost plus method begins with the costs incurred by the supplier and then adds an appropriate mark up to remunerate the supplier for functions performed, assets utilised and risks borne. This mark up should be calculated by reference to similar uncontrolled transactions.

PROFIT METHODS

Profit split method

The combined profit to be split between the associated enterprises from a controlled transaction or controlled transactions is identified, and then split between those enterprises according to an economically valid basis that approximates the division of profits that would have been anticipated and reflected in an agreement made at arm's length between independent parties.

Transactional net margin method

This method is based on comparisons at the net profit level between the taxpayer and independent parties dealing wholly independently in relation to a comparable transaction or dealings.

Importance of documentation

In all of these valuation methods, evidence will be needed to justify the value given. Documentation should be kept to evidence the relevant relationship, nature, terms and prices of the relevant transactions, the valuation method used (particularly how the arm's length price was determined including any functional analysis or comparable study). The basis for any computational adjustment required to reach an arm's length value should be retained, and the terms of relevant commercial arrangements with both third party and affiliated customers. Such documentation should be kept for at least six years from the end of the chargeable period to which it relates.

The extent of documentation should be 'such . . . as is reasonable given the complexity or otherwise of the relevant transaction (or series of transactions)' (HMRC Tax Bulletin 37 (October 1998)).

Assets held offshore

There are two main sets of provisions which would militate against holding intellectual property assets offshore to roll up income on a tax-free basis. These are:

(a) controlled foreign company (CFC) rules (for corporate shareholders);
(b) rules restricting transfer of assets offshore (for individual shareholders).

Controlled foreign company rules

Under the UK's CFC rules if a company resident outside the UK is controlled by persons resident in the UK and is subject to a lower level of taxation than the UK (less than 75 per cent) then the profits of the non-resident company (together with any creditable local tax) can be apportioned to UK tax resident corporate shareholders and charged to UK tax (ICTA 1988, s.747(2)).

Control by UK persons includes cases where a company is controlled by two 40 per cent or more shareholders, at least one of which is resident in the UK.

The rules relating to CFCs are highly technical and there are detailed rules (beyond the scope of this chapter) relating to the computation of any taxable profits apportioned to the UK, how these rules interact with double tax relief when dividends are paid to the UK, anti-avoidance provisions and exemptions from the CFC rules. However, it is worth noting the main exemptions to a CFC apportionment. These are:

(a) the company is not subject to a lower level of taxation than it would have had in the UK (this means it is subject to at least 75 per cent of the corresponding UK tax);
(b) where the company follows an 'acceptable distribution policy' – broadly speaking where it distributes at least 90 per cent of its profits within 18 months of its year end;
(c) where the company pursues certain exempt activities;
(d) where the company meets the public quotation condition (35 per cent of its shares are listed and are actively dealt with on a recognised stock exchange), although it is expected that this exemption will be repealed by FA 2007;
(e) where the company's chargeable profits are less than £50,000 per annum;
(f) where the company is resident in a territory specified in the Controlled Foreign Companies (Excluded Countries) Regulations 1998, SI 1998/3081, and meets any conditions specified in such regulations.

The intention behind these exemptions is to stop the CFC rules catching straightforward commercial transactions. However, due to the complexity of these rules they often do catch what would seem commercial transactions and therefore need to be considered in all cases where companies are owned directly or indirectly by UK corporates.

It is worth noting that the CFC rules, along with the double tax relief rule, are currently subject to consultation and may be radically changed, with a possible effective date of 1 April 2009.

Transfer of assets abroad

The CFC rules do not apply to individual shareholders. However, rules in ITA 2007, ss.720, 727 and 731 (previously ICTA 1988, ss.739 and 740) can produce similar results to the CFC rules for such shareholders.

Sections 720 and 727 apply to prevent the avoidance of income tax by individuals ordinarily resident in the UK by means of a transfer of assets abroad by virtue or in consequence of which income becomes payable to persons resident or domiciled outside the UK. The rules deem such income to be the transferor's income when he has power (either immediately or in the future) to enjoy the income or where he receives or is entitled to a capital sum connected with the transfer of assets.

Similar rules apply under s.731 to tax non-transferors who receive a benefit from assets transferred offshore.

9.3 WITHHOLDING TAXES

Withholding tax on patent royalties

Where a person in the UK pays a royalty or other sum in respect of the use of a patent and the payment is of an income (rather than a capital) nature, the payment is subject to a withholding tax at 22 per cent (ITA 2007, s.903).

This requirement does not apply where the payer had a reasonable belief that the person beneficially entitled to the income is:

(a) a company resident in the UK; or
(b) a company not resident in the UK that carries on a trade in the UK through a permanent establishment and the payment will be brought into account in computing the UK chargeable profits of the non-resident company; or
(c) a body of the type listed in ITA 2007, s.936 (broadly certain public bodies and entities that are generally tax exempt, e.g. charities); or
(d) a partnership comprised of entities that fulfil either the requirements of (a) and/or (b) or (c).

The general exemptions from withholding are contained in ITA 2007, ss.930–7.

If a payer 'reasonably believes' that an exemption applies it may pay gross, but if that belief proves incorrect the withholding obligation is reimposed so the payer is at risk. There is no general mechanism for HMRC to certify that payments may be made gross.

Withholding tax on copyright and design right royalties

A person who pays a copyright royalty or a sum paid periodically for or in respect of that copyright to a non-UK resident copyright owner is required to withhold tax at the basic rate and to account for that tax to HMRC (ITA 2007, s.906).

Similar provisions exist for payments of design right royalties to persons outside the UK. In both cases the statutory exemptions from withholding described above apply.

However, withholding does not apply to copyright payments relating to films or video recordings, or their soundtracks, unless the soundtrack is separately exploited. It also does not apply to payment for copies of works or articles which have been exported from the UK for distribution outside the UK.

Sales of UK patent rights

If a UK person buys patent rights in a UK patent from a non-resident seller which is liable for UK tax in respect of the sale, then the purchaser is obliged to deduct basic rate tax from the purchase price and account for this to HMRC (ITA 2007, s.910). For these purposes 'patent rights' means a right to do or authorise the doing of any thing which, but for the right, would be an infringement of a patent and thus includes licences (ICTA 1988, s. 533 and ITTOIA 2005, s.587).

The statutory exemptions from withholding outlined in **9.3** above apply.

EC Interest and Royalties Directive

From 1 January 2004, the EC Interest and Royalties Directive (Council Directive 2003/49/EC of 3 June 2003 on a common system of taxation applicable to interest and royalty payments made between associated companies of different Member States) introduced a common system of taxation applicable to interest and royalty payments made between associated companies of Member States.

These provisions have force in the UK (ITTOIA 2005, ss.757–67 and ITA 2007, s.914) and provides an exemption from income tax on royalties where:

(a) the payer of the royalty is a UK company or a UK permanent establishment of an EU company; and
(b) the person beneficially entitled to the income is an EU company, but not such a company's UK permanent establishment or non-EU permanent establishment.

Both companies must be 25 per cent associates, that is, one company holds at least 25 per cent of the capital or voting rights in the other or there must be a parent company of both companies that holds such a share in each.

As with the exemptions set out earlier, payment gross is permitted where the payer 'reasonably believes' the exemption applies, but again the payer is at risk if that belief is incorrect. As a practical matter, if the payee is an EU company the payer's risk should be eliminated as the payee company should be making a claim under the applicable double tax treaty that should result in HMRC issuing a payment directive to the payer to apply a reduced or nil rate of withholding (see further below).

Double tax treaties

Royalties paid by a UK resident to a resident of a country with which the UK has a double tax treaty (DTT) may be exempt from withholding taxes as a result of the operation of a royalty article of a DTT. Even if the royalty article does not extinguish the withholding tax liability it will normally impose a restriction on the amount which can be deducted.

'Royalties' generally contemplates payments of any kind received as a consideration for the use of, or the right to use, any copyright of literary, artistic or scientific work including cinematograph films, any patent, trade mark, design or model, plan, secret formula or process, or for information concerning industrial, commercial or scientific experience (OECD Model Tax Convention).

However, relief for UK source taxation under a DTT is not automatic. A non-resident licensor must make an application to its own domestic tax authorities claiming relief under the relevant article of the DTT and demonstrating that it fulfils the requirements of that article. If the parties are unconnected, these will usually be limited to tax residence and beneficial ownership of the royalty payments. Once satisfied, the non-resident's tax authority will certify to HMRC that the licensor is entitled to relief under the relevant DTT and HMRC will then direct the payer to make future payments at the rate specified under the relevant DTT.

Under ITA 2007, s.911 a UK company which makes a payment of royalties otherwise subject to deduction of tax may, if it thinks fit, calculate the sum of income tax to be deducted by reference to the rate applicable in the relevant DTT (if lower than the UK rate) and make the payment on that basis (that is, without receiving a payment direction from HMRC following a DTT claim). However, the company must reasonably believe that, at the time the payment is made, the payee is entitled to relief in respect of the payment under a relevant DTT. As before, the payer is at risk if the payee is not entitled to a reduced rate of withholding under the DTT, and since the payee can make a claim under the DTT that will result in the payer receiving a direction to pay at a reduced rate from HMRC it is difficult to see why payers should take this risk.

Unilateral relief

Where a payment is made by a non-resident to a UK resident and is subject to withholding tax which is not relieved under a DTT, unilateral relief may be given whereby the foreign tax withheld is treated as a credit for UK tax purposes (ICTA 1988, s.796).

To the extent the above mentioned relief does not apply, the foreign tax may, in certain circumstances, be treated as an expense in calculating UK taxable profits (ICTA 1988, s.811).

9.4 VAT

Broadly speaking, VAT is an indirect tax, chargeable on consumer expenditure. It is collected and payable by the supplier on certain supplies including the granting, surrender or assignment of any intellectual property right for value (VATA 1994, s.1).

'Input' and 'output' VAT

The 'cost' of VAT is intended to be borne by the end-user but the tax is collected at different stages in the supply chain. A VAT registered person who only makes taxable supplies is able to offset the VAT it pays on supplies received by it (input tax) against the VAT it charges to its customers on supplies made by it (output tax). It pays to HMRC (generally on a monthly or quarterly basis) the difference between its output and input tax (or receives a repayment where input tax exceeds output tax). Where a VAT-registered person makes both taxable (i.e. vatable or zero rated) and non-taxable supplies (i.e. exempt or outside the scope of VAT), only a proportion of his input tax will be able to be offset ('recoverable') against output tax. This is because input tax is generally only recoverable to the extent it is attributable to taxable supplies.

In particular, the recovery of input tax attributable to exempt supplies is blocked. Businesses which make taxable and exempt supplies are generally referred to as 'partially exempt traders', typical examples of which are banks and insurance companies. The recovery of input tax attributable to 'outside the scope' supplies varies. However, recovery is not blocked in the case of exports of services that would be taxable if made in the UK.

Liability to VAT

For VAT to be chargeable on a particular supply, a number of conditions must be satisfied, namely:

(a) there must be a supply of goods or services (including anything related to that supply);
(b) the supply must be made in the UK at the time of the supply;
(c) the supply is a taxable supply;
(d) the supply is made by a taxable person for consideration; and
(e) the supply must be made in the course or furtherance of a business carried on by him (VATA 1994, ss.1(2), 4).

Supply of services

A 'supply of services' is defined as anything which is not a supply of goods but is done for a consideration (including, if so done, the granting, assignment or surrender of any right) (VATA 1994, s.5(2)(b)). Therefore, intellectual property transactions (such as licences or assignments of intellectual properties) will generally be supplies of services for VAT purposes.

Time of supply

The 'time of supply of services' is when the services are performed (VATA 1994, s.6(3)). An exception to this general rule is where there is a continuous supply of services, in which case the time of supply is the earlier of when the payment is received by the supplier and when the supplier issues the invoice (SI 1995/2518, reg.90(1)).

In the case of royalties, the time of supply is the earlier of when the royalties are received and a VAT invoice is issued (SI 1995/2518, reg.91).

Taxable supply

A taxable supply is a supply of goods or services made in the UK other than an exempt supply (VATA 1994, s.4(2)). There are three rates of VAT on taxable supplies, 17.5 per cent, 5 per cent (on a limited class of supplies) and nil (on zero-rated supplies).

An 'exempt supply' is a supply specified in VATA 1994, Sched.9. Exempt supplies include, for example, financial and insurance services, but suppliers of intellectual property are not generally exempt. Nor does intellectual property fall in the category of basic food and personal items which are zero-rated.

There are two other categories of supply which are important for VAT purposes: 'outside the scope' supplies and other supplies treated as not involving a supply of goods or services with the result that VAT is not chargeable. An example of an 'outside the scope' supply is the supply of certain international services (e.g. a transfer of intellectual property to a customer outside the UK).

Taxable person

VAT applies to supplies made by a taxable person. Therefore, a person who is a taxable person must charge VAT on that supply and a person who is not a taxable person must not charge VAT in respect of any supply.

A 'taxable person' is essentially a person who makes taxable supplies in the United Kingdom in the course or furtherance of a business carried on by him and the aggregate value of the supplies that have been made by him in the previous 12 months or less, or are expected to be made in the forthcoming 12 months (or in the next 30 days alone), exceeds the prevailing registration limit (this is currently £64,000 in the UK for tax year 2007/2008). Businesses may also register voluntarily for VAT (thus becoming taxable persons).

Consideration

While 'consideration' is not a defined term, the legislation does contemplate payments in cash or in kind (VATA 1994, s.19(3)).

In most cases, whether a supply is made for consideration will be quite obvious. Where there is uncertainty, case law suggests that where a direct link exists between the supply and the payment, the payment can be regarded as consideration (Case 154/80 *Staatssecretaris van Financiën* v. *Cooperatiëve Aardappelenbewaarplaats GA* [1981] ECR 445, ECJ).

Course or furtherance

For a supply to be made within the scope of VAT, it must be made in the course or furtherance of a business carried on by the taxable person making the supply (VATA 1994, s.4(1)).

Therefore, the supplier must be conducting some economic activity and the supply must be made in the course or furtherance of that activity.

From an intellectual property perspective, a supply that exploits intellectual property or similar rights will be an economic transaction and hence would be made in the course or furtherance of a business.

However, HMRC take the view that an isolated transaction will not normally be a business transaction for the purposes of VAT (Notice 700 *The VAT Guide*).

Place of supply

The complex 'place of supply' rules determine in which Member State, if any, a supply of goods or services should be taxed. The result is that UK VAT is only chargeable where the place of supply under these rules is the United Kingdom. UK VAT is not chargeable if the place of supply is outside the United Kingdom, even if made by a taxable person. If the place of supply is another Member State of the EU, that Member State has the jurisdiction to charge its local equivalent of VAT on the supply. If the place of supply is outside the EU, no Member State has the jurisdiction to charge VAT on the supply although value added or sales tax may be chargeable outside the EU.

For services, the crucial question is normally where the supplier 'belongs'. A supplier's place of 'belonging' also has a particular meaning for VAT purposes and is broadly the place where that person has its business establishment or some other 'fixed establishment', or (in the UK at least) if it has more than one business establishment, that which is most directly concerned with the supply of services in question.

Schedule 5 services

There are special place of supply rules for certain types of services, in particular those services which are listed in VATA 1994, Sched.5 ('Schedule 5 services'). Schedule 5 services include transfers and assignments of copyright, patents, licences, trade marks and similar rights as well as advertising services, data processing and the provision of information, telecommunication services (and as of 1 July 2003, radio and television broadcasting services, and certain electronically supplied services but these are subject to extra rules).

For these services, the place of supply will normally be the place where the customer 'belongs' if the customer either:

(a) belongs outside the EU (irrespective of whether the customer carries on business or is a private individual); or
(b) belongs in a different Member State to that of the provider, is registered for VAT in that Member State and receives the supply in its business capacity.

In all other cases involving a supply of a Schedule 5 service (for example, where the customer is an EU private individual who does not use the service for business purposes), the general rule for determining the place of supply of services applies and the place of supply will be where the supplier 'belongs'.

Importation of services from other countries

There are anti-avoidance provisions which are designed to prevent 'partially exempt traders' from buying services from outside the UK (which if the services had been provided by a UK supplier would have involved a VAT cost). These provisions are known as the 'reverse charge' and apply to Schedule 5 services. Where the reverse charge applies, the recipient of the services (rather than the supplier of the services) is required to account for VAT at the rate applicable in the Member State in which he belongs to the relevant tax authority. It also gives the right to input tax deduction in respect of purchases related to taxable outputs. The effect of the reverse charge in the UK is to treat Schedule 5 services brought in from outside the UK in the same way as services that are actually supplied in the UK if the recipient of the services is VAT registered.

However, the reverse charge has no effect on recipients acting in a private capacity.

Exports

Exports of Schedule 5 services outside the EU will escape VAT (both UK and EU VAT).

As outlined above, exports of most types of Schedule 5 services from one Member State of the EU to another are chargeable to VAT in the Member State where the recipient of the services belongs if the recipient is registered for VAT purposes in that other Member State and receives the services for the purposes of its business.

Exports of Schedule 5 services from EU suppliers to EU private customers continue to attract VAT in the Member State of the supplier.

There are, however, further special rules relating to the supply of telecommunication, radio and television broadcasting and electronically supplied services, as set out below.

The E-Commerce VAT Directive – from 1 July 2003

Given that the reverse charge only operates on Schedule 5 services supplied to a business customer, non-EU suppliers of digitised products downloaded from the internet were at a competitive advantage to EU suppliers who would need to charge VAT on such supplies. Therefore, on 7 May 2002 Council Directive 2002/38/EC, the so-called 'E-Commerce VAT Directive' was adopted. This Directive amended the special EU place of supply rules for certain services at Art.9(2)(e) (the legislative basis for Schedule 5 services in the UK) so as to establish two additional categories of services, being 'electronically supplied services' (including digitised products and content provision) and 'radio and television broadcasting services'.

Consequently, in the UK the new rules operate under the umbrella of 'Schedule 5 services' according to the special rules already discussed, but with an additional complexity in the case of electronically supplied services. For these services, the place of supply will be the place where the customer 'belongs' if the customer either:

(a) belongs outside the EU (irrespective of whether the service is used for business and non-business purposes); or
(b) belongs in another Member State to that of the content provider, is registered for VAT in that member state and receives the supply in its business capacity, in which case the recipient will account for local VAT under the applicable reverse charge procedure; or
(c) (with effect from 1 July 2003) belongs in a different Member State to that of the content provider, is not registered or liable to be registered for VAT in the UK (or the EU) and receives the supply in a non-business or private capacity from a supplier who belongs outside the EU.

However, as distinct from other Schedule 5 services, the place of supply of electronically supplied services, radio and television broadcasting services, and telecommunication services, may also be determined, in certain circumstances, according to where those services are effectively 'used and enjoyed'.

To avoid multiple registrations, the E-Commerce VAT Directive has introduced a 'special scheme' which provides non-EU suppliers an optional, simplified means of registering and accounting electronically for EU VAT on electronically supplied services, supplying broadcasting or other Schedule 5 services.

The net effect of this is that where intellectual property is supplied by a non-EU supplier to an EU customer in a non-business capacity as part of a digitised product, the supplier may now need to account for EU VAT on the supply. Where the supply is to an EU business customer, the reverse charge procedure will continue to apply.

CHAPTER 10

Digital media and the internet

Lorna Brazell

10.1 OVERVIEW

The activities of file-sharing sites such as Napster, and the reaction of the music and film industries to the infringements facilitated by such activities, have given copyright issues great prominence since the rise of the internet. Similarly, the on-going controversies over domain names incorporating third party trade marks have brought trade mark issues into global rather than national play. But other digital media also give rise to intellectual property issues, and the protection of other forms of intellectual property is also called into question through the operation of the internet.

This chapter focuses on areas where important issues arise: copyright, database right, trade marks and confidential information, and outlines the impact of the digital world on patent enforcement.

10.2 COPYRIGHT

Electronic copies

English law has provided for copyright in electronic forms of traditional copyright works – literary, artistic or musical works for example – since the introduction of Copyright, Designs and Patents Act (CDPA) 1988. The fixation requirement for copyright to subsist in literary, dramatic or musical works is satisfied by a recording in any medium, including electronic media of all kinds, while electronic copies of any category of work, including transient electronic copies in a computer memory, are capable of infringing by virtue of s.17(2) and (6). These sections respectively affirm that an electronic copy is a copy and that the making of copies which are transient or incidental to some other use of the work is copying within the meaning of CDPA 1988.

New issues

Digitisation of copyright works on any medium (such as cassette tape, CD or computer memory) is problematic from the copyright perspective since it gives the average owner of a copy of a copyright work two important powers for the first time. Previously, a person's ability to manipulate a copyright work required the ability to reproduce it, which implied specialist skills and/or equipment. With digital copies, however, came digital applications which give the average user the power to manipulate the work, so that both authenticity and infringement became more complex issues than before. Of greater economic impact is the power conferred by digital recordings to make perfect copies rapidly. Relatively unsophisticated counterfeiters could produce large quantities of CDs of music or software almost as soon as the original was released, and pack up and move on as soon as the operation seemed to be at risk of being uncovered.

The internet brought a new range of copyright issues to the fore, adding to these existing challenges a network which enabled the instantaneous, global publication and transmission of works. Until that point, copyright piracy had been limited to small-scale copying by ordinary users – the taping of records or copying of videos for a friend or two – and to commercial pirates having access to printing and recording techniques on a large scale. Neither of these forms of piracy was without impact on the copyright owner, but the impact could be contained. In many countries a levy on recording media was imposed to compensate copyright owners for private copying, and efforts could be made to track down and prosecute the large-scale pirates.

But once individual copying migrated to the internet, people began sharing their music or video collections worldwide. The economic impact of this is far greater, and far less easy to address. Although it is clear that those concerned are infringing, locating and suing even a small proportion of these people individually is an enormous task with uncertain returns since few will be in a position to pay commensurate damages. Thus the far more attractive option for those trying to enforce copyright would be to find a mechanism whereby the commercial operators providing access to the internet would be responsible for the infringements perpetrated by their customers.

In harness with this approach, technological mechanisms have been developed to track the source of unauthorised copies. The right to enforce copying restrictions is otherwise of limited value in the digital context: the holder of an infringing copy who is not dealing commercially in it or distributing it further is not an infringer. Only the person who made or published the copy can be sued. Rights holders therefore include in any digital copy of a work information such as the authorship, creation date, copyright ownership and so on. The scope of any licence may also be included. Such 'rights management information' can then be used to identify infringing copies and their origins, giving the right holder a point at which to strike to attempt to limit unauthorised copying.

A further approach is to prevent accurate digital copying or manipulation even where a work is made available online. For instance, code may be included which causes each unauthorised copy to be downgraded in quality compared to the original. Other systems include a check as to whether the machine on which the copy is loaded is licensed to use the work and, if not, have the systems have mechanisms to prevent copying. These measures have, however, raised considerable debate as to whether copyright owners are through such techniques extending the protection conferred by copyright beyond the balance – between the public interest in free access and the incentive to create and publish new works – set by the legislators. After all, once copyright has expired then any person possessing a copy of the original would previously have been free to copy and distribute it as they see fit. Degrading or preventing such copying, if effective, extends the protection of copyright works to the eventual impoverishment of the public domain. There has therefore been little respect for such measures, and circumvention devices have been developed and distributed. Although the purchaser of a copyright work in digital form might be contractually bound to respect such measures, this approach suffers from the problem faced by all 'shrinkwrap' licences, as to whether such terms, not being made known to the purchaser before entering the contract, are actually binding.

Finally, since making a transient electronic copy of a work on a computer screen is an infringing act, copyright owners have in respect of digital media a potential additional power: to prevent access to a work at all. In many circumstances, a licence to create that transient copy is implied if not expressly granted. In others, a lawful user of a copyright work is exempted from infringement by the making of such transient copies (CDPA 1988, s.28A) – but only while the use made is lawful, remaining within the terms of any licence for instance. The increasing dominance of digital media as a means for accessing works, particularly sound recordings and audio-visual works, meant that a power to prevent access in these media is effectively a power to prevent and control access altogether.

Copyright in the information society

These and other issues led in 2001 to the introduction of the Copyright Directive, intended to:

(a) harmonise the approach to copyright in digital media;

(b) harmonise the patchwork of exceptions to copyright which existed in the national laws of the EU Member States; and also
(c) deal with the potential liability of internet service providers (ISPs) for the transmission or storage of infringing works by their subscribers.

The E-Commerce Directive (Directive 2000/31/EC of the European Parliament and of the Council of 8 June 2000 on certain legal aspects of information society services, in particular electronic commerce, in the Internal Market) had already tackled the issue of liability of internet service providers (ISPs) by giving an exception from liability for damages if the service provider took down the infringing material upon being given notice of the infringement. The remedy of being able to obtain an injunction to prevent further copying was left. This 'notice and take down' provision, discussed in more detail below, was seen as a temporary solution pending a copyright-based solution. The Copyright Directive builds upon this.

Digital copyrights and associated rights

The Copyright Directive was wide-ranging, not only formalising a copyright exemption tailored to meet the ISPs' position (see the discussion of the Art.5(1) exception below) but also restricting a new act to be the exclusive right of the copyright holder: the right to communicate a work to the public in electronic form. In implementing this right in the Copyright and Related Rights Regulations 2003, SI 2003/2498, Parliament also took the opportunity to align UK law in respect of broadcasts and cable programmes with the approach to copyright in such works which had been adopted on the continent. Thus, the UK's best known internet case (*Shetland Times* v. *Wills* [1997] FSR 604), which had attempted to tackle the question of infringement by internet linking through reliance on copyright law concerning cable programme services, has now been entirely superseded.

The changes involve the introduction of two new rights:

(a) a copyright of electronic communication to the public; and
(b) a related right for performers to make available their performances to the public through on-demand services.

In addition, new legal rights were given to copyright owners and the manufacturers of technological protection mechanisms prohibiting:

(a) circumvention of such mechanisms; or
(b) the removal of electronic rights management information.

Communication of a work to the public

The new restricted act of communication to the public, mandated by Art.3 of the Directive, gives copyright holders the right to control the electronic transmission of particular categories of copyright works. The right applies to literary, dramatic, musical or artistic works, sound recordings, films and broadcasts. Thus, CDPA 1988, s.20, as amended, makes communication to the public of a work a restricted act, alongside copying, publication and so forth. The right governs only electronic transmission, including (but not limited to):

(a) the broadcasting of the work;
(b) the making available to the public of the work by electronic transmission in such a way that members of the public may access it from a place and at a time individually chosen by them.

The Copyright and Related Rights Regulations 2003 define broadcast in a positive sense by excluding internet transmissions altogether save in specified cases. Under CDPA 1988, s.6(1) a broadcast means:

> . . . an electronic transmission of visual images, sounds or other information which –
>
> (a) is transmitted for simultaneous reception by members of the public and is capable of being lawfully received by them, or
> (b) is transmitted at a time determined solely by the person making the transmission for presentation to members of the public,
>
> and which is not excepted . . .

The exception, set out in CDPA 1988, s.6(1A), is for:

> . . . any internet transmission unless it is –
>
> (a) a transmission taking place simultaneously on the internet and by other means,
> (b) a concurrent transmission of a live event, or
> (c) a transmission of recorded moving images or sounds forming part of a programme service offered by the person responsible for making the transmission, being a service in which programmes are transmitted at scheduled times determined by that person.

The intended effect is that, as regards internet transmissions, only those which are of a conventional broadcast character will qualify as broadcasts. However, on-demand internet services, though excluded from the definition of broadcasting, are included in the definition of communication to the public.

Since the new definition of broadcast has subsumed cable programme services within broadcasts for the purpose of copyright protection, the concept of a cable programme as a separate protected work has been abolished entirely.

Unauthorised communication to the public is also a criminal offence (CDPA 1988, s.107).

Making a performance available to the public

The 'making available right' was mandated by Art.3 of the Copyright Directive, which in turn expands on Art.10 of the 1996 World Performances and Phonograms Treaty (WPPT). Article 10 of the WPPT only confers the right in relation to performances fixed in phonograms. Article 3 of the Directive generalises it to all performances – visual as well as aural. Section 182CA of CDPA 1988, implementing Art.3 in the UK, specifies that:

> (1) A performer's rights are infringed by a person who, without his consent, makes available to the public a recording of the whole or any substantial part of a qualifying performance by electronic transmission in such a way that members of the public may access the recording from a place and at a time individually chosen by them.

This echoes the formulation of on demand services used in defining the right of communication to the public. The echo is intentional, since the performer's right is intended to be an equivalent right which required separate treatment only because it is not a copyright but a related right. Performers therefore now have the right to an injunction as well as damages for infringement. The former right of performers to equitable remuneration for such use was simultaneously withdrawn.

This right of making available is a property right in the same way as the reproduction, distribution and rental and lending rights (s.191A), which may be assigned or licensed in whole or in part or transmitted by operation of law (for example, upon death) in the same way as any other personal property. An assignment must be in writing and signed by the assignor in order to be legally effective (s.191B(3)). As with copyright and other related rights, an assignment of future making available rights can be given in advance of a performance (s.191C(2)).

In contrast, the only remedy available to performers for the broadcast of commercially published sound recordings is the existing right under s.182D to equitable remuneration for communication to the public by ordinary (i.e. other than on-demand) broadcasting. The amount of remuneration is fixed by agreement between the parties (which need not be in advance of transmission) or, failing agreement, by the Copyright Tribunal.

The existing rights enabling a performer to control the dissemination of authorised copies of recordings are exhausted once a copy has first been released with the performer's consent. Such copies, once in authorised circulation, are beyond the performer's control and subject to no further remuneration right. In contrast, the new 'making available' right is not subject to exhaustion of rights. Any copy or recording made of such a transmission would be an infringement of the performer's right to control copying of recordings of a performance, under s.182A.

Unauthorised making available of a performance to the public is also a criminal offence (CDPA 1988, s.198).

Technical protection measures

(A) PROTECTION MEASURES FOR COMPUTER PROGRAMS

Under CDPA 1988, s.296 several categories of person have the right to bring proceedings against anyone who manufactures, supplies or advertises devices or information which enable or assist the circumvention of a technical device applied to a computer program. A technical device is defined by s.296(6) as any device intended to prevent or restrict copyright restricted acts which are not authorised by the owner of copyright in the program.

The right to bring proceedings is given to any of:

(a) the copyright holder;
(b) an exclusive licensee of the copyright;
(c) a person who issues or communicates to the public copies of the protected program; and
(d) the owner or exclusive licensee of any intellectual property rights in the technical device itself.

The same persons have the right to apply for delivery up or to execute a seizure of any means for facilitating the unauthorised removal or circumvention of a technical copy-protection device, under prescribed conditions. The conditions are that:

(a) the articles must be on display in a place to which the public have right of access;
(b) the person proposing to make the seizure must notify the local police station beforehand of the intention to carry out a seizure at a particular time and place;
(c) a notice in the prescribed form containing the prescribed particulars as to the person by whom or on whose authority the seizure is made and the grounds on which it is made must be left at the place from which the seizure has been made.

Once infringing devices have been delivered up or seized the claimant can (but need not) apply to the court for an order under CDPA 1988, s.114 that these be forfeited to them or destroyed.

Defendants' rights not to provide information which would incriminate themselves are withdrawn, by amendment of the Supreme Court Act 1981, s.72. However, any information obtained in the course of such an action cannot be used to bring criminal proceedings against the defendants.

(B) PROTECTION OF COPYRIGHT WORKS OTHER THAN COMPUTER PROGRAMS, AND WORKS IN WHICH PERFORMERS' RIGHTS, PUBLICATION RIGHT OR DATABASE RIGHT SUBSIST

Section 296ZF of CDPA 1988 defines technological protection measures straightforwardly: they encompass any technology, device or component which is designed, in the normal course of its operation, to protect a copyright work other than a computer program. Any technological measures which prevent the normal operation of electronic equipment and its technological development are excluded. Protection means the prevention or restriction of copyright-restricted acts where these have not been authorised by the copyright owner. Although software is not expressly mentioned as a technological measure, it is almost certainly included.

Any technological approach will be treated as 'effective' if it achieves the intended protection; complete protection is not necessary.

Under s.296ZF(3)(b) mechanisms which are applied to control a use of the work which is *not* an act restricted by copyright will not benefit from the provisions of the Act protecting technological measures, and can therefore be circumvented with impunity.

Cryptography researchers aside, any other person who does anything which circumvents a technological measure knowing or having reasonable grounds to know that circumvention is the objective will potentially face legal action under s.296ZA. Either the person who issues copies of the work to the public or communicates the work to the public in protected form, or the copyright owner or exclusive licensee can bring the action. The essence of s.296ZA is to prohibit an act or activity (i.e. the circumvention of the technological protection measures), not to give the rightholders rights over any device or mechanism used to perform or enable the activity or over the resulting 'clean' copy. If there is any evidence of its use or intended use for making unauthorised copies, however, then the de-protected copy itself infringes the copyright in the work by virtue of CDPA 1988, s.24. A transmission of a de-protected copy over the internet will also infringe copyright by virtue of CDPA 1988, s.24(2).

The Copyright Directive required Member States to provide some mechanism whereby the beneficiaries of exceptions to copyright protection such as those making a fair use of a copyright work (see **Chapter 2**) could continue to enjoy them. Section 296ZE implements this by means of a complaint system and a power to the Secretary of State to give directions. There are no obligations on the Secretary of State actually to do anything; and it remains to be seen how effective the system is in practice.

(C) ELECTRONIC RIGHTS MANAGEMENT INFORMATION

Section 296ZG of CDPA 1988 gives the copyright owner, an exclusive licensee of the copyright, or a person issuing copies to the public or communicating the work to the public, rights against anyone who either removes or alters electronic rights management information or imports for distribution or communicates to the public copies of a copyright work from which the electronic rights management information has been removed or altered without authority. By s.296ZG(8) the same rights apply to the owner of rights in performances, publication right and database right.

Exceptions to copyright

Transient or incidental copies exception

Article 5(1) of the Copyright Directive introduced a mandatory exception to copyright for:

> transient or incidental copies which are an integral and essential part of a technological process and which have the sole purpose of enabling a transmission of the work in a network between third parties by an intermediary or a lawful use of the work, but having no independent economic significance.

These criteria are complex and there has as yet been no guidance as to how they will be interpreted. The intention is clear, however: as in the E-Commerce Directive, the legislature has decided in favour of ISPs being exempt from liability, provided that they themselves are not knowingly involved in any infringement. Since the ISPs have not in the past had the technical ability to access the traffic flowing through their servers in order to know whether it might include infringing materials or not, this was the most pragmatic solution. Future technological developments making such inspection possible, currently contemplated for instance for the purpose of prioritising privileged customers' traffic over that of lower priority users, may, of course, lead to the solution being readjusted.

Research and education

The former relatively broad exceptions to copyright whereby copying was permitted for the purposes of research and education were restricted by the Copyright Directive. The exception was abolished in respect of commercial research, and narrowed for all non-commercial education to include a requirement that the copier give a sufficient acknowledgement of the source.

Where copying for education is for a commercial purpose, copying is permitted only in respect of works which have been made available to the public, and which is fair dealing (CDPA 1988, s.32(2A)). These exceptions apply equally to digital and non-digital media.

Time-shifting

The only exception which has more relevance to digital than non-digital media is the exception to copyright for recording for the purpose of time-shifting. The UK, unlike most other countries in Europe, lacks a generalised private copying exception and an associated levy on recording media or equipment to compensate rightsholders. It is regarded as politically extremely difficult to introduce a levy into the UK. Instead the only form of private copying exception is a limited 'time-shifting' exception, in CDPA 1988, s.70, which provides:

> The making for private and domestic use of a recording of a broadcast or cable programme solely for the purpose of enabling it to be viewed or listened to at a more convenient time does not infringe any copyright in the broadcast or cable programme or in any work included in it.

The Copyright Directive restricted this permission such that a recording or photograph is exempt *only* if it is made in domestic premises for private and domestic purposes. If the recording is subsequently sold or let for hire, offered for the same or communicated to the public it becomes an infringing copy.

Actions against internet service providers

The Copyright Directive's second objective was to clarify definitively the potential liability of ISPs for material, including infringing copies of copyright works, which passes across their networks. In the Copyright and Related Rights Regulations 2003 a service provider is defined by reference to reg.2 of the Electronic Commerce (EC Directive) Regulations 2002, SI 2002/2013, implementing the E-Commerce Directive in the UK, as:

> any person providing an 'information society service'

which is in turn:

> any service normally provided for remuneration, at a distance, by means of electronic equipment for the processing (including digital compression) and storage of data, and at the individual request of a recipient of a service.

Caching, hosting and transmitting content – exemption from damages

The internet has expanded at astronomical rates since the mid-1990s, as has the number of individuals and businesses relying upon it. Since the early days, the load upon the communications system itself has been an important factor in determining the speed at which information can be accessed from websites. The practice therefore arose of ISPs setting up caches in various locations which would hold copies of remote websites and respond in place of the original website when a local user attempted to access the remote site. Other caches are created by the web browser programmes themselves on a user's own computer once it becomes apparent which websites are likely to be accessed frequently. This reduces the long-distance information traffic, and speeds up access. It also, however, reduces the number of hits on the original site thereby distorting the apparent popularity – a key factor for advertising revenue. Further, where the information on the site is frequently updated, a cache being updated less regularly may affect the perception of accuracy of the original site. The owner of the original site may justifiably object.

Since a cache is not a temporary copy exempted under Art.5(1), creating it is an act of infringement for which the creator could be found liable. However, in the case of ISPs this has been over-ridden by the exception set out in the E-Commerce Directive, Art.12.

This provides a 'notice and take down' arrangement which exonerates the ISP from liability for damages for the:

> automatic, intermediate and temporary storage of information for the sole purpose of making more efficient onward transmission of the information to other recipients of the service upon their request

provided that upon acquiring actual knowledge of infringing material the ISP acts promptly to remove it. To qualify for this exemption, the caching system used must comply with any industry-recognised rules as to updating and must not interfere with any industry-recognised technological means of enquiring as to what usage the cached site receives. The ISP must further not select the information to be stored in the cache.

ISPs are similarly at risk of involuntarily infringing by providing hosting services, whereby their subscribers are able to create discussion groups or other stores of material without the direct involvement of the service provider. This activity is likewise exempted from infringing subject to a notice and take down provision under the E-Commerce Directive, Art.13, such that provided:

(a) the subscriber is not acting under the ISP's authority or control; and
(b) the ISP neither has actual knowledge of the infringing information nor is aware of facts or circumstances from which it would have been apparent to the service provider that the activity or information was unlawful,

then the ISP will not be liable if, once put on notice, it acts expeditiously to remove the information or disable access to it.

Finally, an ISP which acts as a mere conduit for information, transmission of which is initiated and selected by a subscriber to a third party, is not liable for damages or criminal remedies for infringement of any copyright unless the information is stored for longer than reasonably necessary for the transmission (Art.14).

Injunctions

The Copyright and Related Rights Regulations 2003 inserted a new s.97A into CDPA 1988 giving the High Court the express power to grant injunctions against an ISP which has actual knowledge of another person using its services to infringe either copyright or a performer's property right. Actual knowledge can be ensured by the copyright owner notifying the service provider of the presence on their systems of infringing material since in determining whether a service provider has actual knowledge:

> . . . a court shall take into account all matters which appear to it in the particular circumstances to be relevant and, amongst other things, shall have regard to –
>
> (a) whether a service provider has received a notice through a means of contact made available in accordance with regulation 6(1)(c) of the Electronic Commerce (EC Directive) Regulations 2002 . . . and
> (b) the extent to which any notice includes –
>
> (i) the full name and address of the sender of the notice;
> (ii) details of the infringement in question.

The means of contact which the E-Commerce Regulations require ISPs to make available includes an e-mail address, through which copyright holders can give such notice. To be effective, the notice should include the full name and address of its sender and proper details of the infringement in question.

Software copyright

Subsistence and infringement of software copyright

The question of how software is protected by intellectual property has been much debated in the courts, not only in the UK. Early cases were fought on the grounds that the 'look and feel' of the application from the user's perspective has been copied, even though the underlying code has not. In *Richardson* v. *Flanders and Chemtec* [1993] FSR 497, the judge was persuaded by US authorities that this could be an infringement of copyright in the software, but in *Ibcos Computers* v. *Barclays Mercantile Highland Finance Ltd* [1994]

FSR 275 Jacob J reviewed the issues and concluded that the only literary work involved in computer source code was the literary work of the code itself or, at a higher level of abstraction, the algorithm implemented by that code. Neither of these was infringed by producing software which, using a different algorithm and implementing it through original source code, resulted in an application which gave the end user the same look and feel.

Subsequent cases have addressed the extent to which use of a software program other than by literal copying of the source code can amount to copyright infringement. So, for instance, keeping original code open in a separate window on screen while developing the new version – to remind the programmers how particularly tricky development issues had formerly been solved and speed up the development of the new version – has been held to amount to taking a substantial part of the skill and labour that had gone into developing the previous version (*Cantor Fitzgerald* v. *Tradition* [2000] RPC 95).

On the other hand, copying of the user keyboard commands (both individually and as a complete set of commands), and the 'business logic' of an application have been held not to infringe (*Navitaire Inc* v. *Easyjet Airline Company and Bulletproof Technologies Inc* [2005] ECDR 17). Pumfrey J found (following *Exxon Corp.* v. *Exxon Insurance Consultants International Ltd* [1982] RPC 69) that no copyright subsisted in simple commands; that the more complex commands were not recorded as such in the original source code, so were not protected as literary works; and that the command set as a whole had not been systematically designed with an overall structure, so that no compilation copyright subsisted in the set. He held in the alternative that the commands constituted a language, which in his view was excluded from copyright protection by the Software Directive (Council Directive of 14 May 1991 on the legal protection of computer programs (91/250/EEC)) (although that question would ultimately require determination by the European Court of Justice).

As regards the 'business logic', this claim related to aspects of the system such as the relationship between the commands and the screens; the ability to carry out operations with much the same commands and screens as in the original system; and making the same data about all transactions available, and in substantially the same form as in the original. Since there was no dispute that the languages used, the actual code and (other than in respect of the database structure) the architecture of the systems were quite different, this was a claim of non-literal copying. The claimant effectively had to argue that a higher level of designed structure was implicit in the source code since there had been no formal design process, producing higher level flowcharts and functional specifications. However, in view of the judge's finding that the higher level features of the original system were commonplace in airline reservation systems, there was no original work comprising the 'business logic' which could be protected by copyright.

The judge found that the templates for the character-based screens were tables, and thus could have been protected as literary works. However as static frameworks for displaying dynamic data he considered they were ideas underlying the program's interfaces, and therefore excluded from copyright protection by Art.1(2) of the Software Directive.

Indirect reproduction of the original database (such as by studying the maintenance screens) was protected by CDPA 1988, s.50D, since it was necessary for the purpose of finding out what data was present in the database. Section 50D provides that:

> it is not an infringement of copyright in a database for a person who has a right to use it or any part of it to do, in the exercise of that right, anything which is necessary for the purpose of access to and use of the contents of the database or of that part of the database.

Similarly, allegations of copying related to the on-screen appearance of a video pool game failed where there had been no copying of source code, and arguments that the movements of the cue from still to still of the game amounted to a graphic work failed. Drawing inspiration from the general ideas underlying the original game to produce some aspects of the allegedly infringing games does not amount to infringement; ideas are too general to amount to a substantial part of the claimant's work as protected by copyright (*Nova* v. *Mazooma* [2007] EWCA Civ 219).

Software licensees' statutory permissions

The question of the rights which the licensee of a piece of software has to investigate and adapt the software was addressed by the Software Directive in 1991. It was intended to ensure that software houses should not be able to use copyright to establish and maintain a long-term monopoly under which software users would be forever tied to the software and maintenance services of that particular supplier. The Software Directive therefore introduced reforms relating to reverse engineering and to software maintenance which, in particular circumstances, allow lawful users of software to do acts in relation to that software which previously would have infringed.

Broadly, the Directive aimed to ensure that:

(a) programs should be able to work with programs produced by other software houses (that is, should be interoperable);
(b) programs should be able to work with other hardware, either directly or through another's operating system or driver;
(c) programs should be capable of transferring information and data between one computer system and another;
(d) it should be possible to study the program in order to determine the underlying ideas and principles.

Reverse engineering may in some cases be essential for software maintenance, particularly if information concerning the program is no longer available from the software supplier – either wilfully, or because it has gone out of business or ceased supporting that particular product. However, the rights of the lawful acquirer under Art.5(1) of this Directive apply only insofar as they are not excluded by specific contractual provisions in the licence and are necessary for use of the program in accordance with its (undefined) intended purpose.

The right to observe, study or test the functioning of the program in order to determine the underlying ideas or principles is permitted where the user is performing acts that the user is entitled to do. What the user is entitled to do will be wholly determined by the licence, save that the making of a back-up copy and the right to observe functioning cannot be excluded. Further, the Software Directive gives no clues as to what may or may not be done with the information so obtained.

Article 6 gives lawful acquirers the right to decompile for limited purposes and in limited circumstances: only where:

(a) the person decompiling has the right to use the program; and
(b) the information necessary to achieve interoperability has not previously been readily available to that authorised user.

The purpose of decompilation must be to obtain information for creating an independent program (that is, one not substantially similar in its expression to the software being decompiled) which is interoperable with the software in question, such information not being otherwise readily available. However, once the information has been obtained it may only be used for the purpose of creating the independent program: it cannot be given to any other person or used for any other purpose, otherwise the act of decompilation becomes an infringement.

The decompilation right cannot be excluded by contract provided the conditions are complied with. This still leaves the copyright owner the power to restrict the application of these rights by making the limited information necessary for the purpose available. However, Microsoft's long-running battle with the European Commission is in part over how much information it must make available to competitors under this provision to avoid a finding of breach of a dominant position under the EC Treaty, Art.82 (see **Chapter 8**). The CFI has upheld the Commission's relatively broad approach, requiring all information necessary to make it commercially viable to develop interoperable programs to be disclosed (Case T-20Y04, decision of 17/09/07).

As a result of the UK implementation of this Directive, acts of backing-up, decompilation and error correction which might otherwise be regarded as infringement of copyright are not treated as infringing. By CDPA 1988, s.296A any term in a software licence is void insofar as it purports to prohibit or restrict:

(a) the making of any back-up copy of the program which is necessary for the purposes of the agreed use;
(b) decompilation, where the conditions in s.50B(2) are met; and
(c) the use of any device or means to observe, study or test the functioning of the program in order to understand the ideas and principles which underlie any element of the program.

A term permitting the lawful user to copy or adapt the program as necessary for its lawful use (for example, to de-bug it) is implied into the licence by s.50C – but in contrast to the above rights, this right can be excluded by agreement.

Further, s.50BA exempts the lawful user of a computer program from copyright infringement by observing, studying or testing a program for this purpose if he or she does so while performing any of the acts of loading, displaying, running, transmitting or storing the program which he or she is entitled to do. This right cannot be excluded by contract.

It remains unclear, and is perhaps a matter of construction of the licence in each case, whether running a program solely for the purpose of observing its functioning is within the acts which a lawful user is entitled to do. It is, however, clear that the right to observe by running a program does not go so far as to permit general purpose decompilation of the software.

Open source

The open source or 'free software' movement takes as its premise that the products of human creativity should be free for all to use, develop and pass on. It is fiercely opposed to the monopoly rights conferred by either copyright or patents over software, and its lobbying was responsible for the defeat in the European Parliament of the draft Directive on Computer Implemented Inventions, which had as its objective sorting out the difficulties produced by the decisions of the European Patent Office which were arguably inconsistent with the provisions of the European Patent Convention on the extent to which software inventions are patentable (see **Chapter 4**).

Since copyright protection has not proved susceptible to repeal, the open source movement have attempted to create a situation where programmers developing any new program using any open source software are forced to treat their own new work as subject to the open source 'central freedoms'. For instance, the General Public Licence (GPL) (current version 3 is available at **www.gnu.org**), which is governed by US law, states in s.2 that any work distributed or published that in whole or in part contains or is derived from the Program must be licensed under the GPL. In effect, by using any part of a program which is already subject to the GPL, the new work becomes publishable only on the GPL terms. This 'subversion' of copyright law is known as 'copyleft', and code subject to such provisions is sometimes known as 'viral code' since it infects any program of which it becomes a part with the open source obligations.

Not all open source program licences have this quality, but very careful case-by-case analysis is required to ensure that any program intended for commercial distribution does not contain any such code. Where a version of the GPL has become incorporated, the normal non-infringement warranties which a developer may be asked to give that the new program will not infringe any third party intellectual property rights may not address the real problem: by incorporating code subject to the GPL the developer may put the commissioner into a position where it is obliged to publish the new source code and permit its distribution free of charge. Even if not this onerous, it is important to look closely at the precise use and redistribution rights conferred by an open source licence, and what constraints may be imposed, in particular as to:

(a) pricing of further developed versions; and
(b) notification requirements to users and other licensees as to the open source obligations attaching to the software.

Copyright infringement on the internet

Introduction

Although every person who visits a website causes a copy to be made temporarily in their computer's memory, a licence to do so is implied through the mere act of putting the copyright works up in the form of a website. Visiting on its own, therefore, will never be an act of infringement. However, the scope of the licence implied by putting up a website is often ill-defined. Forms of use other than mere viewing of a website may risk infringing.

Web linking and framing

The owner of a website protected by copyright is unlikely to be able to use copyright to prevent linking by other websites, since the only part of a website which is copied in setting up (as opposed to activating) a link is the uniform resource locator (url). The url itself is unlikely to qualify as a copyright work, either under the rule that single words or slogans cannot attract copyright (*Exxon Corp* v. *Exxon Insurance Consultants International Ltd*) or on the basis that a url is in fact a command to a computer and therefore part of a computer language and denied protection by the Software Directive (*Navitaire* v. *Easyjet and Anr*). The user who follows the link copies the target website by causing it to be displayed upon a computer screen, but since this will normally be licensed no infringement occurs.

The position may be different where the link is not to the homepage of the target website or another page recognisable as part of that site, but only to specific works included in that page, by way of in-line links composing a separate page on the linking site. In this case the user viewing the page still loads the material directly from the target site but does not know that they are doing so. As a result, any advertising or other revenue which might have accrued to the target website from the user's action may be circumvented. It is at least arguable (though far from certain, absent any case law) that the implied licence to browse a website does not extend to this sort of inadvertent access. The user may therefore infringe, and the creator of the link may be liable for authorising that infringement. Since authorisation of a restricted act triggers liability irrespective of the infringer's knowledge that the act will infringe, website owners do not need to expressly prohibit such links in order for liability to arise.

Framing is another mechanism enabling the designer of one website to incorporate material from another without the user being aware of the change of source. If a site is designed to display content within several separate frames, a link within one frame will activate material to be displayed within that frame – bypassing, as a deep link does, the home page of the target site and displaying its content surrounded by the material in the remaining frames of the initial site. Applying the same analysis, browsing through such a framed display may infringe and, if so, the owner of the website causing the frames to be displayed may be liable for authorising infringement.

Search engines

In addition to indexing the sites they crawl, search engines sometimes also cache the contents of those sites. The issue as to whether such activity infringes copyright once again comes back to the question of the scope of the express or implied licence granted by the owner of the target website. There is rarely any dispute where the website and search engine are not in competition: search engines are a key service making the internet useful for a wide range of purposes and the benefit is shared not only by users but by the owners of websites indexed, which can normally expect to increase the traffic through their sites as a result. Thus, a licence to index can almost certainly be implied, with any temporary copying that entails. A licence to hold a complete copy may also be implied in many cases. But where the copies are used to compete directly with the website – as for instance to provide a separate source for news reports – then the mere absence of technological barriers (such as the Robots Exclusion Standard) to such copying cannot be used to infer a consent (*Copiepresse* v. *Google Inc* (2007) No. 06/10.928/C, Brussels Court of First Instance).

Nor will the hosting, caching and 'mere conduit' defences provided by the E-Commerce Directive apply in such a situation, since their object is to protect an ISP from liability where a user of their service uploads infringing material, not where the ISP itself is the primary infringer.

Peer-to-peer file sharing

Peer-to-peer (P2P) sites such as Napster or KaZaA do not themselves store any copies of the material which their users exchange. They are essentially a directory service, enabling users to identify files held by other users accessible over the internet where the material of interest may be found. There is therefore no primary act of infringement carried out by the P2P website itself. The UK's 'time-shifting' exception is of such a limited nature that it has no relevance to the issues raised by Napster or its successor systems. Even before the additional restriction that copying must take place in domestic premises for the time shifting exception to apply was introduced, the fact that a commercial interest was involved had excluded it as a defence (*Sony Music Entertainment (UK) Ltd and Others* v. *Easyinternetcafé Ltd* [2003] EWHC 62 (Ch)).

There can be little doubt that the individuals participating in P2P copying infringe, and the only live legal issue is whether those 'behind' the P2P network, enabling the infringing activity to take place, can be said thereby to have 'authorised' it so as to be liable under UK law. The question is likely to come down to the extent to which the P2P site controls any copying. A UK court might well conclude that the continuing element of potential control that a site such as Napster could exercise made this a very different case to *CBS Song* v. *Amstrad* [1988] AC 1013, where the House of Lords found that the sale of double-headed cassette recorders, although these were used mainly to infringe copyright, did not constitute any authorisation so to do. To trigger that form of liability, the authorisation to infringe must be an authorisation to an individual infringer identifiably procuring a particular infringement.

The issue of authorisation becomes more difficult with the more disseminated, and less centrally controlled, P2P networks that have now replaced Napster. Sites such as Grokster, which were found liable for inducing infringement under US law (*MGM Studios Inc* v. *Grokster* 545 US 125 S Ct 267u (2005)), are unlikely to be found to be authorising it under the UK test merely by providing broad advertising and general support.

10.3 DATABASE RIGHT

Definition of a database

The advent of database right, deriving from Directive 96/9/EC, provides a further basis on which a website owner may seek to assert control over those linking to its site. This was implemented in the UK by the Copyright and Rights in Databases Regulations 1997, SI 1997/3032 (Database Regulations 1997), and by equivalent legislation around Europe.

In order to enjoy protection a database must be (CDPA 1988, s.3A(1)):

A collection of independent works, data or other materials which –

(a) are arranged in a systematic or methodical way, and
(b) are individually accessible by electronic or other means.

This definition is sufficiently wide to include a collection of materials on a website. The fact that the database or any of its contents may, or may not, enjoy copyright protection is irrelevant for the purpose of determining whether database right exists.

If the collection qualifies for database right protection, the protection lasts for 15 years from the end of the calendar year in which the database was completed. However, if updates to the database cumulatively amount to a substantial change in the contents which would be considered a substantial new investment, then the updated database qualifies for its own 15-year term of protection (reg.17(3)). The right can therefore last indefinitely, so long as sufficient investment is put into updating it periodically.

Qualifying criteria

Substantial investment

The right subsists in relation to all such databases, provided there has been a substantial qualitative or quantitative investment of financial, human or technical resources in obtaining, verifying or presenting the contents of the database concerned.

The investment must be in producing the database itself and not in a different activity from which valuable data arises. Where claimants had the benefit of a regulatory system which required participants in a particular activity (horse racing in Britain, or the FA's Premier League respectively) to inform the regulator of their fixtures, the information in question came into their possession without any investment being directed to the obtaining or verification of the materials. The resulting databases, though valuable, were not protected (ECJ, joined cases of Cases C-46/02, C-203/02, C-338/02 and C-444/02 *Fixtures Marketing Ltd* v *Oy Veikkaus Ab*, *The British Horseracing Board Ltd and Others* v *William Hill Organisation Ltd*, *Fixtures Marketing Ltd* v *Svenska Spel AB*, *Fixtures Marketing Ltd* v *Organismos prognostikon agonon podosfairou (OPAP)* (OJ 9 November 2004)).

The investment is to be measured either on a quantitative basis or a qualitative one, or by a combination of both qualitative and quantitative. It can be made either at the inception of a database project (obtaining its contents) or during the life of a database (verifying or presenting its contents).

So far, English case law on database right is very scant, although the continental courts have had to consider it on a number of occasions. In *Wegener* v. *Hunter Select* (Electronic Commerce & Law Report (2002) 7(47) 1195) the Dutch Court of Appeal held that what is substantial may be evaluated in the light of the presentation of the contents. The Munich Regional court stated (at an interim stage in *Mainpresse Zeitgungs GmbH*, Electronic Commerce Law Report (2000) 7(30) 776) that a newspaper site did not need to demonstrate the precise investment in producing its electronic format since the technical and personnel expenditures were 'not insignificant' even when the text already exists in print. Interestingly, that court approached the question by comparing this expenditure against that necessary on the part of the defendant to copy. This test, if upheld, would set the threshold for the necessary investment very low. However, in the Dutch case of *PCM* v. *Kranten.com* (*Algemeen Dagblad et al* v. *Eureka* E-Commerce Law Reports Vol.1, issue 2, p.12) concerning the index to another newspaper site, where the defendant produced an equivalent index and provided deep links through it to the relevant articles, the court held that it could not be said that the plaintiffs had invested substantially in the contents of the *index* of titles of news items and articles. The index therefore was not protected by database right.

Nationality

Database right only subsists if the maker (or one of joint makers) is an EEA or Isle of Man individual, partnership or company. Where the maker is a partnership or company it must also have its principal place of business or central administration in the EEA.

Websites as databases

Protection as a database may give the contents of a website protection which is not available to the same content published in hard copy form. An on-line newspaper site may constitute a database even though a paper copy of an edition of the paper does not, since it is not a work of reference and the individual articles are not individually accessible (*Publishers* v. *Euroclip* (Amsterdam District Court, September 2002)). The on-line version, consisting of a collection of articles produced by 'structured systems or methods' and accessible by internet users by various means, may indeed qualify (*Danish Newspaper Publishers' Association* v. *Newsbooster.com ApS* (World e-Commerce & IP Report, August 2002, 2(8) 5)).

Similar conclusions have been reached by the courts of other EU countries in respect of on-line recruitment sites (*Stepstone* v. *Ofir* (Landesgericht Koln Case No.28 O 692/00, 28 February 2001)) or property sales, but the decisions are not entirely consistent between countries even on identical facts. The issue is whether a qualifying investment can be identified in carrying on an on-line version of an existing business, a question of fact on which different courts take differing views. Consequently it is essential to ensure that details of the costs and time spent in setting up and populating a website database are recorded separately from the costs of any parallel business, such that an investment at the least in presenting the database in website format can be identified.

Infringement

Database right is infringed under Art.7 of the Directive if a person extracts or re-utilises all or a substantial part of the contents of the database (Database Regulations 1997, reg.16). 'Extraction' is the permanent or temporary transfer of the contents of a database to another medium by any means or in any form. Re-utilisation means making the contents of a database available to the public by any means (reg.12(1)). What is 'substantial' is of course the key issue. In *News Invest* v. *PR Line* (Tribunal de commerce de Nanterre, 11 April 2002), a French Court of Appeal held that the extraction of no more than 10 communications and two financial reports in six months was not a substantial part of the database.

Repeated and systematic extraction or re-utilisation of insubstantial parts of the contents of a database may amount to the extraction or re-utilisation of a substantial part of the database, and therefore an infringement of the database right (reg.16(2)). The Court in *Danish Newspaper Publishers' Association* v. *Newsbooster.com ApS* (July 2002) had no hesitation in finding that the repeated extraction of headlines, themselves an insubstantial part of each database, infringed and conflicted with the normal exploitation of the databases. This finding, if followed by a UK court, would lead to the *Shetland Times* scenario reaching the same outcome on a completely unrelated legal analysis.

Implied licences are as ever the bane of the rightholder who seeks to enforce. In France, the Nanterre Tribunal of Commerce in considering the *Stepstone* v. *Ofir* case (above) held that the deep links to Stepstone's job vacancies did not infringe since the act of putting the data on the web led to an implied licence to create deep links to it, alternatively that an acknowledgement of the source was sufficient for the linking to be permitted (AIPPI Reports France, Report 168). This analysis is not widely accepted, however. In particular, the acknowledgement of source provision relates only to use of a database by a lawful user for the purpose of teaching or research and not for any commercial purpose (reg.20).

A failure to install suitable technology to prevent linking does not imply a licence for all links to be created (*Der Poet* (Electronic Business Law, February 2002) p.13). The Cologne Regional considered that a website owner should be free to create a website to its own specification; to find otherwise would be to force it to make further investments beyond those in the database itself, in order to obtain the benefit of a legal right which is meant to arise automatically. This is consistent with the Belgian court's more recent conclusion in response to essentially the same defence in the *Copiepresse* copyright case, discussed above.

10.4 CONFIDENTIAL INFORMATION

Overview

As discussed in connection with copyright, information in digital form is far more vulnerable to rapid, perfect copying and transmission than the same information in hard-copy form. Confidential information can now be stored on flash memory, in PDAs or mobile phones in addition to the more traditional (and bulkier) forms of storage such as CDs or floppy disks. In these circumstances anyone wishing to protect such information needs to take precautions as to who has access to the information in electronic form and how and when copies can be taken.

It may also be prudent to consider incorporating in electronic form rights management information, such as copy number, date of creation and so on.

Of course, the safest route where true trade secrets are concerned may simply be not to keep the information in digital form, unless there is no alternative.

Transmission

It is now widely understood that the internet is not a secure system. Transmission of information between computers involves routing that information through a number of unknown, and unpredictable, intermediary computers on each of which a temporary copy of the transmitted information is made. Depending upon the operation of those systems, which is not centrally controlled, the copy may exist for milliseconds, hours or days – during which it may be accessed by third parties using those systems either directly or remotely.

Consequently, transmitting allegedly confidential information across the internet may reduce the prospects of being able in future to defend it against misuse or disclosure on the basis of its confidentiality, even if it is not actually uncovered, published or made use of as a result of the transmission. Transmission over an insecure medium arguably amounts to an admission that the holder of the information is not greatly concerned to maintain its confidentiality, which in turn suggests it may not be truly confidential.

To minimise the risk, any sensitive or confidential information being sent by e-mail should be encrypted with a level of encryption appropriate to its value. The encryption provided by standard applications such as Microsoft

Office are vulnerable to cracking by even slightly competent computer scientists. The two common forms of strong cryptography in widespread use are 'private key encryption' and 'public key encryption', otherwise known as 'symmetric' and 'asymmetric' encryption respectively. In both of these, a complex algorithm is applied to the plain text to produce the cryptogram. In each case, the algorithm calculates the transposition of each letter of the plain text based upon a number which is called the key and randomisation factor e.g. key strokes of user. The only way to decipher particular encrypted messages is by using the cryptographic key. The use of strong encryption based on such algorithms and lengthy keys is likely to reinforce any later claim of confidentiality.

Of course, interception of an e-mail is in itself unlawful under the Regulation of Investigatory Powers Act (RIPA) 2000 so that there is a stronger reason for any unintended recipient to realise the information is not theirs to use. But interception could take place in a lawful manner, either sanctioned by the RIPA 2000 or in a jurisdiction where no such prohibition is in effect. A notice of confidentiality and encryption is therefore essential.

Storage

Confidential information in digital form should always be accompanied by a clear notice that the information is confidential, must neither be copied nor disclosed and is intended for receipt only by the addressee(s), to ensure that any unintended recipient is fixed with knowledge of its confidentiality. It cannot be assumed that encryption by itself amounts to such notice to third parties: if the information is in a public place (even if well hidden in, for example, the bowels of a vending machine) and lawfully accessible by third parties, the owner must accept that it could be decrypted (*Mars* v. *Teknowledge Ltd* [2000] FSR 138).

Highly sensitive information should not be stored on open access systems but on secure drives or standalone workstations, to prevent multiple copies spreading around the system and potentially beyond. Access to the relevant workstations and drives should be technically and, preferably, physically limited to users with a specific need to use the information, and such users' access should be removed once they no longer need it. An audit trail should be maintained as to who has had access, when, and what actions they took while connected to the relevant drive. Such measures will assist the holder to convince a court that the information was being treated as truly confidential despite being in digital form, and also help to prove that any person copying the information without authorisation must have realised from all the circumstances that the information was indeed confidential.

10.5 DOMAIN NAMES AND TRADE MARKS

Introduction

Although the internet is far more than a worldwide virtual shopping mall, the significance of that portion of it known as the World Wide Web for advertising, brand development and product recognition is immense. It offers a global shop-window for informing and attracting consumers, so it was inevitable that trade marks would play an important role as soon as cyberspace began to be commercialised.

The collision between businesses trading under the same names and brands in different countries is exacerbated by the system of domain names, the identifiers by which websites are located. Whereas trade mark registrations are (with the exception of the CTM) purely national, domain names in the top level domains (such as '.com') are effectively global. The result is that several different businesses may all legitimately expect to be able to have a domain name along the lines of 'www.theirbrand.com', and may not readily accept that another trader could have equally legitimate rights to it.

Further, the uniqueness of key domain names made them an early and easy target for so-called 'cybersquatters' who try to register potentially valuable domains ('www.famousname.com') and then either attempt to sell it to the brand owner or await the brand owner's offer for a transfer. Since the early days of the World Wide Web this has been, and remains, a fertile source of dispute.

The hierarchy of domains

The organisation of the internet is governed by a body called the Internet Corporation for Assigned Names and Numbers (ICANN). ICANN is based in the United States, although in its early form it did not have a particularly US-centric view of the net. Its essential function is to ensure that any computer or server connecting into the internet has a unique identifier so that traffic can be routed in a logical and error-free way to the correct address – the Assigned Name or Number. However, once the net began to function in the commercial as well as the academic and military spheres, assigned numbers were rapidly found to be unsatisfactory identifiers: ordinary users, as opposed to students and military specialists, find them extremely difficult to remember. Once the World Wide Web had been established, the system of giving users domain names as descriptors for their internet addresses was established as part of the move to enhance navigability and useability.

Initially three global 'top level' domains were established, '.com', '.org', '.net'. These were expanded in 2001 to add '.info', '.biz', '.name', '.aero', '.coop', '.museum' and '.pro' in order to keep up with the growth in the number of users. Further top level domains are being rolled out progressively.

The assigning of domains within these groups is handled by Verisign Inc, the Registrar appointed by ICANN for this purpose.

In addition, every country has a country 'top level' domain: .uk, .fr, .de and so on, administered by a national registrar under authority delegated from ICANN. The UK's domain '.uk' is administered by Nominet (see **www.nominet.org.uk**). Further, in 2006 the first regional top level domain, '.eu', was rolled out for use by EU businesses and individuals.

Under the top level domains are secondary domains such as .co, some of which, confusingly, are the same as global top level domains. Hence within '.uk' there are '.co.uk', '.gov.uk' and '.org.uk'. Even sticking entirely to the most basic form of its name or brand, no enterprise or organisation can possibly register all possible domain names which might be associated with it. For example, the website address for the law firm Bird & Bird is based around the word 'twobirds', which could lead to, for example, twobirds.com, twobirds.org, twobirds.net, twobirds.co.uk, twobirds.org.uk, twobirds.co.fr, twobirds.org.us . . . However, for commercial purposes '.com' rapidly obtained a higher level of recognition than the country-specific equivalents such as '.co.uk', and '.com' domain names were accordingly perceived as more valuable.

Registration and the rights it confers

The right to use a particular domain name is not an intellectual property right, even though in practice it has a limited monopoly effect preventing another from registering the identical domain name. The registrar which has the right to allocate domains in that class grants a domain name to a user in return for a fee for a specified period of time. Once a particular domain name has been allocated, it cannot as a matter of common sense be allocated to a second applicant while the first grant is still in effect. (In a case where this in fact happened by an error on the part of the registrar, the court concluded that 'first come first served' was the only reasonable way to resolve the dispute, but the conclusion was as a result of the parties' contractual relations with Nominet.)

Like a trade mark registration, a domain name which is not renewed lapses and may be allocated to a different user. However, the registered user does not have a property right in the domain name even while the domain name remains in use; assignability is a matter of the contract with the registrar. Lord Hoffmann in *Douglas* v. *Hello!* [2007] UKHL 21 commented *obiter* that he 'had no difficulty with the proposition that a domain name may be intangible property, like a copyright or trade mark' (Opinion, para.101), but unless and until the system for registration acquires State recognition, it is a purely contractual right.

The registrars have no obligation to investigate trade mark rights which could affect the use of any domain name which they are asked to register, any more than Companies House has an obligation to ensure that the name a newly formed company is being registered under is not the trade mark of an existing enterprise. This is a matter of pragmatism: since a domain, once active, is visible to the whole world, in theory a registrar could be required to check the trade mark registers of every country in the world, and then consider what actual use was being made of any similar marks identified, in order to establish freedom to register. Since identical trade marks are in use by different owners in different countries, disputes between legitimate domain name holders and trade mark owners were inevitably going to arise.

Trade mark infringement

Use of a trade mark in a domain name

Where the goods and services offered by the different parties do not overlap, once the initial outrage has worn off it should in most cases be possible to resolve any dispute by agreeing to co-exist. This can include arrangements such as disclaimers on the respective websites, potentially including links to the other party's site.

If both parties are trading in the same goods and services, but in different geographical territories, the issue is a little more difficult. A UK trade mark can be infringed by the use of the mark on a site which is hosted in another jurisdiction but which is addressed to consumers in the UK. In principle the same solution (a disclaimer, specifically stating that the website is not directed at consumers in the UK) can be effective to avoid infringement. However, this has to be both genuine and consistent with the remainder of the site. The provision of a separate site for UK users may not be sufficient to avoid trade mark infringement if there is other material containing the mark complained of on pages which are also directed to UK users (*Dearlove* v. *Combs* [2007] EWHC 375 (Ch)). The question of when a webpage is directed to UK users is one of fact. Factors such as the website's default language being English, prices being quoted in pounds sterling, the availability of manuals from the site in various European languages including English and the use of testimonials from purchasers in the United Kingdom are likely to lead to a finding that the website is indeed addressed to the UK (*Sony Computer Entertainment* v. *Pacific Game Technology (Holding) Ltd* [2006] EWHC 2509 (Ch)), even if the operator has no presence in the UK. The question is where a reasonable viewer would understand the website's target audience to be (*1-800-FLOWERS* v. *Phonenames Ltd* [2001] EWCA Civ 721). If it is clear sales are intended for the EEA, and the acts, if committed physically within the EEA would have been infringing acts, then the electronic intermediary of a website will not make them any less so. This approach is also consistent with the recommendation of the WIPO Standing Committee on the Law of Trade Marks, published in 2000, which proposed that only a use of a sign which has a commercial effect in a Member State should constitute trade mark use capable of infringing.

Use of a trade mark in other materials on or about a website

Apart from the domain name itself, trade marks may appear in other parts of a website. Their use in the metadata about the site – invisible to the user but visible to web browser programmes – has been another source of disputes. The metadata is the source of the information which a search engine uses to determine whether to include a page in the results of any given search. Accordingly, it can potentially be used to distort the results of such searches. For instance, loading the metadata of a site with the brands of competitors may lead the search engines to list the site prominently in response to searches for those competing brands. Alternatively, the competitor's brand may be used as a keyword to trigger the display of a banner advertisement for the rival site. The user may not realise why their search has produced such a result, or why the banner has appeared, however, since they will never see the text which caused it. In such circumstances, the user is unlikely to be confused as to the origin of the goods or services presented on the site; they will merely consider the search to have been inaccurate – something internet users are well accustomed to. Consequently, this use does not amount to trade mark infringement under TMA 1994, s.10(2) or passing off, since users will not be confused as to the origin of the goods or services they are being offered (*Reed Executive plc* v. *Reed Business Information Ltd* [2004] ECA Civ 159).

Domain name hijacking

Domain name hijacking, or cybersquatting, is an entirely different activity from the clashes between legitimate users of the same marks. It initially had to be addressed through court action based upon trade mark law. The difficulty with this approach is that merely registering a domain including another's registered trade mark may not infringe since there may be no use being made of the mark. However, a pattern of conduct by the registrant of similar registrations and offers to sell is likely to persuade a court that the registrant intends to use the mark and thus amount to actionable threats to infringe (*BT plc and Others* v. *One-in-a-million Ltd* [1998] FSR 265, [1999] 1 WLR 903).

The Court of Appeal held in the same case that the documents registering various famous brands as domain names were instruments of fraud. This last basis for claiming transfer of a domain name will not generally be available unless it is possible to establish a likelihood of deception, which may not be the case where there is mere similarity of names to the trade marks in issue. The criteria were met however in *Global Projects Management Ltd* v. *Citigroup Inc.* [2005] EWHC 2663 (Ch) where a cybersquatter registered the domain name 'citigroup.co.uk' on the day the merger of Citibank and Travelers Group was announced. Global Project Management claimed that it was holding onto the name to enable it to supervise Citigroup for evidence of possible improprieties in the conduct of its business which (if found) would be handed over to the appropriate authorities. The judge found that this was implausible, commented that the sole director appeared to preen himself on his having obtained the domain name (even though he had tried and failed also to register 'citigroup.com'), and that the registration must be an instrument of fraud.

'Sucks' sites

One problematic area is so-called 'sucks' sites, as in 'a-famous-company-sucks.com'. Often disgruntled consumers or protesters set up such sites to air their grievances around some policy or act of a well known enterprise. The targeted organisation not infrequently objects to this negative commentary and may attempt to prevent it by complaining that the use of its trade mark in the domain name infringes its rights or is a ground for transfer of the domain name under the applicable dispute resolution policy.

Such complaints have had variable success. Where the domain name consists solely of the trade mark in question, WIPO panels have reached different conclusions as to whether a criticism site could qualify as a legitimate or fair use. If the disputed domain name is not identical to the trade mark in issue, but includes additional (normally pejorative) words, it may be possible for a registrant to have a legitimate interest in using it. Such a defence is particularly likely to succeed if the respondent does not use the domain name in any way likely to cause visitors to the site to be deceived into believing it is officially associated with the target, nor to cause undue confusion. So for instance in *Ryanair Ltd* v. *Michael Coulston* (2007) Case No. D2006-1194 (WIPO Arbitration and Mediation Center) the respondent registered 'ryanaircampaign.org' for the express purpose of tarnishing Ryanair's reputation, but since the site was clearly a protest site with no commercial overtones at all and limited to genuine criticism rather than attempting to associate Ryanair with any objectionable images or information, the respondent was allowed to keep the domain despite Ryanair's registered trade marks. The panellist specifically pointed out that the outcome of a trade mark infringement action in the courts could well be different, however.

Some 80 per cent of complaints succeed under the Uniform Dispute Resolution Policy (UDRP) (see below), 50 per cent under the '.eu' alternative dispute resolution (ADR) procedure. The high rate of success of such complaints does not mean, however, that the trade mark owners can count on recovering 'their' domain names in all circumstances. The key issue in such disputes is the credibility of the registrant's evidence as to why the particular domain name has been registered. In a complaint about the domain name 'trivialpursuits.net', brought by the holders of the trade mark (and manufacturers of the game) Trivial Pursuit, the defendant's passionate arguments over the right to continue to use a phrase which had been in common parlance before the now-famous board game was ever invented succeeded in persuading the panel that the claimant had not discharged the burden of proof to show that his registration had been in bad faith (*Horn Abbott International Ltd* v. *Macmillan* (WIPO, Case No. D2005-0198).

Dispute resolution

The need for an alternative to court proceedings

Each new top level domain that is established offers a fresh opportunity to hijackers to register potentially valuable domains, and accordingly leads to a fresh round of disputes. The new domains are now introduced for public uptake only after a 'sunrise period' in which owners of registered trade marks have an early opportunity to prove their rights and register their chosen domains before potential cybersquatters have the chance. This has limited, though not eliminated, the extent of cybersquatting in recent launches.

The rapid escalation of disputes between domain name holders and trade mark owners led to ICANN establishing in 1999 a Uniform Dispute Resolution Policy (UDRP) for deciding such conflicts. The UDRP is part of any contract for the registration of the global top level domains; as far as country code top level domains are concerned, the national registrars have their own dispute resolution policies more or less closely modelled upon it.

Under these policies, any dispute over a domain name is referred for arbitration by a panel of one or three arbitrators. A body of case law has built up around the interpretation of three requirements commonly stipulated for a domain name registration to be transferred. These are that:

(a) the disputed domain name is identical or confusingly similar to the complainant's trade mark (which does not have to have been registered, although obviously for purposes of proof it helps);
(b) the respondent has no legitimate right to or interest in the mark; and/or
(c) the respondent has registered and is using the domain name in bad faith (UDRP, .eu ADR rules)/takes unfair advantage of or is unfairly detrimental to the complainant's rights (Nominet Dispute Resolution System (DRS) (see below)).

The need to draft a complaint and file it, and to pay the panellists' fees, means that recovering a domain name, even in uncontested proceedings, involves an outlay in the region of £1,000. As a result a complaint will these days often prompt an offer to sell the domain name for a sum in the region of the unrecoverable costs of taking the cybersquatter through a panel process. Clearly, there are still profits to be made through registering domain names and selling them back to the trade mark owner.

Nominet's dispute resolution policy

The complete policy and procedure can be found at the Nominet website (**www.nominet.org.uk**). The UK registrar defines as an abusive registration a domain name which either:

i. was registered or otherwise acquired in a manner which, at the time when the registration or acquisition took place, took unfair advantage of or was unfairly detrimental to the Complainant's Rights; OR
ii. has been used in a manner which took unfair advantage of or was unfairly detrimental to the Complainant's Rights.

The process involves an informal mediation followed, if unsuccessful, by the appointment of an expert and if necessary after the expert's decision an appeal by way of full review, to a panel.

A complaint can be filed based on any right which is enforceable under English law. The policy specifically points out that a name or term which is wholly descriptive of the complainant's business will not be sufficient to found a complaint; and a generic domain name being fairly used by the respondent will not be found to be abusive. The complainant needs to establish, on the balance of probabilities, that it has rights in respect of a name or mark which is identical or similar to the domain name; and that the respondent's registration of it was abusive.

Factors which may be help to establish that the registration is abusive include the following.

i. Circumstances indicating that the Respondent has registered or otherwise acquired the Domain Name primarily:
    A. for the purposes of selling, renting or otherwise transferring the Domain Name to the Complainant or to a competitor of the Complainant, for valuable consideration in excess of the Respondent's documented out-of-pocket costs directly associated with acquiring or using the Domain Name;
    B. as a blocking registration against a name or mark in which the Complainant has Rights; or
    C. for the purpose of unfairly disrupting the business of the Complainant;
ii. Circumstances indicating that the Respondent is using the Domain Name in a way which has confused people or businesses into believing that the Domain Name is registered to, operated or authorised by, or otherwise connected with the Complainant;

Use of a domain name to pass the respondent's business off as the complainant's will also show abuse, as will evidence that the respondent is trafficking in domain names corresponding to well-known names or trade marks in which the respondent has no apparent rights. Mere lack of use of the domain name is not in itself sufficient to establish abuse.

A respondent may be able to demonstate that the domain is not an abusive registration if it can show that, before becoming aware of the complainant's cause for complaint, it has used or made demonstrable preparations to use the domain name (or a similar domain name) in connection with a genuine offering of goods or services; or made legitimate non-commercial or fair use of the domain name; or been commonly known by the name or legitimately connected with a mark which is identical or similar to the domain name.

Fair use may include sites operated solely in tribute to or in criticism of a person or business.

Once a complaint form has been received by Nominet, the respondent may not transfer the disputed domain name or change the hosting ISP until 10 days after the proceedings have concluded, unless as part of a settlement. All decisions are published in full on Nominet's website. If the expert decides that a domain name registration should be cancelled, suspended, transferred or otherwise amended, Nominet will make any necessary changes to the register.

10.6 PATENT INFRINGEMENT OVER THE INTERNET

An offer to dispose in the UK of a patented product, which is made over the internet, will infringe in the same way as any other such offer. A mere advertisement, on the other hand, may not infringe UK patent rights since it could technically be classified as an invitation to treat rather than an actual offer of sale.

Global corporate websites are often fruitful sources of evidence upon which to base an allegation of joint tortfeasorship by an offshore company with its UK subsidiary which is actually supplying or using infringing products or processes in the UK. The law of common design provides that active furtherance of an infringing act is enough to incur liability as a joint tortfeasor. The tendency of global websites to present the multinational group of companies as a seamless whole, with the parent company's image dominant and local subsidiaries often made to appear merely as sales or support offices for a global enterprise, can provide sufficient foundation for the parent to be joined as a defendant.

A gambling site located offshore was found to infringe a UK patent since it was accessible by punters in the UK through the use of software which was distributed by CD within the UK (*Menashe Business Mercantile Ltd* v. *William Hill Organisation* [2002] EWCA Civ 1702). The patent related to the whole system, host computer and remote terminals, such that only a part of the infringing product was located in the UK. The Court of Appeal concluded that from the point of view of the punter, the invention was being used in the UK since the punter neither knows nor cares where the host computer may be physically located. The supply of the CD in the UK was therefore sufficient to put the invention into effect in the UK. This decision is consistent with the US Federal Circuit decision in the *Blackberry* litigation (*NTP Inc.* v. *Research in Motion Ltd* 418 F.3d, 1382 (Fed Cir 2005), which held that 'it is beyond dispute that the location of the beneficial use and function of the whole operable system assembly is in the United States'. Thus, infringement can take place by the use in the UK over the internet of a patented system only part of which is within the jurisdiction.

Index